Whig principles and party politics

Earl Fitzwilliam and the Whig party
1748-1833

To my wife

Whig principles
and party politics

Earl Fitzwilliam and the Whig party
1748–1833

E A Smith
Senior Lecturer in History
University of Reading

Manchester University Press
Rowman and Littlefield

© 1975 E A Smith

Published by
Manchester University Press
Oxford Road
Manchester MI3 9PL

UK ISBN 0 7190 0598 1

USA

Rowman and Littlefield
81 Adams Drive
Totowa, N.J. 07512

US ISBN 0 87471 680 2

Library of Congress cataloging in publication data

Smith, Ernest Anthony
  Whig principles and party politics

  Includes bibliographical references
  1. Fitzwilliam, William Wentworth Fitzwilliam, fourth Earl, 1748–1833.
2. Whig Party (Gt. Brit.). 3. Great Britain—Politics and government—1714–
1837. I. Title.
DA506. F57S55   1975   329.9′41   74-34447
  UK ISBN 0 7190 0598 1
  US ISBN 0 87471 680 2

Printed in Great Britain
at the St. Ann's Press, Park Road,
Altrincham, Cheshire WA14 5QQ.

CONTENTS

LIST OF PLATES

The author and publishers are indebted to Earl Fitzwilliam and to the National Gallery of Ireland for permission to reproduce the illustrations.

ACKNOWLEDGEMENTS

I have pleasure in thanking the following owners of manuscript collections for permission to work on and to quote from documents: Earl Fitzwilliam and the Trustees of the Fitzwilliam settled estates; the Duke of Devonshire; the Earl of Halifax; the Earl of Harewood; the Duke of Portland; Earl Spencer; the Earl of Wharncliffe; Simon Fraser Esq. (Spencer Stanhope MSS).

I am grateful for a good deal of patient and willing help from the custodians of the many collections I have consulted. I should like to express my thanks in particular to Miss R. Meredith and her staff in the Archives Department of the Sheffield City Libraries and to Mr P. J. King and his assistants at the Northamptonshire County Record Office, Delapré Abbey. I am indebted also to Major T. L. Ingram for help with the Hickleton MSS and to the staff of the Department of MSS at the British Museum.

My major academic obligation is to the late Arthur Aspinall, who first started me on the path which has led to this volume and who gave me the benefit of his knowledge and example during an association of many years. Had he lived to see the typescript, this book would have been immeasurably improved by the benefit of his advice and criticism. I also acknowledge the financial help of the University of Reading which from time to time made grants towards the costs of my research. I am grateful to Mrs J. Cory and Mrs J. Evans for deciphering my manuscript and typing most of the book. Above all, my debt is to my wife who made it possible for me to write it.

A NOTE ON SOURCES AND REFERENCES

The following MS sources have been used:

1 Wentworth Woodhouse muniments, Sheffield City Library. These include the papers of the second Marquess of Rockingham (referred to as 'R' with the finding number of the bundle and document), and the second and fourth Earl Fitzwilliam (referred to as 'F', with the appropriate number), the third and fifth Earl Fitzwilliam ('G'), Yorkshire election records ('E'), collections of accounts, etc ('A'), and the yeomanry and militia papers of the second and fourth earl ('Y'). The collection also includes the major part of the papers of Edmund Burke (referred to as 'B').

2 Fitzwilliam MSS from Milton, now at Delapré Abbey, Northampton. These are referred to as 'N' for the main collection arranged in chronological sequence, or with the box number (e.g. 'x515') for undated and miscellaneous letters.

3 The papers of the second Earl Grey at Durham University, Department of Palaeography and Diplomatic, are referred to as 'Grey MSS'. These are not numbered, as the collection is in process of being recatalogued.

4 The papers of William, first Baron Grenville from Dropmore, lately at Boconnoc and now in process of being catalogued in the British Museum, are referred to as 'B.M., Grenville MSS' (unnumbered at present).

5 Other MS collections used include the following:
Althorp: Althorp MSS.
British Museum: the collections of C. J. Fox, the Adair, Windham, Pelham, Holland House and Hardwicke papers, and the Westminster Association papers.
Chatsworth: Chatsworth MSS.
Garrowby, Yorks.: Hickleton (Ponsonby and Grey) MSS.

Leeds City Library: Harewood MSS, Battie–Wrightson MSS, Ramsden MSS.
North Riding Record Office, Northallerton: Malton estate MSS (these were consulted when they were still at Malton).
Nottingham University: Portland MSS.
Sheffield City Library: Spencer Stanhope MSS, Wharncliffe MSS.
York City Library: Yorkshire Association MSS.

In all quotations from original sources, spelling, punctuation and the use of capital letters have been modernised, except in a few cases where it seemed preferable to retain the original forms.

Reference to secondary sources has been made only where it seemed desirable to refer the reader to further information on precise topics.

A*

INTRODUCTION

It was once suggested that British political organisation in the mid-eighteenth century should be studied without reference to the terms 'Whig' and 'Tory'. Yet it cannot be overlooked that by the end of the American War of Independence there was again an identifiable political group that claimed for itself the sole right to the title of 'Whig' and the function of representing the true national interest, and which based its claim not only on organised connection but on shared political experience, a set of avowed political principles and a political programme for the immediate future. This was the group led by the second Marquess of Rockingham, which had developed out of the political confusion of the early 1760s and which, having experienced a brief interlude of office in 1765–6, maintained its identity and most of its membership throughout the next sixteen years of largely fruitless opposition. This unusual degree of cohesion during a long period out of office is reason enough for regarding the Rockingham Whigs as something of a unique phenomenon in later eighteenth-century politics. There are other reasons, however, for interest in the party, as it called itself. In seeking to define its function and establish its political respectability in an age when 'formed' opposition to the king's government might still be regarded as disloyal and factious, the Whigs had begun to institutionalise a set of common ideas and attitudes previously widespread in eighteenth-century political and social life but, since the days of Sir Robert Walpole, little more than the platitudes to which all public men paid lip service. The formulation of a party creed out of these general principles was not so difficult a process as the application of that creed to successive events and opportunities was to prove to be. The weakness of the Whig party, time and again, was to lie not in any inconsistency of principles but in the difficulty of translating them into practice if the party should ever move from opposition to office.

The Whig party, indeed, was almost the natural opposition as long as George III and his eldest son ruled England. The wonder perhaps is not that they held together in opposition for so long but that they managed to survive the brief interludes of holding office that came their way without complete disintegration. As it was, both 1782–3 and 1792–4 produced changing political alignments that modified the composition of the party, and the period 1801–7 further affected its membership and its alliances. But, though a contemporary wag might remark that

> Naught's constant in the human race.
> Except the Whigs not getting into place,

Whig principles and Whig political attitudes survived from the days of Rockingham and Burke to those of Grey and Russell until their translation into practical politics after 1830 ushered in an equally long period of Whig domination.

The survival and transmission of these principles during this period is the theme of this book. The topic might, and should, be investigated in many other ways. An intensive study of Whig party literature and propaganda would be a valuable contribution to the story, as would a thorough investigation of party organisation. On this occasion, however, the theme is approached through a biography of one of the leading and, it is claimed, most significant of the men who acted as the transmitters of that political heritage from the days of Rockingham to the period of the Reform Act. The man whose active political life spanned all those years, who for many of them held high rank in the party and enjoyed the genuine esteem of most Whig politicians, and for whom the Rockingham tradition was a personal as well as a political legacy, was William, second Earl Fitzwilliam in the English, fourth Earl in the Irish peerage. Fitzwilliam was Rockingham's nephew, and in 1782 inherited his estates and some of his political influence. He was Charles James Fox's closest and lifelong friend from schoolboy days at Eton until the hour of Fox's death, and at the same time the chief representative in the politics of the 1790s of Edmund Burke. For twelve years after Rockingham's death he acted as deputy leader of the party to the Duke of Portland, and though his ill-fated viceroyalty of Ireland in 1795 resulted in a six-year period of political isolation, his reunion with the Foxites after 1801 was instrumental in bringing the rump of the Whig party that had remained in opposition after 1794 back to the heritage of old Whig principles.

When he became Lord Grey's uncle by marriage (and later his father-in-law), the new relationship symbolised Fitzwilliam's position as the chief representative in Whig politics of the Rockingham school and, especially, of the attitudes of Burke: in this capacity he not only encouraged Grey and the post-1807 Whigs to keep to the traditional path of eighteenth-century Whiggism but, after his dismissal from the Lord-Lieutenancy of the West Riding after 'Peterloo' in 1819, he was largely instrumental in preventing the Whigs from officially adopting parliamentary reform as a party principle. Though he held Cabinet office for a total of only eighteen months, and high political office in Ireland for less than three months, Fitzwilliam's political importance was far greater than his contribution to British government. His life not only epitomised but also actively promoted the survival of eighteenth-century Whig principles into the Whig party of the 1820s.

What those principles were will appear in the succeeding chapters. They sprang fundamentally from aristocratic attitudes and from a particular conception of the social order. The Whigs regarded themselves, of course, as the natural guardians of the post-1689 constitutional settlement and protectors of the Englishman's liberties. Yet this was more than a political shibboleth. They looked upon society as an ordered unity, in which birth, rank, and status were vital, but they did not see society as a rigid or authoritarian structure. It was not a society of equals, but it was indissolubly bound together by reciprocal rights and responsibilities, common interests and shared duties. Social discipline stemmed naturally from acceptance of this code, not from legal coercion, and least of all from military force. The powers of government, like the privileges of rank and property, were bounded by law, custom, and humane principles. The focus of attention was not power but the freedom of the individual within this ordered structure to lead his life in his appropriate station, or even to rise above—or fall below—it if he so managed his affairs. The executive government was charged with responsibility for upholding law and order, safeguarding the structure and framework of society, collecting the public revenues, and carrying on foreign relationships (including the regulation, as necessary, of trade). Beyond this, the citizen and his rights—not abstract, philosophical or equal rights, but legal and civil rights related to the practical functioning of society—were the touchstone of political conduct. This was the liberty to which the eighteenth-century Whig dedicated himself. Its protection against ambitious monarchs or statesmen on the one hand, or demagogues and radical innovators on the other, was the major responsibility he accepted. To these ideals Fitzwilliam's life was dedicated.

That the ideals were aristocratic stems from the nature of the society that was to be preserved. To the eighteenth-century Whig nobleman society and the State were the private estate on a larger scale. In microcosm the landed estate represented a social structure found in the nation at large. Its efficient and happy functioning depended upon co-operation, upon a hierarchical yet functional and interdependent set of relationships—upon benevolent paternalism from above, meeting grateful deference from below. Force had no part to play in compelling these relationships, though if there was a threat to their existence force might have to be used—the force that might raise a tenant's rent or, in the last resort, evict him from his tenancy, or the force that had to be used to deal with the law-breaker or the political revolutionary. The ideal, however, remained harmonious co-operation. It is in Burke's writings and speeches that these principles were developed; but Burke was merely translating into political terms ideas already familiar to his aristocratic superiors in the running of their day-to-day affairs. In few periods of history and in few places have these ideals been so unswervingly and unquestionably acted upon as by the English Whig aristocracy of the later eighteenth century; and in few of those noblemen did they so consciously rule a political career as in Fitzwilliam's.

CHAPTER ONE

A Whig recruit
1748–82

Milton House lies immediately to the west of the city of Peterborough, set amongst parkland and meadows in the valley of the river Nene. In the sixteenth century this area of Northamptonshire developed into one of the foremost sheep-rearing counties. Many fortunes were made by sharp-eyed city businessmen shrewd enough to see its potentialities as the establishment of the Tudor dynasty and the suppression of baronial disorder made England a safe country for investment in land and property. Rich London merchants anxious to pass on to their descendants an assured social position and to provide for widows and children from an upward-looking investment rushed into the land market. Among them was Sir William Fitzwilliam, Merchant Taylor, Merchant of the Staple at Calais, and a leading figure in the London wool market.[1] In 1501 he established himself on an estate at Gaynes Park in Essex, and in the following year he bought the manors of Milton and Marholm for 1,200 marks and set about founding a family of consequence. His line already traced its ancestry—a little dubiously—from the knightly Fitzwilliams of Sprotborough near Doncaster in south Yorkshire, not far from the site of the later great mansion of Wentworth House, which, by strange coincidence, became their second home in 1782. A later connexion, ambitious for even more respectable lineage, was to join in the fashion for tracing descent from the companions of the Conqueror—in this case by inventing a bogus William, natural son of William I. The first Sir William, however, was a self-made man. Diligence and prudence were his watchwords as he advanced up the social scale by hard work, native shrewdness and thrift. Born about 1460, in time to catch the great cloth boom of the late fifteenth century, he applied himself to his trade, living above his business house in the City of London. Prosperity qualified him for membership of the City corporation, for

the office of Sheriff in 1506, and for the aldermanic bench a year
later. His business success culminated in the office of Mayor of the
Staple in London in 1518. He also went into politics and was noticed
by Cardinal Wolsey, who made him his Treasurer and High Chancellor, and whose influence carried him into court and the king's
council. By the end of his life the first Sir William's income was over
£400 per annum,[2] while his family was connected with the greatest
in the land. One daughter became the wife of Sir Anthony Cooke of
Gidea Hall, tutor to Edward VI, and one of her daughters married Sir
William Cecil. Sir William's rise was not only swift but also carefully
consolidated.

Sir William the first died in 1534. His son, Sir William II,[3] lived
as a country gentleman, kept sheep, and lost money. Sir William III,
following the precedent of his grandfather, sought to mend the
declining fortunes of mere gentry by seeking office at court. His
distant connexions the Russells forwarded his career with court
patronage, and he cemented the bond by marriage to Anne, sister of
Sir Henry Sidney. This was only the beginning of a distinguished
career in the service of the Tudor dynasty. Not for the last time,
Ireland cast a shadow over the family's political ambitions. In 1555
Fitzwilliam became Keeper of the Irish Great Seal, in 1559 Vice-
Treasurer, General Receiver and Treasurer-at-War in Ireland, and
eventually, in 1571, Lord Deputy. He was also Keeper of Fotheringay
Castle after 1553 and in 1572 he found himself gaoler to Mary, Queen
of Scots, a position of far more responsibility than profit.[4] His
finances suffered rather than grew from political office; when he died
in 1599 he owed the queen £1,000 and, by his son's account, there
was only 11s 3d in his purse and his plate was at pawn for diet and
physic charges. His funeral was 'cheap and shabby'.[5] It was not the
last time that the viceroyalty of Ireland was to be something of a
disaster for the Fitzwilliams. Nevertheless, public office did not break
the Fitzwilliam fortune. The third Sir William left an estate bringing
in a yearly revenue of £1,500, from which his debt to the Crown
was paid off in three years, and he left too a reputation for private
splendour and public service. His son, Sir William IV, established
the family at Milton, Gaynes Park having been left to his mother and
younger brother, and devoted his attention to extending and rebuilding the house and managing the estate. At his death in 1618 the
family's income had risen to £2,500 a year.

After Sir William IV's prudent prosperity came decline, if not quite fall. His son obtained an Irish barony in 1620, becoming the first Lord Fitzwilliam; but this period also marked the beginning of the great slump in wool prices. From the 'long dayes with prosperitie and plentie' to which Sir William IV complacently looked back in his will, his son advanced even more deeply into debt. By 1642 he owed over £20,000, the yearly interest on which absorbed two-thirds of the estate's revenues. The situation was saved only by the second Baron's marriage to a wealthy City heiress, so refreshing the family fortune from its original source, the prospering trade of London.[6] The second Baron also brought the family back into national politics. He became the first of the family to take one of the seats at Peterborough in the Long Parliament, so establishing a political link that lasted for nearly 250 years. The third Baron (1643–1719)[7] sat for Peterborough in the Cavalier parliament from 1666 to 1678, and was also in the first and third Exclusion Parliaments of 1678–9 and 1680–1. A relative, Charles Fitzwilliam of Stamford, represented the constituency in 1685 and in the Convention of 1689. There was no doubt of the family's staunch Whiggism. The distant connexion with the Russells and Sidneys was enough in itself to mark them out as a revolution family, but conviction as well as kinship kept them loyal to the Whig creed. The Hanoverian period saw them emerge again into favour. The third Baron was made an Irish earl in 1716, and his son followed the mainstream of Whiggism, supporting the Stanhope and Sunderland Whigs and later Walpole. Steady loyalty to the Prime Minister rather than political distinction characterised his parliamentary service and that of his son William, who succeeded as third Earl in 1728 but who, as an Irish peer, remained in the Commons. He stuck to the old corps of Whigs in 1741–2 and in the latter year was rewarded with an English barony. Four years later the English viscountcy of Milton and earldom of Fitzwilliam were added.

The decisive event for the family's political and financial fortunes was the first Earl's marriage in 1744 to Anne, the elder daughter of Thomas, first Marquess of Rockingham, which allied the Fitzwilliams to one of the greatest Whig connexions of the century and, the second Marquess having no male heir, was ultimately to unite the Wentworth and Fitzwilliam estates into one of the richest landed fortunes of the day.[8] The beneficiary of this union was the third child and elder son, William, born at Milton on 30 May 1748. The new heir could thus look to an economic and political consequence unmatched in his house since the death of Elizabeth's Sir William in 1599.

William's childhood seems to have been happy but unremarkable. He was a delicate boy, suffering frequent attacks of ill health. Throughout his life he remained subject to crippling attacks of migraine. By 1756 he had a younger brother, George, and five surviving sisters.[9] It was a close family, affectionate and secure. During the Earl's absences on parliamentary business Lady Fitzwilliam, who had some artistic talent and no liking for London life, preferred to stay at Milton with her children and her painting. William's early years gave him a strong sense of family attachment which never left him in later life, when his generosity and sense of duty were often in evidence. They appeared not only in his care for the four sisters who remained unmarried, but also in his repeated responses to the solicitations of the various children of the Sturgeon family, offspring of a runaway marriage in 1764 between his mother's sister, Lady Harriet Wentworth, and one of Rockingham's footmen, William Sturgeon. Lady Harriet's death in 1789 and the failure of Sturgeon's business ventures often threw their children on to Fitzwilliam's charity, which was hardly ever refused.[10]

At 8 years old William was sent up to Eton. Disaster quickly followed; a few months after his arrival his father died, at the age of only 36, and the young schoolboy became the second and fourth Earl Fitzwilliam. His guardian under his father's will was Sir Matthew Lamb, first baronet, the son of an attorney who had been legal adviser to the Cokes of Melbourne Hall; Matthew married the daughter and heiress of the family and inherited the property in 1751.[11] His uncle, Penyston Lamb, had been legal adviser to the Fitzwilliams and manager of the Peterborough interest in the early eighteenth century, and Matthew also acquired that position together with his uncle's fortune. On these inheritances he established an important political family, for his son Peniston (1745-1828) was to become the first Lord Melbourne and father of a Prime Minister. Sir Matthew himself sat for Peterborough on the Fitzwilliam interest from 1747 until 1768, and managed the electoral affairs of the borough for his ward.

Fitzwilliam was not attracted to scholarship and he made no particular mark at Eton, where his tutor, Edward Young, wrote in 1763 only of his 'exceeding good understanding, and . . . most amiable disposition and temper'.[12] Eton, however, had a lifelong influence on him, for he formed here some of the most deeply rooted attachments of his private and political life. Frederick Howard, Lord Morpeth and later fifth Earl of Carlisle, and Lionel Damer, later Viscount Milton and Earl of Dorchester, were exact contemporaries in the same form. Two years later Henry, afterwards third Duke of Buccleuch, joined the school at the same time as the man who was to be, of all Fitzwilliam's schoolfellows and later political associates, the one whose friendship was to be the deepest and longest lasting of all—Charles James Fox. No record exists of their meeting or of the growth of their friendship. It was in many ways a curious association: that Fox, spoilt and indulged from earliest infancy by a doting father, introduced at the earliest age to every pleasure and debauchery, should be so attracted to Fitzwilliam, whose upbringing was sheltered and whose character was by comparison strictly formed, is to some extent incongruous. Throughout their lives they were bound by deep ties of affection and trust, yet their attitudes and temperaments were entirely different. Fitzwilliam grew up to be the typical eighteenth-century aristocrat—a man to whom politics was a natural responsibility due to his order, his family and his country, but not a field for the display of ambition. He was always fonder of the country than the town, of the local rather than the national arena. He saw his role throughout his life as that of leader of his local society and a link between the party and the public. Fox, however, had few connexions with the country-house life of his aristocratic friends: his was the life of the London clubman and politician, and it was lived at the centre of political affairs. Parliament was Fox's only real sphere of political action. Fitzwilliam's world, on the contrary, was that of the great estate owner, whose responsibilities were deeper and more personal. Agents, tenantry, mortgages, leases and properties were his daily concern, and to these his life had in some measure to be dedicated. No one could be a greater partisan or a more willing contributor to party causes, as he was to show in Yorkshire and in other great and small political contests, or as he was to be in the House of Lords as one of the Whig opposition's foremost speakers in the last decades of the century. But national politics had always taken second place to those local responsibilities from which his political engagement sprang so intimately.

For the schoolboys at Eton the late 1750s were a glorious, confident age, unsullied by those fears for English liberty soon to be unleashed by the persecution of Wilkes and the coercion of America. Britain, led by the elder Pitt, was becoming master of the seas and the four continents. It was an age of golden achievements and golden friendships. Lord Carlisle, the most gifted of the young dilettanti among Fitzwilliam's schoolfellows, celebrated in verse the outstanding characteristics of his friends. In Fitzwilliam he found neither burning talents nor outstanding energy, but an amiability and generosity for which his friend was to be noted throughout his life: [13]

> Say, will Fitzwilliam ever want a heart,
> Cheerful his ready blessings to impart?
> Will not another's woe his bosom share,
> The widow's sorrow and the orphan's prayer?
> Who aids the old, who soothes the mother's cry,
> Who wipes the tear from off the virgin's eye?
> Who feeds the hungry, who assists the lame?
> All, all re-echo with Fitzwilliam's name.
> Thou know'st I hate to flatter, yet in thee
> No fault, my friend, no single speck I see.

That Charles Fox should be drawn to such a companion would have surprised no one who knew his genius for friendship. It was to be for both men the deepest and most significant attachment of their public and personal lives.

Fitzwilliam's stay at Eton was not prolonged. He showed only average intellectual ability, and his delicate health was a constant worry. In the summer of 1764, with Europe again at peace and young English lords flocking to the Continent, his mother and guardian decided to send him on the grand tour to re-establish his health and complete his education. To one leaving home and friends at so young an age a congenial and experienced companion was of the greatest importance. Dr Barnard, headmaster of Eton, proposed for the duty of travelling tutor a 41-year-old clergyman, Thomas Crofts, 'an excellent scholar, and a very agreeable companion', with a good deal of experience in accompanying young gentlemen on their continental travels. The next four years were to cement an affectionate friendship between tutor and pupil, and Crofts, though an indulgent taskmaster when it came to the hard labour of learning languages, must have exercised a strong influence in forming Fitzwilliam's taste.[14] The young earl was to begin as a reluctant student of the antique, but he returned from his tour a lifelong devotee of painting and the arts, and with a taste for fine books, for which Crofts was particularly enthusiastic. The grand tour became one of the most rewarding and most formative influences on his development.

The tour followed the conventional pattern now established by at least two generations of grand tourists. The companions embarked for Calais in October 1764, and made their first extended stop at Montauban, when the young milord was to mingle with local society and to take his first steps in learning French.[15] It was 'a most sociable place', Fitzwilliam reported to his mother : he was quickly introduced to 'all the great people of the place' by the senior English residents at a grand dinner party. 'I suppose you would imagine that I was terribly frightened,' he wrote, 'and did not open my lips all dinner; but believe me you are much mistaken, for I spoke French notably; they were not two French people in the room, that I had not some conversation with. I expect to speak most fluently in another month.' Four months later, however, he admitted that 'though I understand, and can say all the common things, I can by no means hold a conversation upon any particular subject'—blaming his misfortune on the prevalence of English company and his tutor's defective pronunciation.

French society failed to live up to its early promise. Fitzwilliam was soon complaining that the French were 'a set of low, mean, impertinent people', and their behaviour 'so intolerable that it is absolutely impossible for me to associate with them . . . it is the opinion of everybody, that I had better quit the place immediately'. Toulouse, the next port of call, was more agreeable. Here, he wrote, 'they are really people of fashion and fortune; there are three or four houses that have assemblies almost every night'. His mother, who had recently received an unexpectedly large account for the first quarter's expenses, took a less enthusiastic view. He assured her :

I have not forgot (as *you* seem to imagine) how small my income is. You may assure yourself, I will not throw my money away *unnecessarily*, but at [the] same time [I] shall not deny myself what is *necessary* : although it may make my expenses larger than were expected.

Three months later, however, Fitzwilliam admitted that he had spent over double his pocket money allowance, mainly on clothes. 'If I was to appear in company,' he wrote, 'it was necessary I should equip myself like a gentleman.' The gaities of Toulouse were accordingly to be abandoned after two months in favour of a quieter resort at Vevay, on Lake Geneva, where, as Crofts wrote, 'there is good French society, and no English'. It was time serious attempts were made to perfect Fitzwilliam's French, and a course of reading was to be begun.

In May, however, the travellers were still in the south of France, visiting Nimes for an introduction to antiquities and Marseilles for a reunion with English friends. Fitzwilliam's first reaction to the classical remains of Nimes was unenthusiastic: 'Mr Crofts instructed me in a number of hard names yesterday, which I endeavoured to remember, but all in vain—I forgot everything in ten minutes', he admitted. Marseilles, too, was surprisingly disappointing: English society there consisted of 'a set of the most stupid people ever got together'. He moved northwards again, taking in Spa in July, where the usual crowd of English tourists had gathered, 'more . . . in number than all the *foreigners* put together', as Fitzwilliam remarked, and including his old schoolfriend Lord Carlisle. In August he travelled to Paris to meet his favourite sister, Charlotte, and her new husband, Thomas Dundas.[16] These diversions both from the planned route of the tour and from its primary purpose of study were the subject of a firm letter received from Lady Fitzwilliam at the beginning of September. 'I coincide with you in everything,' her son admitted, 'and readily agree that my *wants* in almost every branch of science are innumerable; and that nothing can remedy these wants but a steady application.' He promised that the winter would be usefully employed, 'if I am sufficiently master of myself to profit of favourable opportunities'. After toying with thoughts of establishing himself for the winter at Aix, which, however, suffered from cold winds, and even Avignon, whiggishly unsuitable as 'the asylum for every banished Jacobite', Fitzwilliam now fixed upon Lyons as his residence for the next few months, hoping that here at last he might be 'familiarly acquainted with the people, and that I might learn French'. In return his mother promised that he would be allowed to break his tour and return home for a few months next spring, both to see his friends—'naturally the most weighty reason with me', he wrote—but also on sensible educational grounds;

for no arguments can make me believe that it is a wise system of education for a young man to spend the four or five first years after he has left school, abroad; and for him to return at the end of that time without any knowledge of the people or the country, without any connections with the young men of his own age, except those he formed in the dissipations of Italy—and besides for the sake of comparing England with the countries I have seen, a visit is absolutely necessary; for . . . I must necessarily make useful comparisons.

After his winter in Lyons and a short visit to Switzerland he

returned to England early in 1766 for the promised reunion with his
mother and sisters. For a few months the boredom and strangeness
of French provincial society were forgotten in a round of the usual
diversions of the London season. Educational opportunities were not
totally neglected, and in July he made a five-day tour of the Midlands,
visiting Oxford to see the colleges and Birmingham for a look at some
of the new factories. The autumn was spent at home, and early in
December the continental tour was resumed. He returned in a peni-
tential mood, determined both to apply himself to study and to guard
against extravagance. A letter from his mother with a list of his
banker's drafts produced assurances that he would try to 'acquire
that *prudence*, which is so necessary to a person in my circumstances,
and of which I feel I have so small a share. I am conscious how
destitute I am of that quality, but I hope I have resolution enough
to acquire it.' He declared his determination 'to give up at least a part
of the day to reading: but what I shall do, time alone will show'.
Three weeks later he admitted 'we do study a little, how much I will
not pretend to say, but we certainly do jogg on, and turn over a few
pages every day'. His enjoyment of the studious life was evidently
limited; preparing to set out for Italy in April, he wrote: 'after I
have been tied up so long in this dismal solitary place, there can be
no objection to my spending a few sociable hours with my friends,
and therefore I shall do all I can to meet them this summer'. On 29
April he set sail from Nice for Genoa and the last stage of the tour.

The visit to Italy was to be one of the most rewarding and formative influences of his life. He was immediately fascinated by the
country. 'I like this place beyond expression', he wrote from Genoa
a few days after landing. Its delights were immeasurably increased by
the pleasure of meeting again his closest friends. Charles Fox, Carlisle,
Uvedale Price, Buccleuch and a number of other old school friends
were now or shortly to be in Italy, and the summer and winter of
1767-8 were spent mainly in their company. They visited Verona to
see the pictures, Venice for the regatta and its attendant amusements,
Padua, Bologna and Florence for the galleries again in the summer.
It was during these months that Fitzwilliam's love of pictures
blossomed and established itself, while under the guidance of such
cognoscenti as Sir Horace Mann in Florence and William Hamilton
at Naples his taste was cultivated and trained in the predominant
mode of his age. He was to return to Milton no longer a frivolous
boy, eager to escape from the schoolroom to indulge his fancies, but

a connoisseur of discernment and discrimination, with the beginnings of a collection of fine pictures whose extent was limited, for
the time being, only by the shortness of his purse. 'I can never go
through a gallery of pictures, without wishing to be rich', he wrote,
'that I may buy the finest to send to Milton. At Bologna I made a
very pretty collection in my imagination'. By the end of the year he
wrote from Rome that he had 'grown excessively fond of pictures,
and wish very much that I had money to throw away upon painting.'
He was to return home in 1768 with fourteen pictures, including
eight fine Canalettos and a number of the then fashionable works of
the seventeenth-century Bolognese school, such as Guercino and
Guido Reni, who remained favourites with him to the end of his
life.[17] His taste was conventional and altogether that of his age, but
his appreciation of the arts was a permanent enrichment of his life.

Florence also contributed to Fitzwilliam's education. At first it
was 'very dull, no play, no opera, not even a puppet show: the
height of amusement is to walk upon the bridge in the evening'. But
at Sir Horace Mann's celebrated weekly assemblies Fitzwilliam, like
every other grand tourist of the age, found diversion and acquired an
education in manners. Subsequently, with Fox in Rome and elsewhere
he tasted the usual pleasures of the young aristocrat away from the
close supervision of his family. Yet he was sensitive to the cultural
delights of the city. If no companion of Fox could fail to experience
the dissipations of an Italian society geared to the appetites of the
young English milords, no friend of Carlisle could be insensitive to the
visible remains of a classical antiquity with whose art and literature
every boy from Eton was familiar. Though he felt indifferent towards
St Peter's, the 'ancient buildings' attracted him at once: 'The elegance
of their architecture, and the beauty of their sculpture surpass everything, that one sees of modern date'. English painters were set to
work to produce landscapes and a portrait to be presented to Rockingham, and with the visit of the Hamiltons from Naples he was
introduced to the fascination of antique vases, which Hamilton was
presently engaged in describing in a publication which was to be
one of the strongest influences on later eighteenth-century English
domestic ornament.[18] In May Fitzwilliam, Fox and Carlisle followed
the Hamiltons home to Naples, but he found it surprisingly dull;
though the court was lavish, society was only superficially brilliant,
and the notorious cruelty of the King of Naples and his absolutist
system of government could not escape censure from so zealous a

Whig partisan as Fitzwilliam. During the summer, therefore, the travellers set out for the last stage of their journey, returning over the Alps, going through Switzerland and up the Rhine to Mannheim and Spa before the final winter in Paris.[19] In January 1769 the grand tourists returned to England for the last time.[20]

It was an experience never forgotten. Fifty years later, when his own son, Lord Milton, travelled to Italy, Fitzwilliam remembered his youthful experiences, and, recollecting his frustrated ambition, urged him to lay out any sum of money he chose on pictures to bring back to Milton or Wentworth.

I am glad you have found Bologna as replete with beautiful paintings as ever [he wrote]: you must have found in it the finest Guidos and Guercinos, and indeed of all the Caraccis. . . . You ask to what extent I meant to carry the expression, that my purse was yours—5,000 or 10,000 or a larger sum, is at your command : your own discretion must set the limit upon your call on that which sooner or later will be your own.[21]

The grand tour was a formative influence in the lives of several generations of eighteenth-century aristocratic families. It enriched their aesthetic experience, trained them in self-reliance and independence, and moulded their attitudes to their own country and constitution as much as to those of foreign nations. In all this Fitzwilliam shared. He returned still unblemished in personal reputation, despite his association with Fox's set, re-established in health, and prepared to undertake the responsibilities of head of the family, to supervise the estates, and to assume his father's role as one of the leading Whig peers in political life. And beyond his immediate family fortune loomed now the possibility of even greater wealth and responsibilities. His uncle Rockingham, still without a male heir, intended to leave his vast estates intact to the issue of the eldest of his sisters, Fitzwilliam's mother. On his twenty-first birthday in May 1769 Fitzwilliam could already look to a future of far greater consequence than that enjoyed by any of his forbears since the time of Sir William III, Elizabeth's viceroy.

The Fitzwilliam fortune in 1769 was substantial, though not spectacular. The principal estate at Milton produced, during the last seven years of the new Earl's minority, an average clear income rather under £3,000 a year. Other estates in Lincolnshire, Nottinghamshire, Yorkshire and Norfolk and the urban rents in Peterborough produced altogether a further £3,600 on average. In 1768 Fitzwilliam drew over £6,900 from his landed properties. There were, however, many encumbrances. The income of the estates was charged with jointures for his mother, his aunts, brother and four sisters, and the interest on his father's debts; the total debt amounted to £45,000 and the annual charges to over £3,300.[22] However, substantial capital savings had been made during his minority, totalling over £10,000; Lady Fitzwilliam suggested that the debts could be cleared by the sale of the Yorkshire and Nottinghamshire estates, leaving the young Earl to 'begin the world with a titular estate of £8,000 p.a. clear of all deductions except my jointure, which cannot be long before it falls in'.[23] The calculations were optimistic; clearly if the new Earl was to start his majority on a clear footing, land would have to be sold off to pay the debts. The Norfolk estate, for example, producing a clear income of £1,275 in 1768, was burdened with £24,000 of debt. Fitzwilliam sold it for £60,000—a price Rockingham considered 'scarce enough' but sufficient to clear off the encumbrances on the whole estate.[24] Other rearrangements of his properties—the selling off of small outlying estates and the consolidation of the Milton estate by a further purchase in 1775—settled the pattern of the Northamptonshire properties and provided resources to clear the inherited debts. Even before the magnificent Rockingham inheritance of 1782 Fitzwilliam was in sufficiently easy circumstances to be able to play an assured role in Whig politics, though expenses had to be kept within strict limits. In 1780, for example, when Charles Anderson Pelham offered to bring his brother George into Parliament for Grimsby, Fitzwilliam confessed to Rockingham that 'was a dissolution to take place now, I could not advance him a hundred pounds to pay his post chaise to Grimsby' and he had to decline the proposal.[25]

Fitzwilliam's mother did not long survive her son's majority. In failing health for some time, she concealed her state as much as possible from her children, retiring to a rented house at Chelsea 'to put them out of the way at the last melancholy moments', as a relative remarked. By the end of June, Lady Mary Coke was aware that she was not expected to live two months, but Fitzwilliam and his sisters were so uniformed of her condition that they continued to enjoy the season's round of balls, assemblies and amusements in London, and moved to Wentworth for York races in August. All but the youngest of the sisters, Lady Dorothy, who was with her mother, were enjoying the 'gay doings' of York when their mother died on 29 August. Their conduct was regarded as 'indecent, and most unnatural' by a scandalised society. Fitzwilliam, however, was

genuinely shocked and distressed by his mother's death, and quickly
regained the good opinion of the world by his generosity towards his
four still unmarried sisters. Despite his straitened finances, he kept
a promise to his mother to augment the inadequate fortunes left to
them by his father's will, adding £5,000 to each to bring them all
up to £7,000.[26]

His own marriage was now a matter of some urgency. Anything
but a good Whig alliance would have been unthinkable, in view of
the Rockingham inheritance to come and the family's long political
tradition. In any case, the closeness of mid-eighteenth-century Whig
society inevitably threw Fitzwilliam into circles where his choice
was likely to be generally acceptable to its members. It was no
surprise, therefore, when his engagement was announced in May
1770 to Lady Charlotte Ponsonby, second daughter of the second Earl
of Bessborough and a long-standing friend of the family. The Ponsonbys were one of the three great Irish political families.[27] Their
property in Counties Cork and Kilkenny was extensive and their
parliamentary influence was commensurate with it. They were also
prominent office-holders. Their kinship with the leading English Whig
families was one of the closest ties that bound Irish and English
Whiggism together: Fitzwilliam's mission to Ireland in 1795 was to
be partly a product of this relationship, and in some ways it owed
its failure to Fitzwilliam's inability to break through the bonds of
family affection.

In the spring of 1770 these shadows had not yet thrown themselves
across Fitzwilliam's life. Horace Walpole, who knew the intended
bride, was pleased with the news: 'It is a pretty match,' he wrote
to George Montagu, 'and makes Lord Bessborough as happy as
possible.' To Mann he wrote of Charlotte as 'a pretty, sensible and
very amiable girl'. Like her future husband, however, she was often
in delicate health and, wrote Lord John Cavendish in 1783, she had
'much sensibility'. In 1786 Cavendish referred to her recurrent complaint as 'a dropsy of a very particular kind' and remarked that her
health kept Fitzwilliam in a state of constant anxiety. She was
evidently a difficult patient to her devoted husband. 'His over-
tenderness and constant attention has done them both much harm,'
Cavendish remarked, 'but he will not be advised on those points.'
The need to consider her health frequently reinforced Fitzwilliam's
natural tendency to prefer the home life of Milton or Wentworth
to the bustle of London politics.[28]

For the present, the possession of a substantial house and estate
added to a close relationship to the highest Whig circles, and intimate
friendships with leading young Whig politicians made Fitzwilliam
aware from his earliest youth of the political future which might be
his. At the outset political consequence was to be measured chiefly
in the possession of family borough influence. The seat at Peterborough, controlled by the family since Charles II's time, was not an
entirely secure one and Fitzwilliam's first political operations were
designed to consolidate it. The city franchise, belonging to 'scot and
lot' voters, comprised 374 electors, 'and much the greatest part of them
are very necessitous people not influenced by anybody', as Sir Matthew
Lamb remarked after a long experience of managing them. Personal
connexions in the town and the steady support of the cathedral
interest were normally sufficient to guarantee one seat to the family,
but, as Sir Matthew Lamb warned his ward in 1767, it was an interest
'not strong enough . . . to elect a member when different candidates
declare and money and drink is stirring, and that in profusion'.[29] The
major family interest after the Fitzwilliams was that of the Parkers
of Burghberry Manor, near Peterborough, and for eighteen of the
thirty-three years since 1734 Armstead Parker, a Tory in politics, had
filled one seat. In 1767 he announced his retirement and put forward
his son in his place. A third candidate unexpectedly appeared in the
person of Matthew Wyldbore, an old friend and supporter of the
Fitzwilliam interest in the city but on this occasion setting up independently. Sir Matthew Lamb, who was holding the Fitzwilliam seat,
determined to preserve it for the family at all cost; in an expensive
contest lasting four months he succeeded in doing so, though both his
rivals declared 'they matter not money; they keep upon the spot, and
watch every opportunity to gain voters; they both of them have spent
equally with Sir Matthew Lamb'. Fitzwilliam, in Italy, could only
watch from a distance, but, with a characteristic optimism and
ardour, could not help wishing to take a more active part. The
family's neutrality, he thought, neglected an opportunity to help
Wyldbore. If the Parkers won, nothing would be lost, for neither they
nor Fitzwilliam could hope to control the other's seat; if Wyldbore
won, gratitude and self-interest would attach him to Fitzwilliam:

I am now soon going into the world, and into a world of confusion where
an influence over a Member of Parliament will certainly not make me less
considerable. . . . To be sure with my narrow fortune it will be wrong
to run into any expense without good reason to think that it will succeed;

but I own I think it will be worth one or two, nay three thousand: and if it could be secured by that, I am clearly for it.

Fitzwilliam even suggested that, after giving secret encouragement to Wyldbore, he himself should return 'unknown to Parker and to everybody at Peterborough six weeks or a month before the election' to use his personal influence. Such a stratagem, even if wise, was hardly necessary, as Lady Fitzwilliam pointed out; young Parker declined the contest when faced with a potential expense of £4,000 or £5,000, reputedly bought off by Wyldbore for £1,000 in cash. Lady Fitzwilliam, in conference with Sir Matthew Lamb and the bishop, had already determined to follow her late husband's practice of not interfering in the second seat, though private assurances of goodwill were given to Wyldbore: in the event 'each candidate declared himself our friend, an enemy only to the other'. Naturally enough, however, Lamb had to 'spend guinea for guinea with the other candidates' to prevent their stealing his voters, and it cost him nearly £2,500 to secure his position. 'I think you should write to congratulate Sir Matthew,' Lady Fitzwilliam advised her son on Parker's withdrawal, 'to thank him for having so vigorously asserted your interest and to desire he will give you leave to hope you shall see the expense placed to your account when you come of age, which you shall look upon as your quota, the trouble and fatigue having fallen to his share.' Fitzwilliam took the advice, and wrote Sir Matthew a suitable letter 'what he will like, for at the same time that I have thanked him, I have intermixed a little flattery, which with most people generally has a good effect, and not less with him than with others'. For good measure he decided to throw in his portrait, which he was having painted in Rome but which had turned out too disappointingly to be suitable for his uncle Rockingham, its original destination. 'If the picture does not turn out so well as I should wish,' he wrote, 'I should be sorry that my uncle should have it, and the idea of its being done at Rome will please Sir Matthew.' The baronet, unaware perhaps of his young ward's cynicism, begged to be allowed to pay the election expenses himself, and he had to finance another five months of treating the voters before the election in March 1768, when the Parkers put up a third candidate at the polls. This was Edward Littlehales, an attorney recently released from the Fleet prison. 'You will never be free from trouble there,' wrote Lady Fitzwilliam in May. 'If you should be solicited for *anything there*,

no matter what, no matter who, enter into no promises. Fight shy
to everybody: and so keep free to take what part you please when
you come of age.'[30]

On Sir Matthew Lamb's death in November 1768 the Fitzwilliams
set up Lord Belasyse, an old schoolfellow of William's, and a relation
of Sir Matthew's family. The election was fortunately uncontested,
and Lady Filtzwilliam thought it a good opportunity to add to the
family property in the city. £2,500 was spent to buy an inn and
some more houses, whose tenants would swell the interest. In 1773
Fitzwilliam conceived a scheme to secure the position beyond challenge by the exchange of some of his scattered estates in Holderness
and in Lincolnshire for an estate near Peterborough belonging to Sir
Brownlow Cust, part of which was leased to Parker and which in
turn he let to voters from the city. Rockingham advised strongly
against the plan. 'I hope and trust you will not wish to dabble in such
adventurous matters as selling and buying large estates,' he wrote.
'The buying of an estate valued at £68,000 or the selling of an estate
or estates to the amount of upwards of £60,000 value are no light
considerations.' Besides the dubious financial gains or losses, the
political advantages were highly speculative. 'I imagine you mean to
content yourself with *one* member,' Rockingham wrote, 'and if so
your interest is surely strong enough. Lucky events may *sometimes*
give you *two*, but the attempt to have *two* and to keep *two* will I
should fear be an endless trouble and expense to you, and perhaps it
would be wisest to avoid the temptation.' Fitzwilliam, however,
persisted with the scheme, and in August 1776 agreed with Cust for
the purchase of part of the estate for £20,500. In 1790 he bought the
Parker estate for £22,000 and from that time nominated both members. 'It is a place where we have no trouble,' he wrote in 1796, 'but
where we always pay great attention.' There was no more political
opposition at Peterborough until the 1820s.[31]

Nationally too, Fitzwilliam's return from his grand tour and his
assumption of the headship of the family plunged him into the
involvement with Whig party politics that was to characterise the
rest of his career. His eagerness to be of service to the party made
him a valuable recruit to the opposition in the Lords. His twenty-first
birthday came during the summer recess, but he took his seat in the
House along with his friend Carlisle on the first day of the new
session.[32] At once he plunged into the fierce party warfare raging
over the Middlesex election and the reporting of parliamentary

debates. These two issues were related, partly through the championship and activities of John Wilkes but chiefly, in the eyes of the
Rockinghamite and Chathamite oppositions, because they fitted so
neatly into a general advocacy of the cause of 'liberty'—the liberty
of the two Houses from executive influence and—more dangerously
—the liberty of the people to defy a House of Commons whose
attitude (they argued) was so clearly determined by corrupt ministerial domination. The long campaign to force the House of Commons
to accept Wilkes as member for Middlesex, despite the legalistic
grounds on which his thrice-repeated election was voided by the
House, came to a head in 1769 with the Commons' resolution seating
Luttrell, his opponent, who had polled a minority of the votes. In
the general excitement over the issues behind this act—the rights of
electors to choose their own candidates subject only to the law and
the courts, and not to the arbitrary determinations of the Commons
—the opposition saw a chance to rise on a wave of popular support,
manifested in addresses and petitions like the remonstrance from the
City of London presented in March 1770.[33] Nor did they forget that
the original cause on which Wilkes had risen to fame before the
Middlesex elections was that of the freedom of the newspaper press
to criticise the Ministry, and even the sovereign, in the name of
popular rights and opinions. If the Middlesex election case threatened
the rights of electors and conjured up visions of a packed House of
Commons nominated by the Ministry of the day, the refusal of the
same House to permit public reporting of its own debates menaced
the right of the electors to discover and comment on the activities
and opinions of their representatives, once elected. With a zeal and a
vehemence that might have been a good deal less vigorous had their
aristocratic leaders fully understood the radical implications of their
programme, the opposition groups set about the final storming of
Grafton's citadel.

Into this forceful campaign the new recruit plunged with the ardour
of a fully fledged party man. He attended the first big debate of the
session, on 15 January, and was one of the eleven who signed the
first Lords protest of the year. In the debate on the state of the nation
(2 February) the Middlesex election was the major topic: again
Fitzwilliam attended and signed the opposition's two protests.[34] The
pattern of Fitzwilliam's political life was established for the remainder
of the session, and indeed for the whole of the period until the
resignation of Lord North's Ministry twelve years later. Attending,

with the main strength of the opposition Lords, almost every major
political debate; signing almost every one of the protests which the
minority continued to use until the 1780s to put their case before
the public; but never (so far as is known) actually speaking in the
House, he became a regular and reliable partisan of every major opposition cause. His warmth in support of the party sprang partly, of
course, from his close relationship with and deep affection for his
uncle Rockingham, was fanned by pride in a long family tradition of
undeviating Whiggism, and confirmed by a growing and invincible
conviction of the justice and historical rightness of his party cause.
In July 1776, for example, he pressed Rockingham to arrange for a
remonstrance to the king on the outbreak of war in America, to
show the Americans 'that there is still in this country a body of men
of the first rank and importance, who would still wish to govern
them according to the old policy'. Throughout his life he remained a
determined advocate of civil rather than military government. In
opposition to the coercion of America lay the roots of his stand
against the government's approval of 'Peterloo' in 1819.[35] In March
1771 he was one of the ten Whig peers and commoners who demonstrated their support of the London magistrates Crosby and Oliver,
who, along with Wilkes, had acquitted Miller, the printer indicted
for publishing parliamentary debates, and who had been committed to
the Tower. Whether Fitzwilliam played any part in bringing his old
friend Charles Fox into the Whig party in the years 1774–6 is not
known; it is tempting to speculate that the deep friendship between
the two men may have had an influence, but more likely that Fox
found ample motive for his *volte-face* in his own political and
personal interest. There is no doubt, however, that this union gave
both friends great delight. Fox had written in January 1767, on the
grand tour:

I can not help fearing lest two or three years absence, and your different
connections should by degrees make you forget a friendship which I consider as one of the greatest happinesses of my life . . . Though I have not
the honour to know your uncle, everything I hear of him makes me have
the greatest respect for him; but indeed if nothing else did, the affection
I know you bear him would make me interest myself for him; you yourself, I know, are very eager for the success of your party; you cannot
wonder, then, that it gives me great concern to think that I must be
your enemy even in my wishes, and whenever I can be so, in my actions
as to politics, for all the considerations I mentioned, however powerful,

cannot balance the obligations our family has to Lord Bute, and the shocking ingratitude it has met with from the Bedfords.[36]

Thus private affection cemented the close public association which was to last for twenty years without interruption, and to be resumed after a break of only seven years until the end of Fox's life.

The Whig party to which Fitzwilliam found himself inevitably attached by family and tradition was not solely the expression of a conscious political ideology.[37] It was a group of families whose social cohesion, produced by close interrelationships and friendships, expressed a common commitment to ideals of constitutional government and belief in the rights of Parliament against the Crown and executive. They came to see themselves as the guardians of the post-1688 constitutional settlement and the protectors of the liberty of the subject which that settlement had ensured. The cry against the 'influence of the Crown' summed up in a phrase the resentment felt by men excluded from office rightfully theirs, and it provided an explanation of how it came about that both Parliament and administration were apparently unresponsive to national interests. To remedy the national ills it was necessary not only to reduce Crown and ministerial influence over Parliament but also to place authority in the hands of trustworthy Whigs. The Cabinet must be a unity, acting in concert and under a common head, if it were to stand against the divisive tactics of the king and his 'friends'. The Whig party of Rockingham, Portland, Fox and Burke thus provided its members not merely with a set of ready-made moral and political attitudes but with a sense of common purpose and a zeal for the cause of liberty, as they understood the term.

In the 1770s the causes for which their Whiggism stood were epitomised in the conflict with America and the campaign at home to reduce Crown influence over Parliament. These steadily pushed themselves to the front of public attention as the disasters of the later period of the War of Independence became apparent. Military and naval inefficiency, highlighted in Burgoyne's surrender at Saratoga and in the court martial of Admiral Keppel, swung public support against the ineffective government of Lord North. By the autumn of 1781 the Ministry was kept in office only by the king's determination to preserve it. Riven by internal dissension and intrigue, harassed by crises in Ireland, Gibraltar, America and the West Indies, attacked at home by radicals and moderate reformers who saw in its continued

B

existence the symbol of everything corrupt and nationally dishonourable, the Ministry was already breaking up when the final disaster
occurred.

The news of the surrender of Cornwallis's southern army reached
England on 25 November 1781, two days before the meeting of Parliament.[38] The reform movements which had begun to lose momentum
after the Gordon riots and the general election in 1780 were revived
by the news. Addresses seeking an end to the war were voted by
corporations and communities who had previously concerned themselves primarily with reforms at home. On 6 December the liverymen
of the City of London added their weight to the 'stop the war' agitation, and six days later the electors of Westminster voted a similar
address.[39] Public opinion began to stir again, energetically promoted
by the Rev. Christopher Wyvill and his associates in the country and
by the metropolitan radicals in the London area. The rising agitation
was not lost on members of Parliament who represented the sensitive
constituencies—counties and large boroughs—where even the patern-
alistic eighteenth-century electoral system had to allow for a substantial element of independent opinion amongst the voters. Decisive
action by the government—even a show of energy in dealing with
the problems which surrounded it—could perhaps have reassured the
waverers. Far from rallying his supporters by a brave defiance of
adversity, however, North seemed to welcome the demoralisation
which began to set in amongst his following. He begged to be allowed
to resign an office which was distasteful to him and which he knew
he did not fill with credit. By 25 February he was confessing to
George III that he could no longer depend upon the votes of those
members to whom he was sending Treasury letters.[40]

If North was ready and eager to be gone, however, George III had
no intention of releasing him from his post. The king was no longer
the hesitant, unsure boy of 1760, desperate for a 'dear friend' to shield
him from the wicked politicians who engrossed the royal power.
After twenty-one years his experience of politics was as wide and as
deep as that of any man in his dominions, and determination—or
obstinacy, depending on the point of view—was now his major
political attribute. Of the selfishness and corruptibility of politicians
in general he still had no doubt; but he was now aware of his own
advantages and of the strength of his position as monarch in a society
whose cohesion was recognised to lie in the general acceptance of a
monarchial principle. However men might dispute the tactical limits

of the sovereign's day-to-day authority, there were few who contested the necessity of a monarch on the throne. George III had no
doubt that even if North was now too feeble and demoralised to be
propped up again, as he had been propping him up for the past five
or six years, his own intervention would resolve the governmental
crisis and rally the country by a firm designation of authority and
favour into the hands of a new and acceptable leader. The Rockinghams, eagerly awaiting the inevitable capitulation, would be disappointed and routed by a display of 'firmness' if not on North's part,
then on someone else's, and certainly on the king's. At any rate,
there was to be no surrender to the pernicious political doctrines of
the Whigs or to the detestable personal character of Charles James
Fox. George III was not always able to distinguish which of these
was the greater barrier to office for Fox and his associates, but
together they were insurmountable in his eyes. Fox's personal association with the young Prince of Wales, still less than twenty years
old, was blamed by the king for that youth's inexplicably weak
character and decadent morals—neither of which, he was sure, could
be attributed to the example of his parents or the disciplined upbringing to which they had subjected him. Fox, too, was that same young
man who had stalked out of North's Ministry a few years ago over
family resentment against the Royal Marriages Act—a measure
personally promoted by the king—thus adding personal insult to the
injury of 'deserting his post', as any resigning Minister was always
considered by George III to do. Fox, furthermore, had taken up the
cause of the American rebels and flaunted Washington's buff and
blue uniform in the House of Commons itself: and since 1780 he had
been so unscrupulous as to ally himself publicly with extreme radicals
and virtual republicans—dissenters and the rabble of Westminster—
in order to curry favour with a mob taught to shout for universal
suffrage and annual parliaments. If Fox the seducer of the Prince of
Wales needed another title to infamy in his sovereign's eyes it was
provided in the slogan 'the Man of the People'. His admission to
office, George III was convinced, would lead to the subjection of the
royal prerogative to the will, not even of a respectable House of
gentlemen, but of an aristocratic clique whose only title to office lay
in their territorial influence and political unscrupulousness. 'Party' to
George III did not mean what it was to come to mean by the end of
the nineteenth century, or even what it was to Burke in 1770. It was
not a respectable alliance of men bound by public profession of

political principle, a surety to the public for responsible behaviour in office. Rather it seemed, to one brought up as George III had been on the conventional and legalistic constitutionalism of Blackstone, a denial of the fundamental liberties on which the constitution was based. Party government meant the dictation of the executive by the legislature—a legislature which, stripped of that 'influence' which the sovereign legitimately exerted over patriotic and respectable men, would be the tool of faction and narrow self-interest. The balance of the constitution would be destroyed, and the liberties which depended on the maintenance of that balance would be shattered. If the people's interest lay in the preservation of the 'mixed constitution', it was George III, not Charles Fox, who could claim the title 'Man of the People'.

The fall of Lord North's government was to lead, therefore, to two years of almost incessant and unprecedentedly bitter political struggle. It was a conflict in which men were compelled to decide what their political principles really were : and it led to a realignment of parties more fundamental and more significant for a hundred years to come than any political conflict before the rise of organised labour in the later nineteenth century. From the resolution of the crisis now beginning, and in which Fitzwilliam was to play a part, would come the new alignments of Whig, and, eventually, Tory that were to become the almost mythical symbols of nineteenth-century political division.

In the weeks preceding their assumption of office on 1 April the Whigs had been jubilant. At Brooks's, reported George Selwyn with distaste, the language and conduct of Fox and his friends were indecent. They divided the administrative offices amongst themselves and their friends, spoke of the king openly as 'Satan', and, on the verge of entering office as the government of a great empire, sat publicly in the windows overlooking St James's Street playing faro for enormous sums. Selwyn, like many others, found his admiration for Fox as a politician tempered by his distaste for the company he kept. Fitzwilliam, an enthusiastic party man, was as exultant as any of them. On 6 March Selwyn reported that he had been cornered at Brooks's by Fitzwilliam and his brother and made to listen to a forceful diatribe on the state of the country. 'I do not know if he was in earnest,' wrote Selwyn, 'but I suppose that he was. He had worked himself up to commiserate the state of this country, nay, that of the king himself, [so] that I expected every instant that his heart

would have burst'; and on Selwyn's enquiring 'if there was a possibility of salvation in any position in which our affairs could be
placed' Fitzwilliam 'asked me . . . with the utmost impetuosity, what
objection I had to Lord Rock[ingham] being sent for. You may be
pretty sure', Selwyn added, 'that if I had any, I should not have
made it'.[41]

Fitzwilliam's partisanship did not extend, however, to a wish for
office in the approaching Whig administration. As Rockingham's
nephew and Fox's friend he naturally supported all their measures,
but youth, natural diffidence and perhaps family pressures made him
reluctant to press any claim of his own for office. Rank, of course,
forbade his being offered a subordinate office of much business—these
posts were for those who had to make their way and their fortunes
by their own efforts, not to those already endowed with title and
estate. Nor would it have been appropriate for a Whig nobleman to
be offered a sinecure, such as the vice-treasurership of Ireland rejected
by Pitt. Fitzwilliam's role was to be a supporter in the Lords—a silent
one, until Rockingham's death placed him higher in the party
councils—and an active friend in the worlds of London society and
provincial politics. These were the spheres in which he always preferred to operate. Now, as in later life, Fitzwilliam preferred the
private sphere to the public, the supporting to the leading role. Nor
did he receive much encouragement to come forward from his
formidable aunt, Lady Rockingham, who, according to Burke's later
recollections, 'when you were first a public man, was always
repressing and discouraging your early exertions by remarks and
lectures; [saying] that young men ought not to be too forward, till
you became fixed in a habit of doing injustice to your own powers'.[42]
These restraints upon his youthful eagerness deprived him of the
opportunity to acquire experience of administration and of working
with others in office which would have helped him to take a more
positive role in the party leadership in years to come.

The Rockingham–Shelburne administration lasted only three
months. Its end was untimely brought about by the Premier's death,
on 1 July 1782. But like its predecessor, the wonder is that it lasted
so long, for before the end came it was riven by quarrels and dissension within itself. Shelburne, the political pupil and successor of
Chatham, was always distrusted by the Rockingham branch of the
Whigs as one whose attitude towards the Crown's influence in
politics was unreliable, and George III's stratagem in March 1782 in

negotiating with the opposition through Shelburne had served to
confirm their suspicions that he would be the king's tool—suspicions
hardened into certainty by Shelburne's apparent support of the
king's resistance to reform and the way in which George seemed
to regard him as Rockingham's equal in the Cabinet. Fox's well
known remark to Shelburne at the outset of the Ministry that 'He
perceived the administration was to consist of two parts, one belonging to the king, the other to the public' was hardly an auspicious
beginning.[43] A series of disputes over patronage, involving the
question of principle whether Rockingham was sole Prime Minister
and therefore the sole channel of recommendations to the king, or
whether Shelburne, acting as a colleague and not as a subordinate,
had an equal right, bedevilled the Ministry throughout its short life,
and the unfortunate division of responsibility between Fox and
Shelburne for foreign and for home and colonial affairs respectively
made a clash inevitable on the question of the peace negotiations.
Fox, believing that no acceptable terms could be negotiated with
France and Spain, wished to detach the Americans from their allies
by the offer of immediate and unconditional independence, and then
to concentrate on building up a European alliance for a new seven
years' war to regain the lost West Indian and Mediterranean colonies.
Shelburne, perhaps more realistically, saw independence as a bargain-
ing counter which might be used to bring about a similar effect. In
addition, he pointed out that an immediate concession of independence would take the American states out of his department into
Fox's, so that the scheme could be presented as another instance of
Fox's greed for power. The Cabinet hesitated, while Fox's and Shelburne's envoys in France tried to outmanoeuvre each other. Thomas
Grenville, Fox's representative at Versailles, suggested that the situation could be resolved only by recalling them both and placing the
whole negotiation in the hands of one man, and he proposed
Fitzwilliam for the task. In the end, on 30 June Fox was outvoted
in the Cabinet—in Rockingham's absence with an attack of influenza
—and declared his intention of resigning as soon as the Marquess
was well enough to resume his duties.[44] Not for the first or last time,
Fox had chosen his moment badly. On 1 July Rockingham died, and
the king at once offered the Treasury to Shelburne. Fox could not
bring himself to serve under him: it would betray not only his
policies but his party, by endorsing the king's right to determine the
premiership independently of the wishes of the majority of the

Cabinet. Yet Fox had no secure ground to stand on. He could not disclose to the public the full extent of his policy differences with Shelburne without breaking the Privy Councillor's oath of secrecy: his resignation would now appear not as a difference of principle over a matter of public concern but as a fit of pique against Shelburne and as an unconstitutional demand that the king should abdicate his undoubted right to choose his own Ministers. Shelburne lost no opportunity to make these points clear, and when Fox threw up his office on 4 July Shelburne was left in possession, with the support, grudging or otherwise, of those members of the Rockingham group who could not bring themselves to resign with Fox. This was not only the real beginning of the Pitt–Fox alignment of politics that was to last for half a century and more: it was the first stage in the remodelling of the Whig party—a body that had never in Rockingham's lifetime become a party in any but a limited sense, in spite of the magic of the name of Rockingham Whig, but which was to be welded into something like a modern party during the next fifty years, the years of Fitzwilliam's main political life.

Notes
[1] For the details of the early history of the Fitzwilliam family I am indebted to M. A. Finch, *The Wealth of Five Northamptonshire Families 1540–1640* (O.U.P., 1956), pp. 100–34. See also C. Hussey on Milton House in *Country Life*, 129 (1961), pp. 1148–51, 1210–13 and 1270–4.
[2] He was knighted in 1522.
[3] All the eldest sons of the family were Williams until the fourth earl (the subject of this book) broke the succession by interposing the first name Charles (Rockingham's Christian name) for his son, born in 1786.
[4] Mary presented her watch to Fitzwilliam for his courtesy towards her. The watch later passed out of the family's hands but it was restored in 1787 by Lady Godolphin, one of the sponsors of the fourth earl's son, who gave it to him as a Christening present (*York Chronicle*, 6 April 1787).
[5] Finch, p. 110.
[6] One of their daughters became Sir Christopher Wren's wife.
[7] Like his grandfather, the third baron retired from political life to lavish his attention on Milton. Talman, one of the foremost exponents of the classical style in English architecture, was employed to build the fine stable block, though his scheme to pull down the entire house and rebuild in the fashionable idiom was fortunately shelved for lack of funds.
[8] Horace Walpole informed Sir Horace Mann on 22 October 1741 that the third Earl Fitzwilliam was supposed to be a candidate for the hand of Sir Robert Walpole's natural daughter by Maria Skerrett (legitimised by

her parents' marriage in 1738) (*Letters of Horace Walpole*, ed. Mrs Paget Toynbee, V (1904), p. 114). It is tempting to speculate how different the family fortunes might have been if the third earl had married Walpole's daughter and not Rockingham's.

9 A sixth sister, Amelia-Maria, died in infancy when William was four years old.

10 The Sturgeons were married in London by special licence on 21 October 1764. Sturgeon (1741–1831) set up a china manufactory at Rouen but the business did not prosper and it was ruined by the French revolution. I am grateful to the late Professor F. J. W. Roughton, F.R.S., who was a descendant of one of Sturgeon's daughter's, for much interesting information about the family. For Fitzwilliam's later charity see Fitzwilliam MSS, Sheffield City Library (cited hereafter simply by the 'F' number of the bundles), F 112–13.

11 Sir Matthew Lamb (first baronet), 1705–68, MP 1741–68. He was reputedly worth £1,000,000 at his death: *Corresp. of Horace Walpole*, ed. W. S. Lewis, xxx (Yale, 1961), p. 50, n. 25.

12 To Lady Fitzwilliam, 25 July 1763: Fitzwilliam MSS, Northamptonshire Record Office. These MSS are cited henceforth as 'N'. The drawer, box or bundle number is added only where the document does not come from the main chronological series.

13 J. H. Jesse, *George Selwyn and his Contemporaries* (1901), II, p. 165.

14 For a fuller account of Fitzwilliam's European travels see my article, 'Lord Fitzwilliam's "grand tour",' *History Today*, XVII (June, 1967), pp. 393–410.

15 The quotations that follow are from correspondence to and from Lady Fitzwilliam and her daughters, N.

16 Thomas Dundas (1741–1820), second baronet (succeeded 1781), created Baron Dundas of Aske 1794, MP 1763–94. He was 'an amiable, unassuming young man' but later became one of the staunchest supporters of the Whig opposition, shared the management of Scottish opposition interests with William Adam and was a close friend of the Prince of Wales (Sir L. Namier and J. Brooke, *The House of Commons, 1754–90* (H.M.S.O., 1964), II, pp. 364–6).

17 Information from Earl Fitzwilliam; and N vouchers, bundle 856. His sister Harriet wrote on 14 January 1768: Mama says your love of pictures is a touch of the mother in you: to say the truth, I think it a very lucky touch, as it must make Rome very agreeable to you': N.

18 This was *Antiquités Etrusques, Grecques, et Romaines* (4 vols., 1766–7, published at Naples), edited by P. F. Hugues ('D'Harcanville') under Hamilton's direction. 'The work is a very pretty one, and perfectly well executed,' Fitzwilliam wrote, 'but excessively dear, as must be expected when a gentleman dilettante is engaged on it; . . . but the price far exceeds the utility that can ever be derived from the work. However one must subscribe to it, to please Mr Hamilton, because he deserves to be pleased; but I own the subscription sticks in my stomach, for I could lay out the money much more to my own satisfaction' (9 February 1768: N).

19 A year earlier Fitzwilliam had proposed a scheme for a tour from Italy into Greece and as far as Constantinople, but it came to nothing— perhaps from lack of companions willing to risk such an unusual extension of the conventional tour. (To Lady Fitzwilliam, 2 July 1767: N); Lady Harriet Fitzwilliam to Fitzwilliam, 15 September [1767]: N, x516/37).

20 Crofts was paid £850 in total for his services between December 1766 and April 1769 (account book, N, box 964). He received further payments of £200 in July 1769, £300 in 1771 and £300 in 1773 (ibid, misc. vouchers, 7) and in 1769 he was appointed Chancellor of the Diocese of Peterborough, through the Fitzwilliam influence. He died in November 1781 while visiting Milton (Gentleman's Magazine, November 1781).

21 To Lord Milton (at Naples), 6 December [1819]: N, x 1636.

22 To his mother, 16 November 1768: N; statements of yearly income, F 128b. There is another calculation of 1769 in N, x523, which estimates the yearly income at £5,758 and deductions for jointures, interest etc. at £2,980, leaving a clear sum of £2778 p.a.

23 Lady Fitzwilliam to Fitzwilliam [1769] (F 128b).

24 Thomas Hill to Fitzwilliam, 19 November 1771 (N, misc. vouchers, 7); Rockingham to Fitzwilliam, 26 November 1773: N.

25 Fitzwilliam to Rockingham, Friday [1780]: R 1/1921. In 1776 Fitzwilliam paid £2,300 to buy his brother a commission in the Guards (T. Hill to Fitzwilliam, 6 July 1776: N).

26 Letters and Journals of Lady Mary Coke (Edinburgh, 1896), III, pp. 99–100, 126, 139, 143.

27 The second Earl of Bessborough (1704–93) had married the eldest daughter of the fourth Duke of Devonshire, and his brother John Ponsonby (1713–87), Speaker of the Irish House of Commons 1756–71, married Devonshire's third daughter. The second earl's son Frederick (later third earl) married the second daughter of Lord Spencer and sister of Georgiana, wife of the fifth Duke of Devonshire, in 1780 (G.E.C.). The Ponsonbys, Cavendishes and Wentworths were thus at the centre of the tightly-organised 'cousinhood' of aristocratic families which dominated whig politics and society in the eighteenth century. Bessborough's estates in County Kilkenny comprised 17,000 acres. The family estate in County Cork was valued by Wakefield in 1812 at £10,000 p.a. (E. Wakefield, An Account of Ireland, Statistical and Political (1812), II, p. 384.)

28 Walpole, Correspondence, ed. W. S. Lewis, x, p. 304 and Letters, ed. Mrs P. Toynbee, VIII, p. 381; Lord John Cavendish to Mrs W. Ponsonby, 30 July [1783] (Grey MSS), and 27 and 30 May [1786] (Hickleton MSS, A. 1. 2. 6/4–5). The Fitzwilliams were occasional visitors to Strawberry Hill, though Fitzwilliam never had any close relationship with the man who if Fitzwilliam's father had married Sir Robert's daughter would have been his uncle. Lady Charlotte was born on 29 November 1747—she was six months older, therefore, than her husband—and she died on 13 May 1822.

29 Namier and Brooke, I. pp. 347–8; Sir Matthew Lamb to Fitzwilliam, 29 October 1767 (N). The Dean and Chapter had the power to nominate the returning officer, and controlled many votes. For many years they had worked closely with the Fitzwilliam family interest.

B*

³⁰ Lady Harriet Fitzwilliam to Fitzwilliam, n.d. [? July 1767] (N, x516/38) and 29 September (N, x512/25); Fitzwilliam to his mother, 15 September and 21 November 1767; Lady Fitzwilliam to Fitzwilliam, 8, 12 and 27 October 1767, 12 May 1768 (N). Lady Charlotte Fitzwilliam to Fitzwilliam, n.d. (N, x515/75); Lamb to Fitzwilliam, 29 October 1767 (N).

³¹ Rockingham to Fitzwilliam, 26 November 1773 (N); Fitzwilliam to Richard Burke junior [June 1790] (Burke MSS, 37); Sir B. Cust to Fitzwilliam, 13 July, 1 August and 12 August 1775; Fitzwilliam to French Laurence, 18 and 26 September 1796 (N).

³² 9 January 1770: *Journals of the House of Lords*, XXXII, p. 394.

³³ 14 March; *Journals of the House of Commons*, XXXII, p. 804.

³⁴ *Journals of the House of Lords*, XXXII, pp. 417–19.

³⁵ Fitzwilliam to Rockingham, 8 July 1776: R 1–1670. For Peterloo see *infra*, pp. 346–54.

³⁶ 13 January 1767: MS at Milton.

³⁷ For a discussion of the nature of party and of the contribution of the Rockingham Whigs to its development in this period see Namier and Brooke, I, pp. 183–204; A. S. Foord, *His Majesty's Opposition* (O.U.P., 1964), pp. 301–65; G. H. Guttridge, *English Whiggism and the American Revolution* (Berkeley and Los Angeles, 1963), especially pp. 1–57; I. R. Christie, *The End of North's Ministry* (1958), pp. 210–21 and *Myth and Reality in later-eighteenth Century British Politics* (1970), ch I; F. O'Gorman, 'Party and Burke: the Rockingham Whigs', in *Government and Opposition*, III (1968), pp. 92–110; and P. Langford, *The First Rockingham Administration 1765–1766* (O.U.P., 1973), ch VIII.

³⁸ For the weaknesses and collapse of North's government see I. R. Christie, *The End of North's Ministry* and H. Butterfield, *George III, Lord North and the People* (1949).

³⁹ *Annual Register*, 1781, pp. 320–2.

⁴⁰ *Corresp. of George III* (ed. Fortescue), V, No. 3533.

⁴¹ Selwyn to Carlisle, [2], 6, 18 and 19 March [1782]: Historical Manuscripts Commission, *Carlisle MSS*, pp. 586–8, 597, 599.

⁴² F. Laurence to Fitzwilliam, 21 September 1797 (N).

⁴³ Lord E. Fitzmaurice, *Life of William, Earl of Shelburne* (1875) III, pp. 130–2; Fortescue, V, Nos. 3575, 3582, 3589, 3590; General Fitzpatrick's memorandum, *Memorials and Corresp. of C. J. Fox*, ed. Lord John Russell (1853), I, p. 292.

⁴⁴ T. Grenville to Fox, 4 June 1782, and General Fitzpatrick's journal, 1 July: *ibid.*, I, pp. 364, 435.

CHAPTER TWO

The inheritance
1782—4

Rockingham's death on 1 July 1782 was momentous for the Whig party and for Fitzwilliam's position in it. Lacking male heirs, Rockingham's estates and properties devolved upon the issue of his eldest sister, the Lady Anne Wentworth who became Countess Fitzwilliam in 1744.[1] Thus at the age of 34 Fitzwilliam inherited the magnificent fortune and properties of one of the richest men in England, and acquired the greatest house in England as his second home.

Wentworth House[2] was the largest of the eighteenth-century mansions which symbolised the wealth and dominance of the landed aristocracy. Set in a park of 1,500 acres and itself covering no less than three acres of land, with a frontage of over 200 yards, it stands in the midst of a still attractive undulating wooded countryside, some five miles to the north-west of the coal mines and ironworks of Rotherham. Arthur Young described its situation as 'one of the most exquisite spots in the world . . . Which way soever you approach, very magnificent woods, spreading waters, and elegant temples break upon the eye at every angle'. From the top of the hill above the house, looking towards the growing iron manufactories of Rotherham, there was

an immense prospect of vast valleys all scattered with villages, with elegantly cultivated hills arising on every side to the clouds: the house appears in the centre of nine or ten vast hanging and other woods, which have a genuine magnificence more noble than can easily be conceived . . . This view is perhaps the most beautiful in Yorkshire; for the house, park, and woods form a circular connected landscape, more elegantly beautiful than the brighest paintings of *Zuccarelli;* more noble than the grandest of *Poussin's* ideas; while the surrounding country exhibits *Arcadian* scenes smiling with cultivation and endless in variety.[3]

In this still idyllic setting the first Marquess in the 1730s had begun what was to be his major life's work, the reconstruction and vast extension of the Tudor mansion once occupied by Strafford, 'Black Tom Tyrant' of the reign of Charles I and another of Fitzwilliam's ancestors to make his reputation in Ireland.[4] With Burlington's advice and his pupil Henry Flitcroft as architect, Malton created the vast east front with its great portico, and was responsible for the suites of rooms on the main floor leading on both sides from the grand hall, a room 60 ft square and 40 ft high, described by Young as 'beyond all comparison, the finest room in England'.[5] The second Marquess, Fitzwilliam's uncle, succeeded to the house and estates in 1750 and carried on the building. His major contribution was, characteristically, the vast stable block, covering two acres of ground and providing no fewer than eighty-four stalls. Rockingham's great love was for the turf, and his triumphs as a breeder and winning owner were celebrated by Stubbs, whose paintings of Rockingham's horses rank amongst his most impressive achievements. Young also acclaimed Rockingham's merit as a promoter of agricultural improvement.[6] During the second Marquess's tenure Wentworth House became a centre for the social and political life of the whole county, exemplifying at its best the eighteenth-century aristocracy's leadership of and care for the local interests with which they identified themselves. Rockingham was never so happy as when at Wentworth, dispensing hospitality to the nobility, gentry and clergy of the county, overseeing his estates, inspecting his stables, and hunting the surrounding country. Here he built up a fund of respect, affection and goodwill that lay at the basis of his political influence in the north. Where Strafford had ruled as a royal deputy, Rockingham predominated through his 'natural influence' as the leader of county society and hub of county affairs. It was a position Fitzwilliam was to find more difficult to inherit than the wide acres and vast stonework of estates and mansion.

The Rockingham inheritance was far more than a single house and park. The Wentworth estate in south Yorkshire alone comprised some 14,000 acres of agricultural land, woods, mines and quarries producing a net rental of nearly £20,000 a year. The estate of 3,000 acres at Malton in the North Riding, which included the greater part of the town and the right to levy tolls on barge traffic on the Derwent, brought in a further £4,500 in 1783, rising to £10,000 in 1796 and £22,000 by 1810. In Northamptonshire the family properties, including the control of the parliamentary borough of Higham Ferrers, added to the Fitzwilliam estates in the county and to the

Earl's political influence. In Ireland too an estate of some 66,000 acres covered a large part of County Wicklow and yielded about £9,000 a year in rents.[7] Adding these properties to the Milton estate, Fitzwilliam could now look to an annual income of some £60,000; the Rockingham inheritance thus increased his income tenfold and made him one of the wealthiest men in England. No trace of financial insecurity overhangs the remainder of his life: the days when he could not afford £100 towards getting his brother into Parliament must have seemed far away in 1807, when he was to spend close on £100,000 on his son's election for Yorkshire.[8] Altogether, Fitzwilliam now owned over 100,000 acres of British and Irish soil, and in 1804 on the death of Lady Rockingham he acquired the reversion of her dowry of the Bright estates at Badsworth, near Pontefract. His industrial interests also proved an increasing source of profit. In 1780 the two collieries at Lowwood and Elsecar were producing profits of £1,480: in 1796 they yielded £2,978, while two new collieries at Elsecar and Westwood were earning a further £270. By 1801 the total colliery profits were over £6,000, and by 1825 they had reached £22,500, their biggest total in Fitzwilliam's lifetime. The output of coal increased from over 12,500 tons in 1799 to over 122,000 tons in 1823. The family's coal mining interests were already assuming in Fitzwilliam's lifetime an importance sufficient to make him one of the leading coalowners in the kingdom. In 1827 he calculated his net income from all the estates at £115,000.[9] The prosperity of the estate and of the West Riding's industrial development went hand in hand, and Fitzwilliam was always strongly conscious of the importance of the West Riding's industrial interests in county politics.

Fitzwilliam inherited, therefore, a considerable financial, agricultural and industrial empire. The detailed management of the properties was kept in his own hands. Each estate had its own chief steward, but the central direction of the enterprise remained Fitzwilliam's own concern. He corresponded regularly and in detail with each estate steward on the management of the property, letting of farms, repair of buildings, and agricultural methods. The accounts of each estate were sent directly to Fitzwilliam each year, and examined and audited by him. Even though the chief agent at Wentworth occupied the senior position amongst the estate stewards, he was not given full overall responsibility for the estates until later in Fitzwilliam's life.[10] The household steward at Wentworth, Benjamin Hall, and his successor Joshua Biram, not only ran the great house with its army of some

thirty full-time resident servants but also supervised the colliery
interests : and the colliery profits were appropriated to the payment
of household expenses at Wentworth, amounting to over £2,000 per
annum in 1796, plus over £500 per annum for the stables and over
£1,200 for hunting.[11] Like his ancestor Sir William IV, Fitzwilliam
disclosed a talent for estate management that rescued the Wentworth
properties from the disordered state in which Rockingham left them
and made them into one of the best run estates in the two kingdoms.

This achievement was not at the expense of his tenants. Indeed,
Fitzwilliam soon became known as one of the most benevolent and
considerate of landlords. In bad years he was always one of the first
to reduce rents or cancel arrears, to organise supplies of cheap food,
to distribute fish, potatoes or other provisions to the needy, and to
provide such comforts for the aged as free coal or blankets. In good
years he was quick to perform his obligations as a landlord in repairing farms, cottages or outhouses, encouraging progressive methods,
and maintaining reasonable levels of rent that provided the farmer
with an incentive to improve. His charitable subscriptions and donations were extensive and generous, if discriminating. Hospitals were
a particular interest, and an allowance of 'cordials' to 'lying-in
women' in the neighbourhood of Wentworth was benefiting some
two hundred recipients a year by 1820s. In 1795–6 donations of ten to
twenty guineas were given to seven local parishes to assist in the
relief of poverty, and during the bad years of the later 'nineties when
harvest failures, inflation, and war-time trading conditions created
acute scarcities of provisions and high corn prices, measures were
taken on all the estates to provide emergency food supplies. At
Malton the brewing vessels in the Lodge were taken over to provide
'nourishing soup' at one penny a quart (a charge made solely to discourage the abuse of the charity in favour of the tenants' pigs) and salt
fish and potatoes were distributed. These charities were not always
regarded as entirely altruistic—voting rights at Malton, for example,
were confined to those not officially chargeable to the parish, so that
it was in Fitzwilliam's interest to keep his tenant voters off the poor
rate; furthermore his adherence to the principle of the free market
economy meant that he refused to countenance a scheme drawn up
by well-meaning residents of Malton to bring corn to market at below
the current prices. Nevertheless he applied the same discipline to his
own family as that forced upon others, and ordered his steward at
Wentworth to restrict the allowance of bread in the house to 1 lb

per person per day, 'so that the poor may not have the additional pain of seeing wasted, or at least wantonly used, of which they stand in such real want'. By the standards of his time Fitzwilliam set a real example in charity to the unfortunate. He was 'ever giving alms to the poor', his chaplain at Wentworth later noted; 'the tale of woe was never told to him in vain'. Friendly Societies and savings banks also received his support and patronage, as tending to encourage the poorer classes in habits of thrift and self-reliance and helping to avert the social and political dangers of pauperisation and the consequent extension of the authority of the State.[12]

Nowhere was Fitzwilliam's creed of responsible aristocracy better illustrated than on his own estates, where the interests of landlord and dependants were always regarded as interwoven with each other. The hierarchical framework which he always regarded as axiomatic to any stable form of society was clothed with a system of mutual respect and interdependence, so providing a microcosm of the Whig doctrine of the ideal political State. Fitzwilliam personified the best ideals of English aristocracy. A keen huntsman, racehorse breeder and patron of the turf, he enjoyed the traditional country pursuits and regarded himself, first and foremost, as a countryman, his life centred on his estates and his obligations to his tenants the first call upon his time and resources. He practised successfully the difficult art of both upholding differences of rank and yet transcending them, without condescension, by identifying himself with those who provided the infrastructure to support aristocratic privilege.

Fitzwilliam was a proud man, conscious of the dignity of his rank and station; but his pride was for his Whig ancestry and the Rockingham tradition, not for his own pleasure. No man cared less for the outward distinctions of aristocracy. He would have valued the title of Marquess of Rockingham if George III had been willing to confer it on him in 1782 or 1807, but it would have been solely to perpetuate Rockingham's memory and to symbolise Fitzwilliam's commitment to it.[13] The famous story, told by Creevey, of Doncaster races in 1827 illustrates not Fitzwilliam's inordinate pride but his determination never to concede the primacy he felt was due to the house of Wentworth. The Duke of Devonshire, steward of the meeting, appeared on the first day of the races with a coach and six, and twelve outriders, the same as Fitzwilliam; the next day, 'Old Billy' thereupon 'appeared with *two* coaches and six, and *sixteen* outriders, and has kept the thing up ever since'.[14] Fitzwilliam would never concede to any other house the traditional primacy of Wentworth in south Yorkshire.

In his relations with his dependants, therefore, Fitzwilliam demonstrated the liberal Whig creed at its best. He also showed a characteristic distrust of dogmas, of any kind of extremism and of any activity that, however well meant, did not recognise the dignity and freedom of the individual. No better illustration exists than his attitude towards the evangelical 'Proclamation Society' formed in 1786 to reform the manners and morals of the poor, working under the encouragement of a royal proclamation for the suppression of vice. The ultimate objective of the proclamation, Fitzwilliam wrote to the Rev. Henry Zouch, of Sandal, near Wakefield, 'must meet with the wishes of every man : who does not wish that the breast of every subject may be filled with the purest sentiments of virtue?' He disagreed strongly however, with the society's methods. Wilberforce himself had tried to recruit him as a member in the summer of 1787, and, wrote Fitzwilliam,

I agreed with him in sentiment that there was a great deal of debauchery, much looseness of behaviour, and very little religion, but then I could not agree with him, that it ever would be otherwise, as long as there continued a great deal of activity, trade, and riches : that the latter produced the former, and if he wished that the former should not exist, I advised him to apply the proper remedy by annihilating the latter, and I promised him a speedy return of purity of morals in our own home, if none of us had a shilling to spend in debauchery out of doors.

More seriously, he admonished Wilberforce, he should 'consider twice' before attempting to carry into execution all the penal statues for enforcing purity of manners, for he would find that half of them were

a disgrace to our Statute book for their absurdity and folly, whilst the other half was still a greater disgrace on account of the partial, time-serving and hypocritical motives, which had given rise to them. . . . Having seen London in flames only seven years ago, we do not wish to put the potent and zealous arm of enthusiasm under the guidance of hypocrisy so soon again.

He suspected that some of those who promoted the society did so as a punitive measure, to keep the poor in their place : 'I wish not to see all the envy, malice, resentment and deceit of ignorant enthusiasm and disappointed hypocrisy, let loose upon the innocent, under pretence that there is to be found among them some who are vicious, profligate and abandoned.' It would be more effective, he thought, to attend to the morals of the higher orders so that they set a better example: 'let his Majesty dismiss from his service any among his servants who are suspected of drunkenness, lewdness, swearing or Sabbath-breaking, and then we may believe his Majesty is in earnest'.[15] On more than one subsequent occasion, Fitzwilliam's words and actions were to be consistent with this view of the obligations of the higher orders towards the lower.

Once installed at Wentworth, Fitzwilliam set about continuing Rockingham's style of open hospitality in the gatherings which followed the race weeks at York in August and Doncaster in September. The second of these was traditionally the occasion for 'receiving the county' and making contact with local gentry and other men of importance, both to transmit political intelligence from Whig HQ to its local agents and to test county opinion on current political questions for the information of the leadership at Westminster. It was in this role, linking the central and local institutions of the Whig party, rather than in providing leadership in Parliament or Cabinet, that Fitzwilliam now cast himself. His reluctance to take a more positive part and his diffidence in pushing himself to the forefront of the party could rarely be overcome even by the urging of his closest friends. Horace Walpole remarked that he was 'a nephew or Octavius of the late Caesar, but no more likely to be an Augustus, than the Marquess was a Julius'.[16] Far from Fitzwilliam having any such ambition, the difficulty his friends found was to persuade him to stand any further forward than hitherto. Two days after Rockingham's death Burke urged him to take a leading role:

You have his place to fill and his example to follow, and you are the only man in the world to whom this would not be a work of the greatest difficulty. . . . You are Lord Rockingham in every thing. . . . I am so much convinced of this, that I have no doubt that you will take it in good part, that his old friends, who were attached to him by every tie of affection, and of principle, and among others myself, should look to you, and should not think it an act of forwardness and intrusion to offer you their services. . . . I trust (and I am not single in my hopes and wishes) that you will take an early and a very considerable part in affairs. You are much wanted; and you are not a man to deny anything to your country or your friends.

And Fox wrote on the very afternoon of Rockingham's death, 'Do not be satisfied with lamenting but endeavour to imitate him. I know how painful it will be to you to exert yourself at such a time, but it must be done . . . you are one of the persons upon whom I most rely for real assistance at this moment'. Fitzwilliam's response was timid and apprehensive. To Burke he wrote on the 3rd, 'in a melancholy triumph'—Burke's Civil List Bill having passed its second reading that day in the Lords by 44 to 9—but he declared

. . . Why do you write to me so? I can never emulate his character—I will imitate, as I ought to do, at an awful distance—you know my wishes for the publick weal, and you know my inability to further it, more than by the great and venerable name I now with sorrow bear—but I have still courage—I have confidence, that his virtue has spread its seed so far and wide that there is stock of growth sufficient to make honest men respectable, and worthless ones inconsiderable.[17]

Fitzwilliam did not appear in the leading rank of the party for some months. Fox's candidate for the succession to the party leadership and to the premiership was the Duke of Portland, a man of 44 and presently serving as Viceroy in Ireland.[18] Portland had many of the qualities necessary in a leader of the Whig party. Rank, family and estate were indisputably his and his 'revolution' antecedents were impeccable, since his Bentinck forbears had come over with their William the Conqueror in 1688. Marriage alliances with the leading families had long since incorporated them into the English Whig cousinhood, and extensive estates in Nottinghamshire, Lancashire and Ireland qualified them to act on equal terms with the greatest Whig magnates. Portland, too, was a man of high rectitude and integrity, universally respected in an age when the morals of politicians were often their major source of weakness. In model family life, benevolence as a landlord and wide acceptability as a leader he had every qualification for public life except high ability. As a party leader, too, his diligence and application were superior to Rockingham's, as recent investigations into party organisation in the 1780s and early 1790s have shown.[19] Yet, though not so lacking in ability as George Selwyn's contemptuous epithet 'jolter-headed calf' would suggest,[20] Portland lacked political skill, perception and energy, while the administrative grasp of a North or a Grenville was beyond his reach. He served the party faithfully and well according to his lights, but his leadership was to contribute little in the end to its development.

Fox's insistence on Portland's nomination as leader of the Whigs and therefore Prime Minister broke up the administration. Shelburne's appointment to the Treasury on 4 July confirmed Fox's resolution to resign from the Cabinet, and added a further reason for it—namely, Fox's certainty that Shelburne would break up the Rockingham system of Cabinet solidarity against the king and court influence. Fox failed, however, to carry the whole of the party with him. A few, like Burke, urged him to resign if the king could not be forced to appoint a Whig Premier. Others, like Richmond, feared that resignation would play into the kings hands, lead to a readmission of some of North's old Cabinet and be difficult to justify to the public against the accusation of putting faction before country. The issues were debated by the Whig party at a nine-hour meeting on 6 July at Rockingham House, now Fitzwilliam's house, in Grosvenor Square, attended by nearly 150 peers and MPs and harangued for two hours by Burke in one of his most uncompromising moods.[21] Fox and his friends, including Fitzwilliam, attacked Shelburne as being politically and personally untrustworthy, and pressed the Duke of Richmond, the leader of the group who wished to remain in office, to declare whether he could rely on Shelburne's good faith. Richmond confessed his doubts as to Shelburne himself, but stressed the inexpediency of resignation on an issue that could not easily be justified in public. Finally, 'so pressed and stung in this nest of hornets . . . at length he burst into tears, and so the meeting ended'. Richmond, however, persisted in his intention 'to go on till the first breach on fair public grounds'.[22] In the end Richmond, Conway and Keppel remained in office, and only Lord John Cavendish resigned with Fox from the Cabinet, though Portland, Fitzpatrick, Burke, Sheridan, Thomas Grenville and the other leading Rockinghamites outside the Cabinet followed Fox into opposition. Fitzwilliam eagerly supported their secession. Fox declared his hope that they would 'always act together with the same cordiality that we used to do when we had other coadjutors, and that we shall always keep up a standard which all whigs may repair to when they are so inclined'. But for the time being this standard was to fly over a minority in both Houses, unable to make effective progress against the Ministry in power without reinforcement from elsewhere. 'And so,' wrote Sheridan, 'begins a new opposition; but woefully thinned and disconcerted, I fear.'[23]

Placed by Rockingham's death and his inheritance in this leading position in the party, Fitzwilliam made efforts to overcome his diffidence at speaking in the Lords. He began to appear as one of the party's leading spokesmen in the House, and always—now that

Rockingham's moderating influence was removed—on the side of Fox's wing of the party. The incipient cleavage between the more conservative Whigs, represented by Burke, and the more extreme party men like Fox and Sheridan was never absent for long from Whig politics after 1782, and despite his lifelong veneration for Burke's political principles Fitzwilliam always found himself drawn towards Fox. This circumstance alone was to be significant for the future of the party, for Portland too was under Fox's spell. So it came about that Rockingham's death began the decline of Burke's political influence in the party's councils and the beginning of his frustration and isolation which were to be so evident in the party's later years of crisis. Fitzwilliam's immediate instinct was to reassure Burke of his wish to see him keep his position as member for Malton and to continue the financial support which Rockingham had given him over the years. Rockingham's will cancelled the debts which Burke had owed to his patron, but even so, as long as he was out of office and until his retirement brought him that most ironic of rewards, a civil list pension, he remained financially dependent upon the help of his aristocratic friends.[24] He continued to receive Fitzwilliam's patronage for many years, but he never achieved the confidential position within the leadership that he had built up under Rockingham. From 1782 onwards Fitzwilliam's substitution for Rockingham made the Whig party more dependent on Fox and less on Burke. The party crises of 1788–9 and 1790–4 were profoundly affected by this circumstance.

When Parliament reassembled towards the end of 1782 Fitzwilliam's zeal in the Foxite cause was soon in evidence. His first recorded utterance in the Lords was on the first day of the session, 5 December, and in the debate on the address. It was not a set speech, but an intervention taxing Shelburne with a lack of firm principle over the concession of American independence, the issue on which Fox had resigned in July. A week later he raised the question whether the proposed offer of independence to the Americans in the provisional treaty was unconditional and irrevocable, or whether it was dependent on the success of the still uncompleted negotiations with France. This too was a direct reference to the point on which Fox had based his resignation.[25] Fitzwilliam further asserted that 'the principles of those men, in which he had been educated and in which he should die, would never admit that a Prime Minister should be established on such a foundation as the noble Earl had been'. The

opposition in both Houses mustered its fullest strength against Shelburne's peace treaty, and though on 17 February the Lords supported
the government by the narrow majority of seventy-two to fifty-nine,
in the Commons the Ministry was defeated by sixteen votes. The
defeat was brought about by the alliance for this purpose of the
Portland Whigs with Lord North's party; and on 24 February, after
a further defeat by seventeen votes on a motion of censure, Shelburne's resignation was announced to the accompaniment of out-
bursts from the king on 'my lot to reign in the most profligate age,
and when the most unnatural coalition has taken place' and 'the most
extraordinary combination that the depravity of such times as we
live in could alone have given birth to'.[26]

The junction of Fox and North was one of the most remarkable
political events of the eighteenth century.[27] From the first days of
Shelburne's premiership it had been obvious to all experienced
political commentators that the new Ministry's parliamentary position was weak. Shelburne's security lay in the apparent unlikelihood
of any junction between the two other major groups in the
Commons, who together could outvote the Ministry but who were
divided by past animosities and continuing differences of political
principle. The Foxites and the substantial party still following Lord
North seemed as irreconcilable to each other as was either to
Shelburne. The construction of a working alliance between them,
and ultimately of a complete integration of parties, was a slow
process in which mutual suspicion and distrust were only gradually
subordinated to self-interest on both sides. Fox, ready to forget old
scores in new resentments, and North, 'irreconcilable to no man',[28]
were willing enough as individuals to act in concert. Fox would ally
with almost anyone to pull down Shelburne, whose position, as
Fitzwilliam had suggested in the House of Lords, was entirely due to
the king's personal favour. An alliance with North had the additional
attraction that it would prevent a union between North and the new
Ministry, and thus the restoration of the 'old system' in operation
before 1782. Furthermore, North being notoriously averse to serving
again in high office and his party being stronger in numbers than in
individual talents, there seemed every likelihood that the Whigs
would be able to monopolise the most important departmental offices
and control the making of policy.[29] From North's point of view, too,
a coalition with Fox had many potential advantages. It silenced the
major critic of his American war policy, and thus assured his personal

safety. It avoided his adding the responsibility for an unpopular peace
to that of the unsuccessful war. It would prevent a possible Pitt–Fox
alliance against him if he joined Shelburne—Pitt being so hostile to
North as to be a possible deserter to the opposition rather than serve
in the same Cabinet with him. And finally, it was always thought in
the eighteenth century to be true that a party could get better terms
by negotiating with one out of office than with one already in
possession. As the agreement reached between the leaders in mid-
February was to show, North secured from Fox substantial political
concessions which amounted to a guarantee against further economical reform and the leaving open of any measure of parliamentary reform.[30] Fox certainly did not secure North's following at
a low price. Indeed, the desertion of those policies hitherto identified
with the Rockingham Whigs in return for the coalition proved to be
Fox's undoing, for it laid him open to those changes of dereliction
of principle and lust for office which were to be the coalition's major
weaknesses with the public. The new administration, formed after
six weeks' bickering and a desperate search for alternatives by the
king, thus found that it could rely neither on royal favour nor on
public support. In these circumstances its security depended solely
upon the maintenance of the existing House of Commons, elected in
1780. It was open to the king at any time, could he but find an
alternative Minister willing to take office, to solve the problem by
dissolving the House and 'appealing to the people'. Hence George III's
wooing of Pitt and Temple, his only practical resource, from the very
day on which the coalition took office.

Fitzwilliam approved heartily of the new coalition, and his new
standing in the party was shown by the offer now made to him of
the Lord Lieutenancy of Ireland—'the properest man they have to
send', as William Grenville remarked to his brother, Lord Temple, the
Lord Lieutenant in possession.[31] Fitzwilliam was also proposed by
Portland for promotion in the peerage, to a revived Marquessate of
Rockingham. Neither materialised. Lady Fitzwilliam's health was considered too delicate for her to make the journey to Dublin, and Fitzwilliam resisted the pressure to take the office. The promotion in the
peerage he regarded with no more enthusiasm, being largely
indifferent to mere personal dignity. The king, however, hoping that a
publicly known refusal on his part to grant any honours or peerages
at the recommendation of his new Ministers would rally support
against them, received Portland's request with a silent and empty

bow. Fitzwilliam was perhaps the first of 'Fox's martyrs'.[32]

Fitzwilliam's role, even though out of office, was not to remain a minor one. From the end of 1782 he began to accumulate experience in speaking in the House, taking up minor points in debate rather than delivering set speeches or introducing motions. On 1 May he supported a Bill to relieve the East India Company of its financial distress, and on the 5th he spoke in defence of the government's loan. On the latter occasion his speech was praised by the parliamentary reporter for its able reasoning and mastery of financial detail. It was his best performance so far. On 18 June he again spoke on a financial question, moving the rejection of a petition of merchants and traders against the coalition's receipt tax—a measure which was to have unexpected repercussions in Yorkshire before the end of the year. Finally on 30 June he made his first leading speech, introducing the government objections to the second reading of the Bill for reform of abuses in the public offices.[33] This Bill, introduced by Pitt in the House of Commons, was an attempt by the Shelburnites to force the coalition's hand on economical reform and so display to the public Fox's dereliction of principle in giving it up to secure North's alliance. Fitzwilliam showed enough promise as a speaker to be encouraged to go on, though no more speeches are recorded in the last fortnight of the session. By October 1783 Horace Walpole was reflecting a general opinion when he wrote that, though he hardly knew Fitzwilliam personally, 'from what I have heard of him in the Lords, I have conceived a good opinion of his sense; of his character I never heard any ill, which is a great testimonial in his favour, when there are so many horrid characters, and when all that are conspicuous have their minutest actions tortured to depose against them'.[34]

During the parliamentary recess from July to November the coalition's main concerns were the settlement of the Prince of Wales's household and income, and the drafting of the Bill to settle the government of the British territories in India. The first measure nearly brought down the government. The king's refusal to accept the Cabinet's proposals for an establishment of £100,000 a year plus the payment of the prince's heavy debts would undoubtedly have led to a change of administration had Pitt and Temple been prepared to use it as an issue on which to justify their taking office against the coalition. From prudence and calculation, however, Pitt and his cousin made no move to help the king. They were not yet convinced that they had an issue on which the public and the independent members of parliament would give them the necessary support, with or without a general election; nor was Pitt yet prepared to take office without some latitude on the question of parliamentary reform.[35] After a brief crisis the government gave way to the king's indignation, revised its proposals, and resumed its course.

For Burke the great cause of economical reform and the reduction of Crown influence had now given way to another crusade which was to obsess him for the next seven years and more. This was the cause of India. For many years the advance of British power in the sub-continent had raised the question of responsibility for the government of an empire acquired, if not in a fit of absence of mind, as Burke once remarked, at any rate without prior design and purpose. The extension of the East India Company's trading activities and the breakdown in the early eighteenth century of the Mogul power in Delhi coincided with the defeat of French oriental ambitions in the Seven Years' War of 1756–63. The result was to leave a power vacuum which could be filled only by Britain. The home government, however, was by no means anxious to assume the administrative and military responsibilities of so huge an empire, and nothing effective was done until 1773 to control the activities of the company, whose army, civil service and judiciary in India were beginning to acquire the semblance of a political government. In 1773 Lord North's Regulating Act submitted the company's administration in India to the oversight of the British Cabinet, but left the company with the day-to-day responsibility for the government of these territories now directly controlled by it and for diplomatic relations with the native states. The Governor Generalship of Warren Hastings soon demonstrated the unsatisfactory nature of this arrangement. Torn by internal dissensions, largely fomented by the ambition of Philip Francis, but fanned by Hastings's own autocratic manner, the Indian administration was too weak to weather the scandals which inevitably surrounded it, but the home government lacked the power effectively to intervene. By 1782 the situation was so out of hand that a secret committee of the House of Commons was set up to investigate and report on the question. Dundas and Burke, as members of the committee, thus began their long and strikingly divergent connexions with Indian affairs. By 1783 Burke was convinced not only that Hastings was personally culpable of grave crimes in his government of the Indian territories and his relations with the princes, but that the whole moral and political basis of British rule in India must be changed. He engaged Fox's enthusiasm together with Francis's spite to further the cause. By the summer of 1783 it was clear that the government—any government—would have to take action to reform the Indian situation. It was to the credit of the coalition that, recognising from the start that this enterprise would be fraught with the gravest political dangers, they made the most serious and statesmanlike attempt yet seen to deal with the problem.[36]

The main India Bill,[37] on which political controversy was concentrated, was designed to take the political control of Indian affairs out of the hands of the company, which was to be restricted to its original and primary function of trade, and to place it under the oversight of the government. Thus far the measure showed statesmanship and would have been widely supported. The separation of political responsibility from commercial profit was generally accepted as desirable, even by many of the directors of the company. The controversial clauses of the Bill were those which embodied the mechanism for accomplishing the change. Here the Whigs found themselves in a dilemma. The political control of Indian administration, justice, revenue and military affairs necessarily carried with it a considerable degree of patronage. Few eighteenth-century jobs were thought (though often mistakenly) to be so lucrative as a post in India. Few eighteenth-century myths were so prevalent as the myth of the returned 'nabob', enriched by a few short years in India and able to establish himself on a landed estate and in possession of a parliamentary seat bought by the wealth of the orient. Indian patronage was accordingly in great demand and short supply. So long as this patronage was dispersed among the directors of the company, no direct link existed with the 'influence of the Crown'. Administrations naturally sought the alliance of parties among the direction, but no direct power of appointment rested with the king or his Ministers as long as civil or military service in India was service under the company. To transfer political authority directly to the Crown would be, it was thought, to transfer to the Crown a degree of influence and patronage far surpassing all that had been taken away by economic reform in the past eighteen months. And the Foxites, knowing the king's anxiety to be rid of them, naturally feared that on a change of administration this influence would be used against them. The king had made no secret of his dislike for

his Ministers. To give to the Crown a direct responsiblity for an
Indian empire would be, for Fox and Burke, a quick and spectacular
way to political suicide.

To avert this consequence of removing political authority from the
company's control the Whigs conceived a new solution. The control
of Indian affairs and patronage would be vested in a group of commissioners, appointed by Parliament for a set term of years. On the
expiry of that term the commissioners would be appointed or re-
appointed by the Crown. Thus the tenure of the commissioners
would, it was suggested, be independent of political vicissitudes, and
a settled policy for India could be established. Changes of administration at home would not have, as their object or consequence, an
immediate change in the control of India. It was an ingenious attempt
to solve what was, in eighteenth-century conditions, an insoluble
dilemma. What vitiated the whole scheme was the fact that politics
permeated every level of eighteenth-century governmental and parliamentary activity. That the commissioners were to be appointed by
Parliament was no more than a fiction, for eighteenth-century Parliaments, except in times of acute crisis or unusual stress, were
dominated by executive influence. And if the commissioners were
chosen from the political friends of the present Ministers it seemed
impossible that either they or the Ministers could ever be removed.
The term of four years for which they were appointed would ensure
that their office would continue beyond the last possible date of the
next general election.[38] Their political influence might thus be used
on behalf of their ministerial friends at the next elections, and if this
were sufficient, as was widely thought, to counterbalance the
personal influence of the monarch, the Ministers would be virtually
irremoveable. All hinged, therefore, on the composition of the commission. If its members were chosen on a non-party basis, Indian
patronage might not be used as a single political force and the delicate balance of influence not disturbed.

But to ask this was to ask too much of eighteenth-century politicians. If only in self-defence, Fox and Burke felt that the commission should be in reliable hands; and no precedent yet existed for an
administration voluntarily foregoing, let alone surrendering into
hostile hands, any significant amount of patronage which might be
used politically. And on grounds of principle, as Burke argued, it was
unreasonable that they should hand the control of Indian policy to
men who did not share their views on the right way to govern India.

It was no surprise, therefore, that the seven commissioners named in the Bill should be four Foxites and three relatives or supporters of North, nor that Fitzwilliam should be designated their chairman. But, if natural, it was also the fatal circumstance which was, as Loughborough had foretold, to be the ruin of the administration. It gave yet further seeming proof of the insatiable ambition of Fox and his friends; it was tinged with unconstitutionality, for no precedent existed for such an outright declaration of mistrust by Ministers of the integrity of the monarch; and to Pitt, Temple and their friends it sounded a political death-knell. Pitt might declare that the major evil of the Bill was its transfer of all Indian patronage not to the Crown, where it had some constitutional right to be, but to 'Charles Fox, in or out of office'. But his principal motive for acting to prevent the Bill's becoming law was the fear that, if it did, all possibility of his taking office independently of Fox and North would disappear.[39] So Pitt and Temple, who in July and August had been unwilling to make any move towards helping the king to get rid of his Ministers, in December were the first to take the initiative in warning George of the possibilities inherent in the Bill and in urging upon him measures to dismiss the coalition and bring them into office. Fox's dilemma was a cruel one, and whatever he did seemed likely to turn out to his disadvantage. No wonder that he recognised from the start the crucial nature of the Indian business. No wonder, too, that the Whigs should congratulate themselves on surmounting the crisis when the king offered no objection to the Bill and it passed the Commons by comfortable margins.[40] The springing of the trap against them by Temple in the Lords on 17 December, when the Bill was defeated by an unprecedentedly open display of royal influence, accordingly produced a furious reaction.

Fitzwilliam's role in the crisis was a surprisingly passive one. He appears not to have been involved in the drafting of the Bills, nor even in detailed discussion of their provisions. It was not until 13 November that Portland first mentioned to him the proposal to take the chairmanship of the commission, and not until the 16th that Fitzwilliam, replying to the offer, asked for details of the post. 'I must know the extent of my duty,' he wrote, 'that I may guess at the restraint and confinement I am likely to be under.' And his reply showed his almost complete ignorance of the terms of the Bills by asking

Is it intended that the commissioners should undertake the whole duty of the directors, or are they to undertake the *political* affairs of the company *only*, leaving to a committee of directors the management of the detail of commerce? What to be the number of the commissioners, and how many of them to form a quorum? . . . The whole business is meant, I suppose, for a *limited period only*, to reinstate the company's affairs: it is to be a *temporary* dictatorship and the necessity of the case must be its justification.

Fitzwilliam's misunderstanding of the nature of the Bills and of the office for which he was himself designated is astonishing. 'Never having had any conversation with you upon the mode of carrying the plan into execution', as he wrote to Portland, he could not be expected to realise what was involved. But he did appreciate at once what would be one of the most telling arguments against the scheme, 'the clamour against government's taking out of men's hands the management of their own concerns, which will certainly be one way of arguing the case, and perhaps a strong one'. He suggested that the government should offer to buy out, at current market prices, every stockholder who objected to the change; and he even predicted that a profit might be made by selling again at a higher price. Finally, he urged that instead of making the nomination of the commissioners a parliamentary one, they should be appointed by the king, 'for the purpose of creating responsibility in those who advise him to appoint'.[41]

Fitzwilliam's consent to taking the chairmanship was reluctantly given. He suggested that Lord John Cavendish, who wished to retire from the Chancellorship of the Exchequer, would carry greater confidence from the public; if Cavendish would not undertake it, there was Lord Spencer, 'ten times more capable of filling the situation to the satisfaction of his employers than I am'. And above all, 'there is an acquiescence of another person to be obtained before I can think of undertaking anything whatever; without making the thing agreeable to Lady F. or rather without bringing her to look at such an undertaking with some satisfaction, I can never persuade myself to stir one step'. The most that he would agree to was to overcome his 'reluctance to enter into any public situation . . . for a limited period, if I can be of service to those whom I wish to serve out of sincere attachment to them, or if they think I can'.

Portland and Fox were determined not to take no for an answer. 'Fox declares he would not have undertaken the business if he had

not thought himself secure of your assistance,' Portland replied at
once. 'Nothing but your name will do and you may surely lend
yourself conditionally if you can not give yourself to be for the
whole term.' Time was running short. The Duke of Manchester, Fox's
first nominee for the office, had refused it at the end of October.[42]
The names of the commissioners must be inserted in the Bill during
the committee stage in the Commons at the beginning of December.
Two days later Portland once more urged a decision:

Fox's anxiety for your undertaking the E. I. administration increases daily,
and he desires me to say, and I entirely agree with him, that the whole
depends upon your assistance. Lord Spencer will not go down as First
Commissioner, and it is in vain to attempt it.

On the 29th he issued an urgent summons:

the whole depends upon your acceptance, and . . . the success and ruin
of the measure is entirely in your hands. These I acknowledge are strong
words and I would not use them if they were not *facts*. The public looks
for you and calls you to the chair of the new commission, and I venture
to assure you that it can *only* be filled by you. The duration of the commission, its duties, the severity of its confinement I will not attempt to
extenuate, because *we are convinced it cannot exist without you*, and
. . . *what can I say more?* I will only add that we entreat you to come
up to us without delay.[43]

Fitzwilliam arrived in London on Monday 1 December, the very
day that the intrigue by Temple, Robinson and others against the
administration began, four days after the successful second reading
in the Commons of the India Bill. Whatever his sense of his own
limitations, he could not now avoid taking a prominent part in the
debates on the Bill. It had brought him to the centre of public
attention, and the stress by the opposition on the scheme for the
commission as the measure's most undesirable feature inevitably
involved him in this issue. On 15 December the eccentric Lord
Abingdon, speaking in the Lords, declared that the Bill was 'a
proposition to wrest the reins of government out of the hands of the
executive power, and to place it in the hands of a self-created demagogue, supported by a factious and desperate cabal', and that it gave
to the Ministers 'a lease for four years of such means of corruption'
as would enable 'an oligarchical junto in the two Houses of Parliament' to 'purchase a fee simple in the premises, for ever after'.
Similar arguments were urged on the 17th by the leading speakers
against the Bill. Fitzwilliam's speech, in the middle of the debate,

was evidently a long and detailed one, but it was only briefly sum-
marised in the newspapers. His own notes suggest that he intended to
answer the objections expected to be made to the Bill.[44] He was to
stress the necessity of government intervention in the company's
affairs, on the grounds of the company's financial instability and its
improper political activities: to answer arguments alleging improper
influence and the factious nature of the party's aims: and to pledge
government support to the credit of the company. In fact his speech
as reported seems to have been an answer to the company's own
defence of their financial affairs and a castigation on Rockingham
principles of the unconstitutional influence now being excited against
the Bill. 'His mind,' he avowed, 'filled and actuated by the motives of
Whiggism, would ill brook to see a dark and secret influence exerting
itself against the independence of Parliament, and the authority of
Ministers.' The vote, taken amidst great excitement, found the
government in a minority, with seventy-six supporters against ninety-
five opposition votes.[45] Lord Temple's communication to many of the
peers of the king's wishes had had its result. The bishops, the Scots
and household peers, and even one member of the Cabinet itself now
moved into the opposition lobby from fear of the royal displeasure.[46]

The following day the king dismissed the Ministry and appointed
Pitt and Temple to form another one. The central and most profound
political crisis of the reign had begun. Fox declared in the House of
Commons on the 17th that the crisis 'involves the rights of Parliament in all their consequences and extent . . . the deliberations of
this night must decide whether we are to be freemen or slaves;
whether the House of Commons be the palladium of liberty or the
organ of despotism; whether we are henceforth to possess a voice
of our own or to be only the mere mechanical echo of secret
influence'.[47]

Unexpected as the defeat in the Lords was to the leaders of government, they remained confident of their ability to prevent any other
administration from establishing itself. The king's action in interfering with the Lords had raised a storm in the Commons. On 19
December the House assembled in angry mood and passed by a large
majority a resolution declaring that any man advising a dissolution
was 'an enemy to his country'. Clearly, if a dissolution could be
prevented the coalition might batter Pitt's frail government into submission: a failure of nerve, not unexpected in a young man of only
24 so suddenly elevated to the highest office, or the refusal of enough

men of weight and consideration in political circles to join him,
might at any time reopen the door to office for them. Mrs Crewe, the
leading Whig hostess of the day, spoke for many of her friends when
she laughingly christened the new government a 'mince pie' administration that would not outlast the Christmas holidays. If attacks were
pressed home quickly and with resolution, Pitt's administration might
never get off the ground: and until it had established itself in
command of office, it was reckless to think of dissolving Parliament
and holding a general election in which the influential electoral
patrons might hesitate to commit themselves to a futile cause. The
Whigs could be reasonably sure of sufficient time in the existing
House of Commons to re-enter their late offices in irresistible triumph.
During the Christmas recess, with the government clinging pre-
cariously to office, Fitzwilliam and his friends, already heavily
engaged in by-elections in Yorkshire and York city,[48] lost no time in
urging their provincial supporters to rouse the public. In Yorkshire
Sir George Savile's nephew France Foljambe, a candidate acceptable
(for the moment) to both Whigs and reformers, was elected unopposed to his uncle's old seat. Fitzwilliam saw this as an opportunity
to divert the Yorkshire agitation for parliamentary reform, led by
the Rev. Christopher Wyvill, into support for the coalition's campaign against undue royal influence. On 27 December, five days
before the election, he wrote to Dr Henry Zouch, his contact in the
Wakefield district, urging that parliamentary reform was no longer
the real political issue. The cause of the present confusion was 'not
the corruption, not the lack of independence, not the want of
patriotism in the House of Commons, but the unwise and desperate
exercise of the royal prerogative to choose its own Ministers, by the
dismission of those who have the confidence of the people, and the
appointment of those who have it not'. Pitt, he declared, was 'a
young man whose ambition is so restless, and boundless, that nothing
will satisfy him but being first: while to gain the object of his
passion, he cares little by what road he reaches it, and meanly sub-
mits to creep up the backstairs of *secret influence*'. He forecast that
Pitt's attempt would fail, but, he urged, the public must play its part.
'At this crisis, nothing should divert the public from this single
object, a *good government*—till that is again obtained all must be
confusion and distraction in the country: nothing can make it again,
but the return of the old Ministers to the government of the country
. . . any other object, diverting us from that, is at this moment ill

timed, though it may be good abstractedly.' Unfortunately, Wyvill's
adoption of Pitt as the parliamentary spokesman of his Association
movement determined the reformers in the country to support the
new Minister. The Whig claim to be champions of the people against
unconstitutional influence was to be repudiated by the people themselves.[49]

Fitzwilliam always found a party cause, fought on general principle, more to his taste than a combat at closer quarters on questions
of administrative detail, and when Parliament reassembled in January
he threw all his energies into Fox's support. In the upper House he
led for the opposition in the debate of 4 February in his longest
reported speech so far. Lord Effingham had moved a resolution
declaring it to be 'unconstitutional, and contrary to law, for any one
branch of the legislature to assume to itself a right of making any
resolutions which should impede or put a stop to the executive power
of government as by law established' and making particular reference to the Commons' resolutions of 24 December, seeking to stop
the drawing by the Treasury of bills from India, and 16 January,
declaring the continuance of the present Ministry to be 'contrary
to constitutional principles'. Fitzwilliam's reply was a long sardonic
attack on Pitt himself:

his youth, his inexperience, his predilection for court, and seclusion from
those social circles where his equals in rank and fortune and years
commonly resorted, were facts which always would have their weight
in this country. . . . Where were the great or meritorious things he had
yet done, for which he had been so highly and strangely raised? . . . what
mighty schemes of public utility do the public owe to his industry, his
abilities, and his invention?

Surveying Pitt's career, he drew attention to his haughty refusal in
1782 of any 'subordinate situation'; his attempt to acquire popularity
by adoption of the cause of parliamentary reform; his share in
negotiating the 'inglorious' peace preliminaries of 1782; the lack of
any achievements or reforms during his tenure of office as Chancellor
of the Exchequer; and above all, of course, his conduct in December
1783. 'What Minister,' he asked, 'could the history of this country
produce, who had thus held Parliament in defiance, and kept his
situation in opposition to their inclination and express requisition,
with whom the constitution had placed the control of his actions?'
And as for Pitt's refusal to confer upon himself the valuable sinecure

of Clerk of the Pells, which had recently fallen vacant and which, most historians argue, Pitt would have been justified in taking for himself according to the political ethics of the day, Fitzwilliam urged that he had done no more than his plain duty: in taking it for himself he 'would have ruined his character, and blasted it for ever'.[50]

No doubt Fitzwilliam was right to say so: but the impression made on the public was favourable to Pitt. Through the first three months of 1784 Pitt's refusal to budge from office and the coalition's inability to find any practical means of forcing him to do so steadily swung public opinion. Fox's early threats to stop, or even to delay, the voting of supplies and the Mutiny Act were exposed as empty shams. Slowly the independent members, whose attitude was crucial in the end, tired of the inconclusive struggle and left for the country. On 8 March the government's minority in the Commons fell to one: no further resistance was practicable to the Finance and Mutiny Bills, and on their successful passage the Parliament was at last dissolved. George III and his Minister appealed to the people against the self-styled people's champions. Attention switched from Westminster to the constituencies, and here too the Whig cause was to be lost. Fitzwilliam, along with his party, was now to discover the bitterness of defeat and to learn the lessons which complacency had hidden during the months and years since Lord North's fall in 1782: that it was of no use for a group of aristocrats to lay claim to the role of guardians of the constitution and of the people's liberties if their links with the people were forged from above and not from below.

Notes
[1] One of her sisters, Lady Mary Milbanke, wife of John Milbanke, Esq., of Halnaby Hall, received £1,000 from Rockingham's will. The other two sisters, Lady Henrietta Sturgeon and Lady Charlotte Wentworth, inherited £30,000 each. Fitzwilliam's sisters, the Ladies Anne, Frances and Dorothy Fitzwilliam, received £1,000: Wentworth Woodhouse MSS, A 1235B.

[2] Known as Wentworth Woodhouse until the time of the first Marquess of Rockingham and again after 1835, but during this time correctly styled Wentworth House. There is a description of the house by H. Avray Tipping in *Country Life*, LVI (1924).

[3] *A Six-months Tour through the North of England* (1770), I, pp. 278, 294, 301–2.

[4] The Wentworth estate descended to the Fitzwilliams through Lady Anne Wentworth, daughter of the first Earl of Strafford and wife of Edward Watson, second Baron Rockingham of Rockingham Castle, Northamptonshire. On the death of Lady Anne's brother, the second Earl of Strafford, in 1695 the estate passed to her younger son, Thomas Watson-

C

Wentworth (died 1723) and then to his son Thomas, who became Baron
Malton in 1734. In 1746 the barony of Rockingham devolved upon Lord
Malton from his second cousin Thomas (third Earl Rockingham) who died
without issue. Malton was then created Marquess of Rockingham. The
Watson family estates were bequeathed to the third earl's cousin Lewis
Monson, second son of the first Baron Monson by a daughter of Lewis,
first Earl of Rockingham. Lewis Monson took the name of Watson and in
1760 was created Baron Sondes.

5 Young, p. 280; P. Toynbee, 'Horace Walpole's journals of visits to
country seats', *Walpole Society*, XVI (1927–8), p. 71.

6 Young, pp. 307–53.

7 In 1780 the clear receipts from Wentworth, Badsworth and Eccleshall
amounted to about £15,000, in 1796 £20,000, in 1819–20 £36,000. (Estate
accounts, Wentworth Woodhouse MSS, A 269, 285, 331.) In 1801 Fitzwilliam declared his income (after deducting assessed taxes) as £33,570
from the Wentworth and Malton estates, £22,391 from Ireland, and
£6,803 from Milton and Peterborough, plus further items, amounting in
total to £63,574. Outgoings were £13,532, leaving a clear income of over
£50,000.

8 *Infra*, pp. 300–3.

9 Household accounts, 1780 (Wentworth Woodhouse MSS, A 20):
annual accounts of collieries, 1799–1826, F 105a; proposed arrangement as
to the settlement of the estates, 1827 (N). Dr L. G. Mee has calculated that
over the period 1798–1856 the collieries on the Wentworth estate yielded
a net surplus of over £300,000. ('The Earls Fitzwilliam and the management of the collieries . . . on the Wentworth estate, 1795–1857', unpublished Ph.D. thesis, University of Nottingham, 1972.)

10 See my article on the Yorkshire elections of 1806 and 1807, *Northern
History*, II (1967), pp. 86–8, and R. Robson, *The Attorney in eighteenth-
century England* (1959), pp. 88–9.

11 Household accounts, A 54 (1796). Taxes and assessments on the
Wentworth estate amounted to a mere £721. Personal estate inherited
from Rockingham also included Rockingham House (No. 4 Grosvenor
Square), valued at £8,000, which became Fitzwilliam's London headquarters and one of the Whig party's meeting places during the Parliamentary session. Fitzwilliam also inherited a large number of horses,
carriages, racehorses in training and brood mares: accounts of Rockingham's executors, A 1201.

12 See *passim* correspondence with his stewards at Wentworth (Wentworth Estate MSS, Sheffield, Nos. 3 and 4) and Malton (F 75–8) and papers
on poor relief, etc. (F 47).

13 *Infra*, pp. 288–9.

14 Sir Herbert Maxwell, *The Creevey Papers* (1904), II, p. 129.

15 Correspondence with Rev. H. Zouch, 2, 11 and 22 September, 1787:
E 234.

16 To Sir Horace Mann, 7 July 1782: *Letters* (ed. Toynbee), XII, p. 287.

17 Burke to Fitzwilliam, [3] July 1782 (*Corresp. of Edmund Burke*, V,
pp. 6–7); Fox to Fitzwilliam, 'Monday past three' (F 63b); Fitzwilliam to

Burke [3 July 1782] (*Corresp. of E. Burke*, pp. 7–8). A condition of Rocking-ham's legacy was that Fitzwilliam should adopt the surname Wentworth before his own. He signed himself 'Wentworth Fitzwilliam' from this time forward, but he did not legally adopt the addition until 1807, when his son came of age.

18 William Henry Cavendish-Bentinck (1738–1809), third Duke of Port-land from 1762, Prime Minister 1783 and 1807–9: see my essay on him in *The Prime Ministers*, ed. H. Van Thal (1974).

19 D. E. Ginter, *Whig Organisation in the General Election of 1790* (Berkeley, Calif., 1967).

20 Selwyn to Carlisle, 18 March [1782]: *Carlisle MSS*, p. 597.

21 There are several accounts of the meeting, which differ in some particulars. The attendance is reported as between thirty and forty by Shelburne (9 July; Fortescue, VI, No. 3837) and Carmarthen (*Political Memoranda of Francis, Fifth Duke of Leeds*, ed. O. Browning, 1884, pp. 72–3), and Dr J. Cannon accepts this figure (*The Fox–North Coalition* (1969), p. 23). Thomas Pelham, however, said that 150 were present (to Lord Pelham, 14 July: B.M. Add. MS 33128, ff. 83–6). Pelham's informa-tion seems to have come from Richmond: he did not attend himself. Professor Holden Furber (*Corresp. of E. Burke*, V, p. 9n.) accepts the figure of 150. The timing of the meeting is given by Dr Cannon as 12 noon to 9 p.m. on the 6th, but Shelburne wrote of the meeting taking place late at night on the 6th (*loc. cit.*) Professor Furber gives the time as 12 noon to 9 p.m. on 7 July, following Lord Carlisle, who gives the time as 'yester-day morning . . . from 12 o'clock till 9' (to Gower [8 July 1782], *Carlisle MSS*, pp. 632–3). Lord Frederick Cavendish, however, stated to Mrs W. Ponsonby that the meeting was on the Saturday [6th] (8 July, Grey MSS).

22 *Carlisle MSS, loc. cit.*; Temple to Thomas Grenville, 4 July 1782: Duke of Buckingham and Chandos, *Memoirs of the Court and Cabinets of George III* (1853), I, pp. 50–2.

23 Fox to Portland, 6 July: *Memorials and Corresp. of C. J. Fox*, IV, p. 274; Sheridan to T. Grenville, 4 July: *Court and Cabinets*, I, p. 53. The strength of the parties was estimated by George Selwyn as Shelburne 130, North 120, Fox 80 (*Carlisle MSS*, pp. 633–4) and by William Eden as Shel-burne 140, North 120, Fox 90 (Gibbon to Sheffield, 14 October: B.M. Add. MS 34884, f. 275). A modern calculation gives Shelburne 132, North 126, Fox 102 (G.R. Crosby, 'The transformation of the Tory party, 1780–4', Ph.D. dissertation, Radcliffe, 1933, pp. 204–46, quoted in *Corresp. of E. Burke*, V, p. 57, n. l).

24 Fitzwilliam to Burke [3 July]: *Corresp. of E. Burke*, V, p. 8. Rocking-ham's will is in R.

25 *Parl. Register*, XI, pp. 16, 21–7.

26 Fortescue, VI, Nos. 4125 and 4140.

27 For the detailed history of the negotiations leading to the junction and an assessment of its character and significance see Cannon, *op. cit.*, chs. 3, 5 and 12.

28 Loughborough to Eden, 14 July 1782: *Journals and Corresp. of William, Lord Auckland*, ed. Bishop of Bath and Wells (1861), I, pp. 9–10.

29 Portland declared to Temple on 22 February that the coalition would insist upon all the 'efficient' offices being placed in the hands of 'those who are looked upon to be Whigs, and were considered to be such, by our late most excellent friend Lord Rockingham' (*Court and Cabinets*, I, p. 162). Lord North's friends, however, were well represented in the lower ranks of administration.

30 *Memorials and Corresp. of C. J. Fox*, II, pp. 37–8.

31 W. W. Grenville to Temple, 17 March 1783: *Court and Cabinets*, I, p. 232.

32 The description applied to those supporters of the coalition who lost their seats at the general election of 1784, in *Fox's Martyrs; or, a New Book of the Sufferings of the Faithful* (1784).

33 *Parl. Register*, XI, pp. 147–8, 153–4, 168–9, 236, 258–9.

34 Walpole to Strafford, 11 October 1783: *Letters* (ed. Toynbee), XIII, p. 70.

35 H.M.C., *Fortescue MSS*, I, pp. 214–9.

36 Fox to Eden, 7 November 1783: *Journals and Corresp. of Lord Auckland*, I, p. 61.

37 There were two India Bills, but the second (which attracted little notice) was concerned with land tenure in India.

38 The current Parliament was elected in the summer of 1780. It could not therefore run beyond June 1787. If the India Bill were to become law at the earliest possible date (December 1783) the commissioners would have security of tenure until December 1787. Any change of administration would precede rather than follow a general election. The inference is that the king might find it difficult to change his Ministers if the new men were to see Indian patronage remain in the hands of the old ones.

39 Pitt to the Duke of Rutland, 22 November 1783: Stanhope, *Life of Pitt* (1861), I, pp. 140–1. Temple reported to the king on 15 November that Fox had made an offer of coalition to Pitt the previous Thursday (13 November). Pitt had refused without hesitation or discussion (Fortescue, VI, No. 4520). Pitt had made up his mind not to join Fox and North. Dr Cannon has established beyond doubt Pitt's complicity from the beginning in the intrigue which led to the defeat of the India Bill in the Lords on the 17th (*op. cit.*, pp. 128–31).

40 Fox wrote to Eden on 28 November that the vote was 'decisive in every respect' and on 9 December, after the third reading had been passed by 208 to 103, Eden wrote that 'It has purposely been urged as a question on which we rested the fate of our government, and in the result we appear for the present to be very firmly established' (*Journals and Corresp. of Lord Auckland*, I, p. 63).

41 Fitzwilliam to Portland, 16 November: Portland MSS, 618. He cited the strong protest made by thirteen Whig peers, including Rockingham and himself, against the Regulating Act of 1773 on the grounds that 'the election of executive officers in Parliament is plainly unconstitutional, and an example of the most pernicious kind, productive of intrigue and faction, and calculated for extending a corrupt influence in the Crown. . . . It defeats the wise design of the constitution, which placed the

nomination of all offices, either immediately or derivatively, in the Crown, whilst it committed the check upon improper nominations to Parliament' (*Parl. Register*, xiv, p. 30). Portland, however, shrugged off the objection (22 November 1783 : N). Fitzwilliam predicted only too accurately the use that the opposition might make of this protest against the Whigs' reputation for consistency.

[42] H.M.C., eighth report, *Manchester MSS*, appendix, pp. 133, 137b.

[43] Portland to Fitzwilliam, 22, 24 and 29 November (N) and replies, 24 November (Portland MSS, PWF 3758) and [30th] (N). Fitzwilliam's nomination was announced by *The Gazetteer and New Daily Advertiser* on 1 December and by Fox in the Commons on the 2nd.

[44] *Parl. Register*, xiv, pp. 38–40, 103 : memorandum, F 64g.

[45] *Cobbett's Parliamentary History*, xxiv, 193, 196; *Parl. Register*, xiv, pp. 107–8.

[46] Lord Stormont had previously supported the Bill on the assumption, generally shared, that it could not have been introduced without the king's permission. Lord Bute had advised his son to support it in the Commons on a similar understanding (J. Ehrman, *The Younger Pitt* (1969), p. 116). William Eden declared on 16 December that 'the royal disinclination to the Bill was never intimated through the whole of its progress, but every expression held out a contrary idea' (16 December : *Journals and Corresp. of Lord Auckland*, i, p. 69). See also *Windham Papers*, i, p. 54.

[47] *Parl. Hist.*, xxiv, 205–6. Windham wrote on 18 December that Fox had been confident on the 17th of a majority of thirty (*Windham Papers, loc. cit*).

[48] See *infra*, ch. iv.

[49] Fitzwilliam to Zouch, 27 December 1783 : E 234. For Wyvill and the Yorkshire election of 1784 see *infra*, ch. iii. For Savile see pp. 62–9.

[50] *Parl. Register*, xiv, pp. 116, 118–22. Fitzwilliam's attack on Pitt was described at York by James Topping, a lawyer on the northern circuit, as 'a damned blackguard attack on Mr Pitt, and it was received like a blackguard speech in the Lords'. Richard Burke junior, who was present, defended Fitzwilliam's honour in a duel with Topping, which ended with a statement from the latter that he 'meant no insult on Lord Fitz, whom he did not even know'. (*Corresp. of E. Burke*, v, pp. 130–3.)

CHAPTER THREE

The first political test: Yorkshire 1782—4

However diffident Fitzwilliam might be in taking a leading role in the party's parliamentary activity, he could not set aside the legacy which Rockingham left as leader of the Whig cause in Yorkshire. For two years after his uncle's death, through the height of the political crisis at Westminster, it was in provincial politics that Fitzwilliam played his major role. One of the lessons taught by those two years was to be the critical nature of opinion and political management outside the walls of Westminster. Though Fitzwilliam is not wholly to blame for the result in Yorkshire, Pitt's success in 1784 was a triumph in the country as much as in Parliament; and nowhere was that triumph more spectacular and more significant than in the heartland of Rockingham influence. 'Yorkshire and Middlesex,' Fox once remarked, 'between them make all England',[1] and 1784 was to bear him out. It was to take over twenty years for the Whig interest in England's largest county to be brought back to something like its old footing after the disasters that were now to come.

Fitzwilliam lacked one sphere of influence that had belonged to his uncle, in the office of the Lord Lieutenancy of the West Riding. If the administration had continued in Rockinghamite hands it would doubtless have been given to him. Shelburne, who might have aimed to conciliate the Whigs by an immediate offer of the post to Fitzwilliam, with his usual deviousness contrived to offend rather than ingratiate. John Lee, a follower of Rockingham, MP for Malton and Solicitor General in the recent administration, wrote on 10 August to Fitzwilliam that Shelburne was expecting Fitzwilliam to ask for the office himself. Such a step was out of the question, however, and at the end of August Shelburne visited Lord Bessborough, Fitzwilliam's father-in-law, to ask him to transmit the offer of the Lord Lieutenancy to him. Shelburne 'expressed a great esteem for you, as well as a great regard for the memory of the Marquess of Rockingham', Bessborough wrote. Fitzwilliam, however, declared to Lady Rockingham that

Having experienced very closely and very attentively his Lordship's conduct of late, and consequently having formed an opinion of his present principles, I can see no reason to expect that as an honest man I shall ever be able to give support to his administration, and therefore as a fair one I must decline receiving any favour at his hands.[2]

The Lord Lieutenancy might have strengthened Fitzwilliam's political influence in the West Riding, but it would not have solved his major problem—that of retaining Rockingham's old position when a comparative stranger, and at a time when events and opinion were moving against the Whig party there and throughout the country. The old Whig interest in Yorkshire, an alliance of aristocracy and gentry and their dependants clustered round the Wentworth family, was split by controversy over the main political issues of the day. These centred on the question of parliamentary reform, now being agitated by Christopher Wyvill and his allies in the Yorkshire Association, but they also involved other pressing local and national interests. It was an unfortunate moment for a young, inexperienced and untried successor without intimate knowledge of county men and affairs to come to the leadership of the Yorkshire Whigs.

Since the last month of 1779 Yorkshire had been the centre and driving force of a complex movement of opinion in favour of political reform. The origins of the movement seem to have been in the spontaneous activity of a number of gentry and Anglican clergy in the North Riding, stirred to political agitation by grievances against war taxation and weak government.[3] In some respects the movement inherited traditional 'country' prejudices against the court and the institutions of central government. Old cries against sinecurists, pensioners and court favourites, parasites living on the taxes of honest gentlemen, were combined with new resentments against a government incapable of conducting a war with glory or even credit and fears for the stability of a traditional landed society in face of new wealth from trade, industry and imperial development. The vague disgruntlement of country squires and parsons was organised into a political movement by Christopher Wyvill, a non-resident and non-acting Anglican parson who had married into a

landed estate at Burton Constable and who had both considerable
organising talent and the leisure to employ it. Beginning with a
meeting of the gentlemen, clergy and freeholders of Yorkshire on
30 December 1779, Wyvill and his friends proposed a simple
remedy. Economical reform, the restriction of government expenditure on places and pensions, would not only reduce taxation and
purify the State. It would reduce the power of government to interfere in local elections and the ability of the Crown to influence
parliamentary discussion in order to secure approval for a corrupt
government and an ill-run war. The danger of excessive Crown
influence was the major topic of emphasis, and the meeting agreed
to organise a petition calling for public economy and drawing
attention to the 'great and unconstitutional influence [of the
Crown], which, if not checked, may soon prove fatal to the liberties
of the country'. Towards the end of the meeting and after some
of the more conservative element had left, a further proposal was
added for the appointment of a committee to supervise arrangements for the petition and to carry on correspondence with other
interested parties. In January a meeting of thirty-one members of
this committee resolved to propose a County Association whose
object should be not merely economical but parliamentary reform—
in particular, shorter parliaments and a more equal representation.[4]
Rockingham and his friends supported the economical reform proposals, which fitted into their campaign to reduce the influence of
the Crown, but they opposed any extension of the agitation to electoral reform. Wyvill had to move carefully to retain the support of
such basically conservative interests while also building a bridge
towards the radicals of the metropolis whose cry for reform was
based on abstract principles rather than on immediate grievances.
Wyvill's involvement with both radicals and moderate reformers,
however, increased Rockingham's fears about the ulterior objectives
of the Associators. He warned his friend Stephen Croft, an Associator, on 18 May 1780 that 'abstract principles, theoretically right,
will furnish matter for disputation in the Schools of Utopia, till
time is no more. But poor old England may pine away and die for
want of medicines, deemed *slight* ones, and which may nevertheless check her disorder . . . and re-establish her present miserable,
broken constitution.'[5] The Whigs accordingly urged the limitation
of the Association to the original objectives of the first county
meeting.

In pursuit of this strategy Fitzwilliam had accompanied Rockingham and five other Whig peers from Yorkshire to the first meeting.
They did not sign the petition, which was limited to the 'Gentlemen, Clergy and Freeholders of the County of York', the constituents of the House of Commons. Rockingham, however,
arranged that the chairman of the meeting, William Chaloner,
should write a letter of thanks to the peers for their attendance so
that they could send a reply which would make their support
clear.[6] When the committee set up on 30 December produced its
plan of association, including proposals for parliamentary reform,
for approval at a second county meeting on 28 March, the Rockingham group used their weight to discourage the step. Rockingham
wrote to Pemberton Milnes, a leading industrialist, dissenter and
reformer from Wakefield, on 28 February 1780 to point out that
'The grievances we feel, and the cause of our misfortune, arise from
the corruption of men when chosen into Parliament. Cut off the
ways and means of corruption [i.e. by economical reform] and the
effect must and will naturally cease'. Fitzwilliam wrote to Chaloner
on 9 March in a similar vein. 'Adhere strictly to one object', he
advised, 'to reduce the influence of the Crown, as the true source of
every evil.' A better system of representation, he continued, was no
doubt desirable, 'but of all things the most difficult to be brought
about in the absence, so far, of a practicable scheme'.[7]

Outside Yorkshire too Fitzwilliam used his influence on the side
of moderation. He appeared at the county meeting at Huntingdon
on 27 January when the chairman, Sir Robert Barnard, proposed
the adoption of the radical programme recommended by the Westminster Committee. Fitzwilliam led the opposition to the inclusion
of proposals for electoral reform, declaring 'that he could not agree
to annual parliaments or to altering the mode of electing the
members, and that he would oppose those propositions in the House
of Lords'. The meeting nevertheless agreed to a petition similar to
that of the Yorkshire freeholders, and in April a further meeting,
'the most numerous ever known,' according to the *Northampton
Mercury*, resolved in favour of economies in public expenditure,
reduction of Crown influence, shorter parliaments and a more equal
representation, and converted the Committee of Correspondence
into a Committee of Association.[8] In Northamptonshire a more
moderate tone prevailed. At the first county meeting on 29 January
the petition prayed only for relief from the burdens of taxation,

C*

and did not mention parliamentary reform. Instead of setting up a
Committee of Correspondence, the meeting agreed to instruct the
county members to support the adoption of a plan for the abolition
of sinecures, the future prevention of unmerited pensions, the reduction of exorbitant salaries, and the provision of official salaries in
place of perquisites of office. The county was to meet again in the
spring to receive a report from them. At the second meeting, on
29 March 1780, Sir William Dolben proposed to thank the county
members, Knightley and Powys, for their efforts in the Commons
and to ask them 'to express the grateful acknowledgement of that
meeting to the House' for the progress made so far. This was too
weak to satisfy the Rockinghams now that North's majority was
setting to work to destroy piecemeal the opposition's economical
reform Bills. Fitzwilliam therefore led the opposition to the second
part of Dolben's motion and the words objected to were deleted.
'The sensible, lively and candid manner adopted by the speakers
rendered this debate exceedingly pleasing and entertaining to the
hearers,' remarked the reporter in the *Northampton Mercury*; 'the
Assembly broke up with that perfect good nature, which should
always be preserved in a meeting like this, where *the real interest of
our country* is the sole object sought after by all parties.'[9] The Whig
nobility and gentry of Northamptonshire, led by Fitzwilliam and his
friend Althorp, had little to fear from radical sentiment in this more
rural and conservative part of England. Yorkshire and Westminster
were to be the battlegrounds between them and the more radical
reformers.

Not all the Whigs were so cautious in working with the new movement of public opinion. Fox had thrown himself recklessly into
Westminster politics and emerged as chairman of the Westminster
Committee, pledged to a radical reformation. This committee was
originally set up on 2 February 1780, consisting of 103 members and
increased by twenty-four a week later. It represented many different
interests, comprising in 'an uneasy alliance Rockinghamite lords and
gentry, old-style Radicals and new-style revolutionaries', as a recent
writer has remarked.[10] Portland, Derby, five of the Cavendish
brothers, Lord Surrey, Lord Edward Bentinck, Richard Fitzpatrick
and Sir John Ramsden were among the original members, and Fitzwilliam, with seven others, was recruited on 16 February. More
Rockinghamites were added in the next two weeks, including Devonshire, Sir William Milner and General Keppel. But Fox's hope that the

Whigs might thus 'make a strong Whig party in the country' as the only alternative to seeing 'who can make his court best at St James's' was not shared by the aristocratic heads of the party; their fears of radical change were greater than their optimism about their ability to harness and control so dangerous an ally as metropolitan radicalism.[11] The first meetings of the committee resulted in resolutions endorsing the economical reform programme of the opposition in Parliament, but on 15 March it was resolved that

This committee conceive themselves bound to enter into the consideration of every question tending to establish the independency of Parliament on a solid and durable basis [and] that the duration of Parliaments and the state of the representation of the people are questions immediately under this description.

A sub-committee, predominantly radical in membership, reported on 20 March in favour of 'a more equal representation of the people' and annual parliaments. Fox tried to hold the committee together for two purposes : to recruit the support of public opinion for the Whigs, and to serve his own purposes as an electoral machine. It was an impossible strategy, and from 5 April, when the committee was reconstituted as the Westminster Committee of Association, control fell more and more into the hands of political and religious radicals such as Jebb, Cartwright and Brand Hollis. Fitzwilliam and the other Rockinghamite members eventually stopped attending committee meetings and the most Fox could hope to do was to try to restrict the Westminster movement to the more moderate programme of the Yorkshire Association. Even this was becoming distasteful to his party leaders, however, and on 3 November Fitzwilliam spoke on Rockingham's behalf against the plan for adding an extra hundred Knights of the Shire, now the favourite proposal of both sets of reformers. The committee nevertheless resolved in favour of the plan. From this time Fitzwilliam attended few meetings. He went on 14 December, when he was appointed one of the sub-committee to organise a subscription to pay Fox's election expenses, and again on 26 January 1781 to take part in the ballot to choose delegates to the forthcoming meeting of the associated bodies, but he was not present a fortnight later when a mostly radical group of the committee met to brief the delegates to work for economical reform, the extra hundred members and the shortening of the duration of Parliaments. His interest in the committee did not revive until the spring of 1782, when the Rockinghams again tried to use it for their own political ends.[12]

The Rockinghams' failure in 1780 to take control of the Westminster movement was matched by their inability to force their economical reform Bills through the Commons in face of North's delaying tactics. In June 1780 the Gordon riots in London further weakened external support for reform, and the swing of public opinion encouraged North to dissolve Parliament in the summer. He succeeded as a result in holding his position almost unchanged in the new House.[13] The election, however, marked a further stage in the alienation of the Rockinghams from the reformers. In several counties candidates were required by substantial bodies of electors to pledge their support for the Associators' objectives. In Yorkshire Sir George Savile, an independent but hitherto closely associated with the Rockinghams, and his independent colleague Henry Duncombe gave assurances of their goodwill towards reform. Savile exaggerated on both sides when he remarked that 'hitherto I have been elected in Lord Rockingham's dining-room; now I am returned by my constituents'. In fact his position as MP for Yorkshire owed more to his personal reputation for integrity, care for the county's local interests, and standing as a substantial landowner than it did to either aristocratic patronage or popular acclaim. And his attitude towards the Association was ambivalent, to say the least. William Weddell, MP for Malton and Lady Rockingham's brother-in-law, was to remark that Savile 'so mathematically poised his balance, that one did not know whether he was an Associator or not'.[14] Such judicious trimming was necessary to minimise the growing tension in Yorkshire between the aristocratic interests and the reformers. Wyvill's attempt in 1781 to reach a working agreement with the Rockinghams was not successful. His proposals for a programme incorporating the addition of 100 Knights of the Shire to the Commons, with some moderate, voluntary and compensated disfranchisement of boroughs, were approved in Westminster but rejected by the Yorkshire Committee of Association.[15]

1781 marked a lull in the reform movement. Public interest flagged, and in Parliament the reformers failed to make significant headway. The change of Ministry in April 1782 revived enthusiasm. Both Shelburne and Rockingham were committed to some measure of reform, and a series of Bills began the work of reducing Crown influence. Crewe's Bill disfranchising revenue officers and Clerke's Bill dis-

qualifying holders of government contracts from sitting in the
Commons were designed to contribute to the major aim of both
parties in the administration, the reduction of the Crown's political
influence. Burke's Civil List Establishment Act regulated various
branches of civil list expenditure, including the royal household,
and abolished forty-seven offices tenable with a seat in the lower
House.[16] At the same time the parliamentary reformers laid plans to
promote their favourite measure. A meeting at Richmond's house
towards the end of April agreed to depute the young Pitt to sound
out the House on the question, and on 7 May Pitt's general motion
in favour of reform attracted the support of both wings of the movement. The respectable number of 141 members supported his proposal for an enquiry into means of parliamentary reform, against a
majority of only 161. Encouraged by this unprecedentedly close
division, the reformers in Yorkshire and elsewhere resumed their
efforts to procure petitions and other manifestations of public support, while in Parliament the developing alliance between Pitt and
the reform movement drew close together. By the autumn Wyvill
and the Yorkshire Association had not only confirmed their original
proposals for adding a hundred county members to the representation and repealing the Septennial Act but had come out in favour of
abolishing the franchise of fifty obnoxious boroughs, reforming Scottish elections, and enfranchising forty-shilling copyholders in the
counties. A meeting of the Yorkshire Association at the beginning of
November 1782 endorsed these proposals.

This meeting marked the beginning of the end of the alliance,
partial as it had ever been, between the Associators and the Rockingham party in Yorkshire. It was becoming impossible to reconcile
support of the Association with political allegiance to Wentworth.
At the beginning many of Rockingham's followers—men like Stephen
Croft, a prominent gentleman in York and a founder-member of
the Association, and the Rev. Henry Zouch—had shared in the enthusiasm for the movement and had hoped that by joining it they would
help to forge links between the Whig party and a wide spectrum of
important public opinion. Now their ardour cooled. The possibility
arose that at the next parliamentary election for the county there
might be a direct confrontation between the Wentworth interest and
the Association. Only Sir George Savile's rather equivocal stand, with
a foot in each camp, steadied the situation. 'He was the keystone, to
use language nearly his own, by which the nobles and the people, as

parts of the same political arch, were united and kept together,'
wrote Wyvill in 1802.[17] But Savile was getting old, suffered much
from ill health, and was contemplating retirement from the burdensome duties of a member for Yorkshire. His decision to retire, at the
end of November 1783, was the beginning of the crisis in Yorkshire
which culminated in the loss of the general election in March 1784.
The removal of his moderating influence helped to precipitate that
confrontation between the Whig interest and the reformers which he
and Rockingham had tried to avert by diplomacy and even equivocation. Fitzwilliam was as yet less than adept at this conciliatory tech-
nique, and unable to restrain Burke's ill-tempered and uncompromising opposition to parliamentary reform. When Burke visited Wentworth in the summer of 1782, according to Wyvill's colleague
William Mason, by 'wrangling with various of his lordship's visitors
about parliamentary reform, he . . . indisposed several gentlemen of
property and consequence against that noble lord; if therefore he
[Fitzwilliam] has not a quarter of that consequence which Lord
R[ockingham] had (which will certainly be the case) in this county,
he may lay it all to the effect of his friend's eloquence'.[18] Burke or
no Burke, however, Fitzwilliam was quickly to find the maintenance
of Rockingham's power in Yorkshire to be an almost impossible task,
and his own inexperience and unpreparedness were to be as much
to blame for the failure as the tactlessness of his friends.

The crisis in Yorkshire began at the end of October 1783, with the
death on the 26th of Sir Charles Turner, one of the members for York
city. Turner, with his colleague Lord John Cavendish, had been
elected in 1768 with Rockingham's help. York was a large, tumultuous
constituency with an electorate of some 2,000 freemen who were
acutely conscious of the value of their votes and whose hard-headed
practicality needed management. Rockingham and his associates in
the city—men like John Fountayne (Dean of York), Stephen Croft,
William Siddall (a tailor and Lord Mayor in 1783), Robert Sinclair (a
lawyer, later to become Recorder of the city), and Peregrine Wentworth, whose house near Wakefield was a frequent headquarters for
county and city election business, had to combine shrewd knowledge
of personalities and opinion in the city with ability to manage the
organisation necessary in so large a constituency. The first essential
was the support of the corporation, consisting of the Lord Mayor,
twelve aldermen, two sheriffs, the council of twenty-four (consisting
of former holders of the office of sheriff) and the common council of

seventy-two.[19] It was an exclusive body over which there was no effective popular influence: the aldermen in particular were powerful men in city affairs, with a good deal of control over the composition of the councils and, in turn, over admissions to the freedom of the city, which conferred the franchise. From the middle of the century Rockingham secured a foothold in city politics by cultivating the corporation and the Minster interest, and the Dean became his chief representative in the city. The more important freemen were organised into a political body named the Rockingham Club, which at first met monthly, but after 1758 quarterly, to 'keep up the interest', dispense hospitality and maintain a convivial atmosphere. Its membership included the leading Whig gentlemen, clergy, merchants and traders of the city, though by 1782 it also included a number of craftsmen and artisans, and its meetings were occasionally noisy and disorderly. By 1768 Rockingham's organisation had secured control of both seats in the city, though it was a control always susceptible to challenge and expense.

The first danger signs appeared in 1780. Turner, an independent gentleman devoted to hunting and the turf, occupied a position in the city rather like that of Savile in the county. He associated himself with the Rockingham interest more out of constitutional principle than party attachment, and his local prestige was as much an asset to Rockingham as the latter's organisation was to him. Like Savile, Turner avowed his sympathy for the reform cause but he neither joined the Association nor signed the 1780 county petition. Cavendish on the other hand avowed his total opposition to parliamentary reform. Wyvill later declared that Rockingham's delicacy and Savile's good offices had preserved good feeling between the two factions, though Cavendish roundly asserted that the Association was unable to find a suitable alternative candidate and 'saw it was impossible to do anything without our aid'. Wyvill was also attempting to conciliate the Rockinghams in the hope of some joint action, and was naturally averse to anything which would offend the supporters of the Whig interest. As late as March 1783 Fitzwilliam was assured that if Cavendish were appointed Chancellor of the Exchequer his re-election would be 'certain', and his attendance at York merely 'a compliment the citizens will expect'.[20] By the autumn of 1783, however, the Associators and the Portland Whigs were no longer potential allies, and Wyvill's friends in the city were prepared for a trial of strength. Turner's death on 26 October faced

Fitzwilliam with his first real challenge as a political conciliator.

He failed the test. Instead of moving cautiously, seeking the advice
and making sure of the support of his late uncle's friends in the city,
Fitzwilliam acted hastily and without full understanding of the com-
plexities of city politics. The day after Turner's death Charles Duncombe, brother of one of the county members and an Associator,
solicited Fitzwilliam's support for his candidature.[21] Without consulting Cavendish, Portland or any of his York supporters, Fitzwilliam agreed. On the 30th Cavendish wrote, with Portland's
approval, to urge the candidature of Fitzwilliam's brother George,
warning that Duncombe was unsuitable on account of his political
views and his lack of popularity in the city. Duncombe may have
had some claim upon Rockingham, who had tried to find him a seat
in Cornwall in 1780, and Fitzwilliam justified his support partly on
account of 'circumstances of a private nature'. But family piety was
no substitute for political acumen. Duncombe quickly found himself in a dilemma. Fitzwilliam made it a condition of his support
that, as in the case of both Cavendish and Turner, Duncombe must
join the Rockingham Club. This would demonstrate to the city and
to the world Duncombe's alignment with Fitzwilliam and the Whig
interest. Duncombe's brother, a vigorous Associator, urged him not
to join for precisely that reason. Nor would his membership have
pleased some of the leading members of the club, who saw in him a
leading representative of the rival Associating interest in the city.
The canvass was soon reported to be 'uphill work'. Wentworth,
always an optimist, hoped at first that Duncombe would acquire
popularity, but within a few days he was declaring that his first wish
had always been for George Fitzwilliam, and suggesting that Duncombe should yield to the popular clamour and leave the city. In the
event Duncombe, faced by a hostile crowd, took to his heels and
was chased from the city by a mob. His disgruntled remark that the
Rockingham Club was 'no more the firm phalanx as in the time of
our honourable friend, but split into different factions, animated with
a degree of virulence against each other scarce to be believed' was
borne out by subsequent events. Fitzwilliam's attempt to impose his
brother's candidature met with a direct rebuff. The Associators in
the club objected to George's vote against Pitt's motion for parliamentary reform in the Commons on 7 May 1783, and on 10 November a deputation approached Wentworth to declare that if he were
put forward it would divide the interest irretrievably. In fact the

Associators had settled on a candidate. This was Lord Galway, who had made tentative approaches to the corporation on the 30th but had immediately retreated on hearing of Fitzwilliam's support for Duncombe. Now he returned to the city with the favour of the Association and of the reformer members of the Rockingham Club. He arrived on the 13th, was 'dragged through the streets in his coach by the mob', and received the grudging acquiescence of Fitzwilliam and his friends. On 17 November he was elected unopposed. The Dean hoped that in this way the breach would be healed and that 'time will bring things back to the state in which your lordship found them'. This hope was not to be fulfilled for six years.[22]

The reasons for Fitzwilliam's first electoral defeat were complex, but not difficult to discover. The state of politics in the city was already disturbed and the old unity disrupted by the reflection of the national rivalry between the Portland Whigs and the Associators. It was natural that there should be difficulty in York, of all places, in finding a candidate acceptable to both sides. Fitzwilliam, too, was comparatively unknown in the city and he lacked his uncle's ability to conciliate and make a good impression. Unlike Rockingham, who at such a crisis would certainly have visited the city, joined in the convivial entertainment of the most important people, and shown himself to the cheering populace,[23] Fitzwilliam stayed at Milton and conducted his affairs by correspondence. This meant, inevitably, that his confidence seemed to be monopolised by a few. It also made it more difficult for him to assess the characters and motives of those who were advising him, so that his grasp of the situation was less thorough than Rockingham's had been. But above all, it was his rashness in agreeing to Duncombe's request for support, before he could consult his friends on the spot, which led him into the snare, and his inability to moderate the zeal of his more impetuous supporters in the city which entangled him in it. As he himself wrote, 'Perhaps the error of my judgement will have sown the seed of dissension and will be the cause of difference and disunion among that honourable and respectable band of men who never differed and never had but one object while the best and wisest of men still lived'.[24] Those 'respectable . . . men' were no longer so united as in Rockingham's day, but they had not been managed with Rockingham's flair. The political crisis which was immediately to envelop the whole county gave Fitzwilliam another opportunity to prove himself: but here again the force of circumstances was ultimately to be too strong. In

the county by-election which burst upon the Whigs a few days after
Galway's return for York, Fitzwilliam attempted to apply the lessons
learnt in the city, and with some limited success. In the long run,
however, the Whig interest in Yorkshire was unable to overcome the
local effects of the national political crisis which built up as a result
of the India Bill in December.

It was exactly a week after Galway's triumphant election at York
that Savile notified Portland of his decision to vacate the county seat.
It was a decision he had been moving towards for several weeks:
advancing age and ill health were making it increasingly difficult for
him to carry out his parliamentary duties in the way expected of
the member for England's largest constituency. Yet the timing of his
decision seems particularly inept. Portland immediately concluded
that Savile was under pressure from his nephew and close political
associate Francis Foljambe, who nourished the ambition to succeed
him. Foljambe was an Associator, as he declared, 'and *that* upon
principle, not from the persuasions of any man, or set of men whatever'. Portland was sure that Foljambe was 'employed . . . by our
worst enemies the Association' to capitalise on the success at York and
secure the second of the county seats, just at the time when the India
Bill was passing through Parliament and the government needed to
muster its full strength. Perhaps bearing in mind Fitzwilliam's blunder
over Duncombe, Portland immediately urged that a candidate be
found to stand against the Association's interest, suggesting George
Fitzwilliam or Lord George Cavendish.[25] Fitzwilliam, still at this
moment enjoying his hunting at Milton, and pondering whether to
accept the chairmanship of the proposed East India commissioners,
repeated now the mistake he had made over York city. He did not
travel to Wentworth, where he would have been able to influence
events on the spot and manage the electoral business. Nor did he go
up to London, where he could have talked to Portland, Cavendish
and the other party leaders. He pinned his hopes on the possibility
of gaining time by persuading Savile to withdraw his intended resignation, urging him 'if possible to remain as he is and to be satisfied
that his constituents would rather have him, though he never puts
his foot over the threshold of St Stephen's Chapel, than any other
man of the greatest activity and assiduity'. He urged that Savile
should be consulted about his successor, and though Sir George
refused to be drawn into endorsing his nephew's candidature Fitzwilliam made it his aim to present Foljambe either as Savile's choice

or as Savile's nephew, a compliment to the late member for his distinguished services. He himself saw no objection to Foljambe's candidature, provided it were on the Wentworth ticket.[26] These tactics were, in themselves, quite shrewd. The Wentworth interest was still strong, and the Association would certainly hesitate to offer it an outright challenge. Foljambe's apparent hope that he might be called upon as the nominee of the Association was not fulfilled. Nevertheless, as at York, it proved more difficult to persuade Fitzwilliam's friends in Yorkshire to accept the candidature of an avowed parliamentary reformer. To Dr Zouch Fitzwilliam put the question as tactfully as he was able, suggesting that

the attachment of the county to him [Savile], its gratitude for his long, faithful and essential services, may lead the inclinations of most men, to mark their sentiments of his merit by a token that cannot be mistaken, and pretty nearly the only unequivocal token within their reach. . . . It would be a cup of comfort to Sir George in his declining days.[27]

Reluctantly, and with a few exceptions, the supporters of the Wentworth interest swung behind Foljambe. Wyvill, despite the disapproval of the Rev. William Mason, his closest adviser, also decided to accept him, hoping that he too could present him as the choice of his own organisation.[28] At the nomination meeting on 17 December Foljambe's proposer, Lord Surrey, spoke of the candidate's membership of the Association, but his seconder was Walter Spencer Stanhope, not an Associator, who stressed his relationship to Savile. Few of Fitzwilliam's friends attended, principally for fear of a public breach with the Association over the new petition for parliamentary reform which was to be proposed at the meeting, and Croft reported that he 'had many *hands* held up against him'.[29] On 1 January 1784 the formal election was held and Foljambe was returned unopposed.

During the by-election, however, the political climate had suddenly changed. 17 December, the day of the nomination meeting at York, was the very day of the defeat of the India Bill in the Lords; by the time of the election Pitt's 'mince pie' administration had survived the Christmas holidays and the Yorkshire by-election seemed likely at any moment to be nullified by a general dissolution of Parliament. Yorkshire politics were to be profoundly affected by this new development. The prospect of an election fought upon greater issues even than parliamentary reform, in the light of Wyvill's alliance with Pitt, made a direct confrontation between Wentworth House and the Yorkshire Association a matter of probability: and before

Foljambe was even elected Fitzwilliam's friends were discussing the
possibility of putting up candidates for both the county seats—
possibly Foljambe or George Fitzwilliam, together with Fitzwilliam's
brother-in-law, Sir Thomas Dundas. Croft, however, was more despondent, and James Farrer of Leeds put the pessimistic view, all too
soon to be fulfilled, that Foljambe's return had 'given an additional
consequence to the Association, that will require the united efforts
of the independents of every description amongst us to overturn'. He
foresaw that unless candidates were found to stand against the
Association 'the great and extensive interest which your House has
ever had in this county will be in a great measure lost'.[30]

Pitt's decision to delay a dissolution of Parliament and thereby to
prolong his struggle against the coalition's majority in the Commons
has often been debated by historians. A number of reasons no doubt
operated to produce his decision. At the outset the decisive one
appears to have been the discovery that insufficient funds remained
in the Treasury to finance the government during the period of the
dissolution.[31] By the end of January, however, Pitt was prepared to
cut the knot which all his efforts in the Commons had so far failed
to unravel, and on 25 January the Cabinet decided upon a dissolution
—only to discover within a few hours that the time available after
a dissolution for a general election and the passage of the supplies, as
yet withheld by the Commons, in the new Parliament would not
allow the introduction of the necessary annual Mutiny Bill until after
the expiry of the old Act on 25 March.[32] From this point onwards
Pitt had no alternative but to continue his struggle against the
opposition: fortuitously the further delay of two months imposed
by this constitutional deadlock proved to be to his greater advantage.
Not only did it prove conclusively to many who had previously
hesitated to accept him that it was impossible to form a stable
government without a new election: it also gave time for public
opinion to swing against the coalition and for pro-government supporters in 'open' constituencies to organise themselves and lay their
plans. By the end of March the opposition in the Commons had
exhausted its arguments, and many of its supporters; the supplies and
the Mutiny Bill were allowed to pass, and the dissolution was taken.
By chance rather than good strategy Pitt found himself ideally placed
to win a resounding electoral victory far exceeding that forecast by
the cautious and experienced John Robinson in the latter days of
December 1783.

In Yorkshire the delay had one unexpected and extremely important result. It compelled Foljambe, returned by the unnatural alliance of Whigs and Associators, to declare his political position. His uncle had been able to avoid outright commitment to either side. Foljambe entered a House of Commons where neutrality and equivocation were no longer possible. His vote was given to Fox; and in Yorkshire this sealed his fate. 'We must now hope no more from him than a mere support of parliamentary reform, if ever that question should chance to be agitated,' wrote Mason to Wyvill. 'This will not satisfy me, nor do I think it will you.'[33]

Mason's words illuminate the connexion which had now developed between the Associators and Pitt. A year before 'a mere support of parliamentary reform' was as much as Wyvill and his friends would have expected or hoped for from a member for Yorkshire. Now the county Association began to operate as a political machine working on behalf of the new Minister and his supporters. Fox's pledge to North that reform was not to be a government question for the coalition had precipitated this shift of opinion, and from this time onwards it was impossible to separate reform politics in Yorkshire from the national issues raised by the coalition, the India Bill and the appointment of Pitt as first Minister of the Crown.

The story of the Yorkshire and York city elections of 1784 has already been told.[34] In both constituencies events ran a parallel course, and in both the outcome was identical—a resounding and unprecedented defeat for the Wentworth interest. Traditionally, these two constituencies have come to be regarded as epitomising the general character of the 1784 election. Both possessed large and politically aware electorates, and in both there was a good deal of expert electoral management and experience. York itself, the headquarters of the County Association movement and centre of Wyvill's network of correspondents and agents, was a city in which trading and manufacturing interests were mingled, as in the county, with the long-standing influence of many greater and lesser land-owning families and of the Anglican Church. Still Yorkshire's chief city, and traditionally the capital of the north, it provided a centre of assembly during the assizes or at the race meetings for the weighty men of the whole county to discuss local and national politics. A bustling, thriving, dignified and attractive city, it could have stood for much that is traditionally admired in the life of eighteenth-century England. The political supremacy of Rockinghamite Whiggism fitted naturally

into the pattern of later eighteenth-century York. It too combined the
support of land-owning interests with the goodwill of trading and
mercantile elements in society. Its liberal and yet conservative constitutional traditions accorded well with a society that exhibited
an almost ideal balance of interests and social groups. And the
harmony that characterised both the physical appearance and the
social climate of the city was epitomised in the good relationships,
carefully cultivated by Rockingham, between the citizens and the
agents of Wentworth House. Exhibiting the conventional characteristics of the Yorkshireman—hard-headed, businesslike independence,
even obstinacy, and careful husbandry of resources, the citizens of
York, like the freeholders of the county, were not men to be
dragooned or browbeaten, but men whose support had to be won by
conviction and kept by respect. Fitzwilliam was Rockingham's heir
and had the Wentworth blood, but in the eyes of Yorkshiremen he
had not yet proved his political principles. Stephen Croft had written
on 21 December that some disaffected members of the Rockingham
Club 'want a further proof than you have . . . declared of its being a
Whig revolution or constitutional club as well as Rockingham. They
know your uncle's principles but not your lordship's.'[35]

York, and Yorkshire, were therefore ripe for a contest which
mingled constitutional principles with political independence of
judgement. The political tension set up by the by-elections at the end
of 1783 had already alerted the county and city to the new situation,
and the outcome encouraged the Associators and their allies among
the independent gentry and city tradesmen to challenge an interest
hitherto assumed to be impregnable. Wyvill was given material to
work with, allies to organise, and a situation to exploit. As Fitzwilliam wrote,

the real misfortune is, that so many, so very many of our old friends are
themselves Associators, and having their heads so full of all the nonsense
Mr Wyvill was so good as to stuff them with, have hitherto been always
gaping for, and swallowing more: his plausibility and Mason's cunning
are always upon the spot, and having no other object in life, are always
at work to hurt us among our friends. . . . I know not how to fight against
this—that circumstance of their having no other view, and nothing to
divert them for a moment from their object, is an advantage irresistible.

He devoted himself during the Christmas holidays to writing
encouraging letters to his friends and agents in Yorkshire and the
city, sending them bundles of pamphlets to distribute in their neigh-

bourhoods and suggesting tactics and arguments to be used. He had written to several Yorkshire friends in the spring of 1783 to justify the coalition, arguing that 'in the distracted state of things at that period, it became necessary to make a strong, that there might be a *good government*, one independent of the king, and beyond the reach of the country's enemies, *his friends*'. This government, he now contended, 'in time would have restored the credit and prosperity of the country : that nothing could have shaken them, but the restless and desperate ambition of such an unprincipled man as Pitt, [who] . . . was as ready to be the Minister of the king's influence, as the Minister of the people's confidence'. Fitzwilliam avowed that 'I made pretty free with Pitt's character, to instil a jealousy of him, as Mr Wyvill has been turning the eyes of all Yorkshiremen towards him'. However, though he wrote several such letters he received only one reply, which drew the unfortunate conclusion 'that a parliamentary reformation is the only thing'. In his irritation Fitzwilliam confessed that he considered some of his Yorkshire friends to be 'not the most acute reasoners in the world . . . and in short, they have got a twist, and there must be patience to get them right again'. As Robert Sinclair reported from York, however, many of the Associators 'consider Mr Pitt as the champion of their cause, and are therefore not averse to his acquisition of influence however questionably come at', and he discouraged the notion of trying to rouse the county with the cry of 'secret influence', which would be inoperative.

The state of opinion in York, indeed, was now so hostile to the Whig cause that Fitzwilliam's insistence on a trial of strength with the Association was received with horror by his friends in the city. Fitzwilliam wrote to some of them on 28 December to announce his intention to propose his brother as well as Cavendish at the general election, rejecting Galway's overture for a coalition. Croft and Fountayne remonstrated, the Dean declaring that 'strong as my wishes are to show my regard to every branch of your family . . . I could not, as a member of the Association . . . ask a vote for your brother, who (it is said) voted (upon Mr Pitt's Bill) against all reform, unless he has altered his opinion on that subject'. Croft, too, warned of the coming difficulties, and even Sinclair, who, unlike Croft and Fountayne, had no loyalties to the Association, deprecated a canvass for George Fitzwilliam in the present circumstances. His advice to Fitzwilliam was to come to York to hold a meeting of the Rockingham Club, in order to rally the loyalty of his

remaining supporters. Wentworth suggested that the distribution of
some charitable benefaction to the poor of the city during the excep-
tionally hard winter would be timely, while Croft made the rather
lame proposal that Fitzwilliam should patronise the York tradesmen
to counter the activities of Lady Galway, who was furnishing a
house near the city and visiting the shops at frequent intervals.[36]
The defeat of 6 April, when the city poll closed after six days with
Fitzwilliam's two candidates decisively beaten, was already clearly
foreshadowed in January.

During the three months between the new year and the general
election affairs in the county began to follow a similar course to
those in the city. Part of the reason for Cavendish's declining popularity at York during the later months of 1783 was his proposal, as
Chancellor of the Exchequer, of a tax on receipts. The shopkeepers
and merchants of York and of the three ridings joined in the subsequent protest of the commercial interest in London and all over
England. In November 1783 it was found necessary to introduce a
further Bill to prevent evasion of the tax, and Cavendish's constituents attempted to instruct him to vote against it, and formed a
committee to carry on a national agitation against it. The fact that
several members of the Rockingham Club were tradesmen contributed therefore to the society's disaffection from Fitzwilliam's
interest.[37] In the county too the trading and manufacturing interests
were up in arms, the affront to their economic well-being hastening
their conversion to the constitutional case made by the tax's
opponents. Wentworth, sounding opinion in Wakefield, one of the
headquarters of the woollen manufacture, reported that the local
merchants were declaring that Fitzwilliam would never have the
same interest there as Rockingham because of the receipt tax, which,
they said, 'would never be forgiven, as it has done more harm to the
merchant than can be conceived, they were all to a man very clear
that Lord Rockingham had so great a respect for the trade of this
country, that he would never have perservered in so obnoxious a
tax'. Added to their heat and anger 'with Charles Fox upon his India
Bill', this made it impossible to talk to them, and 'half the town',
despite their opposition to the Association, had signed a proposed
address to the throne against the India Bill and supporting Pitt. 'How
to bring about matters in this country, I own, almost distracts me',
Wentworth confessed. Pamphlets were being distributed against the
India Bill, and Zouch alleged that every printing press in York was

on Pitt's side, so that the Whigs were unable to get their case published.[38] The decisive event was to be the county meeting, called by the reformers, Pittities and Tories for 25 March to debate an address to the throne against the coalition. This 'unaccountable *coalition*', as one of Fitzwilliam's correspondents called it, of reformers seeking to protect the people from the Crown and of those wishing to make the Crown absolute over the House of Commons, proved to be an irresistible force. Sinclair lamented that a combination of 'those who used to be advocates for the rights of the people against all encroachments of royal prerogative . . . with the old Tories' had begotten 'this strange monster of county politics', and 'diverted their attention from measures to men—Mr Pitt they consider their champion and therefore, even yet, they can see in him no error. Every wound to the constitution, they foolishly think, will be completely healed by him when his power shall be established and he himself unclogged with opposition or otherwise'.[39]

From all over the county news poured in of public meetings, addresses and resolutions, carrying Pitt and his supporters on an irresistible tide of victory. Fitzwilliam swam as energetically as he could against it, trying to mobilise his supporters to attend the county meeting and to vote against the address. Names were eagerly proposed of lords and influential gentlemen who might be written to, calculations made of numbers of freeholders who might be brought to the Castle yard to support the Whig cause. Fenton, the Banktop agent, wrote drily that he hoped his employer had good evidence for his optimism, for he saw no cause for any. He knew the county well and had watched Rockingham manage it at close quarters for several years, but his good advice was not taken: he pointed out that a challenge to the address which failed to make a good showing would do more harm than good and would expose Fitzwilliam's weakness: an early election was now talked of and 'the strength of your interest ought not to be too officiously brought forward at this period'. Thomas Hill of York calculated that the Whigs had to muster at least 12,000 at the meeting or be beaten, but 'we have not engines at work to bring in the 1,200'; and the vicar of Hemsworth went so far as to declare that the trading part of the county was so unanimously for Pitt that 'I do verily believe that Lord Fitzwilliam by his appearance here at this time will greatly prejudice and lessen that influence I am persuaded he will otherwise soon have in this county'. Fitzwilliam, however, considered the county meeting to be 'upon so serious and important a subject, that I think it my duty to attend'; but his determination to try to focus the debate on the Whig argument of prerogative and influence against popular and parliamentary rights was unavailing.[40] His very presence, as Fox's intended chairman of the East India commissioners, helped to focus the attention of the meeting on the India Bill, and enabled his opponents to turn against the Whigs the same charge of unconstitutional ambition which he was trying to level against Pitt. The distribution in the West Riding of a few copies of Burke's famous speech on the India Bill, in which he depicted Fox as the champion of the oppressed, even to the sacrifice of his 'darling popularity', was insufficient to rebut the charges.[41]

Behind all the disagreements about reform and the agitation against the receipt tax, it was the issues raised by the India Bill which dominated the debate at the county meeting. The Bill was presented as a device for perpetuating the 'unnatural coalition' which had come to epitomise aristocratic domination over king, Commons and people. Walter Spencer Stanhope, seconder of Foljambe's nomination in December 1783, now seconded the proposed address to the throne against Foljambe's party. He set the tone of the meeting with his declaration 'I fear more the tyranny of Venice than of France'; and Richard Slater Milnes, one of the prominent Wakefield family of dissenters and manufacturers previously allied to the Rockingham interest but now Associators and Pittites almost to a man, declared that the coalition ought to be 'remembered to immortality, and posterity have a lesson, that the most amiable men in private life could not resist temptation when public advantage was set in opposition to interest'. He made the distinction now popular with the reformers between influence and prerogative—'Though I would guard against the *influence* of the Crown as dangerous, I am for maintaining its *just prerogative*, which is constitutional and safe'—and so turned back against the Whig aristocracy the chief weapon which Fitzwilliam was endeavouring to use against Pitt.[42] Ignoring the highly dubious tactics by which Pitt, Temple and George III had harnessed the power of the House of Lords to defeat a Bill overwhelmingly approved by the Commons, Wyvill and the Yorkshire reformers focused their attack upon the excessive influence of the aristocracy. As the chief representative of that aristocracy in Yorkshire, Fitzwilliam was peculiarly susceptible to censure on the grounds of his connexion with Fox and with the East India Commission. One speaker indeed went so far as to say to Fitzwilliam's face that he had been designated as chairman of the commissioners 'because he had great influence in this county. . . . He in pretty severe terms made a comparison between Sir George Savile and a great man, who was present, and said, we have for four years been diminishing the power of the Crown, shall we submit to an insolent aristocracy?' Fitzwilliam sprang to his feet to defend himself, but his reply sounded lame, and his attack on Pitt's sincerity made no impression. He attempted in vain to rally old sympathies and allegiances by an appeal to Rockingham's memory—'that most respectable man, whom all revered, was my instructor, every principle in this breast came from him'—but against Fitzwilliam's reasoning his former friend Fauconberg roundly declared that the real issue was 'whether is George III or Charles Fox to reign?' and pointedly referred to 'an oriental aristocracy removed from Brooks's to the Castle yard of York'. Finally Wilberforce, member for Hull and close friend of Pitt, summed up the anti-Fitzwilliam case in his famous speech to the 7,000 gentlemen and freeholders standing in the Castle yard. For a whole hour this slight, frail figure, mounted on a table, his melodious voice buffeted by the wind, arrested the attention of every man in the audience; and at the acute psychological moment a messenger from Pitt galloped into the yard and handed him a letter announcing that Parliament was dissolved. Six hours of debate in the hail and icy wind of a bitter winter prolonged into early spring sealed the fate of Fitzwilliam's Yorkshire influence. The meeting, by a majority on a show of hands, approved the Associators' address to the throne reprobating 'the late attempt to seize the property and violate all the chartered rights of the East India Company' and endorsing 'the calling of a new Parliament' as 'the only true constitutional measure which your majesty in your royal wisdom can adopt to settle the present differences between the several branches of the legislature'.[43]

Carried away by the rhetoric of Wyvill's supporters and the Pittite propaganda circulated throughout the county in newspapers, pamphlets, cartoons and handbills, the freeholders of Yorkshire endorsed the dissolution of the only eighteenth-century Parliament which, under the guidance of Fox and Burke, had struck 'a good stout blow at the influence of the Crown', and demanded a general election in which not only the 'sense of the people' but Crown and Treasury influence was to go to work on behalf of a Minister chosen by the king and appointed through a direct and blatant royal intereference with one House of Parliament. As the events of 1785, and even more those of the early 1790s were to show, the reformers had handed themselves and their cause to a Minister whose power depended above all on the support of the Crown and its influence and whose attempt to fulfil his pledge to the spirit of reform in 1785 neither satisfied the majority of reformers themselves nor laid the basis for any future advocacy of their cause. Fitzwilliam could count himself unfortunate that his friends and supporters in Yorkshire had allowed themselves to be carried away by the emotion of the moment. It may well have been that the Whig predominance secured in 1782 and 1783 might bear the stamp of 'a mere aristocratical republic';[44] but in renouncing Fox, Fitzwilliam, and the Rockingham tradition the freeholders of Yorkshire had done nothing likely to achieve the fundamental aims of the reform movement. The decision of 1784 was not to be reversed until the great Whig victory of 1807 in Yorkshire, and after that it was to take another twenty-three years of struggle against Crown influence and conservative reaction before the heirs of Fox and Fitzwilliam achieved in the 1832 Reform Act something of the aspirations of their opponents in 1784.

Not all the members of the Yorkshire Association were prepared to make this political 'leap in the dark' and to give their undivided trust to the Minister. Indeed, the passing of the address was to be the last act of the old Association. Five days afterwards a considerable minority of the committee resigned, all of them former Rockinghamites now making their decision between Fitzwilliam and Wyvill. Croft, Fountayne, Foljambe, General Hale—one of the three originators of the reform movement in the county four years earlier—and nineteen other members of the committee now threw in their lot decisively with Fitzwilliam again, and a nucleus was recreated round which, eventually, the old interest was to be reformed.[45] The Committee of Association never met again. Wyvill for his part now found himself more and more dependent on the Yorkshire 'Tories' to achieve success in the county election which was to follow. For a short time, indeed, it seemed that the triumph over the address on the 25th might be the end rather than the beginning of the alliance. The victorious parties retired to the York Tavern to celebrate with a great dinner, during the course of which quarrels broke out between Tories and reformers. It was Wilberforce's part in reconciling them which gained him the nomination as Duncombe's colleague to oust Foljambe and secure the county for the 'independent' interest of reformers, anti-aristocratic elements and supporters of Pitt and the Crown. No one could have foreseen this outcome even a few hours before. Wilberforce was young, personally attractive, and an intimate friend of the Prime Minister, but politically he was still a lightweight. He had shown signs as yet neither of the deep religious convictions nor of the parliamentary talents that were together to make him the leader of great moral and political crusades in the 1780s. Boswell's famous description of his speech at the county meeting, when 'the shrimp became a whale', accurately represents his standing until that moment. Wilberforce admitted that when he came to the meeting he could find amidst the throng of Yorkshire's nobility and gentry 'only one gentleman with whom I had the smallest acquaintance'.[46] But so passionate was the spirit raised among the Yorkshire electorate by the events of the past three months that even such an unforeseen and unknown candidate as Wilberforce was able to defeat the organised forces of Wentworth House and its allies.

Fitzwilliam's friends recognised the danger, and on 26 March the Whig committee sent to propose a compromise in favour of the present members. Their message met with an instant rebuff.[47] The Pittites now had two candidates, and the confidence to assure their election. Canvassing began at once, with all the support of the Association's local contacts and agents as well as of many wealthy gentlemen. Walter Spencer Stanhope confidently anticipated a subscription of £25,000 towards expenses.[48] Fitzwilliam on his part had been looking since the end of December for a Whig colleague for Foljambe, in the hope of turning out Henry Duncombe, whom he blamed in part for the fiasco at York in November. No more Rockinghamite a candidate could be conceived than William Weddell, MP for Malton, brother-in-law of Lady Rockingham and one of the richest landowners in the county. All the resources of the Wentworth interest and its allies were mobilised to support Foljambe and Weddell. A subscription of £15,067 was quickly raised, Fitzwilliam promising (in his brother George's name) the sum of £5,500.[49] Agents were retained all over the county, responsible to the central election committee at Bluitts' Tavern, and hurried orders were sent out to them to begin the canvass. The central organisation was hastily set up, and proved seriously deficient. Even so, it was clear that the contest could have only one result. In isolated areas, such as Doncaster, Richmond (where the Dundas influence was predominant) and Skipton, agents and friends wrote glowingly of large majorities for the Whig candidates.[50] But in the crucial areas of the West Riding where the 'independent' vote was strongest and in the outlying areas of the North and East Ridings, where Fitzwilliam's personal interest was weakest, the returns were strongly for Wilberforce and Duncombe. Little reliance can be placed on the canvassing returns on either side, but it was certain enough by 6 April, the day before the nomination meeting, that the Whigs were bound to lose. Foljambe and Weddell accordingly withdrew, to concede victory without a serious struggle.[51]

At York Fitzwilliam's friends made a more persistent effort to regain something of the ground lost to the ministerial party. Here it was Fitzwilliam who had refused Galway's offer of a compromise, and in confidence of unseating him and regaining the former control of both seats the Whigs put up Sir William Milner, a rich landed gentleman from the Tadcaster district, as Cavendish's running mate. The inevitable result, however, was to bring out a fourth candidate, to make the election a straight fight for both seats. This was Richard Slater Milnes, who had spoken so strongly against the coalition at the county meeting on 25 March, and who was a former ally of the Rockingham interest. He had now committed himself firmly to Pitt, and fought the election not on the reform issue but on the question of the factious nature of the coalition, the India Bill, and the preference of Pitt against Fox. He was later to declare that the contest was decided on these political grounds.[52] Milnes, too, may have represented to some of the voters the interests of the commercial element against Milner and Cavendish, representing the landed interest, while his position as an alderman of the city corporation was also an advantage to him. A six days' poll closed on 6 April with Galway 1,083, Milnes 1,024, Cavendish 913 and Milner 812. Milnes attributed his success to the voters' hostility to 'the influence of an aristocratical faction' and the 'defence of the constitutional prerogatives of the Crown, and the rights and privileges of the people'.[53]

Fitzwilliam's analysis of these two crushing defeats was that 'all the upstarts of the county' were massed 'against all the property—Whig and Tory' and that 'we were . . . beat by the ragamuffins'. The truth of such a statement is doubtful. Nearer to reality was Robert Sinclair's remark about 'the passions and caprice of the people'.[54] Propaganda, popular hysteria and the shrewdness of Wyvill and his friends as managers of county politics were responsible. The defeats in Yorkshire were the last results of the rising tide of provincial feeling against factions, traditional corruption and aristocratic dominance that had first given birth to the Association movement in 1779. Though Fitzwilliam had lost Yorkshire and York city, the loss could not be laid at his door personally, and he had done nothing to lose the respect due to his name and rank which was to return with calmer politics in the mid-1780s. The Whig party was the architect of its own misfortunes, and Fitzwilliam suffered again from his association with Fox, whose career was blighted by his talent for being right at the wrong time and in the wrong way. In 1784, clearly enough, it was the national issue that predominated over local questions. As one of Fitzwilliam's supporters in Halifax remarked, it was 'the received notion among the inferiors in many parts that Mr Fox was attempting to dethrone the king and make himself an Oliver Cromwell . . . The name of Fox is enough to make enemies to all who have approved any part of his conduct'.[55]

It was to be the work of the next four years in county politics for Fitzwilliam to attempt to set things right again. By 1788 opinion in the county was more evenly balanced; yet again, however, local effort was to be nullified by the blunders of the party leaders at Westminster. The Whig tragedy of the regency crisis was to ensure a repetition in the county of the failures of 1784, as Fox and his associates proved yet again that the most grievous fault in the party was not so much its aristocratic composition as its almost total inability to gauge the importance or the character of public opinion at large.

Notes

[1] R. I. and S. Wilberforce, *Life of Wilberforce* (1839), II, p. 133.

[2] Lee to Fitzwilliam, 10 August 1782 (F 63b); Bessborough to Fitzwilliam, 31 August 1782 (R164/3) and Fitzwilliam to Lady Rockingham, 4 September (R164/2a). The Lieutenancy was accepted by Lord Surrey, later eleventh Duke of Norfolk, who retained it until 1798 (*infra*, pp. 242–7).

[3] For a full account of the Yorkshire Association and its activities, 1779–85, see C. Wyvill, *Political Papers . . .* (York, 1794–1802), vols 1–4, and I. R. Christie, *Wilkes, Wyvill and Reform* (1962). The contest between the Association and the Wentworth interest in Yorkshire is described in N. C. Phillips, *Yorkshire and English National Politics, 1783–4* (University of Canterbury, Christchurch, N.Z., 1961).

[4] *Wyvill Papers*, I, pp. 7–9, 60–8; Christie, pp. 76, 81.

[5] Albemarle, *Memoirs of the Marquess of Rockingham* (1852), II, p. 409.

[6] Rockingham to E. Burke, 6 and 13 January 1780: *Corresp. of E. Burke*, IV, pp. 185, 192. The petition is printed in *Wyvill Papers*, I, p. 7.

For Chaloner's letter and the peers' answer (drafted by Burke) see *ibid*, pp. 41–2, 44–6.

7 *Albemarle*, II, pp. 395–400; *Wyvill Papers*, IV, p. 127.

8 *Northampton Mercury*, 31 January 1780; Sandwich to George III, 20 April and 8 May 1780 (Fortescue, V, No. 3000); *Wyvill Papers*, I, pp. 382–3.

9 *Northampton Mercury*, 7 February and 3 April 1780.

10 G. Rudé, *Hanoverian London, 1714–1808* (1971), p. 176. Further additions to the committee brought its numbers to over 150 by 1 March, but the attendance at meetings rarely exceeded forty. For details of membership see the committee's minutes, B.M. Add. MSS 38593–5.

11 Fox to Rockingham, 6 May 1781 : Albemarle, II, pp. 435–6.

12 B.M. Add MSS 38593, ff. 13–19, 38594, f.1.

13 Christie, *The End of North's Ministry*, part I.

14 A. M. W. Stirling, *Annals of a Yorkshire House* (1911), II, p. 191; Weddell to Fitzwilliam, 6 December 1783 (F 34b).

15 *Wyvill Papers*, III, pp. 290–328. Savile pointed out that so long as the reformers concentrated their attack on proprietary rather than on corrupt or venal boroughs they could hardly expect the support of a party strong in borough patrons (*ibid*, pp. 305–10, 325–8).

16 Christie, p. 152. In fact only twenty-two of these offices were held by MPs in 1782 (*ibid*, p. 153).

17 *Wyvill Papers*, IV, p. 165n.

18 Mason to Walpole, 18 January 1783 : Walpole *Corresp.*, ed. Lewis, XXIX, p. 281.

19 For some of these details I am indebted to Mr F. C. Price's unpublished M.A. thesis, 'Parliamentary elections in York city, 1754–90' (University of Manchester, 1958).

20 Price, pp. 165–75; *Wyvill Papers*, I, pp. xvi–xix; H.M.C., *Foljambe MSS*, p. 155; Rockingham MSS, R141–12 and R 1–1073; W. Siddall to Fitzwilliam, 17 March 1783 : F 41.

21 Duncombe wrote optimistically, 'I look upon it that, with your Lordship's protection there is no chance of a contest, nor any probable difficulties to alarm me' (27 October): F 35e.

22 Correspondence on York election, October–November 1783 in F 35e.

23 After the 1768 election in York, Rockingham declared 'I was *drunk* at 5 o'clock after dinner—and proceeded on—through more drinking—attending the assembly and supping—and various companies—after supper till near 4 o'clock in the morning, when I *walked home* after in truth having been continually drunk—*or much elevated*—for about eleven hours, without intermission' (N).

24 To P. Wentworth, 'Sunday 6 a.m.' (F 35e). Writing to William Weddell on 3 December, he attributed 'the late discomfiture at York' to 'some bungling mismanagement of my own' (Ramsden MSS, Leeds City Library, vol. II, f. 78).

25 Foljambe to Fitzwilliam, 26 November 1783 (F 34a); Portland to Fitzwilliam, 22 November 1783 (N). The other county member, Henry Duncombe, brother of Charles who was rejected at York, was also an Associator.

[26] Fitzwilliam to Portland [25 November]: Portland MSS, PWF 3758.

[27] Weddell to Fitzwilliam, 6 December 1783 (F 34b); Fitzwilliam to Zouch, 4 December 1783 (E 234).

[28] Phillips. pp. 30–1.

[29] Zouch to Fitzwilliam, 19 December, J. Preston, 21 December and S. Croft, 21 December 1783 (F 34b); *Wyvill Papers*, II, p. 289. Fitzwilliam had tried without success to persuade Weddell and Sir John Ramsden to second Foljambe 'to mark to the meeting the real ground of [his] pretensions' (Ramsden MSS, *loc. cit.*).

[30] Letters from P. Wentworth, 20 and 29 December, J. Preston, 21 December, S. Croft, 21 December 1783, and Farrer, 2 January 1784: F 34b.

[31] Cannon, pp. 148–53, surveys the circumstances; Dr P. Jupp in *Hist. Journal*, XV (1972), pp. 309–13, produces further evidence from Lord Grenville's fragment of autobiography (B.M., Grenville MSS) to show that the financial difficulty was decisive.

[32] *Leeds Memoranda*, pp. 95–7.

[33] Mason to Wyvill, 22 January (*Wyvill Papers*, IV, pp. 353–4). Foljambe voted on 16 January for Lord Charles Spencer's motion for the dismissal of the administration.

[34] Phillips, pp. 33–60.

[35] Croft to Fitzwilliam, 21 December: F 34a.

[36] To Weddell, 26 December 1783 (Ramsden MSS, II, f. 86); Letters from Sinclair, 3 January 1784: Galway, 22 December, Fountayne, 24 December (F 35f); Fountayne, 2 January 1784, Sinclair, 3 January, Wentworth, 7 January (F 35f) and Croft, 9 February (F 34c).

[37] Phillips, pp. 33–5. Of the 120 members who attended the Rockingham Club on 9 October, 1782, with Fitzwilliam in the chair, only forty-one voted for both of Fitwilliam's candidates in 1784, while eleven voted for the two ministerialists and nine split their votes (Price, *op. cit.*, p. 235).

[38] Wentworth to Fitzwilliam, 11 and 16 February, and Zouch, 9 February: F 34c.

[39] J. P. Heywood to Fitzwilliam, 28 February 1784; Sinclair, 3 March: *ibid.* John Carr, the architect, and Alderman of York, wrote that the people 'have no idea but that Mr Fox wants to get the better of the king and be the Lord Protector, and therefore he and all his abettors ought to be opposed' (11 **March**: **ibid.**).

[40] Letters in F 34e; Fitzwilliam to Zouch, 26 February (E 234).

[41] *Parl. Register*, XII, p. 165 (1 December). Fitzwilliam sent copies to Zouch for distribution (2 February 1784: E 234).

[42] The account of the meeting is in *Wyvill Papers*, II, pp. 328–55. The only member of the Milnes family to remain loyal to Wentworth House was Pemberton, R. S. Milnes's uncle.

[43] *Life of Wilberforce*, I, pp. 388–9.

[44] Wyvill to Sir Watts Horton, 30 April 1784: *Wyvill Papers*, IV, p. 387.

D

45 List of seceders, Yorkshire Association papers, York City Library:
Phillips, p. 55.

46 *Life of Wilberforce*, I, pp. 55, 59; J. Spencer Stanhope, 'Memoirs
of the Life of Walter Spencer Stanhope Esq', in Spencer Stanhope MSS,
Sheffield City Library; parts quoted in Stirling, *Annals of a Yorkshire
House*, II, pp. 187–9; *Private Papers of William Wilberforce*, ed. A. M.
Wilberforce (1897), p. 60, n. 1. The individual was the Rev. William
Mason.

47 The message and the reply are in Yorkshire Association papers,
York City Library, M 90/46 and M 90/45.

48 Stirling, II, p. 192. The sum actually promised was £22,351, of
which £16,246 was spent (Yorkshire Association papers, M 90/47).

49 List of subscribers, E 12. Lord Surrey promised £1,000, Pemberton
Milnes £200, the Dean of York £100, Zouch £50, Peregrine Wentworth
£100, Lord John Cavendish £1,300, Stephen Croft £52 10s and Lord
Carlisle £500. The election accounts (E 16) include bills from ninety-six
canvassing agents.

50 Correspondence in F 34f.

51 The Yorkshire Association papers (M 90/53) contain a calculation
of 10,812 promises for Duncombe and Wilberforce and only 2,758
against them. The Whig calculation was 6,000 for, 3,000 doubtful and
neutral, and 1,600 against. 'If they rely upon that,' wrote Jerom Dring,
a supporter, on 16 January 1785, 'they must be equally imposed upon,
and absurd as us, in relying upon ours . . . We . . . must be very
credulous indeed, if we can believe our own account of their numbers.'
(N.)

52 In the House of Commons, 24 May 1784 (*Parl. Register*, XV, pp.
33, 37).

53 *York Courant*, 13 April 1784.

54 Fitzwilliam to Lady Rockingham, 31 March and 11 August 1784
(R164–5 and 6); Sinclair to Fitzwilliam, 12 May [1784]: N 37.

55 R. Parker to Fitzwilliam, 26 April 1784 (N); John Carr of York
reported the same story (11 March: F 34d).

CHAPTER FOUR

A party in opposition
1784–90

The Whig opposition emerged from the 1784 general election demoralised and weakened but by no means destroyed as a potential political force. It is true that Pitt and his supporters scored a number of victories, sometimes spectacular but more often of a routine nature, at the polls. Much of the result, however, was due to the normal processes of the electoral machine. There was a handful of major constituencies whose prestige was far more important than their number in the House, like Yorkshire, York city, and Norwich, where old established Whig interests were unexpectedly overthrown by the effects of the popular 'frenzy', as the defeated liked to call it. These results helped to swell the majority which any new eighteenth-century government could normally expect to win. In such circumstances a general election was designed to remove the supporters of the old administration from seats open to influence and replace them by friends of the new Ministers.[1] And as the opposition in March 1784 included as a major element in its parliamentary strength the following of Lord North, who had been Prime Minister at the time of the previous general election in 1780, there was a good number of such changes to be made. John Robinson, the former Secretary to the Treasury, had forecast most of them without considering that he was dealing with anything out of the ordinary before Pitt even took office in December 1783.[2] Pitt, indeed, relied heavily on the assurance of being able to win these seats when he agreed to condone the dismissal of the coalition and to replace them in office. Most of the defeated candidates in 1784 therefore were 'North's martyrs' rather than Fox's, and their disappearance from the House would have been certain even if Fox had not provided the pro-Pitt electoral interests with propaganda issues which could be exploited against them. Popular excitement and the strength of public opinion aside, there could have been no doubt of the outcome in general of the 1784 elections.

Yet a calmer assessment of the position was not so unfavourable to
the Whig party, had they been prepared to make the necessary effort
to regroup their forces and take advantage of their opportunities.
There were weaknesses in Pitt's own position—his lack of a large
personal following and his corresponding dependence on the 'party
of the Crown' and its body of 'household troops' and placemen,
together with his Chathamite disdain of party management and
manipulation and the inefficiency of his parliamentary organisation,
all placed him as much at the mercy of the independent members
as North had been in 1782. The forces of opposition also remained
strong and, on the whole, united.[3] Dr O'Gorman's estimate of the
Portland Whig strength before the general election is approximately
eighty-two. Of these, twenty-nine disappeared at the election, and
only six new members appeared to replace them. In addition the
party of Lord North, estimated at about 106 in March 1783 (and this
figure included fifty-six 'doubtfuls'), emerged in April 1784 about
fifty-seven strong. The greater part of these losses were caused by
the natural defection to Pitt of pro-ministerial patrons who had provided North's followers with seats in 1780. There were in addition
twelve other members who had sat before 1784, and who remained
adherents of the coalition, and ten new members returned in 1784
on their side. Thus the opposition in 1784 numbered 132 members,[4]
nearly all devotedly attached to 'the party' (as it was now beginning
to call itself). By 1790 the coalition was to gain thirty-four members by change of allegiance or success in by-elections, and to lose
only twenty-two. Thus during the six years of this Parliament the
opposition more than maintained its numbers, and even at its lowest
it still provided a strong force which more than matched the party
following Pitt's administration.[5] Even allowing for the 'party of the
Crown', the Whig party on occasion was to show itself strong enough,
if it could attract a reasonable degree of support from the uncom-
mitted and independent members, or from particular vested interests
on specific questions, to threaten the government's security in the
Commons.

Yet this numerical strength was not in itself enough. Energy and
decision by the leadership were equally necessary if the party was to
make the fullest use of its resources. These were lamentably absent.
Portland's hard work as leader of the party in the post-1784 years
and the devoted toil of William Adam as party manager are now
beginning to be appreciated by historians.[6] But Portland's hesitancy

and lack of confidence in his own judgement made it impossible for him to give the party the clear and decisive leadership it needed to restore morale and to keep the membership united. When faced by the centrifugal influence of its parliamentary orators, Burke, Fox and Sheridan in particular, Portland made little apparent effort to resolve jealousies or to exert the discipline which every political party must occasionally require from its leaders. His deputy, as Fitzwilliam was now considered to be, had an equal distaste for political prominence and preferred a local and personal role to that of a national leader. His loyalty to Portland and his own natural diffidence made it difficult for him to realise the political potential of the Rockingham inheritance. Throughout the later 1780s the Whigs suffered as much from deficiencies in the party leadership as from the effect of Pitt's successes or the public distaste for aristocratic faction.

In the immediate aftermath of March–April 1784, Fitzwilliam and his friends had two major tasks. One was to attempt to hold the party together in Parliament and to give it strength and direction. The other was to attend to its local organisation, to repair the damage done to its local influence, and to restore as far as possible the public image of the party as one dedicated to the true Whig principles of liberty and constitutional government. The second of these was to be Fitzwilliam's major sphere of operation, though he continued to act as a parliamentary speaker and participant in central party councils. It was Fitzwilliam who frequently opened the opposition's attack in the first debates of the session. In May 1784, for example, he was the only peer to speak on the address, apart from the proposer and seconder. Though the opposition leaders had agreed not to debate or divide against the address, Fitzwilliam made a protest against the section of the address 'replete with sentiments of gratitude to HM for the late dissolution of Parliament' and declared 'He thought HM's exercise of the prerogative reposed in him at the period of the dissolution unnecessary and unwarrantable'.[7] In the routine debates of the session, however, Fitzwilliam came forward less frequently, leaving the leadership to Loughborough, Carlisle or Stormont as the principal opposition speakers in the Lords. No speech of Fitzwilliam's is reported on Pitt's India Bill in 1784, nor did he sign the protest against it.

The other sphere, apart from India, with which Fitzwilliam's name was coming to be associated was Ireland, and in 1785 he took a more prominent part in the debates on Pitt's Irish commercial propositions. This attempt to place the economic relationship between the two kingdoms on a new footing involved not only the interests of Irish landowners and merchants but also those of English manufacturers and traders.[8] On both counts Fitzwilliam was involved. His own Irish connexions and estates reinforced his general concern, as a member of the Anglo-Irish Whig alliance, for the special interests of the sister kingdom, while his Yorkshire interests were involved from the English side. The opposition which Pitt's revised proposals of 1785 stimulated among English manufacturers fearful of possible low-cost Irish competition was shared by England's leading industrial county. The merchants and manufacturers of Sheffield set up a committee to agitate against the project, as did those of many other industrial and commercial centres, and Fitzwilliam urged them to petition against it. The manufacturers of pig and bar iron, among whom south Yorkshire interests were prominent, also came forward.

With this backing, Fitzwilliam presented the opposition's case against the scheme on 18 July. He described the propositions as 'a system that overturned the whole policy of the navigation and trade of Great Britain', and went on to draw together the commercial and the constitutional and political aspects of the problem. Echoing some of the arguments already advanced by Fox in the Commons, Fitzwilliam stressed the unsatisfactory nature of Pitt's plan to both Irish and English interests. It was a measure thought up by the Minister, not one urged upon him by Ireland; indeed, the original proposals had been so strongly objected to in Ireland that they had had to be drastically altered and mutilated, to the extent that they now raised equally forceful opposition in England. From this point Fitzwilliam developed the theme of the propositions as an unhappy compromise, giving both countries the worst of the bargain: speaking 'as an Englishman', he deplored the opening to Ireland of Britain's home and colonial markets, and foresaw Irish engrossing of the colonial trade at Britain's expense. Speaking also 'as an Irishman', he complained of the heavy burdens Ireland was to be laid under in return for the dubious commercial advantage she was to receive. He also brought in the political aspects of the Anglo-Irish problem, and pointed out that the present discontents of Ireland were not economic so much as constitutional; and he particularly instanced the grievances over the government's attempt to prevent public meetings 'for the purpose of deliberating on great national questions' in Ireland at a time when in England 'a circular letter was sent about the kingdom, under the sanction of the Minister, and signed by a gentleman of some consideration (the Rev. Mr Wyvill) inviting the people to conventions and associations of a similar nature, and for the same purposes as those which were the objects of such intemperate persecution in Ireland'.[9] The speech was one of his best parliamentary performances. It drew together all the threads of opposition to the proposals and presented them as a coherent whole. At the opening of the next session when Fitzwilliam opened the debate on the address he was able to look back with satisfaction to the withdrawal of the scheme in face of continued Irish resistance. 'The wisdom of Ireland,' he declared, 'had accomplished what the prudence of this country could not achieve.'[10]

The choice of Fitzwilliam to open the opposition's attack in the Lords in 1786 was no doubt promoted by the success of his Irish speech in 1785. This too was an impressive performance. Going on from his remarks on the failure of the commercial propositions, he drew into his speech opposition criticisms of financial, colonial and foreign policies: he objected to the Minister's taking responsibility for the improvement in public credit, which he pointed out had merely risen back to its natural level; he alleged that, far from foreign powers being 'peaceably disposed', as claimed in the speech, Britain was faced by strong commercial hostility from France and the German princes; and he commented on the 'wretched' state of India and the difficulties facing the East India Company over the Commutation Act, which had drastically reduced the import duty on tea in order to check smuggling but which had not yet begun to achieve the success it was eventually to attain. Once more, however, after providing themes for development against the Ministry, Fitzwilliam retired into the background. There was again no division on the address, and no sign of a real effort by the Whig peers to press home the attack or to bring up specific issues relating to the general criticisms made. Again it was the former Northite peers—Loughborough, Carlisle, Stormont—who led in the Lords, while those who looked upon themselves as the representatives of the true Whig cause sat silent. In 1787 again there was no division and this time not a single speech is recorded in opposition to the address. The opposition case was upheld mainly by Stormont, with help now from the Duke of Norfolk, who led the debates on the major question of the session, the French commercial treaty. Fitzwilliam is recorded as speaking only once, on the alarm of the Yorkshire manufacturers at the

possible repercussions on trade with Portgual.[11] Not a single speech
is reported from Portland during this session, and even the former
habit of composing regular protests against divisions favouring the
Ministry was falling out of use. The House of Commons was now
incomparably the more important political arena. The personal
rivalries of Pitt, Grenville and Dundas against Fox, Burke and
Sheridan added a further dimension to the political conflict of the
age and concentrated public attention on the lower House. Yet the
Whigs remained essentially an aristocratic party, and behind their
House of Commons activities the leadership and direction of the
party's national and local interests remained in the hands of the
'great men'. It was in this behind-the-scenes activity of management,
organisation and influence that Fitzwilliam found his true role in the
party, and there that he peformed his most valuable service to it.
Wentworth House again became what it had been in Rockingham's
day, the organisational centre for Whig interests in the north, while
the yearly round of county race meetings and assizes provided opportunities both for party rallies and for quiet and intimate discussion
of political tactics and local arrangements.

Even in the immediate aftermath of the defeat at the polls in 1784,
Fitzwilliam and his friends were looking to the future and to the
re-establishment of the Whig strength in Yorkshire. On 8 April, only
two days after the close of the poll at York, Portland told Lady
Rockingham that he had received a letter from Fitzwilliam expressing 'the sentiments of a wounded but undaunted and unconquerable
mind'; within a few days Fitzwilliam was interesting himself in
suggestions from some of the Whig supporters in York for setting up
a dining club to keep their friends together. A Yorkshire Club was
also formed for gentlemen from the county to dine monthly in
London, and to meet at York every August during the assizes. This
York meeting, wrote Fitzwilliam, would 'show that though we were
defeated, we do not look upon ourselves as conquered'. Further
dinners and meetings were to be held around the county to rally
supporters. Sinclair quickly regained his optimism and was soon
reporting from York that

the infatuation and delusion are wearing out—that the passions and
caprice of the people are nearly evaporated—and that their judgements
are at length beginning to reassume their ordinary functions. . . . Our
old steady friends are still firm—some lukewarm people are enlisting with
us, and I have little doubt but many apostates will shortly wish to be

reinstated in our confidence. . . . We have all the better sort of people
with us and therefore it is to be hoped they will by degrees draw the
others in to join our parties.

The meeting of the Rockingham Club on 17 May to celebrate the
anniversary of Rockingham's birthday was attended by the 'bulk of
the respectable tradesmen in York' and 'I never saw a greater appearance of steadiness, unanimity and cordiality than actuated the whole
company'.[12] In the meantime there was hope that the unity of their
rivals would soon disintegrate. 'The Association is in a great measure
broke up,' wrote a supporter from Doncaster; '. . . the republican
spirit of the Dissenters and the arbitrary notions of the High Tories
(for such was in great part the late assemblage) can never hold long
together, indeed it is only surprising they ever joined.'[13]

These signs were encouraging. The meeting at York, Fitzwilliam
reported to Lady Rockingham in August,

brought sixty people together, and it went off exactly as [I] could have
wished : much harmony, and good understanding among us, without an
idea of any political resolutions or anything of that sort: however I
believe we will agree not only in our county views, but likewise in
general opinions.

The meeting agreed that Whig gentlemen should muster the strongest
possible attendance at the forthcoming races, traditionally the
occasion for displays of party strength, in order to show that
morale remained high. Fitzwilliam afterwards confessed, 'I felt it a
bitter pill, and it required a good gulp to swallow it, when I resolved
to go to York races'. He determined, however, 'to do everything as
formerly, and not to give the enemy the triumph of beating us out
of anything . . . but . . . to show ourselves as usual, and appear to
follow our own diversions and our views as if nothing mortifying
had happened'. After the races he wrote, 'the event has turned out
exactly as one could have wished'. There was no great 'appearance
of any families on their side' and 'on the whole it went off most
excessively to my satisfaction'. Pitt's popularity, he concluded, 'has
seen its full tide'. After Doncaster races in September, too, there was
a gratifying gathering at Wentworth :

The recollection of old attachments to the house brings hither almost all
our neighbours : the very few who absent themselves, probably do so
on the ground of the late circumstances in politics; but though these may

D*

affect some few of the neighbourhood in this manner, they lead at the same time to rivet others the more firmly to their old connexions.

From the secure vantage ground of his Yorkshire palace, away from the bustling streets of York or London, Fitzwilliam could look with pleasure on a scene of traditional deference and loyalty. Yet even here his sense of realism did not desert him.

After the late frenzy [he wrote] it is not to be wished that so sudden a change should take place as to produce an immediate opinion in favour of, and a call for the service of those they so lately decried and fairly run down; it would be unbecoming and disgraceful for the publick to appear so volatile and unsteady—let us then hope to see the popularity of our friends follow a general discontentment with the present rulers.[14]

Fitzwilliam's strategy in Yorkshire was therefore to lay the organisational foundations for a later recovery, and to work quietly in the meantime to recover lost ground in public opinion. As a first step the lessons of the general election campaign were to be thoroughly learnt, so that on future occasions an expert and fully organised electoral machine would be ready for action. Charles Bowns, clerk to Fitzwilliam's Wentworth agent (and later his successor) was set to work to build the skeleton of an organisation for future county elections,[15] while Fitzwilliam gave his attention to turning public opinion against the new government. Opposition pamphlets were distributed in the county through Fitzwilliam's friends and opportunities were seized to emphasise the unpopularity of Pitt's new taxes, particularly the increased window tax introduced in order to enable the tax on tea to be lowered and smuggling discouraged. The battle for public opinion was fairly joined on this issue, Fitzwilliam declaring to Zouch that the tax was 'a grievous imposition upon the community at large, for the purpose of making the balances of his friends and makers at the India House appear better upon paper at the next review', and so to divert public attention from 'these evils, made by the India Bill'. The tax, Fitzwilliam maintained, was 'levied with no other view than that of benefiting the Company—it may fairly be said to be transferred from the pocket of the individual to the Treasury in Leadenhall Street'.[16]

Parliamentary reform was now less of a public advantage to Pitt. Lacking the king's support or that of most of his Cabinet colleagues on this issue, and knowing therefore that the attitude of the public and the independent members would be crucial, Pitt hoped that

Wyvill would again provide him with evidence of a widespread popular agitation to which Parliament might be induced to give way. All too plainly, however, it appeared that public opinion had cooled considerably since 1783. The Fox–North coalition had shown that the balance of the constitution might be threatened more by the power of the House of Commons than by the prerogative of the Crown, and Pitt's success against the coalition owed at least as much to the support of reactionary 'tory' elements as it did to reformers and Associators. His undertaking parliamentary reform again now threatened to expose the extent to which he depended on support which was fundamentally anti-reform, if not actively pro-tory. Unless he were backed by the utmost strength of the reforming element in the House and in the public at large, Pitt stood to expose his major and fundamental political weakness—his lack of a committed party or even personal following large enough to counter the Whig accusation that he was the mere tool of court influence.

Wyvill's sense of realism was strong, but his tactics were not always over-scrupulous. He was called to London by Pitt in December 1784 to concert plans. He was either misled by Pitt's natural optimism or convinced that something more than the usual trumpet call to old reform battle stations was needed. He put out a series of letters to his friends declaring, as from full authority, that Pitt was pledged to bring in a measure of parliamentary reform and to pursue it 'as a Man and as a Minister' and one of the letters, addressed to the secretary of the Committee of Citizens at Edinburgh, was published in the London press. If the phrase 'as a Minister' meant anything at all it must mean that Pitt had the king's authority, and the support of his colleagues, in making this measure one of the government's official Bills, and that the official supporters of administration would be required to vote for it. As both Pitt and Wyvill well knew, neither the king nor the majority of the Cabinet would have endorsed such a step. Wyvill therefore attempted to explain away the phrase by stating that it merely meant that Pitt would support reform whether he personally were in or out of office, and when Pitt was challenged in the Commons he confirmed this interpretation. Wyvill's more private correspondence gave a different impression. He wrote to Walter Spencer Stanhope on 5 January 1785:

I can now say, not indeed from authority as I before conveyed Mr Pitt's manly declaration, but from my own conjecture grounded on what I

have observed in various conversations with *men in power* since I first
wrote to you on the subject that the intended propositions for the reform
of our representation are not to be considered merely as *Mr Pitt's
propositions* but *as one of the principal measures of the present government*. This is merely my unauthorised opinion, and I beg you to consider
it as *entrusted to you alone*, for I have not ventured to commit this
opinion to paper till this evening.

Given this further assurance of likely success, as Wyvill wrote,
'surely it would be strange if Yorkshire were neutral, when the
Minister brought the subject forward, and all the other friends of
reform gave their earnest support?'[17] He urged his friends in the
north to prepare for a county meeting.

Fitzwilliam shared the opposition's scepticism on Pitt's position
and motives. Always inclined to see and believe the worst in the
young Minister who had clambered into power up the backstairs of
Crown influence, he was not disposed to accept Pitt's idealism at
its face value. He anticipated that Pitt would have to either disavow
Wyvill's statement or explain it 'as meaning nothing more than this,
the support of a Minister is the support of a man, and the support
of a man is the support of a Minister—in other words—three blue
beans in three blue bladders'. As Fitzwilliam pointed out, the phrase
'as a Minister' must mean the power to order the placemen to vote
for reform, and that was incredible. 'If Mr Pitt has made that promise
which Mr Wyvill declares he has made, he is bound as an honourable and honest man to exercise this authority, or to relinquish his
situation, if that is not permitted him.'

Reform was nevertheless still a dangerous issue, and the Yorkshire Whigs decided not to intervene if any county meeting were
called. 'The business is of a most ticklish nature,' Fitzwilliam confessed, 'and may do a deal of mischief, if unskilfully handled; but
I am sure we shall not have the power to prevent it, and therefore
let those who offer themselves as undertakers in it carry it in their
own way.'[18] Fitzwilliam neither wished to reopen old controversies
among his own friends in Yorkshire nor to expose his friend Fox,
who was still pledged to reform, to disagreement within the party.
And he was right to judge that even if a county meeting were called
it could have little influence on the ultimate decision. The old
enthusiasm was dead, and though a petition was eventually sent up
in support of Pitt, few other communities followed Yorkshire's lead.
The Minister's proposals were defeated in the Commons, even with

the grudging support of Fox and several other reformers who were prepared to vote for reform in principle but who warned Pitt that they would insist on radical amendments should the Bill reach the committee stage.[19] Parliamentary reform was not only dead but seen to be dead as an immediate political issue.

The cooling of reform sentiment in Yorkshire provided an opportunity for the re-establishment of the old interest. In both county and city Fitzwilliam and his friends lost no time in exploiting the advantage. Dissatisfaction with Pitt's financial and commercial policies was promoted whenever possible among the trading and manufacturing elements. Paragraphs were inserted in the county newspapers against the commutation tax and the French commercial treaty, meetings were organised or supported to pass resolutions, addresses or instructions to members of Parliament against the government's policies, and pamphlets were distributed in the county.[20] In York the Rockingham Club resumed its old function of keeping the interest together with annual dinners and meetings, while for the 'inferior' sort smaller local gatherings in alehouses round the city were financed by Fitzwilliam's contributions to local electoral expenses.

The corporation, whose political influence was bound to be extensive in a constituency where admission to the freedom of the city conferred the vote, was also cultivated. The loyalty of the bench of aldermen, Fitzwilliam's stronghold, was enhanced in November 1785 by the election to it of Sir William Milner, one of the Whig candidates in 1784. In 1786 Galway's position was further weakened by the sale of his estate in the county to the Duke of York for £100,000; this was followed a few months later by a declaration that he did not intend to offer himself again for election. Sinclair at once suggested that the Whigs should let it be known that they would set up a candidate. As a preparatory measure £400 of Fitzwilliam's money was distributed as a Christmas present to the 'lower voters . . . as a gift from Sir William Milner'. Both Fitzwilliam and Cavendish counselled caution, however, deploring any disturbance to the peace of the city with electioneering four years before election time, and advising that no mention should be made of any individual candidate beyond the assurance 'that at a proper time some of us would stand forward to prevent the town being dictated to by the Association or persons of still less pretensions to intermeddle'. Fitzwilliam assured Milner that although last time 'you fought with

staves against musquetry and bayonets—you talked about law,
sobriety and purity to men with beer and gin in their heads and a
guinea in their hands—all this at the very moment a popular delusion
was waking against you', this time the influence of 'the better sort'
would be exerted over the lower classes and the election would be
decided by the respectable voters.[21] Neither Fitzwilliam nor his supporters foresaw that this promising outlook was to be severely modified by the renewed outburst of Pittite feeling over the regency crisis
a year later, and in the end the York Whigs were thankful enough
to reach a compromise agreement with their rivals to return Milnes
and Milner in 1790.

By the later months of 1787 public affairs seemed to be settling
into a dull routine. In February 1786 Fitzwilliam had remarked that
'The present session has opened with a degree of quiet and inactivity,
not within any parliamentary memory', and though the opposition
had tried to whip up popular agitation against the political implications of the French commercial treaty during the later weeks of 1786
and in 1787, the treaty's commercial advantages were too apparent
to those trading interests to whom the party had to appeal. In
Yorkshire an attempt to rouse the woollen and worsted manufacturers against the potential competition of French textiles was
unavailing. The opposition's assertions that the country would be
'irrecoverably ruined if Eden's treaty should take effect' were clearly
wildly exaggerated.[22]

Nevertheless, by the spring of 1788 the political atmosphere in
Yorkshire seemed more favourable to the Whigs than at any time
since Rockingham's death. Pitt's failure to carry parliamentary
reform and the cooling of public enthusiasm for associations had
diminished the appeal of this issue, particularly among those former
supporters of the Wentworth interest who had wavered in their
attachment in 1783 and 1784. After four years of office, too, Pitt's
cause was naturally less appealing to the public than it had been in
the exciting days of 1784, when it had been identified with deep
issues of constitutional principle. Then, as now, it was natural for a
government in the mid-term of a Parliament to lose popularity, and
for an even moderately active opposition to be successful in promoting dissatisfaction with the burden of taxes or with particular
governmental measures. And by the spring of 1788 Pitt's record of
successes, though solid in more mundane matters of financial
administration, was generally less spectacular than his failures had

appeared to be. In almost every session of Parliament since 1784
there had been some check to the government's policies. In 1785 the
Irish propositions had met virtual defeat. In 1786 a proposal to fortify
the dockyards and arsenals at Plymouth and Portsmouth against
naval attack had foundered on the unpopularity of the Duke of
Richmond, the responsible Minister, and the dislike of the independent country gentlemen for standing armies.[23] In the early months
of 1788 an issue more politically important perhaps than all these
arose in the shape of the East India Declaratory Bill. This was a
particularly sensitive issue, for it was Fox's India Bill, rather than
the legitimacy of the Fox–North coalition, which had been the predominant issue of the 1784 election. Pitt had won immense public
support, with the assistance of the East India Company's money and
propaganda, by campaigning against the supposed confiscation of the
company's property and the abrogation of its chartered rights
through the appointment of Fitzwilliam's commission to control
Indian administration and patronage. His own measure of 1784,
under which Indian affairs were now supervised, had been presented
to Parliament and public as one of an entirely different character
from Fox's.[24] The Board of Control which was set up under the act
was, unlike the commission proposed in 1783, a government agency,
composed of six official members, though the real authority of the
board quickly devolved upon Henry Dundas. To meet the objection
that such a direct control by the government would immeasurably
increase the patronage influence of the Crown, however, Pitt had
proposed that the board should have only an oversight of administration and policy, and that all powers of appointment should remain
in the hands of the directors. This compromise had satisfied the company, who had accepted the Bill, and it had therefore aroused little
comment or opposition in the country as a whole. Even in Parliament
the opposition, dispirited by the general election, had made little
more than a token resistance. No serious attempt had been made to
present to the public the real defects and disadvantages of the Bill,
though the opposition speakers in both Houses had declared its
true character to be equally confiscatory and oppressive to the company's interests as Fox's Bill had been alleged to be. It was not until
February 1788 that the opportunity arose to expose the India Act in
its true light.

The occasion of the new declaratory Bill was a dispute between
the Board of Control and the company over the power claimed by the

board to issue direct orders for the defence of India and to deploy
armed forces for that purpose, and to order the company to bear the
expenses involved. The Dutch crisis of 1786–7 had led to a degree of
mobilisation against the possible threat of a renewed French war, and
in the course of this mobilisation the board had ordered four regiments to India. The government then presented to the company the
bill for the transport of these troops. The court of directors had at
first agreed to the proposal, but now retracted its consent and protested that they could not be compelled to pay for operations about
which they had not been consulted, and that the government's action
was *ultra vires*. The government replied that the Act of 1784 gave
the Board of Control the power to act as it had done; and the Cabinet
decided to introduce a declaratory Bill to clarify the position. The
Bill was bitterly attacked in the Commons, first by a number of the
company's directors and then by several of the independent members
who had been roused to criticism of the government in 1786 over the
dockyard fortifications. The opposition naturally joined in, stressing
the point that this Bill exposed the true character of the 1784 Act as
oppressive and confiscatory, whereas Fox's measure had contained
important political safeguards missing from Pitt's Act. The direct
nature of the government's political control under Pitt's Act had
been mitigated by assurances as to the powers, including patronage,
which were to be left in the hands of the directors. The declaratory
Bill seemed to make these assurances illusory and to show that the
Board of Control could claim unlimited authority to override the
directors at any time. The real issue which the opposition seized
upon was, of course, Pitt's integrity. The debates in the Commons on
the declaratory Bill were couched in particularly personal terms;
and in the propaganda which now appeared in opposition pamphlets
and newspapers Pitt's good faith became the central question. Well
might Thomas Steele describe it as a 'frightful question'; though
William Grenville's fears that the government might be beaten on
the Bill were averted by timely amendments and Pitt's brilliant
speech in recovery on the third reading, the damage had been done.[25]

The debates on the declaratory Bill thus revived issues which had
been debated in Parliament and in the country four years previously.
Fitzwilliam was involved at both levels. Now, in the Lords, he joined
in the opposition's detailed attack on the separate clauses of the
declaratory Bill and signed the protest against its passage. In Yorkshire no pains were spared to draw the parallel between 1784 and

1788. Loughborough had referred in the debate on the third reading
of the Bill to a story of two Yorkshire freeholders in 1783 discussing
Fitzwilliam's intended role as administrator of India patronage and
speculating that he would 'bring a good deal of it down to Wentworth'. Now the contrast between Pitt's present interpretation of the
1784 Act and the propaganda formerly issued by his supporters against
Fox's Bill was pointed out, to considerable effect. John Beckett of
Leeds wrote to Fitzwilliam on 24 March that the declaratory Bill had
'operated almost like a miracle' on provincial opinion, and had
'almost . . . completely cured' the 'delirium' of 1784, so that, 'together
with the inveteracy against us having subsided in a great measure
by the lapse of time', there were grounds for confidence that 'an
election now would most assuredly be determined upon very
different grounds from that of '84. . . . Taking things as they are,
except they can raise the devil again in some new frightful shape, I
really think the question may be considered generally as between
party and party only, and that ours is the stronger'.[26]

The issue had a particularly immediate significance for the Yorkshire Whigs, for early in 1788 Wilberforce became seriously ill.
There were rumours of his approaching death, or at least his enforced
retirement from politics, and a by-election for the county became
the immediate subject of conversation and correspondence. Neither
Foljambe nor Weddell, the Whig candidates in 1784, was likely to
stand again—Pemberton Milnes, one of Fitzwilliam's important links
with the West Riding trading community, went so far as to suggest
that it would be inadvisable for them to do so—and Foljambe
remained pessimistic about the state both of public opinion and of
the party's organisation. 'There seems an infatuation in the people
in general for Pitt and a jealousy of opposition that blinds them to
everything' he wrote; '. . . I hope our friends will not let their feelings for the last defeat hurry them rashly to another contest.' Fitzwilliam's natural optimism was not to be discouraged, however.
'Whatever effect the declaratory law may have produced in the
country,' he wrote to Zouch, 'in London and its neighbourhood it
has lowered Pitt in men's esteem most exceedingly,' and he suggested
a resumption of efforts to get suitable paragraphs inserted in the
provincial newspapers.[27] As potential candidate for Wilberforce's
seat Fitzwilliam chose John, fifth Viscount Downe in the Irish peerage, whose family was long established at Cowick in the south-
eastern part of the West Riding. His candidature was approved by

many of Fitzwilliam's friends in the county, but Downe himself would not be committed to more than a willingness to stand either at a by-election or a general election in case of Wilberforce's retirement. Fitzwilliam urged him to come forward for the next general election in any case, arguing that a declaration of his intention to stand might frighten Wilberforce off, but by September, with Wilberforce recovered and understood to be intending to stand at the next dissolution, Downe had retired from the lists.[28] An attempt to find a substitute had not gone far when the news of the king's illness and the beginning of the regency crisis changed the situation radically both in Parliament and in the county.

The Whig connexion with the Prince of Wales after 1783 was a curious political anachronism. In the reigns of George I and George II the quarrels between the reigning monarch and the heir to the throne had been exploited by politicians eager to find an alternative base to that of royal favour. The 'reversionary interest', though never the only, nor even the major, section of opposition during that period, had been a well known device for providing politicians out of office with both present benefits and future prospects. The Prince of Wales's household had provided a number of offices for impecunious oppositionists, and a base for political planning such as that indulged in by the 'Leicester House' group in the later 1740s.[29] By the 1780s, however, such tactics were of questionable value. The growing importance of public opinion among the middling classes, who were apt to look askance at aristocratic morals and princely debts, made a connexion with the irresponsible and extravagant eldest son of George III a liability. If the Whigs had realised the true character of that public opinion they were doing so much to cultivate they would have avoided an embroilment with the notoriously disreputable circle around the young prince and would have tried to dissociate themselves from the factious tradition of 'reversionary interest'. To claim to be the chief antagonists of the 'influence of the Crown' and yet to be courting the future favours of the heir to the throne was not an easy position to justify to the public.

As early as 1781 the king had complained to his eldest son that 'some unpleasant mention of you is daily to be found in the [news]papers'.[30] The prince's notorious amours, his escapades and his irresponsible extravagance blighted his reputation from the start. In Fox he found a congenial companion, so that before long the king was beginning to associate Fox's malign influence over his son with

Whig political principles. Fox created not so much a Whig reversionary interest as the need for one; by 1784 the king was determined
never, if possible, to employ him in government again. In June 1783
Portland and Fox had tried, so it seemed, to use their ministerial
positions to obtain for the prince a financial settlement far in excess
of all precedent, and at a time when the country was deep in the
financial consequences of the American war. George III stoutly
refused to condone this attempt 'to gratify the passions of an ill-
advised young man', and the government was nearly brought down
over the issue, so that in the end the prince had to accept the king's
terms. He remained nevertheless a zealous partisan of the Whig
cause, and in 1784 gave an ostentatious fête to celebrate Fox's victory at Westminster—though he rather spoiled the effect by getting
drunk, falling flat on his face and vomiting in public when attempting to dance a quadrille. Whig society still flocked to Carlton House,
that monument to aesthetic taste and unbridled extravagance, while
the prince remained a frequent visitor to smart Whig households
such as that of the Duke of Devonshire and Georgiana at Chiswick.
Indeed, the prince seemed to assume that he was regarded by the
Whigs as their political leader. He had written coyly to his brother
Frederick in May 1782 that he had had 'a great deal of business of
late' on account of the circumstance that 'the new administration
seem to wish me better than the former one'. The Whigs, realising
in the 1780s that the royal disfavour was a powerful obstacle to their
return to office, perhaps inevitably cultivated the royal favour to
come; but they found it difficult to combine the hope of their own
future benefit with detachment from the present needs of the prince,
while their championship of the prince's interests placed them more
than ever in the king's bad books. 'Believe me,' the king had declared
to North in June 1783, referring to the government's proposals for
the prince's income, 'no consideration can ever make me either forget
or forgive what has passed, and the public shall know how well
founded the principles of economy are in those who have so loudly
preached it up.'[31]

Later in 1784 and in 1785 the prince's infatuation with Mrs Fitzherbert landed him in a new set of scrapes. His extravagant exhibi-
tions of affection not only made him ridiculous but also helped to
increase his rapidly growing debts. In August 1784 he declared to
his father his intention of living abroad, ostensibly to economise but
in reality to pursue Mrs Fitzherbert, who had fled from his atten-

tions.[32] Ultimately, by staging an attempt at suicide, he persuaded
her to go through a form of marriage ceremony in December 1785,
in the teeth of a remonstrance from Fox, who pointed out the grave
consequences, both private and public, that might be involved in an
illegal union with a Roman Catholic.[33] As Fox refrained from pointing out, the possibility of the prince's exclusion from the succession
to the throne under the terms of the Act of Settlement would also
wreck the hopes the Whigs were placing on a tangible return for
their partisanship. The Whig leaders refused, therefore, to recognise
the marriage, and the Duke of Portland forbade his duchess to receive
Mrs Fitzherbert.[34] Meanwhile the negotiations between father and
son for the payment of the prince's debts and a more satisfactory
regulation of his household finances dragged on inconclusively, with
intransigence on both sides. At length, in April 1787 one of the
prince's friends in the Commons, Alderman Newnham, moved for
a consideration by the House of his financial affairs. Sir Gilbert Elliot
declared that this was brought on against the advice of Portland,
Fox and the other leading Whigs; and a Tory backbencher, John
Rolle, MP for Devon, took advantage of the opportunity to hint in
the House of constitutional difficulties in the way of a settlement. To
save himself the prince gave Fox an assurance that no marriage with
Mrs Fitzherbert had taken place—which was true only in the sense
that their union was illegal under the terms of the Royal Marriage
Act, the prince being under 25 years of age at the time and not having
his father's or Parliament's consent. Fox, however, spoke firmly and
from authority in the House: 'He denied it *in toto*, in point of fact,
as well as law. The fact not only never could have happened legally,
but never did happen in any way whatsoever, and had from the
beginning been a base and malicious falsehood.' As a result of Fox's
declaration Pitt persuaded the king to agree to a financial settlement,
which was announced on 21 May.[35]

However, the prince was not out of the toils of his own equivocation. Mrs Fitzherbert, who was openly living with him, was now
publicly branded as an immoral woman. She evidently gave her
'husband' an uncomfortable time, for the prince called in Charles
Grey, a young recruit to the Whig party and its inner social circles,
and asked him to make some counter-statement in the House which
might take off the effect of Fox's declaration without actually con-
tradicting it. Grey not only found it impossible to construct such a
masterpiece of casuistry but told Fox about the prince's request.[36]

The result was a breach between Fox and the prince, Fox resenting the way in which the prince had tricked him into lying to the House of Commons. For over a year social relations between the prince and the principal leaders of the Whig party were broken off. Only Sheridan, of the Whig 'front bench', remained an habitué of Carlton House, while lesser men like Jack Payne, an old crony of the prince's, were able to secure a strong influence over him. The regency crisis was to be complicated for the Whigs by their temporary eclipse at Carlton House.

On 5 November 1788 the king, whose health and manner had been causing anxiety for some little time, lapsed into a state of mental derangement. Whether, as was thought at the time and for nearly 200 years afterwards, this was an attack of insanity in some form, or whether, as the latest investigators into the case have concluded, it was an acute outbreak of one of the metabolic disorders known as the porphyrias, is irrelevent to the story. The immediate prospect was that he might die; at best, it seemed that his mental health and political capacity would be impaired for a considerable time and perhaps for the remainder of his life. The Whigs caught a glimpse of the promised land all the more intoxicating for being so unexpected.[37] Fox, on holiday in Italy, was hurriedly summoned by express, and performed the considerable feat of rushing more than a thousand miles to England over eighteenth-century roads in nine days—to the severe detriment of his health and perhaps his judgement. Meanwhile his colleagues hastily convened to discuss their tactics and their future prospects. Fitzwilliam characteristically remained in the country—at Wentworth until mid-November, and then at Milton, to be nearer London in case of need. His main preoccupation was the attempt to set up Lady Fitzwilliam's nephew Lord Burford as a candidate for Hull at the next election, and he also acted as a channel of information from other parts of Yorkshire about the state of public opinion and the prospects in case of a dissolution of Parliament. He did not arrive in town until early December, ready for the beginning of parliamentary discussions of the measures to be taken to deal with the deficiency in the royal authority. In the meantime Portland had been persuaded to make up his breach with the prince, while Sheridan had stepped forward as the prince's right hand man in opening a negotiation to win over the Lord Chancellor, Lord Thurlow, whose relations with Pitt were far from cordial. He was willing to listen to overtures which might

enable him to stay in office under a regency, and by the time of
Fox's arrival on 24 November the party was virtually committed to
an agreement to that effect. In early December Thurlow veered back
to the ministerial side under the impression of the king's likely
recovery, but Portland and Fitzwilliam never forgave Sheridan's
initiative in the intrigue, and their resentment at his coming forward
as the prince's chief adviser reappeared in greater depth when
Sheridan and Burke quarrelled in 1790. Throughout the regency crisis
the Whigs were hampered by internal squabbles and jealousies, and
the reluctance, or inability, of the leadership to construct a planned
strategy to deal with the crisis resulted in a policy of drift and
opportunism that played into Pitt's hands. At the beginning of the
king's illness the Whigs confidently expected to be in office under
the prince's regency within two or three weeks, and as a result they
devoted more time to planning the distribution of offices amongst
themselves than to concerting a plan for achieving victory. The
counter-claims and rivalries of their members for particular offices
further hampered their political planning, till by the time of their
apparently fast approaching accession to power in late January they
seemed more like a party about to break up under the strains of
internal jealousies than an opposition sweeping triumphantly into
office.

The crisis thus created internal tensions which were to contribute to the party split in 1791–4. In particular it opened a gap
between Burke and the rest of the party, who, virtually ignoring
Burke's attempt to provide them with a reasoned and defensible
strategy, spent most of their time and effort in fruitless attempts to
retrieve the results of Fox's indiscretions. Burke's defence of the
principle of hereditary succession was worked out on grounds
defensible to a protagonist of the constitution of 1689; Fox's rash
declaration in the Commons that the Prince of Wales had a hereditary right to assume his father's full prerogatives without any parliamentary interference merely handed the political initiative to Pitt.[38]
Locally, as well as in Parliament, the effect was disastrous. In a short
time, as Fitzwilliam's Yorkshire correspondents began unanimously
to report, provincial opinion reverted to the state of 1784. By Christmas news was coming in of almost total support for Pitt; John Dixon
of Leeds lamented that 'the neighbourhood hereabouts seem so
horridly infatuated in their opinions of the rectitude of Mr Pitt's
conduct', and Peregrine Wentworth, writing on Christmas Day,

mentioned Sir William Milner's opinion that the popular cry 'was very much against us', and concluded, 'Believe me, my dear lord, I do not know what can be done, our friends seem low'. Even Sinclair could not find a favourable interpretation to put on local opinion, for though he attributed the general mood to Pitt's 'plausibility and hypocrisy', he admitted that these had brought the Minister great popularity in York. Francis Foljambe, declining Fitzwilliam's offer to put him up again for the county, confirmed that 'the question of right has done much harm and shakes some of our steadiest friends and that in case of a county meeting the sense of the people would be full as strong against us as in 1784'. Zouch, too, advised lying low when Fitzwilliam suggested an attempt to procure a popular address in favour of the prince's right; it would be a 'very hazardous experiment'. Indeed, Zouch went so far as to suggest that it would be imprudent to attempt to oppose addresses in support of Pitt. From Leeds Beckett reported on 12 January that even if the prince were to become regent and bring in his friends a dissolution of Parliament to give them a majority would be unwise so far as the Leeds area was concerned. 'The ground which Mr Fox unfortunately took upon the question of right has once more raised a storm about our ears,' he wrote, 'and sorry, very sorry, I am to say that it takes much the same direction now that it did in '84.' Ominously, the local dissenters, led by the Milnes family, were again on Pitt's side, despite the Minister's recent vote against the proposal to repeal the Test and Corporation Acts. Beckett accordingly thought it 'bordering on insanity to offer to stir at this juncture'. At York, where preparations for setting up a candidate to replace the retiring Galway were now under way, even Sinclair deprecated Fitzwilliam's suggestion of an address. 'An immediate attempt to summon the people together,' he wrote on 21 December, 'would have an injurious effect upon the general interest, . . . and also . . . probably would rekindle a little of that spirit among the mob which was so injurious to us upon the last election, and which it has been our constant inclination and endeavour to extinguish altogether'. Indeed, so violent was the spirit against the Whigs in York that several handbills and posters sent up by Fitzwilliam had 'produced some inflammatory and violent retorts which, if carried much further, we all think will produce a contest of that nature which would do us more harm than service—we therefore have employed people to pull down as soon as discovered all squibs and papers of the kind'. Beckett, too, suppressed a number of

handbills sent to him for distribution in Leeds: 'Whatever may be
the operation of these bills in the metropolis,' he wrote, 'I am sure
in the country they hurt your lordship exceedingly, for wherever
they originate, they are all traced up to your lordship by the people in
the country.' The other side's handbills, however, seem to have been
everywhere. A supporter in York reported on Christmas Eve that
bills containing personal references to Fitzwilliam were appearing
all over the city.[39] The hard work of Fitzwilliam and his friends to
recover the ground lost in Yorkshire in 1784 was thrown away
almost overnight by Fox's blunders.

Nevertheless, in Parliament Fitzwilliam loyally followed Fox's
line. On 10 December Fox's declaration that '. . . the Prince of Wales
had as clear, as express a right to assume the reins of government,
and exercise the power of sovereignty . . . as in the case of His
Majesty's having undergone a perfect and natural demise' had been
met by Pitt's insistence that 'the Prince of Wales had no more right
(speaking of strict right) to assume the government than any other
individual subject of the country'. The House supported Pitt's proposal
for the appointment of a committee to search for precedents, while
the Minister was able to insist upon a debate on the question whether
or not the prince did have such a right to the sovereign power. The
initiative now passed into Pitt's hands, whence it never subsequently
fell. The Whigs were reduced to attempts to explain away Fox's
assertion, and tried to prevent the discussion of the prince's right. It
was on this theme that Fitzwilliam based his speech opening the
debate in the Lords on 15 December. The prince's right, he contended, was 'a question which . . . could not be brought under discussion without producing effects which every well-meaning and
considerate individual must wish to avoid'. His efforts were unavailing, and in both Houses the opposition suffered the tactical disadvantage of losing the first divisions. Late in January, when the
resolutions passed by the Commons as a basis for a Regency Bill came
up to the Lords, Fitzwilliam came forward again to try to take the
offensive. He declared that the tendency of the proposals was 'to
reduce the constitution from the principles of a limited monarchy,
and change it to the principles of a republic'. In particular he contested Lord Camden's remark that the restriction on the creation of
new peerages by the regent could be mitigated by the grant of
peerages, if necessary, on the authority of the two Houses. This
opinion, Fitzwilliam contended, was 'in the highest degree uncon-

stitutional, and he should, in consequence, think it his indispensable duty to come forward with a declaration condemning all such doctrines as repugnant to the principles of the British constitution'. Camden was eventually obliged to withdraw his remark.[40] Such minor victories in the debating chamber were hollow, however, in the face of the government's unshakable majorities. The final irony of the king's recovery as the Regency Bill was going through the committee stage in the Lords was an apt comment on the hopelessness of the opposition's tactics and strategy since the beginning of the crisis.

The loss of the prospect of office soured relationships within the party still further. Fitzwilliam, who always professed an indifference to, and indeed shrank from, the labours of high office, was more relieved than angry at his release from the proposed office of First Lord of the Admiralty, for which he was destined in Portland's prospective Cabinet.[41] It was one of the most important as well as one of the most burdensome of eighteenth-century Cabinet offices, and Fitzwilliam possessed neither the administrative experience nor the naval background that would have been necessary to the efficient performance of its duties. It was with some relief, therefore, that he turned his attention from the flood of applications for naval patronage that was already beginning to flow to the more congenial sphere of local politics, devoting the major share of his attention to the attempt to repair the damage done to the Whig interests in Yorkshire by the crises of 1784 and 1788.

To counter the political damage suffered by the Wentworth interest in the regency crisis needed much effort and expense. In the late summer the Prince of Wales was persuaded to embark on a tour of the northern counties in an attempt to rally loyalty to his person and to counter the demonstrations of affection for his father now taking place all over the country. On 31 August he and his brother, the Duke of York, arrived at the race ground at York, where, after riding about on horseback 'to gratify public curiosity with a sight of their persons', they entered Fitzwilliam's carriage for the drive into the city. The crowd took out the horses at Micklegate Bar and drew the carriage into the city. The following day the princes were presented with a congratulatory address in a gold box, and on 2 September they were received by the Fitzwilliams at Wentworth, where a lavish entertainment was provided for them and for a good part of the county. There were 247 guests to dinner in the princely

presence, including prominent party men such as Norfolk, Loughborough and Carlisle, local worthies and relatives such as the
Dundases, Weddells, Ramsdens, Foljambes and Milners, persons of
electoral importance such as John and Pemberton Milnes, the Dixons,
Fentons, Osbaldestons, Stricklands, and the Lord Mayor of York.[42]
In addition to the distinguished assemblage of house guests, a lavish
festival was organised in the grounds for some 40,000 persons, at
which fifty-five hogsheads of ale were drunk. 'Nothing could be more
superb and sumptuous than the whole of the arrangements', reported
The Oracle on 8 September. 'It was in the true style of ancient
English hospitality. His gates . . . were thrown open to the loyalty
and love of the surrounding country. . . . The diversions, consisting
of all the rural sports in use in that part of the kingdom, lasted the
whole day; and the prince, with the nobility and gentry, who were
the noble earl's guests, participated in the merriment.' The day's
festivities concluded with a ball, described in the *Annual Register* as
'the most brilliant ever seen beyond the Humber'.[43] The occasion
made Wentworth the focus of county society and began to lay the
foundation of a new revival of the family's electoral interests. Burke
thought that the prince's visit had been of some political use, though
regretting that he had not stayed longer 'to shew himself to the
manufacturing towns which are the headquarters of the enemy. It
is very probable that he might have dislodged them'. In the county
generally, however, the visit was 'the happiest thing imaginable, and
the best adapted to dispel prejudices in that county which was
cruelly poisoned with them'. The prince had been 'properly attentive
and civil to those who were adverse in their politics, so as rather to
please than to offend them, without losing a marked preference to
his friends', and his action in holding up Fitzwilliam's infant son
Lord Milton in his arms before the crowd had 'charmed the people
within and without the House'.[44] For once the prince's connexion
was of some benefit to the party.

The general election of 1790 was nevertheless a testing time for
the Whig party in Yorkshire. Fitzwilliam's former hopes of being
able to recover one of the county seats were quickly abandoned.
Sinclair admitted that 'we stand very ill in the county and that, as
things now are, we must rest content. Every report from that quarter is somewhat unfavourable'.[45] It was to take another sixteen years
to bring public opinion round once more to the Whig cause. In York
and Hull, however, the two largest and most important urban con-

stituencies in Yorkshire, the Whigs were able to take advantage of local circumstances and in both cases to recover one of the seats lost in 1784. At York Galway's retirement presented Fitzwilliam's friends with an opportunity to negotiate a compromise which enabled them to avoid a test of their renewed unpopularity. The only question was which side would first offer the compromise, and so risk offending the greedy voters who would be deprived of their opportunity for profit. Secret negotiations were carried on, resulting in an agreement between the agents of both sides in early June 1790. Milnes and Milner were to be returned without opposition, and each agreed 'not to join with any other candidate—to prevent any third person standing as far as lay in each other's power—and *bona fide* to assist each other as far as possible without showing the appearance of a compromise'. The final agreement was concluded at Fryston, Milnes's residence, on 10 June and the election was peacefully carried through on the 18th.[46]

Hull required a different approach. The town had a large, unruly and demanding electorate, generally little responsive to political argument and consequently fickle in its allegiance. Government, the corporation, the Dock Company and Trinity House all had interests among the voters, and several local families of gentry had more or less extensive influence. The balance, however, was always liable to be tilted by judicious corruption. The reformer Thomas Oldfield calculated that two thirds of the voters regularly took two guineas for a vote. Any 'third man' who came along to challenge sitting members and provoke a contest was accordingly popular, and no one could expect to represent the town for any length of time without profuse expense. Rockingham had acquired an interest in the borough by his normal method of working through local gentry families. Sir George Savile's local prestige was also influential. In 1784, however, the deaths of Rockingham and Savile, the change of government and the swing of county opinion against the coalition resulted in a clean sweep for the Pittites, Wilberforce and Samuel Thornton being elected by a large majority. On Wilberforce's translation to the county seat Walter Spencer Stanhope, a leading member of the Yorkshire Association, was returned unopposed in June.

Stanhope found his seat at Hull precarious, and had no relish for an expensive contest. His known unwillingness to spend money on the scale required for an election at Hull was his weak spot, and Fitzwilliam determined to exploit the advantage.[47] The prospective beneficiary was Lord Burford, the eldest son of the Duke of St Albans (an old schoolfellow) and nephew of Fitzwilliam's wife through the duke's marriage to her elder sister, Lady Catherine Ponsonby.[48] In addition, Burford's marriage in July 1788 to Jane Moses, niece and heiress of Sir Henry Etherington, a wealthy country gentleman from the Hull district and an alderman of the city, gave him the foundation of an interest of his own. If Etherington could be persuaded to back his new nephew his prospects would be assured. Burford's association with Fitzwilliam, however, was not welcome to Etherington, who was a supporter of the present Ministry and well disposed towards both sitting members. Fitzwilliam was nevertheless eager to take advantage of a local dispute over the activities of the Hull Dock Company, a body set up in 1774 by Act of Parliament to build and administer a new dock. The dock was completed by 1778 but had quickly proved inadequate for the rapidly increasing trade of the town, and in 1785 the leading merchants and shipowners petitioned for an extension. The company, though willing to undertake another new dock, was not prepared to finance it out of the profits of the first one, and produced a scheme which would have required the town to contribute £1,000 a year in perpetuity to the company in addition to the perpetual tolls levied by the company on users of the docks. The corporation, who resented the company's statutory autonomy, led the opposition to the scheme, and its friends accused the members of the company of taking excessive profits from the traders of the town. The sitting members of Parliament supported the corporation, so that Fitzwilliam and Burford were able to win the support of the Dock Company.

The election took place on 21 June 1790, and Fitzwilliam's tactics won the day. Burford's arrival to canvass the voters a week before polling day immediately frightened off Stanhope, who resigned on the 14th, left Hull on the 15th before five in the morning, and retired to his bed to be out of the way of the election. Fitzwilliam had succeeded in re-establishing some of the former Whig influence in the town. His chief weapon, however, had undoubtedly been money. His chief local supporters had noted an absence of party spirit in the election—neither Pitt nor Fox had been mentioned. The only way to raise the Whig interest, Joseph Sykes asserted, was 'by being charitable'. Etherington had declared that 'nothing can carry the point but to have it given out . . . that whether he [Burford] succeeds or not two guineas will be given to all those that give him a vote and four guineas for a single vote . . . he must bring at least 5,000 guineas with him and lodge it in the bank, this will give *immediate credit* and may turn the die in his favour, nothing else I think can make him succeed'. The cost of this electoral bounty amounted to £6,200, over £2,000 being in cash paid to the burgesses. That this distribution of electoral alms had not made Fitzwilliam especially popular, however, was suggested by some of his local friends, who advised him to defer his intended visit to Hull races on 29 June until the disagreements and disputes of the election had subsided.[49]

In other parts of Yorkshire, too, the Whigs' electoral fortunes showed signs of revival in 1790. Fitzwilliam's friends were also active at Beverley, another large and rapacious borough in the East Riding, and Hedon, near Hull, where the ministerialists had also triumphed in 1784. At each of these places one seat was recaptured. All in all, therefore, the four Yorkshire borough constituencies in which the Wentworth interest had been defeated in 1784 now each returned one member to swell the Whig numbers in the Commons. It was some reward for the energy, skill and money that Fitzwilliam had contributed to the party cause since 1784. His financial contributions alone were outstanding. In addition to payments of £1,705 towards the county canvass and £1,000 for the York city election in 1784, he had contributed generously to party expenses elsewhere. He had given nearly £2,000 towards the costs of Fox's Westminster election in 1784 and the subsequent scrutiny, and £6,000 for the Westminster by-election in 1788 when Lord John Townshend was successful in winning the second seat for the party. He was then one of the few Whig Lords who not only promised and subscribed to the amount of his first undertaking (£2,000) but trebled his original subscription to help make up a deficit in the sums actually collected. He contributed several hundreds more between 1784 and 1788 towards expenses in Bedfordshire, Buckinghamshire, Middlesex and Lancaster, in none of which constituencies he had any personal property or interest. He had contributed equally generously to the party's plan for a general election subscription in 1790 of £20,000 in forty shares. As Lord Robert Spencer admiringly wrote in 1788, 'I should always expect you to do everything that is handsome about money', and Fitzwilliam's generosity in supporting the Whigs' political activities marked him out as the most zealous of their members.[50] The party's central political organisation, developed in the years immediately after Rockingham's death, owed much to the financial contributions of their great lords. An annual subscription had been arranged to subsidise the opposition press, and William Adam had been installed at Burlington House as party agent and whip to administer the political fund and co-ordinate the party's electoral activities.[51] Nevertheless, the central organisation remained dependent on the initiative and activity of local magnates, and tended merely to try to fill the gaps between their semi-autonomous spheres of influence. Fitzwilliam remained the party's chief representative in Yorkshire, and contributed much more to the electoral successes of the party there in 1790 than he drew in assistance from any central office. He took supplies of opposition literature from the London headquarters for distribution in the county, but his electoral activities there were carried on independently and through the old-established channels of personal and family influence running outwards from Wentworth. In 1790, for example, he helped to finance the setting up of the *York Herald* as a new Whig paper for the county, paying for copies to be distributed to most of the public houses in Yorkshire until it was securely established.[52]

So, despite the paucity of their achievement in national and local politics, by the end of 1788 the Whigs had come a long way from the disasters of 1783–4. They were now a party in a very real sense, with acknowledged leadership, a considerable degree of organisation, and a responsible political attitude if not yet a complete political programme.[53] They were strong in debating talent in the Commons, and by no means contemptible in the Lords. Their best speakers could make up to a considerable extent in parliamentary opportunism for the deficiencies of their leaders in concerted strategy before the opening of the session. As Fitzwilliam wrote in April 1788 of the prosecution speeches in the Hastings impeachment, 'disgraced, degraded, run down as they were, scarcely suffered to speak in the infancy of the present Parliament, this very Parliament has already conferred on them the distinguished duty of vindicating the justice of the nation, and of rescuing the name of Englishmen from the obloquy of tyranny over the inoffensive and the impotent'.[54] Despite the regency crisis, the Whig party was beginning again to show a vitality and feel a well-being it had neither shown nor felt since Rockingham's last days. In these developments Fitzwilliam played a leading part. In the lavish hospitality of Wentworth during the summer and autumn, or through the careful but liberal administration of his Yorkshire estates, Fitzwilliam also began to recover some of the old loyalty to the Wentworths that had been under strain in 1782–4. The prestige of Wentworth House again stood high in York-shire, and Fitzwilliam, by his personal liberality and benevolence, benefited from and promoted this renewed attachment. His family, now well known in the county from their annual residence at Went-worth during the summer months, was much respected; and the long-delayed birth of his only son and heir, Charles William, Viscount Milton, at Wentworth on 4 May 1786—only a few days from the anniversary of Rockingham's birth—promoted new demonstrations of affection, and relieved the family from the immediate threat of the succession to the Rockingham estates of the son of the runaway match of Lady Harriet Wentworth with her footman, William Sturgeon. The joy of the family and their friends at the now unexpected event was unbounded, and it was a joy shared by most of the old partisans of Wentworth in the West Rid-ing. No longer was Fitzwilliam a stranger in Yorkshire. Accepted as the true heir and successor of Rockingham, his efforts had helped to revitalise the Whig interest in the county as well as to support the party's activities in national politics.

Notes
¹ See M. D. George, ' "Fox's Martyrs" : the general election of 1784' in *Transactions of the Royal Historical Society*, 4th series XXI (1939), pp. 133–68.
² *Parliamentary Papers of John Robinson*, ed. W. T. Laprade, Camden 3rd series, XXXIII (1922). Robinson's calculations and the results are dis-cussed in Cannon, pp. 207–27.
³ I am indebted for much of what immediately follows to Dr F. O'Gorman's valuable study. *The Whig Party and the French Revolution* (1967), ch. I, 1784–90 (pp. 1–31) and appendix I, pp. 244–9. Dr Cannon, pp. 216–19 and appendix, pp. 244–5, comes to slightly different totals.
⁴ O'Gorman, pp. 245–6. Dr O'Gorman omits William Eden from the list of defectors between 1784 and 1790, nor does he count him among the Northites returned in 1784.
⁵ Pitt's personal following in the Commons was calculated in 1788 to be only fifty-two (*English Historical Documents*, vol. XI ed. A. Aspinall and E. Anthony Smith, repr. 1969, p. 253).
⁶ O'Gorman, ch. I, and D. E. Ginter, *Whig Organisation in the General Election of 1790* and 'The financing of Whig party organisation, 1783–93', *American Historical Review*, LXXI (2), January 1966, pp. 421–40.
⁷ *Parl. Register*, XVI (ii), p. 3. On 4 February and 18 May 1784 and 24 January 1786 Fitzwilliam was the opposition's first, or only, speaker in the debates at the opening of the session. There was no debate on the

address in the Lords in January 1785. (*Ibid.*, XIV (ii), 118–22; XVI (ii), 3; XVIII (ii), 1–4; XX (ii), 4–5.)

8 For the detailed account of the scheme and the debates on it in the Commons see Ehrman, pp. 197–213.

9 Fitzwilliam to R. Parker of Halifax [1785] (F 65b); *Parl. Register*, XVIII (i), pp. 253–4, (ii), 101–4.

10 *Ibid.*, XX (ii), p. 4.

11 *Ibid.*, XXII (ii), p. 96.

12 Portland to Lady Rockingham, [8 April 1784] (Portland MSS, 628); T. Plummer to Fitzwilliam, 12 April (N); Fitzwilliam to Zouch, 9 June (E 234); Sinclair to Fitzwilliam, 26 May and 2 June (N).

13 R. Hay Drummond to Fitzwilliam, 5 July 1784 (N).

14 Letters to Lady Rockingham, 11 August 1784, Scarborough, Sunday [Sept. 1784], 11 August 1784 and 3 November 1784 (R 164).

15 J. Dring to Fitzwilliam, 10 November and 6 December 1784 (N).

16 7 and 21 January 1785: E 234. Fitzwilliam co-operated with Zouch in the composition of a pamphlet, *Plain Facts Submitted to the Common Sense of the People of England* (1785), which attacked the Ministry's financial policies, justified the coalition's India Bill, and censured Pitt's treatment of the Westminster scrutiny, an attempt to prevent Fox's return as member for Westminster in 1784–5. Fitzwilliam had the pamphlet printed and circulated in March 1785.

17 Correspondence in *Wyvill Papers*, IV, pp. 14–15, 118–123; *Later Corresp. of George III*, I, p. 119; *Parl. Register*, XVII, pp. 10–13 and 24–5: Spencer Stanhope MSS, Sheffield City Library: Wyvill's italics.

18 To Zouch, 7 January 1785: E 234.

19 *Wyvill Papers*, II, pp. 356–71, 446–50 and 460–2; *Parl. Register*, XVIII, pp. 42–83.

20 See *York Chronicle*, 2 July 1786. Fitzwilliam wrote to Portland on 26 November 1786 that the Yorkshire manufacturers were not yet roused against the French treaty, 'but probably few or none of them understand [its] effects. . . . A great deal of continued comment upon it in the newspapers is the true mode of explaining [it] to them. . . . I do not think till the newspapers have been full of comment and observation for at least that period [a fortnight], it would be advisable to sift for their opinion'. (N.) There was a meeting of the inhabitants of York on 2 July 1784 against the window tax, and one in January 1787 at Bradford concerning the Bill to prevent the export of wool (*York Chronicle*, 9 July 1786 and 12 January 1787). There were also widespread meetings against Pitt's shop tax in 1785–6 (Fitzwilliam to Zouch, 6 February 1786: E 234).

21 *York Chronicle*, 12 January 1787; Sinclair to Fitzwilliam, 14 November 1787, and reply, 15 November 1787 (N) (Fitzwilliam had contributed £1,000 towards the cost of the 1784 city election: account books, N); Cavendish to Fitzwilliam, 'Friday' [16 November 1787] (N, X512/19); Fitzwilliam to Milner, 31 December 1787 (N).

22 Fitzwilliam to Zouch, 6 February 1786 (E 234); Portland to Fitzwilliam, 3 February 1787 (N 38). Isaac Hawkins-Brown reported to Wilberforce on 18 June 1787 that the people at Sheffield were 'much pleased

with the commercial treaty' (*Corresp. of William Wilberforce* (1840), I, pp. 32–4). Fitzwilliam and his friends also encouraged the agitation of the West Riding clothiers in favour of the Wool Bill of 1787, to enforce more strictly the prohibition on the export of raw wool for foreign manufacture.

23 *Parl. Register*, XIX, pp. 170–227.

24 *Ibid.*, XVI, pp. 1–16 (6 July: wrongly dated as 17 July). The Act is printed in *Eng. Hist. Docs.*, XI, pp. 826–31.

25 Ehrman, pp. 451–5: *Parl. Register*, XXIII, pp. 244–54, 289–359, 385–405, 415–45; Steele to Wilberforce, 30 April 1788 (*Corresp. of William Wilberforce*, I, pp. 54–5); W. Grenville to Buckingham, 14 March 1788 (*Court and Cabinets*, I, p. 357).

26 *Parl. Register*, XXIV, pp. 295–9, 310–15, 334, 341–4; Beckett to Fitzwilliam, 24 March 1788: F 34g.

27 P. Milnes to Fitzwilliam, 27 March 1788 and Foljambe to Fitzwilliam, 21 March (F 34g); Fitzwilliam to Zouch, 8 April (E 234).

28 Fitzwilliam to Downe, 29 August and 16 September 1788 (F 34g). Downe (1764–1832) was the son of a former associate of Rockingham's, MP for Malton 1768–74 (Namier and Brooke, II, pp. 305–6). His candidature was approved at a meeting presided over by Fitzwilliam at York assizes in July 1788 (W. Radcliffe to Fitzwilliam, 21 July: F 34g).

29 See A. N. Newman, 'Leicester House politics, 1749–51', *Eng. Hist. Review*, LXXVI (1961) pp. 577–89 and 'Leicester House politics, 1750–60', in Royal Historical Society, *Camden Miscellany*, XXIII, pp. 85–94.

30 *Corresp. of George, Prince of Wales* (ed. A. Aspinall), I (1963) p. 60.

31 *Ibid.*, pp. 88, 95, 123.

32 24 August: *ibid.*, p. 155.

33 *Memorials and Corresp. of C. J. Fox*, II, pp. 278–83. The prince replied on 11 December with a categorical assurance that no marriage was in contemplation (*ibid.*, pp. 283–4). Ten days later the ceremony took place.

34 T. Orde to the Duke of Rutland, 16 May 1786: H.M.C., *Rutland MSS*, III, p. 300.

35 *Life and Letters of Sir G. Elliot*, I, pp. 155–9; *Parl. Register*, XXII, pp. 230 and 251–6.

36 *Memorials and Corresp. of C. J. Fox*, II, pp. 288–90.

37 For the king's illness see I. Macalpine and R. Hunter, *George III and the Mad Business* (1969), pp. 1–107 and 172–5. For the details of the crisis see C. Chenevix-Trench, *The Royal Malady* (1964); J. W. Derry, *The Regency Crisis and the Whigs* (1963); Ehrman, pp. 644–6; and the correspondence in *Corresp. of George, Prince of Wales*, I, pp. 352–500.

38 W. W. Grenville to Buckingham, 11 December 1788: *Court and Cabinets*, II, p. 54.

39 Letters to Fitzwilliam from John Dixon, 24 December, P. Wentworth, 25th, R. Sinclair, 28th, F. Foljambe [n.d.], H. Zouch, 27 December 1788, Sir J. Beckett, 12 January 1789, Sir T. Gascoigne [n.d.], Sinclair, 21 December 1788, Beckett, 2 January 1789, Harrison, 24 December 1788: F 34h.

E

40 *Parl. Register*, xxv, pp. 22–32; xxvi, pp. 26–8, 111–13, 119–20.

41 Fox to Portland [21 January 1789]: *Memorials and Corresp. of C. J. Fox*, iv, p. 283.

42 T. Allen, *A New and Complete History of the County of York*, i (1829), pp. 122–3; list of company at Wentworth House, 2 September 1789: F 127/25.

43 1789, p. 221.

44 *Corresp. of E. Burke*, vi, pp. 15, 23. The princes returned to York on the 3rd and went on to Castle Howard on the 5th.

45 Sinclair to Fitzwilliam, 19 April 1789 (F 115a).

46 W. Markham to Sir W. Milner, 7 June 1790, enclosed in Lady Milner to Fitzwilliam [June 1790], and Sir W. Milner to Fitzwilliam [12 July 1790] (N).

47 Sir J. Beckett to Fitzwilliam, 11 November 1788: N.

48 *G. E. C.*: Burford's mother died in 1789. He was born in 1765 and succeeded his father as sixth Duke of St Albans in 1802. Lady Robert Manners described him in 1788 as 'a sensible prudent young man in endeavouring to get a woman with a fortune to support his rank, or at least to enable him to live suitable to it during his father's life' (Etherington to W. Spencer Stanhope, 7 May 1788: MS, 'Memoirs of the Life of Walter Spencer Stanhope, Esq. of Cannon Hall' by John Spencer Stanhope, vol. iii: Spencer Stanhope MSS, 60645).

49 For the Hull election see correspondence in N 39–41; election account N, x523; Spencer Stanhope's diary (Spencer Stanhope MSS, 60635, vol. 10); G. Hadley, *A New and Complete History of . . . Kingston-upon-Hull* (Hull, 1788) [sc. 1790], ii, pp. 483–681.

50 Account books; Lord Robert Spencer to Fitzwilliam [September 1788], 18 September 1788 and [13 October 1788] (N); Lord Cholmondeley to Fitzwilliam, August 1789 (F 115a).

51 D. E. Ginter 'The financing of Whig party organisation, 1783–93', *loc. cit.*

52 Sir William Milner to Fitzwilliam, 2 April 1788 (F 34g) and T. Wilson to Fitzwilliam, 22 May 1790: F 115a.

53 Portland, writing to his son Lord Titchfield on 25 December 1786, put forward 'a rule for your own conduct, which is never to oppose or support any question of public importance when you are out of office which you would not treat exactly in the same manner if you were entrusted with all the powers of government, and in the trial of every measure which is proposed by this test the characteristic difference or distinction between a party and a faction will be found to consist' (Portland MSS, PWF 319).

54 Fitzwilliam to Rev. H. Zouch, 8 April 1788 (E 234).

CHAPTER FIVE

A party in disintegration
1790—2

By the summer of 1790 the political situation in England was beginning to be affected by the French revolution. Once again the apparent recovery of the Whig party from its political misfortunes and miscalculations was to be turned into near-disaster, and in this case into personal tragedy for Fitzwilliam. The opening rift between Fox and Burke was of deep concern to him as both Fox's friend and Burke's patron. The one embodied for Fitzwilliam all the qualities of close friendship and affection, the other all the political principles to which his life was dedicated. The choice between the two was to be an agonising one.

Fox's impulsive welcome to the revolution in France as 'how much the greatest event it is that ever happened in the world! and how much the best!'[1] was not shared by Burke, who quickly came to see the revolution as a threat to the established order of society all over Western Europe. Their common zeal for the cause of civil and religious liberty now became an issue of division rather than of unity. Fox could never desert the view, which he identified with basic Whig principle, that the purpose of his political life and the *raison d'être* of his party was the protection of constitutional liberties against the Crown and executive. This led him to offer an instinctive welcome to the French revolution in 1789 and, while condemning the violence and excesses of its later phases, to see it always as the embodiment of the principle of liberty against tyrannical government. He refused to accept the view that the revival of reform agitations in Britain after 1790 was a threat to the established order of property and rank, seeing them as a continuation of the respectable reform movements of 1779–85 and as a necessary stage in the guardianship of liberty against the Crown. To him the supreme question was not whether France was to fall under a levelling totalitarianism and so become a centre of revolutionary infection for all

Europe, but whether the reaction against Jacobin principles in
England would lead to a defection from native constitutionalism as
drawn from Locke, Sidney and the men of 1688. Fox's error was to
see French politics in terms of English political ideas, and to see in
the revolution the transference to France of English Whiggism. To
Burke, however, the revolution in France was important mainly for
what it signified for England. It came to stand for a threat to
rank, property and the traditional ordering of society throughout
Western Europe. The principles to which he appealed were those
of the Locke whose ideas had become the holy writ of eighteenth-
century Whiggism—the principles of government established for
the preservation of the rights of property and the social order
founded on rank, wealth and deference. Whereas Fox's attitude to
events in France was, as one recent writer has remarked, one of
'sympathetic detachment',[2] Burke's was one of passionate involvement. And though the personal ties which bound Fitzwilliam and
Portland to Fox were strong and long-lasting, Burke's powerful
appeal to and redefinition of Whig principles in terms of aristocratic
self-interest and historical tradition were to prove too strong in the
end to be resisted.

The Whig party's crisis over the French revolution was delayed
until 1792. Fox refused at first to be drawn into a contest against
Burke which would split his friends into two acrimonious camps, while
Portland and Fitzwilliam followed a similar strategy of avoiding
confrontations wherever possible. Others were less disposed to be
moderate and less anxious to avoid a breach with Burke, for whom
Fox still retained much affection. To Sheridan, Francis and some of
the younger recruits to the party Burke was a tiresome liability. He
had run the party into the political dead end of Hastings's impeachment for the sake of an abstract principle, and his hysterical denun-
ciations of the French revolution seemed likely to alienate popular
opinion. Both to protect the party's new strategy of appealing to
the public against Crown influence and to assert its role as leader of
liberal reform sentiment they seem to have wished deliberately to
drive Burke from its ranks and to establish a new, liberal (but
moderate) Whig party untrammelled by outdated ideas. Fox's
anxiety not to lose contact with the newer generation of more out-
ward-looking Whigs led him to identify himself with them, while
Burke could not shake off the resentment which he had formed
against Sheridan during the regency crisis, when the latter had

apparently been attempting to build up his own influence at Carlton
House against that of the accredited leaders of the opposition.
Sheridan's championship of the French revolution seemed deliberately provocative, and it led to the famous quarrel with Burke in
the debate on the army estimates on 5 February 1790 and to a
subsequent party conference at Burlington House at which the lines
of the later division in the party began to be drawn.[3]

As both Burke's patron and one of Fox's closest friends Fitzwilliam
was to fill a crucial role in the crisis. In November 1789 Burke had
turned to him as one of the first recipients of his concern about the
possible consequences of the revolution for Europe. Now Burke's
son Richard, who had recently been appointed as Fitzwilliam's
London agent, wrote to urge his intervention, in the hope that Fitzwilliam's influence might turn Fox against Sheridan. Taking the
opportunity of the meeting at the Crown and Anchor tavern in the
Strand to celebrate the first anniversary of the fall of the Bastille,
Richard suggested that the Whig leaders should 'come to town and
lay their heads together a little at this crisis'. The French revolution
was 'a usurpation obtained by fraud and sustained by force; a most
horrible tyranny, in the most execrable hands . . . abetted by the
furies of a ferocious mob'. Sheridan, he declared, had deliberately
'put himself at the head of the spirit of innovation in this country'
in order to satisfy his 'deep and systematic ambition', and his aim
was to draw the party away from its fundamental policy of 'adhering to and maintaining both the form and substance of our present
constitution. . . . You know the facility of Fox. You know that he
is surrounded and in many things governed by those who have not
a hundredth part of his parts, no share in his judgement, and principles absolutely bad. . . . If Fox engages in it, will you not also be
committed; and he is not far from it.' He concluded by urging that
if Fitzwilliam did not directly forbid Sheridan and Fox from taking
part with the radicals the reform movement would get out of hand,
the respectable leadership, as in France, would give way to
extremism, and the country would be taken over by 'Methodist
preachers, mountebanks, writers of newspapers, strolling players. . . .
Think when you walk the streets of Peterborough that they lie under
the stones, and that they will come out of the rotten tenements you
have purchased of Mr Parker to lord it over the lord of those
tenements'.

Fitzwilliam was sufficiently concerned both about the party's

constitutional doctrine and about Sheridan's conduct to give Richard
the assurance that he agreed about 'the propriety of entering a *caveat*
against the enthusiasm, or the ambition of any man whatever leading us into the trammels of Dr Price, Parson Horne, or any reverend
or irreverend speculator in politics, be his intentions, or be his
declarations what they will', and he promised, 'I shall certainly take
an opportunity of saying something upon that subject where I think
it ought to be spoken about'. He was aware, however, of the use that
Richard might make of any open declaration, and concluded by
warning him: 'don't say anything about my intentions, or even of
my sentiments, for I think it is better to be perfectly reserved upon
the subject'. Fitzwilliam's letter to Fox has not survived. Richard
later complained that Fox had merely pocketed it without an answer
and that it had not affected his conduct; but its terms could scarcely
have been strong enough in any case to satisfy the Burkes without
risking a breach with Fox.[4]

Fitzwilliam's tactics reflected the official line of the party leadership at this period of the crisis. Though intellectually convinced of
the rightness of Burke's principles, and utterly opposed (as in 1780)
to reform on the speculative doctrines of the radicals, Fitzwilliam
was neither prepared to split the party nor willing to endanger his
friendship with its recognised leader in the Commons. His financial
and political patronage of Burke made him one of the chief confidants of Burke's developing alarms, but he held aloof from a public
commitment to his views which might force a definition of the
party's standpoint. Like the other Whig leaders, he withheld any
public sign of approval of Burke's *Reflections on the Revolution in
France*, published in November 1790, though Burke declared on 29
November that Fitzwilliam and the 'old Stamina of the Whigs' had
acclaimed it and Fitzwilliam had written to Richard Burke in August
and September to express his agreement with the general principles
of the work. On its publication, Fitzwilliam wrote of the pamphlet
as being 'almost universally admired and approved', and there can
be no doubt that he felt it to be, in general, a statement of his own
political principles. Tactically, however, he may well have shared
Fox's view that the publication was ill timed to serve party interests.[5]
The aim of the opposition was still to attack Pitt's Ministry and, if
possible, secure its downfall by parliamentary measures and the
support of public opinion. Anything which might divide the party
or alienate the public was to be avoided, and Burke's insistence on

what must as yet seem a hypothetical threat to the principles of the constitution was merely an unwelcome diversion from the real business of politics. To Burke's chagrin, the party leaders seemed determined not to take him seriously. The prospects of a successful attack in the new Parliament on Pitt's foreign or financial policies or the possibility of successful intervention in the internal divisions within the Cabinet held precedence over theoretical disputes about the nature of liberty, so long as no concrete evidence of a real threat to liberty or property in England appeared to exist.

The new session of Parliament therefore opened quietly, with no major debates to enliven the political scene. The dispute with Spain over rival claims to Nootka Sound on the west coast of Canada, which the opposition had attempted, with little success, to make into a general attack on Pitt's foreign policy earlier in 1790, had been settled by a convention in October. The dissenters' agitation for the repeal of the Test and Corporation Acts in 1789 and 1790 had shown up divisions of opinion among the Whigs but had not led to any serious consequences. Fox had welcomed the proposal, declaring to Fitzwilliam in November 1789 that 'I feel myself so much inclined to the *cause* of the dissenters that without any further consideration I should be very glad to take any part they desire of me and not at all sorry that they should apply to me'. Even Burke, at that stage, had approved the policy of Whig support of the petitioners, who, as he pointed out to Fox, were 'a set of men powerful enough in many things, but most of all in elections'. Portland was inclined to reject the proposal for repeal on principle, since, in power, he would not wish to alienate the established Church, but Fitzwilliam supported Fox's view.[6] Twelve months later Fitzwilliam argued the case on the merits of the measure, writing to rebuke his Yorkshire supporter the Rev. Henry Zouch for taking a leading part against the proposal at a public meeting. He argued that the only ground on which the application could be refused would be 'an undeviating adherence to *that which is*—a principle to which I feel a strong attachment in most cases, because alteration and innovation is so seldom proposed to me, without a great alloy of experiment and uncertainty', but a change would not carry those dangers in this instance because by the practice of occasional conformity the dissenters were already able to circumvent the Test and Corporation Acts. The Church, then, gained nothing in practice by the maintenance of the Acts save the hostility of the dissenters. Fitzwilliam

added that 'the tone and temper of their meetings' and 'the publications and professed principles of some of their most eminent leaders'
on other questions were distasteful to him, but he contended that
these leaders—men like Price and Priestley—would lose their
influence if they were not able to play upon the grievances of their
followers against the penal Acts. From a party point of view, he
thought the opposition could never expect 'support or assistance
from the Dissenters as a body', but that the removal of their common
grievance would weaken their cohesion in politics and reduce their
hostile leaders to the weight of mere individuals.[7]

Fitzwilliam's letter explains some of the attitudes he was to take
up towards reform and reformers in subsequent years; radical innovation was to be avoided because of the unknown dangers and
consequences that might follow, but the removal of grievances and
abuses was to be recommended, not only on liberal principles but in
order to deprive dangerous extremists of the opportunity to propagate their doctrines. The belief that the best way to deal with radical
movements was to take the control of them out of the hands of
extremists and so teach the general public to look to the Whigs for
leadership became the party's conventional thinking. In 1791–2 the
Foxites advocated this method of dealing with parliamentary reform
agitations, as did Grey and the liberals in the 1820s; and on the
Catholic question it was to be Fitzwilliam's consistent policy for over
thirty years. Fox's attitude in 1790–2 was explicable in these terms,
and on this argument it was Burke's passionate dedication to principle that was responsible for the Whigs' dissensions.

Not all the political issues of the early 1790s divided the Whigs.
In 1791, indeed, they came nearest since 1784 to inflicting a serious
political defeat on Pitt, on the issue of the Russian armament. The
Russo-Turkish war which had broken out in 1787 had resulted in the
Russian occupation of the strategic base of Ochakov on the Black
Sea. Pitt's foreign policy was to support the Turkish empire as a
barrier against Russian penetration to the Mediterranean, and efforts
were now made to force a Russian withdrawal. On 27 March an
ultimatum was sent to Russia and the navy was mobilised. The
opposition attacked the government's measures on grounds set out
by Fitzwilliam in a speech on 29 March which opened the campaign
in the Lords. He set out the constitutional objections to giving the
government discretionary powers to order an augmentation of the
armed forces without full disclosure of the circumstances, but prin-

cipally he based his speech on the alternative Whig foreign policy
that had been put forward by Fox since 1780. This policy was based
on a northern alliance, and in particular on friendship with Russia,
whose ruler, Catherine the Great, had been much courted by the
Whigs. Fitzwilliam embarked on a long and comprehensive review
of 'the relative situations of the continental powers in Europe, and
the advantages or disadvantages that must attend Great Britain from
being more or less connected with each', and drew the conclusion
that a war with Russia would be 'unjust, impolitic and in every way
detrimental to the interests of this country'. On 3 April he moved
three resolutions, declaring that the country was not bound by an
alliance with Prussia to intervene in the Russo–Turkish war, which
he termed an aggressive war by Turkey on Russia, nor was it in
Britain's interest to do so, nor was she bound to do so in the interests
of justice. Ochakov, the second resolution declared, was neither an
adequate nor a just cause for war against Russia. In the Commons
the opposition's attack on the government's policy ran closer to destroying Pitt's Ministry than on any issue since 1784. Fox, Sheridan,
Grey, Whitbread, and indeed all sections of the party rallied to the
conflict, and Pitt's spokesmen were trounced in a series of brilliant
debates that raised Whig oratory once more to its height as a
political instrument. Furthermore, the opposition had found an issue
on which public support was unmistakable. In a further speech in
the Lords on 9 May Fitzwilliam was able to refer to reports from
Manchester, Norwich and the West Riding of strong public feeling
against war, and of widespread concern for the important Russian trade
in industrial raw materials. The opposition's morale rose to its height,
and the independent supporters of the administration were wavering. On 12 April the minority in the Commons against the government numbered 173, against the ministerialists' 253.[8] Faced by the
storm at home and lacking support abroad, the Cabinet's resolution
wavered, and Pitt, declaring that 'it was the greatest mortification he
had ever experienced', decided to retreat.[9] The Foreign Secretary,
the Duke of Leeds, who had hitherto been content to leave the
determination of foreign policy in his chief's hands, refused, however, to sign the new despatches and on 21 April he resigned. The
Cabinet seemed on the verge of breaking up. Thurlow's ill humour
with Pitt and his other colleagues was notorious, and the relationship
between the two was already at breaking point. Leeds's departure led
to a reshuffle which demonstrated the paucity of talent open to the

E*

Ministry. Only the unwavering support of the king and the continued reluctance of the independent members in the Commons to trust Fox once more in office saved Pitt from disaster.

Pitt was shaken by the Ochakov crisis, and by the demonstration in the debates that the opposition had recruited several young men of talent and had been able to mobilise the support of public opinion. The temptation to interfere in their growing divisions to his own advantage was now a strong one, and the Minister began to watch more closely the progress of the Whig split. If the influential Whig lords could be detached from Fox and the more radical wing, and if their support could be obtained for the government, Pitt's problems would be solved. As early as 1791 Pitt and Grenville were toying with schemes for a coalition with the moderate part of the Whig opposition.[10] Burke, indeed, was already turning to the Ministry. Obsessed by the Hastings impeachment, Burke grew ever more impatient with the coolness which the party was beginning to show towards it. No political dividends had accrued to the opposition from the case, and its tortuous technicalities bored both the public and the newer young members of the party who looked 'out of doors' for the basis of Whig strength. Sheridan and Fox in particular, who had at first thrown themselves wholeheartedly into the impeachment, were now tired of it and would have liked to rid the party of its toils. Burke found a readier response from Dundas, the effective head of the Board of Control, who was anxious for Hastings and his policies to be condemned. Dundas and Pitt, in turn, set out to draw Burke and his immediate supporters away from the Foxite part of the opposition. They began to lay stress on those matters on which the Whigs' disagreements would emerge, and to give every possible opportunity for Burke and Fox to confront each other. Even during the Ochakov debates, on 15 April, Pitt had provoked Fox into another panegyric on the French revolution as 'considered altogether, . . . the most stupendous and glorious edifice of liberty, which had been erected on the foundations of human integrity in any time or country'.[11] Burke had risen to reply, but the House refused to hear him. He determined, however, to make clear his dissent from Fox's view as soon as possible, and announced his intention to speak in the committee stage of the Quebec Bill on 20 April, when an opportunity would arise of comparing the British and French systems of government as they might be applicable to French-speaking Canada. The Quebec debate was postponed, the

Whigs being anxious to give time for the situation to cool, Pitt
perhaps in hopes that they would fall out more acrimoniously in
private than in public. Fox and Burke were brought together on 21
April to discuss the situation, and parted amicably, though still of
contrary opinions respecting the revolution. Portland warned Burke
that an outright quarrel with Fox could only promote the interests
of the Ministry, and suggested that it was Pitt's deliberate intention
to provoke one. He feared, he told Fitzwilliam, 'such a political
schism and division as may end in the dissolution of the party', and
he suggested that he and Fitzwilliam should also see Fox before
Parliament reassembled. Tom Grenville also urged Fitzwilliam to
intervene: 'Your prudence and advice will be at this moment of
peculiar advantage to all your friends. . . . If Burke could be
persuaded to discharge his mind upon this subject by writing and
publication, I know nobody so likely to persuade him as yourself'.
Nevertheless, as Grenville admitted, the only hope lay in the prevention of any public debate on the 'general principles of government',
and Burke was attempting to provoke just such a discussion. He
resented Fox's implicit assumption that his approval of the French
revolution represented the view of the considerable majority of the
party and its supporters in the country, and was anxious to dissociate the Whigs at both levels from the pernicious doctrines of
Paine. He was deeply concerned about the increasing circulation and
public approval of Paine's *Rights of Man*, which was both a contemptuous reply to his own *Reflections* and also an extreme statement of the pro-French view on the issue of principle. The Unitarian
Society had recently endorsed Paine's book and condemned Burke's,
and the spring and summer of 1791 saw an upsurge of public
interest in reform at home, with the foundation of a number of
popular societies and clubs in London and the larger provincial
towns. To Burke these societies seemed subversive in intention, and
he was determined that, if the party would not speak out against
them, the party must break up. It was more important than anything
else that all public men of influence should declare where they stood
on this issue. Fitzwilliam's arguments that the 'debating of mere
abstract rights' would involve the party in dangerous internal
squabbles of no real importance therefore merely convinced Burke
that necessity was now about to drive him out of his association
with the Whig party.[12]

On 6 May the confrontation took place in the House of Commons,

Burke repudiating, and Fox defending, the doctrine that the rights of man were basic to the British constitution, and the debate culminating in the dramatic—indeed melodramatic—scene in which Burke declared his friendship with Fox at an end and Fox, his face streaming with tears, protested that it need not be so.[13] Fitzwilliam's distress was as great as Fox's, and his dilemma even more cruel. Burke symbolised for him the Rockinghamite tradition to which his political life was devoted and of which he was, in a sense, the main legatee. Burke, too, sat for Malton, and only two and a half years previously had been the receipient of Fitzwilliam's financial generosity.[14] Yet friendship with Fox remained Fitzwilliam's deepest emotional tie, and Fox's studied moderation in the dispute seemed to place Burke tactically in the wrong, at least. It was a conflict between personal bonds going back to Eton and the grand tour, born in the emotional attachments of youth and strengthened by the intimacy of shared experiences over many years, and political principles derived from equally deep and long-lasting attachment to family tradition and the social order. For Fitzwilliam the choice between Fox and Burke was an agonising personal conflict, a choice between two parts of himself. It took three years for him to make it.

To Burke, about to make the discovery that the men who for him had embodied the principles of a lifetime were unable to respond to a moral crusade which cut across their personal friendships, the choice was simpler and, though not easy, inevitable. His son, who often put Edmund's view more bluntly and with less feeling than his father's emotional nature would have allowed, had written from a committee room in Parliament on the day of the public break with Fox that his father 'considers the principles of the French revolution as opposite to those of our government as light and darkness' and that if 'the fear of dissolution of the party' should induce the Whig leaders 'to acquiesce in everything that Fox does or says . . . my father will be under the necessity of declaring his disconnexion with the present opposition'. For the present Fitzwilliam was not prepared to accept such an argument. 'You see things in a way in which I do not feel them,' he wrote to Richard about this time. When he renewed his offer of financial help to Burke at the end of May he therefore received in reply a long justification of Burke's conduct and a refusal of assistance from a party to which Burke could no longer belong. 'It was an exhibition absolutely new,' Burke wrote of the debate of 6 May, 'to see a man who had sat twenty-six

years in Parliament not to have one friend in the House. . . . I have
the misfortune totally and fundamentally to differ with that party
in constitutional and public points of such moment, that all those,
on which I have hitherto ever differed from other men and other
parties, are, in comparison, mere toys and trifles.' He declared that
he could receive no further obligations of any kind 'out of a party
whose public principles are the very reverse of mine, and who have
recorded an account of my public and private character which, if
admitted, must reflect on me and on all my posterity'. The conclusion of the Hastings impeachment alone detained him in Parliament; 'My seat . . . will probably be at your lordship's disposal early
in the next session; and you will naturally be led to consider of a
person more capable of giving credit to your recommendation and
of doing service to your party than I am, or than I can be'. It was
a strong and determined letter but not one designed, nor likely, to
win Fitzwilliam over, though Burke concluded with professions
that 'there is not living one who more respects your virtues public
and private, or that loves you with a more warm, true and grateful
attachment than I do'.[15]

Fitzwilliam's affection for Burke, and his kindness to him and
his family, were not interrupted by the event of 6 May nor by
Burke's refusal of his help in June, but friendship with and
attachment to Fox were equally unaffected. Indeed, Fitzwilliam
went out of his way to demonstrate that fact. In August Fox
stayed at Wentworth, and the two friends visited York together
for the race week. Their carriage was drawn into the city by the
cheering populace, and on the 25th Fox received the freedom of the
city in a gold box as 'a proof of the high respect and sincere gratitude
of this corporation for the constant and beneficial exertion of his
brilliant and unrivalled abilities, in support of the British constitution, upon the true principles of the glorious revolution; of the just
rights of every degree of citizens, and the peace, liberty, and happiness of mankind'. This endorsement, in one of Fitzwilliam's strong-
holds, of Fox's constitutional position was galling to Burke. 'You
see on what topics they choose to magnify him at York,' Burke
wrote to his son. 'It is a slap at me.' He had intended to visit Wentworth, but changed his mind because of Fox's reception. Fitzwilliam's true opinions were, however, moving towards Burke's
position. French Laurence, Burke's close friend and disciple, declared
that he had spoken out in support of the *Reflections* 'in a large,

mixed company [and] . . . in a manner which made it understood to
be his wish that his opinion should be as publicly known as possible'.
The tide of events was beginning to carry him into Burke's camp.[16]

Fitzwilliam's attitude was made even more explicit by his reception of Burke's second major pamphlet on the issue, the *Appeal from
the New to the Old Whigs*, published on 3 August 1791. In this work
it was Burke's design to contrast the 'old' Whiggism of 1688 and the
Rockingham party with the 'new, republican, Frenchified Whiggism'
of Fox and the *Rights of Man*, and so to force the party to a clear
choice between them.[17] It was a provocative step. Burke was now
convinced that the time had come 'for the weighty men of all parties
to declare themselves, not only in favour of our constitution . . . but
. . . against the French business'. The party leadership was dismayed.
Loughborough and Portland tried to persuade him not to publish,
but young Richard told Loughborough outright 'that one great object
of the publication was to compel those who approved his principles
to make a public profession of them, in opposition to what he . . .
holds to be the doctrine of others, and under the sanction of their
name imputed to all the party'. Portland, while privately approving
of Burke's interpretation of true Whig principles, deeply disapproved
of the 'general censure' which it seemed to pass upon the party,[18]
and the leadership in general studiously refrained from commenting
publicly on the pamphlet. Fitzwilliam, however, decided to break
the silence, and assured Burke of his sympathy:

I thank you heartily for the pamphlet [he wrote on 18 September] and
for the authorities you give me for the doctrines I have sworn by, long
and long since: I know not how long, they have been my creed: I
believe, before even my happiness in your acquaintance and friendship,
tho' they have certainly been strengthened and confirmed by your conversation and instruction—in support of those principles I trust I shall
ever act, and I shall continue to attempt their general propagation.

He declared that he would make it his concern to counter the doctrines of Paine and Priestley 'in the mode I myself think the best
to resist their mischief—private conversation and private insinuation may best suit the extent of my abilities, the turn of my temper,
and the nature of my character—and if the best proof of wisdom is
to accommodate modes to means, it is the only way of producing
effect in ordinary hands'. He ended: 'I have no sentiment but regret
for everything that I have seen happen—adieu, never hesitate one
instant to doubt my affection esteem and admiration'.[19]

Fitzwilliam's generosity of mind and deep affection for Burke would not allow him to remain silent, much though he deplored the breach between his two friends and political mentors. Mere party interests or tactical considerations were beginning to seem too trivial to restrain his true opinions and natural affections from breaking out. And his letter served to confirm Burke's view that the party 'agree with me to a tittle; but they dare not speak out for fear of hurting Fox'. As Burke declared to Weddell in January 1792, he was confident that 'I had not wandered very widely from the sentiments of those with whom I was known to be so closely connected.[20] So during the summer of 1791, though Fitzwilliam, from his vantage point at Wentworth, strove to reconcile the opposed views of his friends, to keep the Yorkshire Whigs in a moderate frame of mind and to prepare the ground for a possible reconciliation of views in the autumn, when the party would again assemble for the new session, new influences began to work upon his mind, to push him from Fox's confident liberalism nearer to Burke's alarmist conservatism. As leader of the Whig interest in the West Riding he began to find local opinion moving disconcertingly towards the radical position as new influences and new centres of opinion began to impinge on Yorkshire politics. No longer were local politics capable of interpretation in purely electoral terms, as a struggle for supremacy between the Rockingham interest on the one hand and the unnatural alliance of Tories and reformers on the other. New dangers to the established order of society now seemed to appear, and the Whigs in Yorkshire began to find themselves faced with local issues which paralleled and reflected the divisions in the party at Westminster. For the next two years, as in 1782–4, Fitzwilliam's stand on national and party questions was to be closely intermingled with his concern about the political situation in the West Riding.

The new and growing industrial centre of Sheffield symbolised the new, as the still mainly medieval city of York stood for the old political attitudes. By the end of the eighteenth century the cutlery industry was well established in the confluence of the valleys of the Sheaf and the Don, providing water power for the cutlers' workshops. In the middle of the century the population of Sheffield was about 12,000 persons. The growth of the town accelerated when the Don was made navigable to Tinsley, about three miles to the east, and road improvements encouraged the carriage of more raw materials and finished goods into and out of the area. In 1758 works

for making red and white lead were set up, and shortly afterwards
a silk mill, later converted to cotton manufacture, was introduced.
There were already forging, slitting and rolling mills to provide the
iron and steel for the cutlers, and in 1758 the Sheffield plate industry
was brought in to develop on a large and increasing scale. By 1795
the historian of the northern industrial area could write that 'since
that time this branch has been pursued by numerous companies to
great advantage, and has since contributed very considerably to
promote the wealth and population of the town'.[21] An assay office
was established in Sheffield in 1773, and by the 'nineties cutlery and
the production of Sheffield plate were the town's major industries.
The amenities of the town were also expanding rapidly. The
Assembly Rooms and theatre were built in Norfolk Street in 1762,
the first local bank opened in 1770, and a new market was erected
by the Duke of Norfolk in 1786. There were four breweries, and five
stage-coach routes linked the town to other parts of the country. The
population of the town alone had now increased to nearly 30,000
and that of the whole area to some 45,000, served by four Anglican
churches, one Methodist chapel, seven dissenting meeting houses and
one 'Romish' chapel. It was not yet, however, an incorporated
borough, and until 1835 there was no single local government
authority except that of the parish vestry. The Cutlers' Company
had jurisdiction only over the trade and its concerns, and there was
no resident local magistrate as late as 1831. The manorial Courts
Baron functioned as a rudimentary local government until an Act
of 1818 set up a Board of Improvement Commissioners. Police and
watch services were perfunctory. It says much for the inherent
orderliness and discipline of eighteenth-century society that such a
rapidly growing industrial centre could function with so little in
the way of law enforcement. The men of Sheffield, however, prided
themselves on their sturdy self-sufficiency. The cutlery trade in
particular was carried on in hundreds of small workshops, where
the master, with a few journeymen and apprentices, carried on an
independent business subject only to the rules of the Master Cutlers.
This system bred a hard-grained self-reliance that made the Sheffield
working master and craftsman a by-word for thrift, hard work and
independence of mind. In the 1790s there were fears that it might
also make him a republican and a revolutionary in politics, for the
social and political structure of the area made it peculiarly receptive
to the new ideas of Paine's *Rights of Man*, while a temporary slump
in trade created economic conditions which fed discontent and

aroused questioning of the economic and social system. Fitzwilliam, only a few miles to the north-east of the town at Wentworth, was quickly aware of the dangers that might arise from the spread of Paineite radicalism among the intelligent Sheffield craftsmen, and his political course for the next three years was strongly affected by his assessment of the situation there.

Troubles in Sheffield began on 27 July 1791, when opposition to the enclosure of land at Stannington and Hallam led to riots in the town itself.[22] The debtors' prison was broken open, treasonable inscriptions were allegedly written on the walls, and threatening letters were sent round. Fitzwilliam at once hastened to the town, spending several days there enquiring into the disturbances. The arrival of his copy of Burke's *Appeal* and Fitzwilliam's public avowal of his support for Burke's doctrines almost coincided with these events on his own doorstep. Though he assured Burke that the riots were not political and that 'practical Painism has not extended itself that way',[23] there were soon ominous signs of disaffection among the artisans of the town. Thomas Paine himself had only recently left the district, where he had been engaged—ironically, on Burke's recommendation to Fitzwilliam—to design an iron bridge to be erected by Samuel Walker near Rotherham.[24] In the summer of 1791 the reformist newspaper *The Sheffield Register*, founded in 1787 by Joseph Gales and David Martin, began to take up Paineite ideas. In November 1790 the *Register* had criticised Burke's *Reflections*, and in the summer of 1792 articles and quotations from appropriate authors were introduced in approval of the French revolution. Events in France were beginning to make English observers look on the revolution in a new light. The early enthusiasm for liberty and constitutionalism, perhaps on the English model, was now tempered by anxieties about the security of property, religion and the Church, and the future of the French monarchy itself. In June 1791 Louis XVI embarked on his ill fated flight to the frontier, to be arrested at Varennes and brought back a prisoner to his own capital city. The death of Mirabeau in April 1792 seemed to mark the end of realistic hopes for a moderate constitutional settlement. Control began to pass into the hands of extremists. Stories of the Paris 'mob' and its unruly disrespect for persons of quality mingled in apprehensive English minds with the memories of London's own Gordon riots of 1780, when Fitzwilliam had helped to defend Rockingham's house in Grosvenor Square against the crowd.

In 1790 the conservative reaction was already gaining strength.

Henry Flood's attempt to catch the rising tide of reformist sentiment
by introducing a proposal for moderate parliamentary reform into
the House of Commons had been met by Pitt's opposition and Windham's famous speech about the folly of repairing one's house in the
'hurricane season'.[25] As the second anniversary of the fall of the
Bastille approached, opinion in England began to polarise dangerously. Preparations for dinners and public meetings to celebrate the
anniversary were matched by a rising current of hostility against
political radicals and religious dissenters—the two were increasingly
becoming identified in the popular mind, as they were to Burke. A
thousand of the 'friends of liberty' met on the 14th at the Crown
and Anchor tavern in London to celebrate the occasion 'in a manner
as peaceable as solemn', and drank twenty toasts, including a
sarcastic one to Burke 'in gratitude for his having provoked the great
discussion which occupies every thinking person'. At Manchester a
similar celebration passed off peaceably, despite an anonymous hand-
bill threatening to mingle the brains of the diners with the bricks
and mortar of the building in which they met.[26] At Norwich and
at Birmingham, however, opposition to the reformers was aroused
into riot, in which religious prejudice was at least as evident as
loyalty to the constitution. For four days Birmingham was at the
mercy of the 'Church and King' mob which sacked and burned
Priestley's house as well as a number of Unitarian meeting houses
and the homes of sympathisers with reform or nonconformity. It
was in this changed atmosphere of tension that reformers in London,
Manchester, Norwich and Sheffield began to organise themselves into
societies avowedly peaceable and constitutional in method and aim,
but bound to seem provocative to the alarmists who saw their
activities as a threat to the public order. At Sheffield the Constitutional Society seems to have come into existence late in 1791,
starting with 'an assembly of some five or six mechanics' meeting
in each other's houses to discuss such matters as 'the enormous high
price of provisions, etc', 'the iniquitous Corn Bill' of 1791, and the
doctrines of Paine's *Rights of Man*.[27] By the beginning of 1792 the
movement was beginning to spread, and a fully organised society
came into being, holding monthly general meetings and smaller fortnightly gatherings in public houses to study Paine's book and discuss
its implications. By January the membership of the society was .
reported as upwards of 200, and a general meeting on 30 January
was said to have been attended by 600. In March the society claimed

'nearly 2,000' members, and on 24 May 2,400. Tracts and pamphlets were circulated, a cheap edition of the *Rights of Man* was published, and a fortnightly newspaper, *The Patriot*, was established, with an extreme radical tone. Despite the society's *Address to the Public* in December 1791, which stressed the peaceable and orderly nature of its intended proceedings,[28] alarm was taken at the possibility of disaffection spreading from the more responsible middling ranks to the 'lower orders' of society, whose activities were less likely to be restrained by an interest in peace and social stability.

Fitzwilliam was closely informed of the society's activities from the start. His frequent correspondent, the Rev. Henry Zouch, who lived at Sandal, near Wakefield, was a close observer and his correspondents in Sheffield sent him frequent reports which he passed on to Fitzwilliam.[29] In late December an anonymous correspondent was taking alarm at the growing numbers in the society 'of the lower classes of manufacturers', amounting to 'several hundreds', and professing 'to be admirers of the dangerous doctrine of Mr Payne, whose pamphlet they distribute with industry and support his dogmas with zeal'. At the same time rumours reached Fitzwilliam's ears of a supposed plan to march on Wentworth to destroy the house as a symbol of privilege and oppression, and he warned his steward to prepare means of defence. 'The levelling of the fortunes, the rank, and every outward mark of distinction belonging to the classes above them' was their aim, he wrote. Others stressed the economic aims and preoccupations of the movement. An account of a meeting on 30 January, for example, attended by some 600 persons, mentioned speeches against parliamentary abuses, ministerial corruption, the lavish expenditure of public money, and the recent Corn Bill, which was presented as a measure to raise the price of bread to the poor. The lower classes, this observer reported, were mainly concerned with the cost of living and the reduction of public expenditure. In the spring of 1792 Zouch viewed with increasing apprehension the spread of grievances among the journeymen over wages and the spread of agitation amongst the soldiery. 'There are few regiments', he wrote on 14 April, 'which are not filled with recruits from Sheffield, Leeds, Halifax, etc. (the very sweepings of the streets).' On 29 May one of Zouch's informants referred to a meeting of the society as consisting

mostly of the lowest and most ignorant classes, led by several desperate

adventurers who are looking up to profit from confusion. . . . The
doctrines of Mr Payne seem to have laid strong hold on the minds of the
lower classes, who have everything to win and nothing to lose, and they
look up to great expectations from a *Revolution* for a *Reform* only, will
not satisfy their ignorant hopes.

Another Sheffield correspondent lamented that 'the first fruits of the
liberty the lower classes of manufacturers [i.e. artisans] wish for
shows itself in their want of all subordination and their open contempt for their masters'.

To Fitzwilliam the spread of radical sentiment amongst the
industrial workers of Sheffield was not in itself dangerous. As long
as the movement seemed merely a local and spontaneous reaction to
economic distress, limited to the 'lower orders' of society and lacking
respectable leadership, it was unlikely to have any serious political
repercussions. By the early summer of 1792, however, far more
ominous developments were taking place, which seemed about to link
popular agitations throughout the industrial areas with political
leadership from among the ranks of Fitzwilliam's own party.
Hitherto Fox, though singled out by Burke as the major threat to
the conservative tradition of Whiggism, had refrained from connect-
ing himself with the reformers. During the latter part of 1791 and
in the early months of 1792 he showed a studious moderation in all
political questions.[30] Partly as a result, Burke's *Appeal* in August
had not rallied the leadership to his side, despite Fitzwilliam's
declaration of support for its principles. Portland, indeed, had complained bitterly of the pain which Burke's new pamphlet had given
him,[31] and Fox, while carefully avoiding any commitment to the
radical cause, tried to impress on his aristocratic friends the irrele-
vance of events in France to English political conditions. On 15
March 1972 Fox and Fitzwilliam met for a long discussion which
ranged over the whole state of the Whig party, and Fitzwilliam
confided to his friend his anxieties about the spread of radical ideas
among the people at large. On the following day Fox wrote to
amplify and clarify his attitudes, and to urge that the differences
between him and the party leadership were confined to specific
measures.

Our apprehensions are raised by very different objects [Fox wrote]. *You*
seem to dread the prevalence of Paine's opinions (which in most parts
I detest as much as you do) while *I* am much more afraid of the total
annihilation of all principles of liberty and resistance, an event which I

am sure you would be as sorry to see as I. We both hate the two
extremes equally, but we differ in opinions with respect to the quarter
from which the danger is most pressing.[32]

As to the matters on which they differed, and on which Fox admitted
'I know that I have not the general support of the party', he maintained that the differences were of emphasis and not of principle. On
religious toleration, Fox asserted that 'you differ from me very
little if at all in theory and not at all in practice', and that resistance
to the repeal of the Test and Corporation Acts came largely from
'the other wing of the coalition'. The second issue on which Fitzwilliam did not share his friend's liberal views was the abolition of
the slave trade, to which Fox had instinctively and deliberately committed himself from the outset of Wilberforce's campaign in 1788.
Fitzwilliam shared the doubts and hesitations of the anti-abolition-
ists, not on any anti-humanitarian principle but partly on account
of the strong economic arguments about interference with the rights
of property and the possible disruption of the West Indian economy,
and partly on the new grounds that the abolitionists were working
hand-in-hand with popular radicalism and that the abolitionist campaign was designed to further the cause of democracy. Fox regretted,
he wrote, that Fitzwilliam should connect abolitionism with 'those
foolish and wicked opinions which your Sheffield neighbours wish
to propagate'. As for himself, he admitted that 'I think so seriously
and so warmly that I should prefer the abolition . . . to any political
good that can be gained or even wished, for the party or the
country'; but this alone was no reason for there to be any other
difference between him and the party leaders than one of opinion
as to one specific measure. Finally, on parliamentary reform, Fox
admitted that 'I am more bound by former declarations and consistency than by any strong opinion I entertain in its favour . . .
and I much doubt whether the part which you have taken in the
question be not upon the whole the most manly and judicious'. The
French revolution, he wrote, was not an issue on which the party
should divide: 'I never can allow that while we agree about what
is and what ought to be the constitution of our own country, it can
be of any importance how far we do so about what passes in France.'
He repeated his own view that the revolution started as 'the greatest
event that ever happened for the happiness of mankind' but
admitted that he was disturbed about the present state of France,

and particularly about the danger of a successful 're-establishment of the ancient despotism', which might be 'a decisive blow to all liberty in Europe'. This, however, was not an important enough issue on which to wreck the unity of the party; on the contrary,

It is our duty to maintain it by every exertion and effort. . . . However, if our party is useful we must not forget that its foundation is *Whig*, and that upon that principle only we are necessary or even useful. If a Tory party is necesssary for the support of the constitution, God knows there is one and strong enough and too strong in my judgement, but if I am wrong, let us go to it and strengthen it, which can only be done by our party becoming *part* of a Tory party, and that by being dissolved.

Fox's letter identified the issues on which he felt the beginnings of a breach arising between him and the party leaders, but it did not resolve them, and it showed no disposition to meet anyone half-way. It begged the question, at the very least, as to whether the party *was* agreed 'about what is and what ought to be the constitution of our country', and his assertion that the French revolution was of no significance for English politics was diametrically opposed to Burke's most passionate conviction that it was. Fitzwilliam, however, felt encouraged enough to approach Burke with a further proposal for a reconciliation. Fitzwilliam was now the crucial figure in the Whig hierarchy, for his ties of affection with both men were the strongest link which now existed across the gulf in the party's political thinking. His impulsive welcome to the principles behind Burke's *Appeal* in August contrasted in Burke's mind with Portland's cold disapproval of the timing and expediency of the publication, and though Burke had twice rejected Fitzwilliam's renewed offers of financial help, in June and November, he had done so on political and not on personal grounds. His 'most sincere and zealous affection, the most perfect esteem and the warmest gratitude', Burke assured Fitzwilliam, continued to make their friendship of supreme importance to his life.[33] A week after his conversation with Fox, Fitzwilliam gave a dinner for three of Burke's leading emigré friends at which Portland, Fitzwilliam's brother-in-law Sir Thomas Dundas, Fox's friend Lord Ossory, and Burke's close disciples Walker King and French Laurence were also present. Twice during the evening Fitzwilliam and Burke talked privately and at length, Fitzwilliam urging a reconciliation, 'or at least some steps towards it', with Fox; but, Burke wrote, 'I gave him such reasons why it could not be, yet at least, as made him not condemn me, though he left me, after our last conversation, in a mood sufficiently melancholy. He is, in truth, a man of wonderful honour, good nature and integrity'.[34]

The failure of Fitzwilliam's efforts at mediation was to be expected. Burke's obduracy in the debate of 6 May, when he had refused to respond to Fox's tearful protests that their friendship could continue, had not been softened either by what he considered to be the party's neglect and rejection during the succeeding months or by the progress of events in France, in the West Indies and at home.[35] Fitzwilliam's distress at the continued breach between his two closest political connections was profound. And he himself was shortly to have to begin to make the choice which all his efforts hitherto had been designed to avert, for at the beginning of April the crisis in the party came to a head with the foundation of the Association of the Friends of the People. The question of parliamentary reform now ceased to be an academic one, on which Fox could no longer dodge meaningful commitment.

By any account the formation on 11 April 1792 of this Association was the decisive event in the Whig split. It made it impossible for Fox, however much he disapproved of the foundation of the society at that moment, to run with the hare and hunt with the hounds. And it convinced Fitzwilliam that the moment of crisis had arrived. The action of Grey, Lauderdale and several other young recruits to the party in setting up the society and issuing a manifesto in favour of reform was not, of course, designed to split the party, nor was it the mere aristocratic prank described in Lord Holland's later *Memoirs*.[36] It was an attempt to win for the party the growing public support for moderate reform, to revitalise the party's image as the leader of liberal sentiment, and to give it a programme for the next session of Parliament to follow up the success of the Ochakov campaign in 1791—a success which seemed in danger of being dissipated by the relative inactivity of the party in 1792. But to Fitzwilliam and the conservatively inclined members of the party the new pressure group seemed at best a rash, thoughtless and irresponsible prank, at worst a conspiracy to take over the leadership and direction of the party and use it for subversive purposes. Fitzwilliam inclined to the latter view, seeing the grey eminence of Sheridan behind this challenge to Portland's leadership, and he quickly connected the Association with the dangerous potentiality of the radical movement in the country. He wrote to Zouch on 5 June that the societies in London, Sheffield, Manchester and Norwich were hitherto contemptible, but they took a very different aspect when they were headed by a new Association, formed by some of the first men in the kingdom in point of rank, ability and activity—when members of Parliament began to tell the lowest orders of the people that they had rights of which they were bereaved by others; that to recover these rights they had only to collect together, and to unite; that if they were anxious to vindicate those rights they had the power of doing so, and to effect this, advocates and leaders were ready at their call.

This was all the more dangerous because of events abroad:

Now there is nothing but revolutions, and in that of France is an example of the turbulent and the factious instigating the numbers . . . to the subversion of the first principle of civil society . . . the protection of the individual against the multitude. . . . The French revolutionists are just as anxious to bring into England their spirit of proselytism as they have been to carry it into every other part of Europe.

And he drew attention to the election of two deputies by the Manchester Constitutional Society to visit the Jacobin Club in Paris 'to engage in one common cause with them for confusion in each country'. At Sheffield, too, the recent disorders had given increased cause for alarm, while the clamour amongst the journeymen for an increase in wages seemed even more ominous than the rhetoric of radical orators.[37]

The foundation of the Friends of the People therefore presented Fitzwilliam and his party with the need to choose and to avow their political standpoint. In doing so it inevitably restored Burke's influence over their minds and embarrassed Fox by taking away the middle ground on which he had tried to stand. Fox's dilemma lay in the circumstance that all the leading Associators were his close friends, drinking and gambling companions at Brooks's who were generally looked on as Fox's 'set', and whom it was not in his nature to desert, or even to discipline or rebuke. The fact that Fox himself was the original 'Man of the People' of 1780 made it harder for him to abandon the reforming principles to which he had committed himself then and in 1785, despite his private admission to Fitzwilliam that he no longer felt strongly about the question. Fox supported Grey's motion on the reform of Parliament on 30 April despite a speech in which he deprecated the raising of the issue and stressed his disapproval of Paine's radicalism. This seemed to accord ill with the decision of a meeting of party leaders at Burlington House on

the eve of the debate that Grey's proposals should not be allowed
to appear as party policy.[38] Fox's vote was undoubtedly a gesture
of sympathy for his young friends and an attempt to prevent them
from becoming outcasts from the party, but to Burke and the party
leaders it seemed an avowal of political principles which they could
no longer tolerate, and a defiance of party discipline. It also created
the opportunity for which Pitt had been waiting to drive a wedge
between the Whig factions and dismember the opposition to his
government. By the end of April Pitt and Dundas had sketched out
a strategy to tempt the conservative Whigs, if not into coalition with
the Ministry, at any rate into such co-operation as would lead to a
schism with the reformers.[39] As their intermediary they chose Loughborough, ambitious for the Great Seal and, as a Northite, apt to take
the conservative rather than the liberal view. Pitt here made an
advantage of what might otherwise have been a near-disaster for
his Ministry, the growing disaffection of Lord Chancellor Thurlow
and the approaching ultimatum from the Premier to the king to
choose between them. Thurlow's departure would open the prospect
of the chancellorship to Loughborough, and make him more anxious
to negotiate an arrangement between the Ministry and his present
friends that might cover his personal change of sides.

During the next few weeks there was intense political activity.
The Cabinet decided to issue a proclamation against seditious writings, ostensibly to warn the reform societies against the circulation
of such offensive publications as the second part of *The Rights of
Man* and to encourage the magistrates to take firm action, but in
reality, as the Foxite Whigs believed, to present the opposition with
an issue on which conservatives and liberals must fall out. Portland
was given a preliminary account of the intended measure, asked to
consult his friends about it, and even invited, with whichever
colleagues he chose, to attend the Privy Council meeting at which
the proclamation would be ordered. The last proposal was rejected.
The leaders were still distrustful of Pitt, whom Fitzwilliam especially
regarded with distaste as the author of Whig misfortunes in 1783
and the upholder of Tory principles of prerogative. He for one was
not yet prepared to forget past political animosities. The Cabinet,
however, was receptive to changes in the wording of the proclamation suggested by the Whig leaders in order to make it seem less
'personally hostile to our old friends', and in amended form it was
issued on 21 May, and debated in the Commons on the 25th. The

debate showed that the Whigs of all shades were anxious not to play Pitt's game. Fox, though opposing the proclamation as a mere political trick, was moderate enough to avoid giving offence to his colleagues.[40] Nevertheless, Burke and some of the extreme right of the party—Windham, Loughborough and Spencer—now began to work as a pressure group to detach the Whig leadership from Fox and to work in co-operation with the government on all matters concerning public order and the preservation of the constitution. A few months later Fitzwilliam was to trace the disintegration of the party to this moment.[41] The Whigs were gradually ceasing to be an opposition. The next few months were to make it clear that the only future for the conservatives in the party lay in coalition with the administration to make, as Fox had foretold in March 1792, a stronger Tory party than had ever yet existed. The making of that coalition was distasteful to Fitzwilliam. despite his deep commitment to Burke's aristocratic principle. His long resistance to it was to have a profound influence on its character, and his ultimate inability to accept its consequences was to lead to the tragedy of Ireland in February 1795, and ultimately to the reconstitution under Grey and Grenville of a Whig party which could still, through Fitzwilliam, look back to Rockinghamite principles.

Notes

[1] Fox to Fitzpatrick [30 July 1789]; *Memorials and Corresp. of C. J. Fox*, II, p. 361.

[2] L. G. Mitchell, *Charles James Fox and the Disintegration of the Whig Party, 1782–94* (1971), p. 155.

[3] *Ibid.*, pp. 155–6.

[4] E. Burke to Fitzwilliam, 12 November 1789, (*Corresp. of E. Burke*, VI, pp. 34–7); R. Burke junior to Fitzwilliam, 29 July 1790 (Burke MSS, Northampton, A IV 71, part printed in *ibid.*, pp. 125–30), and reply, 8 August (*ibid.*, p. 130).

[5] Burke to R. Burke junior, 29 November 1790 (*ibid.*, p. 178); Fitzwilliam to same, 8 August and 15 September (Burke MSS, Sheffield, 1) and to Lady Fitzwilliam (F 41); Mitchell, p. 158.

[6] Fox to Fitzwilliam, 13 November [1789] (F 115a); Burke to Fox, 9 September 1789 (*Corresp. of E. Burke*, VI, p. 15), Portland to French Laurence, 14 September 1789 (Portland MSS): Fitzwilliam to Weddell, 2 March 1790 (Ramsden MSS, Rockingham correspondence, vol. II, f. 90). Weddell nevertheless declared his intention to vote against repeal (*ibid.*).

[7] Fitzwilliam to Rev. H. Zouch, 28 April 1791 : E 234.

[8] *Parl. Register*, XXX, pp. 56–8, 82–98, 158–73; XXIX, pp. 153–7.

[9] J. Holland Rose, *Pitt and National Revival*, p. 617.

[10] Memorandum, 28 March 1791, Grenville MSS, Bucks R. O., AR 41/ 63, D 56. The document suggests a cabinet reshuffle, with Pitt as Secretary of State, Lord John Cavendish Chancellor of the Exchequer, Fox Secretary of State or First Lord of the Admiralty, Portland Lord Privy Seal and Fitzwilliam or Stormont Lord President of the Council.

[11] *Parl. Hist.*, XXXIX, pp. 243–4 and 248–9.

[12] Portland to Fitzwilliam, 21 and 26 April 1791, and T. Grenville to Fitzwilliam, 22 and 28 April: F 115d.

[13] *Parl. Register*, XXIX, pp. 318–53.

[14] Fitzwilliam's account books show a payment of £100 to Burke on 8 November 1788 and of £500 to Portland 'towards liquidating a friend's debts' when Burke's financial distress was most acute. In 1791 Fitzwilliam gave £1,200 for Burke's use (N). It has been suggested that Burke may have been indebted to Fitzwilliam to the extent of some £5,000 by 1795 (*Corresp. of E. Burke*, VII, p. 551, n. 2).

[15] R. Burke junior to T. O'Beirne, 6 May 1791 (*Corresp. of E. Burke*, VI, pp. 253–8); Fitzwilliam to R. Burke junior [May 1791]: Burke MSS. Sheffield, 37 (quoted in *ibid*, p. 272n); E. Burke to Fitzwilliam, 5 June 1791 (*ibid.*, pp. 271–6).

[16] T. Allen, *History of Yorkshire*, I (1829), p. 123; *Morning Chronicle*, 29 August 1791; E. Burke to R. Burke junior, 1 September 1791 (*Corresp. of E. Burke*, VI, pp. 377–8); F. Laurence to Burke, 8 August 1791 (Burke MSS, 1–648).

[17] E. Burke to W. Weddell, 21 January 1792: *Corresp. of E. Burke*, VIII, p. 52.

[18] E. Burke to R. Burke senior [24 July 1791] (*ibid.*, VI, p. 306); Loughborough to Fitzwilliam, 1 August 1791 (F 115a–25); Portland to French Laurence, 23, 25 and 30 August 1791 (Portland MSS, PWF 6239–41).

[19] *Corresp. of E. Burke*, VI, p. 402. Burke replied on the 28th with thanks for Fitzwilliam's encouragement. As for 'the best mode of giving effect to your sentiments,' he added, '. . . the reasons of personal disqualification, which you give for the plan you adopt are such as no person who knows you can possibly subscribe to' (*ibid.*, p. 416).

[20] E. Burke to R. Burke junior, 18 August [1791] and to W. Weddell 31 January 1792: *ibid.*, VI, p. 360 and VII, p. 52.

[21] J Aikin, *A Description of the Country from Thirty to Forty Miles Round Manchester* (1795), pp. 548–51. For a description of the town see also T. Allen, *New and Complete History of the County of York*, III (1831), pp. 26–9.

[22] For the political events in Sheffield in the early 1790s see A. W. L. Seaman, 'Reform politics at Sheffield 1791–7' (*Transactions of the Hunter Archaeological Society*, VII, 1955, pp. 215–28), J. Taylor, 'The Sheffield Constitutional Society (*ibid.*, V, 1940, pp. 133–42) and G. P. Jones, 'The political reform movement in Sheffield' (*ibid.*, VI, 1929–30, pp. 57–68).

[23] Quoted in Burke to Fitzwilliam, 4 August 1791: *Corresp. of E. Burke*, VI, p. 313.

[24] *Ibid.*, n. 3.

[25] *Parl. Register*, XXVII, pp. 196–209.

[26] G. S. Veitch, *The Genesis of Parliamentary Reform* (repr. 1965), p. 181; T. Walker, *A Review of some of the Political Events which have occurred in Manchester during the last five years. . . .* (1794), p. 23.

[27] Letter from the Sheffield Constitutional Society to *The English Chronicle*, 15 January 1792; quoted in Seaman, *op. cit.*, p. 216. For the membership and organisation of the Society see Seaman, p. 217, Taylor, p. 134, and Jones, pp. 58–60.

[28] *Wyvill Papers*, II, pp. 576–8. The address concluded with a declaration to be accepted by all members of the Society, abjuring 'all conspiracies, tumults and riotous proceedings'.

[29] The quotations which follow are from correspondence in F 44a and in Wentworth estate MSS, Stewards' Corresp., No. 3.

[30] L. G. Mitchell, *C. J. Fox and the Disintegration of the Whig Party*, pp. 171–6.

[31] Portland to French Laurence, 23 August 1791: Portland MSS, PWF 6239.

[32] Fox to Fitzwilliam, 16 March 1792: N.

[33] *Corresp. of E. Burke*, VI, pp. 271–6 (5 June 1791) and 449–53 (21 November 1791). From 1790 Fitzwilliam provided Burke with an annuity of £800 for the remainder of his life (Fitzwilliam to Richard Burke junior [21 August 1790]; B 37).

[34] Burke to Richard Burke junior, 20 March 1792: *ibid.*, VII, p. 107.

[35] Burke complained to his son in October 1791, when the news arrived of the revolt by the freed slaves in St Domingo and the massacre of the white colonists, that Portland and Fitzwilliam could not be brought to see the relevance of these events to the political conflict in England (*ibid.*, VI, p. 439).

[36] *Memoirs of the Whig Party During my Time*, I, pp. 13–15.

[37] E 234.

[38] O'Gorman, pp. 84–6; *Parl. Register*, XXXII, pp. 466–71; Windham, *Diary*, p. 253.

[39] O'Gorman, pp. 86–8.

[40] Minto, *Life and Letters of Sir Gilbert Elliot*, II (1874), pp. 23–6, 28–33; *Parl. Register*, XXXIII, pp. 457–89.

[41] Fitzwilliam to W. Adam, 28 August 1793: Blair Adam MSS.

CHAPTER SIX

The making of a coalition
1792—4

Pitt made overtures to the Portland Whigs through Loughborough for a possible coalition of parties in May 1792. Portland at once consulted Fitzwilliam and Fox, both of whom advised him that the proposals were 'utterly inadmissible'. The number of posts offered was too small, their patronage insignificant, their responsibility slight. The great departments of state, 'one only excepted, [were] . . . carefully reserved to the present possessors: nothing like a situation of equality in the House of Commons or indeed in either House'. Though Loughborough pointed out that Pitt's proposals had been only 'a rapid sketch' and not a definitive offer, he admitted 'it is evident, however, that the chief department could never come in question'.[1] Neither of the Whig leaders had yet formulated precise terms for a junction, but they could not yet bring themselves to desert their connexion with Fox for so flimsy a share of power. They professed themselves prepared to support from the opposition benches measures necessary to preserve public order and the constitution, but they were determined that any formal coalition would have to offer the Whigs a substantial, or even an equal, share of power and patronage. This remained Fitzwilliam's attitude throughout the next two years. He never wavered in his determination to use all his influence in support of the anti-Jacobin cause, but he remained equally obdurate that he was not prepared to become a mere individual follower of Pitt's Ministry. Thus though his anti-radical views steadily drew him away from Fox, he resisted the attempts of Burke and the alarmists to commit him to Pitt. At a meeting of party leaders at Burlington House on 9 May, when Burke violently attacked Fox as tainted with Jacobin principles and accused him of preferring 'a new set in the party' to its established leaders, Fitzwilliam limited his support to expressing 'a strong wish for Government being supported in all measures which tended to strengthen the country', quoting recent reports of proceedings at Sheffield to justify his alarm. As regards Fox, he agreed with Portland and Malmesbury

that Fox's conduct had been very ill judged, and very distressing; that to separate from him would be highly disagreeable, yet that to remain with him after what he professed was giving their tacit approbation to the sentiments he had avowed in the House of Commons on the parliamentary reform, which sentiments were in direct contradiction to theirs. The state of the times was amply discussed, and it was agreed that they called out for a junction.

Fitzwilliam nevertheless supported Fox's stipulation, made in an interview with Portland on 13 June, that any junction with Pitt must be on level terms, with equal shares of power and patronage. This would involve the replacement of Pitt as Prime Minister by some 'neutral head'—possibly the Duke of Leeds—and giving Fox an office comparable to Pitt's. Fox himself pointed out the unlikelihood of Pitt's consenting to leave the Treasury and roughly declared his conviction that Pitt was out only to divide the party. Malmesbury turned to Fitzwilliam to try to argue Fox into a more co-operative frame of mind. He found Fitzwilliam's 'sentiments perfectly right', and his mind full of resentment against Sheridan and the others who, he considered, had led Fox astray in their own interests. He was even willing to cease regular opposition, but he seemed still disposed to demand Pitt's resignation of the Treasury. Loughborough, to whom Malmesbury reported the conversation, thought it a most unreasonable stipulation to make and tried to argue Fitzwilliam out of it. But Fitzwilliam refused to give up his long distrust of Pitt, and in the end the negotiation was broken off, though Pitt told Portland of his wish to regard it as 'suspended rather than abandoned'.[2] Portland remarked to Fitzwilliam that Pitt and Dundas had acted

on the hope . . . of its being a favourable opportunity for breaking the opposition and dividing us and F., and that when they found us insist upon F.'s being not only a member of the Cabinet but of his being placed there in as respectable and efficient a situation as he held in the years '92 and '93 [sic] they were totally unprepared.

Fox's view that Pitt's intention was not to strengthen government so much as to set the opposition at loggerheads with each other prevailed on the Whig leaders. Burke found it supremely irritating that

'Mr Fox's coach stops the way', but it needed a darker threat to the
English constitution than had yet appeared before Portland and
Fitzwilliam were prepared to go on without him.[3]

That threat seemed to develop in the latter half of 1792. At the end
of July Prussian forces under the command of the Duke of Brunswick massed for an invasion of France to rescue the royal family
from their virtual imprisonment in the Tuileries. On the 25th Brunswick issued his famous manifesto, threatening the sack of Paris if
any harm were done to the king or his family, and five days later
his army began its ponderous movement towards France. In Paris
the threat of foreign invasion produced a violent reaction. On 10
August the Paris mob stormed the Tuileries and massacred the Swiss
Guards. Less than a month later, on 2 September, the Prussians captured Verdun, and in a panic reaction in Paris the 'September
massacres' took place, when hundreds of political prisoners, including many clergy, were murdered in the goals.

English reaction to these events was dramatic. Burke, of course,
regarded them as final proof of his contentions about the nature of
the revolution, and looked to their effect on his former friends to
force a separation from all who condoned it. Fitzwilliam, along with
Portland and the majority of the Whigs, was deeply shocked and
alarmed. Burke took the opportunity of the news from the Tuileries
to urge upon him the danger to England, and to declare that for the
past two years the Morning Chronicle, 'Mr Fox's paper', had 'stimulated the French to all their excesses' by pretending to represent as
sympathetic the views of 'the Independent people of England'. How
much more important, he wrote, was the influence of 'the first
and most splendid names in this country carrying with them the
weight and sanction of great parties'. Fitzwilliam, however, now
hoped that the violence in Paris might induce Fox to rejoin his old
friends in condemning the excesses of the revolutionaries.[4] At the
end of August Richard Burke junior had some conversations with
Fitzwilliam at Buxton, where Charlotte was recuperating after an
attack of rheumatic fever. He found him reserved and non-commital
on the subject of a coalition. As regards Fox,

He said that he would safely and conscientiously trust him with a
considerable trust in government, but I think he said it with a little hesitation. It is clear that he is not quite at ease about him, tho' as far as I
can see determined not to abandon him. . . . The combat in his mind

between the candid interpretation of his friend's actions, and his own conviction deprives him of half the benefit of his understanding.

Both Fitzwilliam and Portland pinned their hopes on Brunswick's manifesto and the Prussian invasion to restore the French monarchy, and on the disorders in Paris to produce a favourable reaction in the minds and conduct of Fox and the Associators. Portland, writing on 26 September, said that he had seen Fox at the end of August and that he was confident 'that if the courts of Vienna and Berlin adhere to the terms of their declarations that he will *be right*'. It was not to be expected that he would retract his earlier approval of the principles behind the revolution, but he had declared to Portland 'in speaking of the state of it and the events that had lately happened . . . that it is horrid and horrible'. In the circumstances any coalition with Pitt would have to be a full coalition of parties, not an accession to Pitt's government of a few respectable individuals, which would force Fox back into the arms of the reformers. To Burke, Portland declared his willingness for the former, but not the latter:

They [the government] know not what *party* is, but for the desire of annihilating it, and suppose favours emoluments and patronage a compensation for the loss of consistency of character. Whenever their mode of thinking is reformed I shall be willing to take them by the hand. But till then I can hold no connexions with them.[5]

Locally, too, Fitzwilliam was cheered by signs of a revulsion of opinion against the French revolution. Writing from Doncaster, where the September race meeting provided an annual opportunity to test county opinion on political questions, he noted hopefully that

their [the French] cause is now looked upon with execration, and the fallacy of their system as universally admitted, as the wickedness and cruelty of their proceedings abominated. You will recollect the change of sentiment in the public upon the subject of the American war: on this occasion, the vane has veered not only more suddenly, but more completely too.

It was all the more important, then, that nothing should be done to re-engage Fox's sympathies with the radicals. When in mid-October Lord Carlisle, the old school friend of Fox and Fitzwilliam and their companion on the grand tour, wrote to voice his concern about the

state of the party, Fitzwilliam replied that though he agreed that
the true aim of the Associators was not to achieve parliamentary
reform but to split the party and to supplant its existing leadership,
he remained convinced that the party should be held together as
long as possible. Of the reformers he wrote,

They are certainly not unimportant men: and perhaps it may appear
desirable that such men should not be irretrievably driven into the hands
of the professed levellers. . . . Putting aside all personal predilection in
his favour, all affection and friendship . . . is he [Fox] to be shaken off
from his connection with sound constitutional men, and forced into the
arms of the Tookes and the Paines? We must be sure that the Colossus
is theirs before we take a step to make him so.

It was unfortunate that Burke's 'purest patriotism' and 'depth of
foresight and philosophy' in standing forth against the French revolution had led him into an attack on Fox, and had pinned words and
sentiments on to him which he could not easily repudiate; without
such notice Fox's original praise of the revolution would have been
of little account except as 'the flourish of the period'. Fox, indeed,
was now an anxious advocate of a coalition, while Pitt's veto upon
him led Fitzwilliam to doubt the Minister's sincerity in offering it.
'If he [Pitt] is in earnest,' Fitzwilliam wrote, 'sacrifice must be made
on his part. . . . In my opinion he ought not to hesitate about
putting the Treasury in the D. of P.'s hands . . . [but] in my opinion
Pitt wishes to detach and I take that to be the *utmost extent* of his
aim.' As for his own views,

I am one of those who feel that one country has a self-interest in the
events of another, and therefore for its own sake it is entitled to watch
over them. . . . France ought to be watched, not altogether on account
of the spirit of universal interference and conquest which she manifests
but on account of the weapons she uses . . .; it is not the red-hot balls
of her cannon that are to be dreaded, but the red-hot principles with
which she charges them. An invasion from these is what you and I dread,
and if we feel that an universal junction is necessary in order to repel
them, the foundation of that junction must not be founded in exclusion.

His strategy, therefore, was to maintain the links across both wings
of the party in the hope of ultimate reconciliation and to avoid the
traps laid for them by Pitt to serve his own advantage.[6]

The Whig leaders' confusion and perplexity were increased by the
unexpected retreat of the allied armies after the battle of Valmy on

F

20 September, and the resulting prospect of a French victory and the spread of revolutionary doctrines throughout Europe. It was at this point that Burke, together with Windham, Loughborough and a few fellow extremists, decided that the Whigs must be made to commit themselves against the French, if necessary to the point of war. Fitzwilliam became one of their targets. His willingness to express his sympathy with the anti-revolutionary ideals of the conservatives made him an obvious channel for them to work through to the party leadership. Burke opened the offensive on 23 October, writing to thank Fitzwilliam for a generous donation to a fund to assist the French emigré clergy who had fled from the September massacres. Urging the danger of French aggression throughout Europe and the Mediterranean, he foresaw the necessity of war by Britain, which would be undertaken more disadvantageously the longer the delay in beginning it: 'Never can any combination of Continental powers act with success against France, nor have they ever, without Great Britain', he wrote. 'But no time ought to be lost.' And Windham, fresh from meetings with Ministers to discuss possible steps against France, determined to set out in late November for Milton, bearing a copy of Burke's memorandum 'On the present state of affairs' which had been handed to Hawkesbury. Thomas Grenville took immediate alarm at the disclosure of the Burke–Windham group's plan to force British intervention in Europe, and wrote to Fitzwilliam to urge the continuance of the policy of neutrality. To declare war now, he wrote, would be 'ruin and madness'.

Fitzwilliam, however, was already moving towards an interventionist position. His reply spoke, as Grenville put it, of 'giving greater latitude to the principle of interference in internal governments of foreign countries, than I am prepared to give, and . . . looking for greater advantage from an interference that I should know how to hope or expect'. However, pleading ill health, he did not go up to town to join in the party councils, relying, as so often, on Portland to represent his views. Meanwhile Portland talked to Fox on 24 November and found him unaffected by the recent 'horrors' in France:

He is so hostile what he calls the cause of kings and consequently so satisfied and pleased with the failure of the Prussian and Austrian powers that he is in a manner insensible to the effect of the power of France. . . . His eyes appeared to be not at all more open than they were in the spring to the danger to which this country is exposed by the inundation of levelling doctrines and the support they derive from the success of French arms: the interest he used to profess for the preservation of the constitution seemed much less lively, and I am sorry to say that I fear I observed symptoms of no very strong indisposition to submit to the experiment of a new and possibly a republican form of government.

His hopes that Fox might be coming round to a moderate point of view were now shattered, and that on the eve of the crisis which was to lead to the outbreak of a war of which Fox was now bound to disapprove. Burke took the opportunity to widen the breach. Writing at great length to give Fitzwilliam an account of the discussions with Ministers, he declared that Fox had spoken in favour of recognising the French Republic, Catholic emancipation, the repeal of the Test Act, and Scottish burgh reform, and that 'as to the rest, a regular opposition was to be carried on as usual'.[7] It was time, he suggested, that the Whigs should consider 'putting yourselves in some proper array; knowing who are or are not with you—and making yourselves rather a small, well ordered phalanx than an apparently great but confused and radically discordant corps'.

The government, meanwhile, had decided to act. The proclamation of the French Republic and the announcement of the king's trial determined Pitt to recall Parliament at once. To do so before the date to which it had been prorogued required some exceptional measure; the only constitutional way was to issue a proclamation calling out the militia, which would require the assembly of Parliament in order to approve it. The only ground on which the militia could be called out was that there was a danger of insurrection inside the country. This was clearly not true. Fitzwilliam's contacts in Sheffield had only recently reassured him on the state of local opinion, which had been much more favourable since the proclamation against seditious writings in June. Such alarm as there was, his correspondents reported, was more attributable to the proclamation itself than to any existing danger. Indeed, at Barnsley the populace had to be restrained by Fitzwilliam's representative from burning Paine in effigy.[8] Armed with news such as this, Fitzwilliam was sceptical of the government's alarmism and regarded the proclamation as a mere device to work on the fears of the conservative Whigs. Nevertheless, he was equally alarmed at Fox's extreme reaction. On 4 December, at a Whig Club meeting, Fox not only joined in such newly provocative toasts as 'the friends of liberty all over the world' but also professed himself 'an advocate for the rights of

the people' as the foundation of all legitimate government. As Fitzwilliam wrote two days later, his words, 'when taken abstractedly,
we all might, and all do cordially subscribe to, but I must say, when
coupled with the times . . . his commenting upon them at all does
not meet with my approbation'. Arriving in town the following day,
Fitzwilliam went straight to dine at Burlington House, where he met
Fox. 'I by no means like him,' he confided to Charlotte.[9] He seemed
to be little concerned about the French threat to Holland, but
obsessed by the government's 'breach of law' in calling out the
militia and accused them of 'converting riot and disturbance upon
common causes into insurrections and civil commotion'. He attacked
'the wickedness of their attempt to inflame man against man, by
insinuation of treasonable practices which they neither attempt nor
do prove'.

Fox, in fact, had made up his mind that he could no longer act in
harmony with his old friends on the French question, and he behaved
now with a lack of restraint that dismayed and distressed them. 'I
grow doubtful,' he had written to his friend Adair on 26 November,
'about the possibility of preserving those connexions which I love
and esteem as much as ever'. The blame, he thought, lay not upon
himself nor upon those friends, like Grey and Sheridan, who were
alleged to have led him astray, but upon 'those on the aristocratic
side' who had set themselves 'to pervert the Duke of Portland, Fitzwilliam, Windham, etc'. His and Grey's words on parliamentary
reform, he protested, were no different from those he had used ten
years ago, nor did Grey's proposal for reform differ materially from
those supported then by Lord John Cavendish in Yorkshire. He saw
no reason why Portland and Fitzwilliam should not accept the differences between them and him on reform, as they had done between
1782 and 1785, as a purely personal difference of opinion. 'Indeed,
indeed, instead of my making strides forwards towards new opinions,
. . . they are adopting systems of conduct entirely *new*, and in so
doing are, I am convinced, the dupes of those who have the worst
intentions.'[10] It was thus to save the Whig party from extremists and
alarmists who would betray it to the Tories that Fox now adopted
his intransigent line towards the administration's policies.

The Whig leaders assembled at Burlington House on 11 December
in a mood of some trepidation. Fox attacked the militia proclamation
as a political trick, but failed to win support. Fitzwilliam, again
quoting events in the West Riding, thought the Ministry's procedures

irregular but its actions justified by the necessity of rallying public opinion to the 'cause of order'. The following evening, at the eve-of-session meeting of Whig peers to decide on tactics in the opening debates, it was agreed that there should be no official amendment to the address but that individuals should be free to speak as they wished. After the meeting, however, Fox burst in with a copy of the king's speech, and 'with an oath declared that there was no address at this moment Pitt could frame he would not propose an amendment to and divide the House upon'. This open threat to party discipline was met by conciliation. Portland and Fitzwilliam hoped, even yet, to reclaim the old Charles Fox from his new and dangerous allies. Fox's amendment, moved in terms which attributed all the dangers to liberty to the designs of the Minister and the Crown, was supported by only fifty votes, but of the fifty it was alleged that several, 'from an excess of good nature in Lord Fitzwilliam and the Duke of Portland, voted at their particular request, in order to avoid, if possible . . . an irreparable breach with Fox, and to leave open for him a door to return'. Fox, however, was no longer interested in compromise. Convinced that the party was lost to him, he went to further extremes, moving on the 15th to recognise the French Republic, proclaimed with the deposition, and shortly to be followed by the sentence of death, on Louis XVI. His friends, declared Malmesbury, were 'hurt beyond measure'. Portland, under repeated attack now by Windham, Elliot and their friends to declare the party's separation from Fox, took refuge in silence and in tears 'benumbed and paralysed', as Malmesbury put it, and muttering only 'that he was against anything that could widen the breach, and put it out of Fox's power to return, and drive him into desperate opposition'. Fitzwilliam, equally shocked by the sudden crisis in his relationship with Fox, could do nothing to resolve Portland's dilemma. On the 18th he left town to spend Christmas at Milton, but, as Malmesbury alleged, 'from difficulty how to act, and distress of mind relative to Fox', leaving Portland to cope as best he could with the angry swarm of Burke and Windhamites who tried to sting him into a positive declaration in the Lords.[11]

Nevertheless, much depended on Fitzwilliam at this point. He was still the closest of the Whig lords to both Portland and Fox; his attitude, though firm on the constitutional principle, remained flexible as regards individuals. He had no wish to drive Fox irrevocably into the hands of the radicals, and remained always eager for any sign of a reconciliation. He encouraged Portland to stand firm, and assured him of support for the middle course which he was still trying to steer. Returning to town shortly after Christmas, he took Portland's side in resisting the attempt of Elliot, Windham and others to force a separation from Fox, and rebuked Elliot for his speech in the Commons on 27 December which implied that such a division had taken place. Fitzwilliam's action seemed to convince the extremists that nothing further could be done until the end of the session, and Loughborough decided to accept the Great Seal at the end of January, despairing of carrying Portland and the party over with him. Elliot, however, could not bring himself to take office as well.[12] Fitzwilliam's solid support of Portland may well have been decisive in averting the final break even at this late hour, while his efforts to keep Fox in reasonable check were equally strenuous. 'Fox appeared to me much happier and better disposed in all respects after you saw him last,' Portland wrote on 17 January, 'and I should think he would approve all the political doctrines laid down by Lord G[renville]'.[13]

Fox's other friends, however, were not disposed to allow him to slide back from his commitment to reform, and Portland went on to warn Fitzwilliam that a proposal had been made to vote a short address of thanks to Fox by the Whig Club for his speech on 4 December, in which he had so indiscreetly, in Fitzwilliam's view, praised the cause of popular rights. Portland had written to William Adam, the party's political agent, expressing strong disapproval of the idea:

those thanks would only tend to confirm the disadvantageous ideas that had been entertained of that speech and to give the credit and sanction of the club to opinions which I believed the majority of its members . . . highly disapproved; . . . If the Club runs riot we must not let them carry our names along with theirs.

A more moderate declaration was drawn up by Robert Adair, which asserted the club's continued loyalty to the principles of its foundation in 1784, and attempted to rally the Whigs once more to the old cause of opposition to the despotic designs of the king and court as then revealed to the world. The present troubles were 'distinctly imputable to the unconstitutional advice given to His Majesty in the year 1784. . . . To this point we trace . . . the rise and progress of those fatal discontents which alarm and agitate the minds of all good

men'. No good purpose would be served by a junction with the
present administration, which was 'so constituted as to be incapable
of receiving strength to any useful purpose. . . . Trust and confidence
can alone be claimed by a national administration, founded upon
national principles, and directed to national objects'. The draft concluded with a panegyric on Fox for his constancy in defending the
monarchical system, in supporting 'in all their due privileges and
authorities, the hereditary aristocracy of the country', and asserting
'the invaluable rights and privileges of the House of Commons,
which are one and the same with the rights and privileges of the
people'. Adair suggested that such a general declaration would 'get
rid of a restless and pernicious faction with whom I see it is quite
impossible even to act' and also 'preserve the connexion between
the aristocracy and the people on its true, and legitimate foundation'. In the event a shorter and simpler resolution previously
approved by Fox, Portland and Fitzwilliam was proposed, though
Serjeant James Adair feared 'we shall but skim over without effec-
tually healing the wound'. Portland attended the meeting of the club
on 20 February at which this resolution was passed, but shortly
afterwards a number of the more conservative members, led by
Burke and Elliot, resigned in protest. The Whig Club now became in
effect the instrument of the radical, soon to be the Foxite, wing of
the party.[14]

The breakdown demonstrated that Fitzwilliam's efforts to bridge
the gap between the two sides of the party had failed. Writing to
Lady Rockingham in February, he identified three major sections in
the party.[15] There were, first, those who 'give a considerable degree
of approbation to the revolution, and much sanction to the revolutionists in France' and who deprecated any armed intervention
designed to destroy the new French constitution. Others, on the
contrary, considered the revolution 'so hostile and dangerous to
everything that is established, peaceable and tranquil' that there
could be no safety for Britain unless it were put down by force.
For that purpose they were prepared for 'something [only] little
short of systematic support of the Ministers, or of the court', even
though they considered the present Ministry and its policies to be
'weak, inefficient and contemptible'. Fitzwilliam, however, identified
himself with the third element—'a few, and but a few, . . . who,
thinking French principles . . . wicked and formidable, are ready to
resist them' by supporting 'measures of vigour' on the part of govern-

ment but 'engaging for nothing further'. The responsibility for the
divisions in the party he laid at the door of the Friends of the People
—'that society formed out of our party for the purpose of breaking
it up'. He deplored Fox's action in giving the Friends his protection
and countenance and censured Fox's failure to see that parliamentary
reform, a relatively harmless proposition ten years ago, had now
become a subversive issue. The raising of the question had alarmed
some of the party, and led to negotiations between them and the
Ministry, and eventually to Loughborough's taking the Lord Chancellorship after sowing 'the seed of jealousy, suspicion and mistrust
of those he spoke of as his friends, allies and associates'. Such was
Fitzwilliam's version of the events of the past twelve months. For
the future, his hopes that 'the true old stuff of the Whig party'
would surmount the difficulties 'by exercise of their patience' seemed
likely to be vitiated by the wide differences which had now grown
up amongst them on 'that great measure, relative to France, which
certainly fills the political eye altogether in the present moment—
there we differ widely, upon principle and policy'. Since December
1792 the support or condemnation of the French revolutionaries'
actions in proclaiming a republic and deposing their king had
become, for Fitzwilliam, the dominating issue, superseding the quarrels
over reform which had been at the centre of controversy for the
previous nine months. There could now be no question that Fitzwilliam must repudiate Fox politically, and avow his support of
Burke. The Rubicon was crossed, and the only resource for the
future was 'to hope for better times'.

Fitzwilliam's previous policy of maintaining the link between the
extremes in the party thus collapsed. He had now become almost
pathologically hostile to the Associators, placing the whole blame
for the disaffection of the country and the break-up of the party on
them. When in July 1793 William Adam, anxious to square his
accounts for the party's general fund for the year, wrote to ask
Fitzwilliam for the arrears of his subscription and to suggest an
arrangement for the future, he received a blistering reply, the more
surprising in view of the writer's past record of generosity. Fitzwilliam refused to pay a farthing towards the support of newspapers which, he asserted, had poured out republican propaganda.
'I trust,' he wrote again on 2 August, 'I was always found as ready
to make my proportionable deposits for services done as any of my
associates,' but 'the party was broke up a year and a half ago' and

'from that period . . . I must be understood . . . as free from all demands for existing or future services.' He was ready to pay his share only 'if there still remain any old scores to be wiped off, such as you have accrued, while we were still acting upon party principles'. Portland, to whom Fitzwilliam referred the correspondence with Adam, heartily agreed:

I will not, upon any account whatever, contribute a single farthing for the benefit of writers or printers of newspapers. I have long thought that the public would be infinitely more benefited by the suppression than by the encouragement of *such* vehicles of *such* intelligence, and that in particular which is generally supposed to be in the pay of opposition is so composed, and is so avowedly enlisted in the cause of anarchy, that it behoves us to do everything in our power to convince the world that we have nothing to do with it.

Thus ended the Whig party's efforts since 1784 to cultivate public support through the newspaper press.[16]

As for Adam's suggestion that Fitzwilliam and Portland might explore the possibility of acting together again with Fox against the conduct of the war, Fitzwilliam stiffly declared, 'I never will *act in party* with men who call in 4,000 weavers to dictate political measures to the government—nor with men whose opposition is laid against the constitution more than against the Ministers'. He avowed his complete disagreement with Fox over the principle of the war, for he supported the doctrine of 'interference for the purpose of settling the internal government. . . . France must start again from her ancient monarchy', he added, 'and improving upon that is her only chance of establishing a system that will give happiness to herself, and ensure peace and security to her neighbours'. Further discussions with Fox could lead only to a deeper disagreement. The only hope left was 'a completely successful termination of the present war', for it was this, and not reform, that now divided them.[17]

Nevertheless, though convinced of the impossibility of an early reconciliation with Fox, the Whig leaders persisted in keeping open a way for his return. When a public subscription was set on foot in June 1793 to pay Fox's private debts—then standing at over £60,000 —Portland and Fitzwilliam contributed generously and gave it the support of their influence in the country, despite the political overtones which might be read into it.[18] And in the summer of 1793 Fitzwilliam had a further opportunity to profess his attitude towards

F*

the divisions in the party when the seat at Higham Ferrers became
vacant by the death on 5 August of Jack Lee, an old and faithful
member of the Rockingham party who had continued to symbolise
Fitzwilliam's political inheritance as one of his members in the
Commons. There is no doubt that Richard Burke junior confidently
expected to be offered the seat, and it is equally certain that had
Fitzwilliam done so Richard and his father would have blazed it
forth as a symbol of Fitzwilliam's devotion to their section of the
party. Despite his evident affection for Richard himself, therefore,
Fitzwilliam wrote at once to make it clear that the offer would not
be made. Using the pretext that, in a recent conversation, Richard
had declared that if he were a member of Parliament he would
expect his patron to allow him complete freedom of judgement,
Fitzwilliam declared that events had proved Richard's sentiments
and his own to be widely at variance. Under these circumstances,
'though painful to me not to gratify your wishes, I am obliged to
say that I cannot bring myself to offer a seat to a young man on
those terms on which alone you have declared your intention to
receive it'.

Richard took a week to compose his reply. It was an extraordinary
document coming from an aspirant to the political arena to a senior
member of the party leadership and to his own employer and patron,
for Richard had been Fitzwilliam's London legal and financial agent
for three years. 'Your lordship's letter,' he began, 'does not appear
to me as clear as your style of writing usually is.' He denied that
he had laid down any conditions as to his freedom of action; but, he
remonstrated,

there are many conditions of connexion—from the abject one pres-
cribed by Lord Lonsdale, up to that which your lordship indulges to my
father. I flattered myself that . . . my situation might have approached
more nearly to the latter; and that in this respect you would have
considered me as my father's son.

As to the differences of opinion to which Fitzwilliam referred,
Richard professed that the only one between them was that relative
to Fox's intentions and conduct. Thus Fitzwilliam must be insisting
upon no less than that Richard should be prepared to support Fox
against his own father. Pointing to the numerous issues during the
last session on which Fox had voted in a way distasteful to Fitzwilliam, he maintained that Fitzwilliam was indulging in

that impossible attempt, to separate men and measures—persons and principles. . . . The whole matter between us reverts to this. You will not bring me into Parliament because I do not pledge myself, against my principles, and against *your* principles, to vote with a man whom you yourself do scarce in any instance vote or are likely to vote with. It is really afflicting almost to distraction.

Appealing to their mutual professions of friendship and attachment, transcending 'the inequality of rank and fortune (great as it is)', and to the connexion, first between Edmund Burke and Rockingham, and since 1782 between Burke and Fitzwilliam, which made their friendship 'doubly hereditary', he remonstrated almost frantically that 'I am indeed sacrificed to Mr Fox'.

To have rejected the only son of Mr Burke and your own friend, not in favour of Mr Fox himself, an only son or a son of his, but in favour of some of his partisans—will be undoubtedly in a very authentic manner setting the seal of your lordship's approbation on *his* conduct and passing a sentence of condemnation on that of my father for these last two years.

All this, and much else, poured from Richard's pen in a stream of disappointed chagrin, and served not only to irritate Fitzwilliam but to confirm the wisdom of his judgement in withholding the seat from him. Portland, when shown Richard's letter, commented sadly that it confirmed 'the disqualification which I have long, I might say I have *always*, thought young Burke laboured under of being brought into Parliament' and classed the outburst as a 'very extraordinary performance'. Fitzwilliam replied ten days later, after the distractions of York race week and 'the din of six to four and three to one', that he sincerely lamented having written at all.

The less that is said the better respecting the terms upon which you declared in that conversation your expectation of being brought into Parliament: they are now become matter of fact, and what that fact is rests upon recollection: fearing . . . that our recollections do not quite tally, it is better to waive all reference thereto.

Richard must certainly act in concert with his father; and so,

why, my dear Burke, have you so little feeling for my respect, my attachment, my affection for your father, why are you so cruel as to wring from me, as to force me to commit to paper, what I hardly confided to my own bosom, that he and I materially differ in politics? I may

give an occasional support to Mr Pitt . . .; I do and mean to give such
support to the measure of the present war, to its propriety, its necessity,
its justice . . . ; but systematically I continue to be, and am, in opposition to him and his Ministry: there exists many a knotty point to be
adjusted between him and me, many difficulties very important in their
nature to be smoothed, much obliteration of facts not easy to be affected,
and the general face of things strangely to be altered, before I retire
from my watch upon his Ministry.

Burke, however, had 'delivered himself over into the hands of Pitt,
formally and professedly, last November. . . . He became the
standard-bearer of his empire. . . . He possesses in as full and ample a
degree as ever my respect, my attachment, my affection, my
veneration for his virtues, but in this instance he has failed to carry
my conviction. . . . We differ upon a fundamental point in politics'.
To bring Richard into Parliament, then, would be to declare not
against Fox but against Portland. As long as the two lords were
trying to hold the middle ground it would be impossible for Fitzwilliam to commit himself in this way. Richard responded with an
equally spirited defence of his father's conduct, denying that Burke
had held up 'Mr P.'s standard or anybody['s] standard except his
own', and claiming that he had been supported during the last session
'by a large majority of the Duke of Portland's party' in urging Pitt
to declare war on France. 'He therefore held up *his own* standard,
Mr P. joined him and not he Mr Pitt.' And the cause on which he
had embarked was not Pitt's but 'it is yours and was so long before
it was his. It is . . . the cause of everything that is good—against
everything that is evil'. Richard indeed claimed that Portland himself
had subscribed to Burke's doctrines as lately as on the occasion of
his installation as Chancellor of Oxford University at the beginning
of July, and denied that it would have offended Portland for Fitzwilliam to have patronised Burke's son. As for continuing to regard
himself as in regular opposition to the government, Fitzwilliam
should recognise that he

might have been of infinitely more service to the common cause in
carrying the weight of your property and character to those who are
fighting the battles of true aristocracy . . . than you can be by standing
sentinel in the watchhouse of opposition; a sort of business for which,
with great deference, many others are better cut out than your lordship.

According to William Elliot, Sir Gilbert's cousin, Edmund too was
hurt by Fitzwilliam's letter, and wrote 'a severe remonstrance' which

affected his patron 'so much that he was actually ill for some days', until Burke himself, hearing of it, went to see him and 'the whole affair was completely made up'.[19] There is no record of either such a letter or such a meeting, however, in the Fitzwilliam archives. Certainly the whole affair had severely shaken Fitzwilliam's composure, for he was still as deeply attached to Burke as ever on the fundamental issues. Yet he could not allow even Burke to tear him away from his equally close and affectionate ties with Fox, and his efforts for a reconciliation continued. In fact it was only Richard's utter insensitivity to the feelings and reactions of others that had brought about this *imbroglio*. A man of greater discretion and understanding would not have written the letters he sent to Fitzwilliam, nor thought it necessary to try to force his hand in such a way. Fitzwilliam's relationship with Burke himself was unaffected by the affair, however. In November he evidently renewed his offer of financial assistance, drawing from Burke the profession that 'whilst honour, virtue and benignity are entitled to the love and esteem of mankind you ever must have an uncontrovertible title to my cordial and respectful attachment'. It says a great deal for the love and friendship that Fitzwilliam was able to inspire that, almost at the same time, Fox was also writing to Adam that Fitzwilliam's

unremitting kindness to me in all situations quite oppresses me when I think of it. God knows, there is nothing on earth consistent with principle and honour that I would not do to continue his political friend, as I shall always be his warmest and most attached private friend.

There could have been few, if any, others at that moment in time who would not only have been found eager to use their wealth to offer financial support both to Fox and to Burke but who could have been regarded by both with equal affection.[20]

Yet, as Richard had too bluntly but truly remarked, Fitzwilliam was engaged in an 'impossible attempt, to separate men and measures —persons and principles'. Even his warm good nature could not bridge the gap of profound political divergence which had opened up in the party, and Fitzwilliam was ill equipped for sitting on fences. In the end his own convictions were too strong to be smothered even by his friendships. This was shown by the terms of his offer of the seat at Higham Ferrers to James Adair, a moderate who was both a friend of Fox and a close confidant of Portland. The seat was offered on 3 August, and Adair's acceptance on the 8th was conditional only upon one question. He wished it to be clear that 'I cannot prevail upon myself to concur in any systematic opposition to government on the subject of the war with France'. 'Our sentiments coincide perfectly upon the subject of the war,' Fitzwilliam replied:

No person entertained a more decided opinion of the wisdom and necessity of it than I did, long before it began. . . . I shall therefore give a fair and honourable support to the *measure;* but I will not engage to give applause to its management. I think the first and great end of it has been neglected and neglected because Ministry are not honourable enough to avow it as an object, for fear of unpopularity . . . that we are at war for the purpose of overthrowing the reign of anarchy, and of re-establishing government and law and order in France.[21]

Fitzwilliam was now as enthusiastic as Burke himself for the prosecution of an ideological war against the French revolution. He deplored the constitution of 1791, which 'was built upon the declaration of the rights of man, which admits no distinction between man and man, between the orders of men in society, and whilst it pretends to give to the virtues, in truth confers all power upon the vices of mankind'. Only his long and deep-seated abhorrence of Pitt and his continued affection for Fox held him back in general opposition; Pitt, too, still represented a threat to Whig constitutionalism, and Fox might yet be reclaimed for it. In the autumn of 1793, therefore, Fitzwilliam still tried to hold Portland to his middle line. Pitt had opened tentative negotiations with Windham, leader of the 'third party' which was trying to bring the moderate Whigs into alliance with the Ministry. Fitzwilliam urged Portland not to trust Windham, who, he declared, had a year ago made a 'proffer of his party to Pitt without communication with you'. The unhappy Portland, who needed constant stiffening to keep his chosen course, bewailed that 'it is difficult to steer between the extremes of *good* motives' and confessed that 'I never saw nor can I yet see Burke and Windham's visit to Pitt in the same light in which it has always been viewed by you'. He admitted that he had been thinking over further hints from Windham and Spencer about the possibility of joining the government, and that he had been only deferring 'the intention I have long had, and have long determined to carry into effect . . . of giving him [Windham] a very full and explicit statement of my sentiments on the subject'. Fitzwilliam immediately responded with a warning shot across his leader's bows, and Portland hurriedly reassured him that he had not meant to suggest that Pitt's offers could be seriously entertained 'upon those principles and that basis upon which alone I ever could take a part in it [the government] myself or advise any one for whom I had a regard to embark in it'. His present view, Portland wrote, was that the Minister should not be attacked for the misconduct of the war, and he would certainly profess his utter opposition to any connexion with 'the members of any of the associations for reform'—though he feared that this individual course would lead him straight, as he put it, 'to *Coventry*'. Two days later he admitted that though he remained opposed to acting under Pitt in principle, it was neither surprising nor unreasonable that Pitt should refuse to step down from the premiership: 'The reality of his power may be much to be lamented, but if he possesses it, as I am persuaded he does, I can not think it very unnatural in him to desire to retain it.[22]

These ominous remarks suggested that Portland had now virtually made up his mind for a more direct support of the Ministry. The occasion for this change of heart was undoubtedly to be found in the events in the Netherlands, where the Duke of York's expedition to capture Dunkirk had been unexpectedly turned back by a disastrous defeat at Hondschoote. Not only did this once again arouse the spectre of French domination of the strategically vital Low Countries, but it aroused a storm of criticism at home of the government's handling of military operations and further weakened the Cabinet's already tottering condition. The Portland Whigs' contention that the present Ministry was incapable of handling the war with success seemed to be justified, but it was less easy to see what was to be done about it unless Portland and his friends would take office to strengthen it. Elliot was the first to go, accepting in September the post of Civil Commissioner at Toulon, captured by Hood's fleet a month previously. Spencer was being offered the viceroyalty of Ireland, and Windham, though anxious not to accept office without Portland, was urging his party leader to take a decision.[23] On 25 September Portland went to see Pitt, and came away temporarily convinced of the Minister's willingness to accept his terms. It was Fitzwilliam who pulled Portland back from the precipice and, possibly, saved the party from capitulation to Pitt's designs. Portland accepted Fitzwilliam's view that a coalition must only take place on an equal basis, and that it must not be under Pitt's premiership. And on those terms no coalition, clearly, could take place.

The efforts of Burke and his group now turned again to Fitzwilliam. On 29 October Tom Grenville, who had now come round to
agreement with Windham, wrote to renew contact with him. He
reminded Fitzwilliam of his earlier declaration that the war was to
be justified on the grounds that the intentions of France were
'evidently directed to the establishing here the same principles of
anarchy which prevailed there', and warned him that the disaster
of Dunkirk and other failures of the first year of the war, together
with resentment at higher taxation, seemed likely to produce disaffection among the British public. 'We are as much beat by the
French if we are disarmed by popular clamour,' he wrote, 'as if we
had literally been disarmed by the success of their arms, and from
that event whenever it happens I think we shall have to date the
struggle in this country between the English constitution and the
bloody code of French anarchy.' He concluded by urging 'the indispensable duty of all who wished success to the war . . . to speak the
warm and decided language of men who know that upon the event
of this contest all that is dear to them is at stake'. Fitzwilliam replied
that he was discouraged by the evident unpopularity of the war,
which he had expected to be approved of by the public: 'to fight
its battle is an uphill game', he wrote: 'I have found it so daily—
its wisdom and its principle are everywhere doubted . . . and here
the misfortune is, that this doubt arises among men, naturally,
properly, and really, aristocratic'. The stagnation of trade had also
made the war unpopular with the business community, who were
already inclined to disaffection because of 'the immeasurable quan-
tity of abuse daily poured out indiscriminately upon the whole body
of dissenters, that is upon the whole body of merchants and manufacturers'. Pitt's refusal to declare that the restoration of the French
monarchy was the object of the war was, he considered, 'the true
cause of any doubt about its support at this moment', and it was the
major factor in Fitzwilliam's advocacy of a continued independent
strategy for the Whigs. He had no hesitation in avowing his own
complete support for the war,

but bearing at the same time as little good will to Government as ever:
perhaps less: because I feel the greatest part of the difficulty we, true
supporters of the good cause, have to combat against, arises from their
original want of system, or rather from their false system upon the
subject.

He could neither join a government whose war policy was weak and unacceptable nor support an opposition whose commitment to reform was repulsive. He thought, however, that on these grounds, as Tom Grenville reported after a conversation at Milton, 'a very respectable corps of public men' might be formed.[24] Portland shared this view at the time, but bad news from abroad hastened events. On Christmas Day the news of the loss of Toulon arrived. Portland wrote at once to Fitzwilliam that he intended to go to St Anne's Hill to tell Fox of his determination 'to support the war with all the effect and energy in my power' and to end all connexion with the Friends of the People, and on this basis 'to collect in the best manner I can all the force which the old Whig party can supply'. Tom Grenville had already told Fox that he could no longer act with him, and Fitzwilliam as well as Portland now declared their decision 'to take a more decided line than they had hitherto done, in support of the administration'.[25] At the Whig party's eve-of-session meeting at Burlington House on the 20th (to which Burke had, significantly, received a personal invitation from Portland) the duke made a strong and decisive speech, declaring his support for the Ministry and urging the same course on his followers. As Fox recognised, this event marked the separation of the official party leadership from him and foreshadowed a future junction with the Ministry. Though the party remained seated on the opposition benches, they supported the address against Foxite amendments in both Houses, and Portland made a rare speech in the Lords to avow his adherence to the justice and necessity of the war. Spencer went so far as to declare the separation of the party, a statement which was not contradicted by any of his colleagues. Socially, too, the old closeness between Fox and Fitzwilliam was diminishing. Charlotte told Lady Ponsonby in March 1794 that they now rarely met. Fox thought 'it seemed some way as if I had the world to begin anew', and threw himself more energetically than ever into opposition to the government's measures.[26]

So the events of the session drew the Portland Whigs inexorably towards coalition. The disclosures of increased radical and, possibly, treasonable activity in the country were coupled with further disasters for allied armies on the Continent and corresponding alarms for the subversion of all the European monarchies. On 12 May Thomas Hardy and other leading reformers were arrested, and a committee of secrecy of the House of Commons, containing fourteen

ministerialists and seven of the most alarmist Whigs, was appointed
to enquire into the reformers' activities. In the Lords a similar committee of nine included Portland, Carlisle and Mansfield. Both Houses
endorsed the suspension of Habeas Corpus by 22 May. Fox's continued intransigence over this measure and his motion of 30 May,
repeated in the Lords by Bedford, to end the war brought Fitzwilliam
to his feet to declare his expectation that England must intervene in
the internal affairs of France. He had already declared on 17 February, speaking against Lansdowne's motion for peace with France,
that

with regard to peace with France, we could have no hopes of it under
the present system, unless we were prepared to sacrifice everything that
was dear to us. . . . His Lordship contended that the safety of the
country, the preservation of the constitution, of everything dear to
Englishmen and to their posterity depended upon the preventing the
introduction of French principles, and the new-fangled doctrine of the
rights of man; and that this could only be effected by the establishment
of some regular form of government in that country upon which some
reliance might be placed.

On 30 May he repeated his conviction that the war was a defensive
one on England's part and remarked:

It had been urged that we had no right to interfere in the conduct of
France. He denied the position. It became a great and magnanimous people
to become the defenders of mankind. It had been the glorious province of
England at all times. Our great King William had, in the same manner,
risen up the defender of mankind against the ambition of Louis XIV. . . .
We had now the same object. . . . We had a right to interfere in the
internal affairs of France, until those internal affairs should be so regulated
as to give security to mankind. He should withdraw his feeble support
from Ministers if they were to abandon this principle. Nor had he any
hesitation in declaring that he was an advocate for the re-establishment
of monarchy in France, because that was an intelligent means of restor-
ing order. It was not from his mere love of monarchy that he did this,
for he admired the simple and beautiful superstructure of America . . .
but it was because he wished to have something solid to repose upon for
the peace and happiness of mankind.

Fitzwilliam went on to defend the measures taken by the government for the better security of the country, declaring that, from
his knowledge of the West Riding, 'the rigorous measures of sus-
pending the Habeas Corpus and other Acts were in unison with the
opinion of the country'.[27]

Very little now divided Fitzwilliam from the government except a continued inability to make up his mind to trust Pitt and break finally with Fox. Yet there were still crucial questions. Portland had clearly made up his mind to a junction, and Fitzwilliam was prepared to allow his loyalty to the party leader to carry him into support of government, if not into office himself, but he did not wish to assume any personal responsibility for the step. Portland, for his part, was equally unwilling to take the decision to join Pitt unless Fitzwilliam would concur in, and even advise, it. For almost the whole of June, therefore, the Whigs trembled on the brink of a coalition which they could see no way to avoid but which they could not yet wholeheartedly accept. During this period Fitzwilliam acted as the conscience of the party, and it was the need to win his approval of the step which alone delayed Portland's taking it. From the point of view of party advantage this delay might well have worked in favour of the Whigs, for Pitt was made to raise his offer in order to secure them. Fitzwilliam's reluctance, however, stemmed not from party calculation but from a genuine inability to overcome his ingrained prejudice against the present Ministers and from the still powerful tug of affection for Fox.

Portland summoned Fitzwilliam on 25 May to confer on the situation at Burlington House. He had seen Pitt on the 24th, and the Minister had declared his wish for a coalition on the common ground of 'the expulsion of that evil spirit [of Jacobinism] . . . and [said] that his wish and object was that it might make us act together as one great Family'. Pitt 'lamented the scantiness of Cabinet employments he had it in his power at this moment to offer to us' but said that others would be offered as they became available. The original meeting planned for 30 May had to be postponed till 13 June owing to the sudden death of the Duchess of Portland. Fitzwilliam, however, declined to attend. He was busily engaged in organising the new Volunteer forces in the West Riding, but in any case he could not bring himself to a decision. 'However frequently I have thought on the subject . . . it never occurs to me without presenting itself in some new point of view, which generally tends to render decision more difficult.' In particular he wished for clarification as to whether the Whigs were to receive only the offices at present vacant or whether they were to be given a fuller share of power 'to direct the management of these weighty measures'. Until this was clarified he could not bring himself to decide. He took refuge in a willingness to trust Portland's 'excellent judgement' and in the condition that, before deciding, Portland would consult the Duke of Devonshire and Lord Mansfield.

The meeting on 13 June consisted of Portland, Spencer, Mansfield and Tom Grenville. Portland reported to Fitzwilliam his intense regret at his absence, and declared that

without knowledge of your sentiments . . . I must fairly say I cannot proceed. . . . I feel myself in a most unpleasant dilemma, very sincerely distressed at being under the necessity of closing the overtures made us by Pitt, without the power of assigning any other reason than the impossibility of obtaining your opinion on them.

The meeting, after two hours' discussion, had agreed that a junction with the administration was now timely and proper, and that

the basis and *sina qua non* condition must be the re-establishment of order and good government in France as described by you in your last speech in the H. of Lords . . . which I understood to be, in other words, the restoration of the French monarchy and restitution of property or at least a government of which property forms the basis.

Portland avowed that he was the most strongly of all in favour of the union, and that he no longer doubted Pitt's sincerity in proposing it. Besides, 'Ireland may be saved by it and made a powerful and useful member of the British empire. . . . The true spirit of aristocracy and the true principles of Whiggism may be revived and re-established . . . [and] the liberty of Europe may be secured'. Fitzwilliam, however, '*must be* a party, a very efficient party, in this business and . . . without you I *cannot* stir'. Fitzwilliam's response was cautious. He wished for an explicit declaration from Pitt of the principle that the basic war aim was the restoration of the monarchy and of order in France. Even in coalition with the Whigs, he pointed out, the present Ministers would be in the majority in a new Cabinet, so that their present policy towards the war would prevail. If Portland was prepared to accept the coalition under the terms offered, Fitzwilliam would support it; but he would not take office himself. 'I peremptorily decline being a party in the arrangement,' he wrote. Like many of his Yorkshire friends, he still thought the appointment of Pitt in 1783 was 'a severe blow to the spirit of the constitution and to Whiggism, which is the essence of it'.[28]

Portland took Fitzwilliam's objections to Pitt, and at an interview on the 18th the Prime Minister conceded 'that the re-establishment of the Crown of France in such person of the family of Bourbon as shall be naturally entitled to it was the first and determined aim of the present Ministry'. Furthermore, though the Cabinet did not consider this to be the best moment to recognise 'Monsieur' as regent, as Fitzwilliam had urged in his letter of the 15th,

if upon a full view and examination . . . you should be of a different opinion, so far from finding any obstinate resistance or pertinacious adherence on the part of the administration he could assure me that you would meet with every possible inclination to be convinced by you.

The diversion of Moira's intended expedition from La Vendée to Flanders was, Pitt had assured him, a merely temporary one: indeed, it was to the royalists in France that he looked for the successful restoration of the monarchy. All these points Pitt was anxious to discuss personally with Fitzwilliam, 'being convinced that it was in his power to give your mind the fullest satisfaction upon every one of them, and our conversation ended with his entreating me to urge by every possible argument your return to town at your earliest convenience'. Mansfield too was fully in favour of coalition, and Portland urged Fitzwilliam to consider that 'our acceptance of office will be the means of rallying, reuniting and incorporating the Old Whigs and of setting up and fairly establishing the standard of true aristocracy'. As for Fitzwilliam's wish to restrict his sphere of activity to the West Riding, 'If you are not a principal . . . they will not . . . look up to you as they ought and you will not have that weight, that influence, that authority which is so very desirable at all times'.[29] Fitzwilliam declared his satisfaction that the administration had now come round to the Whig point of view, and announced, 'for my own part I am now ready, not only to adopt the opinion that a junction should take place, as your sentiment, but to advise it as the genuine offspring of my own judgement'. The only condition he would make was that

as much weight and sway should be given to us as possible. . . . In my humble opinion, this junction will not produce half its effect if it is not opened to the world by such marks of real substantial favour and confidence on the part of the Crown towards us as will mark beyond dispute the return of weight, power and consideration to the Old Whigs.

In particular, 'after thirty years' exclusion from patronage in the line of peerage' they should receive a number of peerages. As for

himself, however, he repeated his disinclination to take an office
in the Cabinet:

I can be of ten times more service to the common cause out than in
. . . let me act in my sphere: leave it to work without doors: I shall not
fail to do it zealously and assiduously. I am now at it every day, attempting, and I think with some effect, to prepare men's minds to see things
as they ought to be seen, and as they are to be acted upon. . . . I am
preparing them to think that everything that assumes to itself the name
of Liberty is not therefore Liberty if it does not carry with it the first
and last characteristic of Liberty, Protection: and that everything that
is branded with the name of Monarchy is not therefore oppressive and
ought not . . . to be held as odious. . . . In this line, I feel I act usefully
. . . but in no other can I be of real use. The only one I think of would
be in going to Ireland, but important as I think that consideration, with
shame I say it, it is impossible. Leave me, then, where I am: I feel I am
not injuring the general cause by peremptorily repeating that I cannot
take office.

Both Portland and Mansfield, however, insisted that Fitzwilliam
must enter the Cabinet, as a condition of their own agreement to
do so. When Fitzwilliam arrived in London on Saturday 28 June
Mansfield had a 'short but earnest conversation' with him in the
street, and reported that he was 'strongly inclined to do what was
best upon the whole. I could not remove his doubts [but] . . . I
brought him to admit that if *ever* he was to take office this was the
time'.[30]

Fitzwilliam's crucial interview with Portland took place on the
following day. 'I see little prospect of escaping office,' Fitzwilliam
wrote to Charlotte:

the duke . . . seems so intent upon my accepting, as almost to say that
he will not, if I do not—I left him last night my reasons for thinking
that I should be more serviceable out of office, than in . . . if I find I
have not persuaded him, *I must submit*.[31]

Portland went to see Pitt again on 1 July, and Pitt, possibly considering that Fitzwilliam's reluctance merely disguised an ambition
for the Irish viceroyalty, agreed to offer him that post as soon as
provision could be made for its present incumbent, Lord Westmorland. Fitzwilliam's objections were now overborne, and on 3 July
he accepted the terms. 'It is a time when private affection must give
way to public exigency,' he immediately wrote to Lady Rockingham.
His wish to give support merely from the country, 'where I think I

can do it with some degree of advantage,' had been overborne by Portland's 'earnest request,' and he had accepted the Lord Presidency. On the 4th Portland was granted an audience at St James's to receive the king's authority to confer with Pitt. Only the last-minute hitch about the arrangement of Dundas's offices in the Cabinet now delayed the formal junction until the 11th.[32]

Yet Fitzwilliam's acceptance of office still weighed heavily upon him. It involved not only the abandonment of Fox, to which he had already reconciled himself because of the impossibility of agreeing with him any longer on the French war. It also involved the reversal of a lifetime's political convictions.

I am just got home to tell you the business is done [he wrote to Charlotte.] I am President of the Council, and I must not let you hear it by a newspaper. I do not receive this honour (if it is one) with much exultation; on the contrary with a heavy heart. I did not feel great comfort in finding myself at St James's surrounded by persons with whom I had been so many years in political hostility, and without those I can never think of being separated from, publicly or privately, without a pang.

His only comfort was that 'I do not see in the countenances of those I really regret either shyness or indignation'. Fox too regretted rather than resented Fitzwilliam's step. A few days earlier he had written:

Nothing ever can make me forget a friendship as old as my life and the man in the world to whom I feel myself in every view the most obliged. . . . Whatever happens I never can forget, my dearest Fitz, that you are the friend in the world whom I most esteem, for whom I would sacrifice every thing that one man ought to sacrifice to another. I know that the properest conduct in such a situation would be to say nothing, nor to inquire any thing from any of my old friends, and so I shall do in regard to all others, but I feel you to be an exception with respect to me to all general rules, I am sure your friendship has been so. God bless you, my dear Fitz.

Writing to his nephew a month later, he declared:

I cannot forget that ever since I was a child Fitzwilliam has been, in all situations, my warmest and most affectionate friend, and the person in the world of whom decidedly I have the best opinion, and so in most respects I have still, but as a politician I cannot reconcile his conduct with what I (who have known him for more than five-and-thirty years) have always thought to be his character.

And he added:

I think they have all behaved very ill to me, and for most of them, who
certainly owe much more to me than I do to them, I feel nothing but
contempt, and do not trouble myself about them; but Fitzwilliam is an
exception indeed.

Towards Fitzwilliam, he wrote, he felt as Lord Rochester had
expressed it, that 'to be ill used by those to whom we owe obligations which we can never forget and towards whom we must continue to feel affection and gratitude is indeed a most painful sensation'. But if Fox's emotion was sorrow rather than anger, Lady
Rockingham's first impulse was to the latter. On receiving Fitzwilliam's letter she sat down to write her lament that he and Portland 'are taken in, in every sense of the word, to prop up misfortune
and mismanagement', but, as she afterwards wrote to Fitzwilliam's
aunt, Lady Charlotte Wentworth, 'I durst not send all, and . . .
when I became more calm I wrote, not perhaps as I ought, but I
wrote a good deal of what flowed'. Her memories ran back irresistibly to 1782, when her husband had taken office:

I never yet saw cause to rejoice at coming into Administration [she
wrote] and I am persuaded that I never shall. . . . I feel not quite at ease,
that two such dear friends should (as it seems to me) be binding themselves at such a moment to *His Majesty* and *Mr Pitt*; Think of Mr Pitt!
Who, when he had but just left school, disdained to be a colleague with
Lord John Cavendish in a *subordinate situation*. . . . If you are to *guide*,
there may be good hope; but if you are oftener *only* to *concur*,
it seems trusting too far. They will borrow your zeal and uprightness;
and will pay you back again *only* in *honours* and *compliments*.[33]

Burke, however, was delighted, and his pleasure was sealed by the
achievement of one of his oldest surviving ambitions—to see his son
succeed him as member for Malton. He had sent Fitzwilliam his
letter of resignation on 21 June, and five days later Fitzwilliam
replied that

however much to my satisfaction, and however honourably to the
borough it may be hereafter be represented, certainly the days of its
greatest lustre are now gone past, and in no case shall I ever feel the
same degree of satisfaction in the exercise of my influence there.

Fitzwilliam's decision to offer the seat to Richard was certainly
expected by Edmund, but there were fears among his friends that
Richard's response to Fitzwilliam's refusal of Higham Ferrers would
prejudice his chances. Indeed, Richard himself had told French

Laurence, his father's chief confidant, that he would not accept
Malton at Fitzwilliam's hands, and in March 1794 he had resigned
as Fitzwilliam's London agent. But Fitzwilliam needed no prompting,
though Laurence, convinced that 'nothing would so wound him
[Edmund] to the soul as a disappointment in this respect', went to
see him to suggest Richard's nomination. Richard promptly accepted
the seat as 'an instance of a true generosity of mind and of personal
friendship' in Fitzwilliam, and the latter wrote triumphantly to
Charlotte that

the old one is pleased beyond conception that I made the offer, and he
is pleased too in as great a degree at the short letter I wrote to him in
answer to his notification of his retreat . . . he has found something in
it that has delighted his affectionate heart. The young one seems exceedingly pleased too, and everything has passed between us as might be
wished, not a word of what passed before.[34]

So the Pitt–Portland coalition of July 1794 took shape. Fitzwilliam
had been responsible for much of its character. His doubts and hesitations, the product of a sincere lifetime's devotion to the Old Whig
creed, had secured for the Whigs a greater share of power, office and
patronage than Pitt would have originally offered or Portland
accepted. His own reluctance to enter the Cabinet, and the influence
of his doubts on Spencer, who had given up the intended viceroyalty,
had resulted in the understanding, as part of the bargain, that he
himself would go to Ireland; and that circumstance was to provide
the crucial test not only of the character of the new coalition but
of the lines of future party divisions. Fitzwilliam's inability to shake
off a lifetime's devotion to Rockinghamite principles and to abandon
his instinctive distrust of Pitt and all he stood for lay behind the
failure of his Irish viceroyalty, and even doomed it from the start.
That failure resulted in Fitzwilliam's alienation from the other
conservative Whigs and, paradoxically, helped to cement more
firmly the alliance between the Pittities and the rest of the Portland
group into the nucleus of the Tory party of the future; it also led,
inevitably, to a future reunion of Fitzwilliam with Fox and the
liberals, a reunion which, as later chapters will show, was significant
for the political attitudes and prospects of the Whig party of the
early nineteenth century. Ireland was now to shape both Fitzwilliam's future and his party's destiny.

Notes

[1] Portland to Loughborough, 25 May 1792, and the reply: Portland MSS, PWF 9220. For the negotiations see O'Gorman, pp. 90–7; Mitchell, pp. 184–9; Malmesbury, *Diaries and Corresp. of James Harris, first Earl of Malmesbury* (1845), II, pp. 418–36.

[2] *Ibid.* Portland refused Pitt's subsequent offer of the Garter, declaring to Loughborough on 27 July that he could accept it only as part of the arrangements for a broad based administration, including his friends (Portland MSS, PWF 9222).

[3] Portland to Fitzwilliam, 27 June 1792 (F 31a); Malmesbury, *Diaries*, II, p. 433.

[4] 17 August 1792: *Corresp. of E. Burke*, VI, pp. 170–3. For Fox's comments on the attack on the Tuileries see his letter to Holland, 3 September 1792 (*Memorials and Corresp. of C. J. Fox*, II, p. 368). On 12 October, he wrote of the September massacres that they admitted of 'no excuse, no palliation for such cruelty and such baseness' (*ibid.*, p. 374).

[5] Richard Burke junior to Edmund Burke, 1 September 1792 (*Corresp. of E. Burke*, VII, pp. 185–8); Portland to Fitzwilliam, 26 September 1792 (N); Portland to Burke, 12 September 1792 (*Corresp. of E. Burke*, VII, pp. 206–7).

[6] Fitzwilliam to Burke, 27 September [1792] (*ibid.*, p. 228, n. 4); Carlisle to Fitzwilliam, 19 October 1792 and reply, 31 October (N). For Carlisle's correspondence with Fox in July 1792 on the question of the relationship between the 'Friends of the People' and the party see *Memorials and Corresp. of C. J. Fox*, III, p. 22, and Carlisle MSS, p. 696.

[7] Burke to Fitzwilliam, 23 October; Windham to Burke, 14 November (*Corresp. of E. Burke*, VII, pp. 276–8, 288–9); T. Grenville to Fitzwilliam, 15, 17 and 24 November 1792; Windham to Fitzwilliam, 17 November; Portland to Fitzwilliam, 30 November (N); Burke to Fitzwilliam, 29 November 1792 (*Corresp. of E. Burke*, VII, pp. 306–18).

[8] Letters from J. Wilkinson, [December 1792], R. A. Athorpe, J.P., 12 December and C. Bowns, 13 December: F 44b.

[9] Mitchell, p. 201; Fitzwilliam to Lady Fitzwilliam, [6 December 1792]: N 45.

[10] Fox to Adair, 26 and 29 November 1792: *Memorials and Corresp. of C. J. Fox*, III, pp. 257, 259.

[11] Malmesbury, *Diaries*, II, pp. 440–6. Among the fifty voting with Fox were two of Fitzwilliam's five members, Lord Milton (MP for Malton) and Lionel Damer (MP for Peterborough). Other moderate Whigs who voted in the minority included Lord Edward Bentinck, William Plumer, Lord Robert Spencer, and Tom Grenville (*Parl. Register*, XXXIV, pp. 73–4).

[12] Portland to Fitzwilliam, 29 December 1792 (F 31a); Malmesbury, *Diaries*, II, pp. 463–5; *Life and Letters of Sir G. Elliot*, II, pp. 89, 106–7.

[13] F 31a. Portland refers to Grenville's answer to the letter from Chauvelin, the French Minister in London, explaining the French decree of 19 November, promising aid to oppressed peoples (*Annual Register*, XXXV, pp. 114–9).

[14] Portland to Fitzwilliam, 17 January 1793 (F 31a); Robert Adair to Portland, [7 February]; James Adair to Portland [19 February] (Portland MSS, PWF 32 and 21); O'Gorman, pp. 120–1.

[15] Fitzwilliam to Lady Rockingham, 28 February 1793: R 164/14.

[16] Adam to Fitzwilliam, 4 July 1793 (N); Fitzwilliam to Adam, 21 July (Blair Adam MSS) and 2 August (N); Adam to Fitzwilliam, 19 and 20 September; Portland to Fitzwilliam, 28 September (ibid.).

[17] Fox to Adam, 18 September 1793 (Blair Adam MSS); Fitzwilliam to Portland (draft), 22 September (F 31a); Fitzwilliam to Adam, 15 November (Blair Adam MSS); and see O'Gorman, pp. 158–62.

[18] O'Gorman, pp. 142–3. Fox called the subscription 'the most honourable thing that ever happened to any man' (Memorials and Corresp. of C. J. Fox, III, p. 40).

[19] Fitzwilliam to R. Burke junior, 8 August 1793, and reply, 16 August (Corresp. of E. Burke, VII, pp. 394, 396–410); Portland to Fitzwilliam, 22 September (F 31a); Fitzwilliam to R. Burke junior, 27 August (Corresp. of E. Burke, VII, pp. 416–9), and reply, 31 August (Burke MSS, Northampton, A iv 16); Life and Letters of Sir G. Elliot, II, p. 8, and Corresp. of E. Burke, VII, p. 419n.

[20] Burke to Fitzwilliam, 29 November 1793 (ibid., pp. 494–7); Fox to Adair, 15 December 1793 (B.M. Add. MS 47569, f. 25).

[21] Adair to Fitzwilliam, 8 August 1793, and reply 11th: Adair MSS, B.M. Add. MS 50830.

[22] Fitzwilliam to Portland, [September 1793], Portland to Fitzwilliam, 22 September (F 31a) and 26 and 28 September (N).

[23] Memorandum by T. Grenville of conversations with Lord and Lady Spencer, 18–19 November 1793: B.M. Add. MS 42058, ff. 128–9; O'Gorman, pp. 155–6.

[24] T. Grenville to Fitzwilliam, 29 October 1793 (N 45), and reply, 7 November (B.M. Add. MS 42085, ff. 120–3); T. Grenville to Spencer, 6 December 1793: Althorp MSS, second Earl Spencer, misc., box 12.

[25] Portland to Fitzwilliam, 25 and 31 December 1793 (F 31a); Windham to Burke, [18 January 1794] (Corresp. of E. Burke, VII, pp. 525–6); T. Grenville to Fox, 29 December 1793 (Memorials and Corresp. of C. J. Fox, III, p. 62); Fox to Holland, 9 March 1794 (ibid., pp. 64–8). Fox replied to Grenville on 6 January 1794 that 'I think you all—I mean the D. of P., Fitz., and yourself—very very wrong not only in your opinions but in your conduct', and pleaded for a continuation of general opposition even while supporting Ministers on the war. The course they were taking was 'abandoning all the principles of your former political life' (B.M. Add MS 42058, ff. 135–8).

[26] Portland to Burke, 19 January 1794 (Corresp of E. Burke, VII, p. 526); Windham to Pitt, 20 January (B.M. Add. MS 37844, f. 19); Parl. Register, XXIX, pp. 13–15; Lady Ponsonby to Louisa Ponsonby, 31 March [1794] (Hickleton MSS, A. 1. 2. 1. 96); Fox to Holland, 9 March 1794 Memorials and Corresp. of C. J. Fox, III, p. 65).

[27] Parl. Register, XXIX, pp. 94–5, 364–6. Albemarle declared that Fitzwilliam's speech made it 'necessary for every one to avow his

sentiments'. He, Grafton and Lauderdale supported Bedford's motion, Lauderdale remarking of Fitzwilliam's declaration for monarchy in France, that 'it was the first time he had heard that language from his Lordship, and he sincerely trusted it would be the last' (p. 375). Fitzwilliam, however, repudiated the suggested that he advocated the restoration of 'the ancient despotism of France'.

28 Portland to Fitzwilliam, 25 May 1794 (F 31b); Fitzwilliam to Portland, 12 and 15 June, and Portland to Fitzwilliam, 14 June (Portland MSS, PWF 3761–3).

29 Portland to Fitzwilliam, 19/20 June 1794: F 31b. Grenville reported Portland's conversation with Pitt to Spencer on 21 June, and told him that Portland had sent an account of it to Fitzwilliam, 'so that we expect by the return of the servant on Monday morning a letter announcing our coy correspondent's approaching return' (Althorp MSS, second Earl Spencer, misc. box 15).

30 Fitzwilliam to Portland, 23 June 1794 (Portland MSS, PWF 3765); Portland to Fitzwilliam, 25 June 1794 (F 31b); Mansfield to Portland, 25 and 29 June 1794 (Portland MSS, PWF 7029–30).

31 Fitzwilliam to Charlotte [June 1794] (N).

32 Pitt to Portland, 2 July 1794 (Portland MSS, PWF 7703); Fitzwilliam to Lady Rockingham, 3 July 1794 (Ramsden MSS, I, f. 94); O'Gorman, pp. 204–8.

33 Fitzwilliam to Charlotte, Friday [11 July 1794] (N X512); Fox to Fitzwilliam, July 1794 (F 115a), and to Holland, 18 August 1794 (*Memorials and Corresp. of C. J. Fox*, III, pp. 79–80); Lady Rockingham to Lady C. Wentworth (Ramsden MSS, I, ff. 96, 98), and to Fitzwilliam, 7 July 1794 (F 128h).

34 Burke to Fitzwilliam, 21 June 1794, and Fitzwilliam's reply, 26th (*Corresp. of E. Burke*, VII, pp. 552–3, 555); W. Elliot to Sir Gilbert Elliot, 6 September 1794 (Minto MSS, M 67); R. Burke junior to Fitzwilliam, 18 March 1794 (Burke MSS, Northampton, A vi 4); Laurence to Portland, 24 June 1794 (Portland MSS, PWF 6246); R. Burke to Fitzwilliam, 27 June 1794 (*Corresp. of E. Burke*, VII, p. 556); Fitzwilliam to Charlotte, n.d. (N 512/23).

CHAPTER SEVEN

Lord Lieutenant of Ireland
1794—5

To understand the character of Fitzwilliam's mission to Ireland it is necessary to see his viceroyalty in relationship to his own temperament and background, to the Whig attitude towards the war and the Irish situation, and to the state of Anglo-Irish relations.[1] Religion, as such, was of lesser significance. The mission was born of political considerations and it failed for political reasons. Fitzwilliam represented Burke's passionate conviction that only the twin measures of Catholic emancipation and the ending of the political control of the Protestant ascendancy could avert the threat of a Jacobinised Ireland allied with France to overthrow the British constitution. He had to work through the Ponsonbys, who were mainly interested in using him to climb back into office. In his path lay the many vested interests of the Protestant ascendancy and their connexions with Pitt's government at home. To steer a course through this tangle would have taxed the most experienced and the most patient of statesmen. Fitzwilliam was neither. He lacked the strength of character to control the situation and the flexibility of mind to accommodate principles to practical circumstances. Yet above all he was the victim of the political incompatibility between Pitt's system of government and Whig doctrine, developed on a basis of moral principle and nurtured in years of regular opposition. Pitt, like any statesman caught up in the necessities of government in a time of national crisis, had to work according to a system of priorities. The conduct of an increasingly difficult war and the problems of financing it at home necessarily took precedence over the more complex but ultimately more long-term question of the Anglo-Irish relationship. That question needed to be solved, as Pitt himself recognised, and the lines along which he would have attempted a solution might, in better times, have been not unlike those urged by Fitzwilliam in 1795. In a conversation with Sylvester Douglas, newly appointed Chief Secretary in Ireland, in January 1794 Pitt laid down the principle that 'the Catholics, being the great majority of the inhabitants, must in justice and policy be admitted by degrees to a full participation of all the advantages now held exclusively by the Protestants; but, he added, 'this must be done by degrees, to avoid confusion and a sudden shock'. Pitt admitted that the Protestant monopoly of offices was 'unjust and cannot long be maintained, but that on the other hand it is natural that those who have it should be very unwilling to relinquish it, and that it would be impolitic, and also even in some degree unjust to wrest it from them with violence'.[2]

Pitt's attitude reflected the general character of his statesmanship and embodied the root of the differences between him and the Portland Whigs. In the past Pitt had avoided taking a doctrinaire attitude on political issues. Similarly, he viewed Irish questions on a basis of practical expediency. It was both his great strength and his great weakness as a statesman that he should constantly do so. The Whigs, however, found this attitude unbearably lacking in principle. The French war, which Pitt seemed to regard as no more than a traditional Anglo-French contest for European security and imperial aggrandisement, was to Burke and the Whig leaders a crusade on behalf of property, liberty and all that was worthwhile in eighteenth-century society. They had joined the coalition not to strengthen Pitt's authority and endorse his policies but to infuse into his system of government at home and the conduct of the war in Europe a greater element of ideological commitment. They believed that the new administration was formed to resist Jacobinism at home and to destroy its roots by waging a vigorous war for the restoration of the Bourbon monarchy in France.[3] Portland, Fitzwilliam, Spencer, Mansfield and Windham were all men who believed passionately in the 'cause of kings' and in the Whig party's special mission to preserve the aristocratic order of society. In Ireland, as elsewhere, their enemy was Jacobinism. The Protestants of Ulster were already infected through the Society of United Irishmen, which flourished in the northern province. The seduction of the Catholic south, already resentful at the religious, political and economic disabilities imposed by the alliance of British government and the Protestant ascendancy, would raise up the spectre of a truly united Ireland seeking to avenge centuries of English exploitation and oppression by alliance with France. A French occupation of Ireland would disrupt British sea power and would open the way for a French army to march into England. Concessions to the Catholic claims were designed mainly to avert this threat. The Whig tradition of 'civil and religious liberty all over the world', so frequently toasted at opposition dinners, was not the major source of Whig policy in Ireland. The chief aim was to reconcile the Catholic gentry and moneyed class to the British connexion and to cement a 'union of property' against subversion. The Protestant ascendancy primarily represented not a religious tyranny over the mass of Catholic Irishmen but a narrow political monopoly of power which both limited the freedom of the British government and alienated the leaders of Catholic society from their natural role as upholders of order. It was in pursuit of Burke's ideal of an ordered and disciplined society, not primarily for the sake of religious toleration, that the Whigs advocated the removal of the Catholic disabilities. This was the root of Fitzwilliam's policy as Lord Lieutenant, and it represented merely an application to the Irish situation of those fundamental principles by which he guided his political life. It was impossible for him to compromise without betraying those principles, hallowed by the memory of Rockingham, fastened upon him by the responsibilities of his inheritance, and still represented by Rockingham's living political representative, Edmund Burke. All these circumstances made Fitzwilliam perhaps the most unsuited of all the Whig politicians for the task which he now undertook in Ireland. But his conduct of the office highlights, as does no other single issue of the decade, the true nature of the division between the political systems of Pitt on the one hand and the Whigs on the other. Fitzwilliam's Irish viceroyalty was far more than a mere episode in the politics of the 1790s.

The first suggestion that Fitzwilliam might find a political role in Ireland came from Richard Burke junior in October 1792. Acting as agent to the Irish Catholic Committee, Richard was trying to persuade the British Cabinet to make concessions to the Catholic claims. He became convinced that the Catholic community was innately loyal, pacific and hostile to Jacobinism and that the British government would like to escape from dependence on the Protestant ascendancy but lacked the courage 'to grapple with the Irish factions'. The only hope for Ireland lay in 'a total, abrupt and immediate interruption of all the measures, policies, plans and ideas now prevalent among the governing part of it'. A new Viceroy should be prepared to exert a firm authority over the Irish government; without such a step, Ireland would remain a grave danger. Fitzwilliam, urged Richard, should turn his thoughts towards this role for himself.[4]

Fitzwilliam gave no hint of any wish to undertake such a mission. Spencer was the Whig Lord Lieutenant designate, having been offered the post by Portland at the time of the regency crisis, and it was not until the very eve of the coalition in June 1794 that he finally withdrew his claims. Portland, who had served under Rockingham as Viceroy in 1782, seems to have wished to take the office again in 1794, but he was persuaded by Mansfield that his presence in the Cabinet was essential. Fitzwilliam was therefore the natural candidate for the post, and he had already declared that it was the only leading office he was prepared to contemplate.[5] Ireland attracted him principally because it seemed to offer an opportunity to put Whig principles into practice. He also felt a personal interest in the country where he possessed a large estate, and in which his wife's relatives, the Ponsonbys, represented the Whig interest.[6] For these reasons Fitzwilliam was prepared to overcome his perennial distaste for departmental office.

Fitzwilliam's installation in the office of Lord Lieutenant was delayed by the necessity to find a suitable retreat for the current Viceroy, Lord Westmorland. Pitt was insistent that an office of equivalent standing to that which he had held before going to Ireland should be found for him. Until this could be done Fitzwilliam was to hold the office of Lord President of the Council, carrying membership of the Cabinet without departmental responsibilities. No specific time was set for the transfer of offices, and indeed Pitt and his friends seemed to consider the matter not to be urgent.[7] To his new Whig allies it was far otherwise. Fitzwilliam at once began to consider the details of future arrangements and policies in Ireland. Grattan and William and George Ponsonby, the leaders of the Irish Whigs, were called over for consultations.[8] These steps, taken before Fitzwilliam's appointment to the viceroyalty was announced or even confirmed by the king, have been adduced as early evidence of his rashness and indiscretion. However, it was Portland who took the first steps to inform the Irish Whigs of Fitzwilliam's impending appointment, to hint at the intention to change policies and appointments in Ireland, and to call Grattan and the Ponsonbys to London.

PLATE I

Fitzwilliam aged 16, by Sir Joshua Reynolds (Milton)

PLATE II

Fitzwilliam in middle life, engraving by J. Grozer after Sir Joshua Reynolds
(National Gallery of Ireland)

On 14 August, writing to express his relief at Fitzwilliam's acceptance of the viceroyalty, Portland remarked that 'I communicated
immediately to Ponsonby, but have not had an opportunity yet of
talking to Pitt upon it. You will suppose consequently that I have
not mentioned it to the king'. Portland thus disclosed the appointment to the Irish Whigs before it had been officially mentioned even
to the Prime Minister. Dr Walker King, Lady Rockingham's chaplain and a leading Whig clergyman, later asserted that it had been
'with the entire approbation or rather at the express desire of the
D. of P. [that] he [Fitzwilliam] immediately sent for Mr Grattan and
Mr Ponsonby to come to England. In concert with them, the whole
plan of the future administration for Ireland was settled and
arranged and all with the D. of P.'s privity and consent'.[9] As Fitzwilliam was later to argue, the whole of his Irish mission was concerted from the beginning with Portland, and Fitzwilliam throughout regarded himself as acting solely as Portland's agent in putting
forward measures on which they had agreed at the outset.

It was, of course, widely believed that the coalition would lead
to a 'change of system' in Ireland. James Adair remarked to Portland on 5 August—a week before Fitzwilliam finally accepted the
viceroyalty—that 'the expectations of your Irish friends are pretty
highly raised by seeing your Grace at the head of *that* very important
department [the Home Office]. You will probably not think it prudent
wholly to disappoint them'. And Portland made no secret of his
motives for taking that department, which included in its sphere the
responsibility for Irish affairs. Back in 1792 he had written to Fitzwilliam that the Irish Catholic Committee had given George Ponsonby 'assurances of confidence which they would be disposed to
place in us were we in power, an exception which I entertained so
strongly as to feel it a great inducement among others for wishing
for the ministerial arrangement I thought there was a possibility of
effecting in the beginning of the summer'. Now in July 1794 he not
only told Fitzwilliam that the establishment of a Whig regime in
Ireland was 'a principal inducement for our accepting office' but
also declared to Windham that he could not 'suffer the government
of Ireland to continue to be administered by any person in whom I
have not an implicit confidence'.[10] According to William Ponsonby's
later account, Portland had insisted

that the direction of Irish affairs should be entirely given up to him, for
G

the purpose of enabling him to put an end to the system of government which then existed in Ireland, by nominating a Lord Lieutenant, and putting the management of public affairs into the hands of his friends there—he informed me that this arrangement for Ireland was his principal inducement to agree to Mr Pitt's proposal, and the *sine qua non* of his junction with him.

Pitt, according to this account, had 'perfectly understood' the implications of Portland's demand, and the junction had 'taken place, precisely on the terms which he had stated to me.[11] Though it would certainly be injudicious to accept on Ponsonby's authority the suggestion that Pitt and Portland came to any such precise agreement on the future of Ireland, there seems little doubt that Portland's language to his Irish associates was indiscreet and over-optimistic. No British Prime Minister, and certainly none with so lofty a view of his office as Pitt, could agree to pass over the entire control of any department of government to any group of colleagues, and certainly not to such untried hands as those of his new partners in 1794. Furthermore, there were other parties than the Whigs to take into account. Men who had served Pitt's administration in Ireland could not be lightly handed over to the vindictiveness of their personal rivals or sacrificed to the needs of political expediency in England. If Pitt had been prepared to forget these obligations there were others who were ready to remind him. In particular the Marquis of Buckingham, Pitt's cousin, Lord Grenville's elder brother, twice Lord Lieutenant of Ireland since 1783, was a man with a dominating sense of what was due to him for his past services and a ready sense of outrage at any sign of a slight upon his honour. Buckingham had immediately realised the significance of the coalition for Ireland. Writing to Grenville on 8 July, he declared his disapproval of 'a Cabinet formed from the ranks of the ancient enemy, so nearly complete that it wants only the accession of Mr Fox to render it an efficient administration', and remarked that he expected 'most unpleasant consequences to the public, to Mr Pitt, and most certainly to myself'. In September he complained of 'the measure which you have adopted of surrendering that kingdom to Lord Fitzwilliam and the Duke of Portland, under the government of Mr Ponsonby'. He still smarted under the recollection of 1789, when, as Lord Lieutenant during the regency crisis, he had failed to restrain the Irish House of Commons, led by the Ponsonbys, from voting to address the Prince of Wales to take the unrestricted powers of a regency over Ireland. He no doubt remembered too that the Irish commissioners who then came to London to present the address were feted by the Whigs and entertained by Fitzwilliam himself. He considered that he could not honourably desert the system he had operated in Ireland nor the men who had served him during his viceroyalty. His warnings to Pitt and Grenville now showed that the partisans of the old system in Ireland were not without friends in the sister kingdom and not without influence in high places.[12] Indeed, his outcry against the new Irish arrangements was strong enough to block the first of Fitzwilliam's intended official preparations, the offer of the chief secretaryship to his brother Thomas Grenville. Grenville at first accepted, but when he consulted Buckingham on his return to England in October he found his disapproval so violent that he decided to decline the post, writing to Fitzwilliam of 'the peculiar difficulties which apply personally to me and to me only, [which] make me of all men in England the only one who should not be thought of to undertake the office of Irish Secretary'.[13] Fitzwilliam's final choice for the chief secretaryship was George Damer, Viscount Milton, son of the Earl of Dorchester and an old friend at Eton, who was now one of Fitzwilliam's members for Malton in the British House of Commons. Milton's inexperience as an administrator and parliamentary speaker made him a less effective secretary than Grenville would probably have been, and deprived Fitzwilliam of the sort of experienced advice which Grenville could have given. Buckingham's intransigence helped to cripple Fitzwilliam's Lord Lieutenancy before it had begun.

These were by no means the greatest difficulties which Fitzwilliam had to contend with in the early weeks of his new official career. During August his discussions with the Irish Whigs over policies and appointments advanced rapidly, with complete agreement as to the 'new system' which was to be introduced. Yet no sign came from Pitt. Never the most patient of men, by the end of August Fitzwilliam was complaining of the long delay in making public his forthcoming office. It was clearly becoming more difficult as the weeks went by to maintain even the appearance of confidentiality about the post, and his Irish friends—including Burke—were becoming anxious lest Westmorland and his friends should use the interval to appropriate all the patronage about to fall due across St George's Channel. On 8 September Fitzwilliam impatiently asked whether anything had yet been mentioned to the king, who was at Weymouth, and who,

if he did not know of Fitzwilliam's intended destination, must be
'the only person not admitted to the secret'. A month later he drew
attention to rumours in Ireland that Westmorland was to continue
in office for the coming Parliamentary session, and, suspecting that
this might indeed be Pitt's intention, he determined to bring matters
to a head. Either his appointment must be speedily announced, he
declared, or he would resign from the Cabinet. 'The present state of
uncertainty is mischievous to government in innumerable ways,' he
wrote: 'it is to me irksome in the greatest degree.' When Windham
went on 11 October to press upon Pitt the need for Fitzwilliam's
appointment to be made, however, the Prime Minister, as Portland
put it, not only 'harped' on the need to find a satisfactory office for
Westmorland but complained of the Whig demand for the removal
of Fitzgibbon, the Irish Chancellor and bulwark of the Protestant
ascendancy faction. Pitt, reported Portland, 'rested much upon the
sacrifice of the Chancellor . . . as contrary to the spirit of our
coalition'. Grattan, on the other hand, had declared at the outset
that not only could he never act with any of the leaders of the
Protestant faction but that 'should he ever enter Lord Fitzwilliam's
Cabinet, it should be only on condition that while he entered on one
door, Fitzgibbon should go out on the other'. Fitzwilliam responded,
therefore, with an angry declaration that he would not undertake
the Lord Lieutenancy unless he were given a free hand with respect
to both men and measures. It seemed, he complained, that he was
after all to be required to 'step into Lord Westmorland's old shoes—
that I put on the old trappings, and submit to the old chains'. These
were not the terms he understood when 'upon negotiation the
management of Ireland was transferred to the care of the Duke of
Portland'. For the sake of his own honour and that of his Irish
friends, whom he had taken into his confidence, he felt 'bound to
make clear in the most unequivocal and most overt manner that if I
have misled and duped [them], I have done so because I was misled
and duped myself'. He accordingly declared his intention to resign.[14]

Neither Portland nor Windham thought this reasonable. Portland
had already, rather timidly, suggested that Pitt's refusal to give up
Fitzgibbon was 'perhaps not without reason'. Windham too thought
that Pitt's attitude was understandable, since no suggestion of the
Chancellor's dismissal had been made when the coalition was formed.
'The evil has been,' Windham truly remarked, 'that things have been
suffered to lie, under a supposed general understanding, which . . .

were not of that sort, that an agreement on them should have been presumed.' Strengthened by the hesitations of Portland and Windham, Pitt firmly declared that Fitzgibbon's removal 'would be both dangerous and impolitick', adding that 'the very idea of a *new system* . . . is in itself what I feel it utterly impossible to accede to; and it appears to me to be directly contrary to the general principles on which our junction was formed'.[15]

It was clearly time for explanations. Burke, frantic at the thought that the deadlock over Irish arrangements might jeopardise the whole future of the coalition, proposed a full and frank discussion of the question, free of recrimination: he urged that the Minister should understand Fitzwilliam's position and the impossibility of his sacrificing his honour and dignity. He admitted that Fitzwilliam had 'in some respects acted with a degree of indiscretion', but pointed out that both the Whig leaders had understood that the government of Ireland was to be in their charge and that they were to have full responsibility for men and measures there, 'without any other reserves than what are supposed in every wise and sober servant of the Crown'. In his perplexity and anxiety, his mind almost unhinged by the recent tragedy of the death of his son Richard, Burke veered between suggestions that Pitt should give way, or that Portland and Fitzwilliam should stand their ground and force Pitt to turn them out of office.[16]

Pitt had no intention of allowing Burke or anyone else to settle the matter for him, and he now intervened by calling Grattan to Downing Street. He did not mince his words. According to Grattan's account, 'Mr Pitt don't agree to those extensive powers which we were taught to believe the Duke of Portland had', and he referred to the understanding that Portland should nominate the Lord Lieutenant of Ireland as '*a great original* mistake'. Fitzwilliam, taking Pitt's phrase to refer to himself, roundly declared that he would resign from the government altogether, deferring only the act until Spencer's return from Vienna. 'A flat negative,' he wrote, had been put on any 'powers to alter the face of Government.' 'I shall not go,' he assured Charlotte, 'unless I go with that authority I ought to have, and unless I feel a confidence in the support I shall receive here.' After further discussions with Grattan and the Ponsonbys he repeated his view that there would be 'a total rupture, and there is no doubt of our going out together'.[17]

As London buzzed with rumours of a new ministerial crisis Burke

rushed up to town to mediate, but it was Grattan who provided a
way out. He withdrew his objection to Fitzgibbon's continuing in
office, declaring that he had no wish for office himself. He was prepared to work with anyone so long as Portland and Fitzwilliam were
ultimately in control. In consequence Fitzwilliam authorised Burke to
assure Pitt that he 'never had an idea . . . of considering Ireland as
a thing separate from the general mass of the king's government'
and that 'as to the introduction of any thing which could properly
be called new systems, you [Fitzwilliam] had formed nothing at all
definite in your mind' and would in any case act only 'in concert
with Mr Pitt'. In return for these assurances, Fitzwilliam expected
that Pitt 'would think himself bound to support your Lordship's
government in Ireland, in efficiency, dignity and honour'. Loughborough reported that Pitt was reassured by this declaration and,
Fitzwilliam now wrote to Charlotte, 'I have little doubt of its ending
in our going', though he repeated his conviction that Pitt had
'granted without reserve' Portland's stipulation that he should have
the management of Ireland, and that the arrangement of offices there
was part of that stipulation. 'The scene is not yet closed,' Fitzwilliam
concluded; 'it remains still quivering in the balance : but be assured
I will not go if I do not go in all the dignity of proper power.'[18]

At length, on 15 November, the principal Whig leaders met to
discuss with Pitt and Grenville the precise terms of Fitzwilliam's
mission. Portland, Spencer and Windham accompanied Fitzwilliam
to Downing Street, where a long and frank meeting thrashed out
some kind of understanding. No minute was kept except for
some rough notes by Fitzwilliam and, presumably, others by Grenville, who drafted an account of the discussion late in March 1795
for the approval of all those, except Fitzwilliam, who had been
present. These two documents together provide the only written
evidence of the understanding reached between the Whigs and Pitt
as to Fitzwilliam's instructions.[19] They dealt with five major questions.
First, the provostship of Trinity College, which seemed likely soon
to fall vacant by the death of the current incumbent, was to be
filled on Fitzwilliam's nomination. Secondly, Fitzwilliam urged that
his cousin William Ponsonby should be given a prominent place in
his administration, and proposed that he should become Secretary
of State.[20] Pitt and Grenville objected strongly, mainly on grounds'
that this office should not become politically important in itself, and
it was agreed that the office should be amalgamated with the chief

secretaryship and that Ponsonby should become Keeper of the Signet. Thirdly, the disposal of the Irish law offices was argued at great length. Fitzwilliam wished to make George Ponsonby Attorney General, in order to make him the leading government spokesman in the Irish House of Commons. It was objected that the bringing forward so prominently of both Ponsonby brothers would 'countenance the opinion of a change of system in Ireland', to which Pitt and his friends had so much objection. At length it was agreed that Ponsonby might become Solicitor General, the lower ranking of the two law offices, the present holder, Toler, being compensated by removal to the judicial bench. Wolfe, currently Attorney General, was not to be removed, at any rate for the time being. Fourthly, Pitt and Grenville resisted suggestions, originating from Fitzwilliam's Irish friends, for the abolition of some offices created by Buckingham, mainly in the Revenue boards and, allegedly, for purposes solely of patronage. It was suggested that he should study the question on the spot and make recommendations accordingly. Nothing was said about the position of John Beresford, First Commissioner of the Revenue, who was generally regarded as the leading representative of the Protestant faction and who had built up a commanding influence in the Irish administration.[21] When Fitzwilliam later attempted to dismiss him Pitt and Grenville argued that the intention should have been discussed at this meeting. Fitzwilliam, however, maintained that he had mentioned the matter personally to Pitt on another occasion and that no objection had been stated at any time to Beresford's dimissal.[22]

Finally the meeting came to the Catholic question. Grattan had already indicated his intention to move for a further measure of Catholic relief which would extend the concessions made in 1793, when Catholics otherwise qualified for the franchise had been given the parliamentary vote and allowed to hold military commissions up to the rank of general on the staff. It was now to be proposed that they should become eligible for membership of Parliament and for most higher military and civil offices. The Catholic Bill was to play a decisive part in the history of Fitzwilliam's viceroyalty, and it is all the more surprising that it was not thoroughly discussed on 15 November. However, it had been a long and exhausting meeting and no one was anxious to prolong it. As often happens on such occasions, the item at the tail of the agenda was hastily dealt with and a formula found which enabled the participants to postpone a real decision, without providing proper machinery for that further discussion which was obviously necessary. According to Grenville's record,

The subject was considered as one of much delicacy, and no decided sentiment as to the line which it might ultimately be right to adopt upon it was expressed by any person present. The result of the discussion was an unanimous opinion that Lord Fitzwilliam should inform himself in Ireland as to the state and disposition of the country in this respect, and should transmit that information, with his opinion, to the king's servants here; that he should, as much as possible, endeavour to prevent the agitation of the question during the present session; and that, in all events, he should do nothing in it which might commit the king's government here or in Ireland without fresh instructions from hence.

Fitzwilliam, however, went away with a rather different impression. His note of this item simply read : 'Roman Catholick [question] not to be brought forward by Government, that the discussion of the propriety may be left open.' And he later interpreted this to mean that, though he was not authorised to bring Catholic relief forward as a government measure, he was not to obstruct any unofficial attempt to do so and, if that proposal was strongly supported in the Irish Parliament, he was empowered to allow it to pass. Fitzwilliam here relied upon Grattan's declaration that at his meeting with Pitt on 15 October he had been given a positive assurance that Fitzwilliam was authorised to yield to a Catholic relief Bill if it were pressed strongly in the Dublin Parliament. In the debate on the Union in the Lords on 19 March 1799 Fitzwilliam reiterated this view, to be contradicted by Grenville, who maintained that Fitzwilliam was instructed to go no further than to collect opinions and transmit them to London for a decision.[23] It was on this misunderstanding that the fate of Fitzwilliam's viceroyalty was partly to rest.

Thus, as a set of instructions—which, as it was not reduced to writing until four months later, it was not in fact intended to be— the record of the meeting of 15 November had many obvious deficiencies. It can certainly not be said, however, that Fitzwilliam was guilty of flouting precise instructions laid down for him by the Cabinet.[24] There is no evidence that the Cabinet, as such, ever discussed the Catholic question or any other Irish matter connected with Fitzwilliam's office until early in February 1795, by which time Fitzwilliam had been repeatedly asking for more precise instructions for over a month. Fitzwilliam claimed that he had at all times kept

London fully informed of his actions and repeatedly and unsuccess-
fully demanded the Cabinet's authority for steps which he wished
to take. Fitzwilliam should perhaps rather be blamed, as an observer
in Ireland was later to remark, for *not* obtaining from the Cabinet
beforehand a more precise written understanding of what he was or
was not to do.[25] He was to argue that the Ministers at home failed to
realise the urgency of the crisis which he found on his arrival in
Dublin, and that it was their dilatoriness in attending to the situation
that forced him into independent action : and even then, that nothing was done to commit the government to the Catholic Bill before
the Cabinet could take the final decision. Whatever mistakes he
made during his stay in Dublin, Fitzwilliam always maintained that
he acted within a legitimate interpretation of the discussion of 15
November.

The outcome of the November meeting did not, in fact, satisfy
Fitzwilliam. He wrote to Burke that he was to go 'not exactly upon
the terms I had originally thought of, and I mean particularly in the
removal of the Chancellor, who is now to remain'. He referred the
conditions placed upon him to his Irish friends, believing that it
would be dishonourable to accept the Lieutenancy on terms other
than those he had agreed with them. 'Grattan and the Ponsonbys
desire me to accept,' he informed Burke. 'I left the decision to
them.'[26] Their willingness to settle within the terms of the discussion
of 15 November made it possible for Fitzwilliam to accept the
viceroyalty, but the crisis which had at one time seemed about to
destroy the coalition had only been postponed. Before the union
of Pitt and the Portland Whigs was finally cemented, more concessions would have to be made to the 'old system' than Fitzwilliam
and his Irish friends were prepared to give. His reluctance to come
into the coalition in June 1794 was to be tragically vindicated by the
events of January and February 1795.

As soon as the new year arrived the Fitzwilliam household set off
for Dublin, landing at Balbriggan after the usual rough crossing on 4
January. They were welcomed by eager crowds, full of rumours that
at last Ireland was to have justice and liberty. At the castle Fitzwilliam's staff and advisors awaited him, while his Irish relatives and
their dependants found themselves in the lately unaccustomed position of attenders at the Viceroy's court. Encouraged by these tokens
of goodwill and support, Fitzwilliam threw himself energetically into
his new role. No time was to be wasted. French armies were sweep-

G*

ing over Europe to the Netherlands and British shores were once
again menaced by threats of invasion.[27] Ireland was to be defended
by conciliation, and England herself protected by winning her
loyalty. Fitzwilliam devoted himself to the service of his country
—forgetting, perhaps, that all those on whom he relied might not be
so single-minded or so public-spirited. Too many of those who called
themselves the friends of Ireland wished to serve only their own
interests.

Among those who sought to establish an influence over Fitzwilliam was the man who, as his private secretary, was one of the
first and closest of his contacts in Ireland. This was Thomas Lewis
O'Beirne, born a Catholic but now a clergyman of the established
Church and Portland's private secretary in Dublin in 1782. A staunch
Whig, he had commended himself to the party in Ireland by writing
several political pamphlets and he now looked to his friends in office
for advancement in his profession. A man of rapacious ambition,
completely lacking in tact or discretion and a stranger to all notions
of compromise, he was utterly single-minded in his devotion to the
Irish Whig cause—or, at any rate, the cause of placing Irish Whigs
in offices of power and wealth. His own appetite for patronage was
predatory and insatiable. On the death of the Archbishop of Tuam in
mid-August 1794 he had urged on Portland a complicated reshuffle
of the Irish bench that would allow him to take a seat on it, and he
had warned the Home Secretary that the Beresfords were plotting
to secure the archbishopric for one of their protégés. 'You have not
a moment to lose', he urged. 'Whoever is to come [as Viceroy]
ought to come directly . . . to assume the government.' A few days
later, on hearing from George Ponsonby of Fitzwilliam's intended
nomination, he wrote to both Fitzwilliam and Portland to offer himself as the Lord Lieutenant's private secretary, declaring again the
need for 'speedy and decisive measures' to conciliate the Catholics,
to put the country in a proper state of defence, and to make 'above
all an *immediate* change of *men* . . . amongst the heads of that
faction, with which it is impossible that he [Grattan] ever could
act'. He ended with an assurance that his own appointment as private
secretary would not debar him from being also made a bishop, since
there were two precedents for the combination of these offices.

When Fitzwilliam, seeing O'Beirne as a useful link with Portland,
offered him the private secretaryship O'Beirne replied with a long
letter of advice, mainly concerned with the absorbing subject of Irish

patronage. The Primate and two other bishops were either at death's door or approaching it, the Provost of Trinity College was in 'desperate' health, and a Commissioner of Customs was 'on the point of death'. If Westmorland were not speedily replaced this otherwise fortunate onset of mortality would redound to the benefit of his creatures, 'whose enmity and opposition to everything connected with the Duke of Portland and his principles no change of circumstances or of times can remove or diminish, . . . who . . . will be ever on the watch to thwart and overturn your government'. Westmorland, he alleged, was 'despicable and despised, and surrounded by a set of men . . . who are universally odious' and who (unlike their opponents, presumably) were now 'scrambling for whatever they can secure'. Fitzwilliam must do everything possible to expedite his appointment, and his first step must then be to get rid of Fitzgibbon and the Beresfords. Without their removal nothing could be accomplished. The disaffected state of Ireland could not be dealt with while they remained in power. A few days later O'Beirne again pressed on Fitzwilliam the necessity of taking all efficient and powerful offices into reliable hands, and on 1 November he urged that, in any discussions with Pitt, the Whigs should not sacrifice their aims in Ireland even in order to preserve the coalition. The news, which reached him later in the month, that Fitzgibbon was to stay, produced another missive in which he predicted that this would be 'a fatal measure' and would be interpreted as a sign that Fitzwilliam was to be a prisoner of the 'old system'. Three weeks later, as Fitzwilliam prepared for his departure, O'Beirne wrote again to press the dismissal of Sackville Hamilton and Edward Cook, the civil and military Under-Secretaries at Dublin, as members of 'that faction, whose system it is your Lordship's interest, and will be your glory, to destroy'. And in preparation for Fitzwilliam's arrival he composed a long memorandum, marked 'Most secret and for your Lordship alone', which he placed on Fitzwilliam's desk to be the first document for his attention in office. This once more pressed the necessity of a 'change of system', arguing that the Irish people would interpret the continuance in office of the Beresfords and 'the whole junto' at present in power as evidence of Fitzwilliam's impotence to carry out any changes of policy. 'The support of these men will be your weakness, as their enmity would be your strength', O'Beirne declared. He must give to his friends 'places conferring power sufficient to support your government', and in particular 'such offices as are considered to be *ministerial* in the House of Commons'—the offices of Attorney and Solicitor General and the civil and military Under-Secretaries. O'Beirne also urged the abolition of Buckingham's additional Revenue offices as they became vacant and the replacement of the Postmaster General and his two subordinate postmasters. Finally he added that 'it will be a most dangerous thing to leave Beresford at the head of the Revenue Board', and he gave the impression that all these changes would be accepted and were indeed expected by the office-holders themselves, who either already had ample provision to fall back on or could be satisfactorily compensated by pensions or sinecures.[28]

Thus Fitzwilliam found himself from the outset under heavy pressure from his Irish advisors to carry into effect that clean sweep of offices and policies that had been the original intention of the Whigs. The assertions 'of O'Beirne and the Ponsonbys that new policies, to which Fitzwilliam felt himself committed, could be carried through only after a sweeping change of personnel in office and that those changes must be carried through before the meeting of the Irish Parliament on 22 January lay behind the apparently precipitate action on which Fitzwilliam now embarked. He quickly allowed himself to be convinced that the situation was urgent, indeed desperate, and that the caution of the Ministers in London was based upon a lack of understanding of that fact. Nothing but a change of policy in Ireland, it seemed, could avert a rebellion and reconcile the respectable men of both religions to the British connexion : and the unanimous advice of his Irish friends was that such a change of policy could not be carried out without a previous change of men in office. It was for this reason that Fitzwilliam's first attention was given to what, in London, seemed to be merely matters of place and patronage. In his mind, however, they were no more than the preliminaries to his real task, the pacification of a disorderly and increasingly disaffected part of the empire at a moment of exceptional peril.

The day after Fitzwilliam's arrival in Ireland was spent in recovering from the journey. On 6 January he set about making the necessary official arrangements. The vacant Primacy of Ireland was offered to the Bishop of Waterford, and the Bishopric of Ossory was conferred on O'Beirne. The provostship of Trinity College was offered to Richard Murray, one of the fellows, as Burke had urged some weeks before. These recommendations, Fitzwilliam wrote to

Portland, would be popular all over Ireland and would set his vice-royalty off on the right footing. He also began his intended reconstruction of the administration by making a proposal to Wolfe, the Attorney General, to retire to make way for George Ponsonby. He interpreted the agreement of 15 November as precluding only Wolfe's dismissal. His voluntary retirement was another matter, and an inducement was now offered in the tempting shape of promotion to a Chief Justiceship at the first vacancy, in addition to the imminent falling in of a reversion, which Wolfe already possessed, to a place worth £2,300 a year. A peerage was offered to Mrs Wolfe, and Fitzwilliam reported that with these promises and 'some other little douceurs . . . the Attorney General will retire very well contented.' He also asked for a peerage for Yelverton, the Chief Baron of the Exchequer, so that he could become government spokesman in the Lords and keep an eye on the Chancellor, while Ponsonby would take his place as the leading government representative in the Commons. On the 13th Portland replied with a prompt approval of all these suggestions, expressing some reservations only about the possible impropriety of appointing Wolfe to the bench after so long an absence from the Bar.[29] Even this, however, did not amount to an objection to Fitzwilliam's plan, and no mention was made of any breach of the agreement on 15 November (to which, of course, Portland had been a party).

Fitzwilliam did not wait for Portland's approval of his first proposals before going on to the next. On 9 January Beresford was informed that he was to be relieved of office, with the grant of a pension equal to the amount of his salary. Fitzwilliam asserted to Portland that Beresford was 'satisfied, and himself and his family promise support'. Toler, the Solicitor General, was asked for his resignation on the 10th, as agreed in November, and according to that agreement was promised the first vacant seat on the bench. His request for a peerage for *his* wife was also agreed to. Fitzwilliam reported that he thought himself well taken care of. He also declared that he intended to appoint William Ponsonby Secretary of State for a few months only, after which interval the post was to be amalgamated with the chief secretaryship as agreed in November. A week later he announced his intention to cancel the grant by Westmorland of the reversion of the Clerkship of the Hanaper, one of the most valuable of Irish sinecures, to Lord Glentworth and to give it to the Duke of Leinster, head of the Irish Whig connexions, 'to mark by this ostensible act his decided support of Government. I have offered it to him and he has accepted'. The following day he recommended Grattan's nephew, the Bishop of Clonfert, to the see of Waterford, and proposed George Ponsonby's appointment as Attorney General, pointing out that he was 'certainly . . . the most rising man at the Bar, and . . . Mr Grattan excepted, is indisputably the best speaker in the House of Commons'. On the 15th Lord Milton told Hamilton and Cook, the Under-Secretaries, that they too were to be removed, assuring Cook that no imputation of misconduct was implied against them and that an 'honourable compensation' was to be offered.[30]

As the Whig revolution in Ireland got under way consternation spread through the Protestant faction and their friends in London. Bad weather was delaying the Irish mails,[31] but on 2 February Portland wrote to remonstrate at length against the plan to give Wolfe a chief justiceship and to appoint George Ponsonby in his place, though he had given his tacit consent to these measures on 13 January. No mention was as yet made of the other arrangements, all of which Fitzwilliam had notified promptly to London.[32] On 5 February Fitzwilliam wrote to Pitt, as First Lord of the Treasury, to press for the grant of a sinecure in reversion to Yelverton's son, to complete the arrangements for the peerage proposed for the Chief Baron. He took the opportunity to mention his dispositions so far as steps necessary 'to give strength and credit to my administration', and added, 'I have every reason to expect a great degree of unanimity in support of my administration : nothing can defeat those expectations unless an idea should go forth that I do not possess the fullest confidence, and cannot command the most cordial support of the British Cabinet'.[33]

The dispossessed friends of the old administration had already set to work to influence opinion in London against Fitzwilliam. Beresford wrote immediately after his dismissal to Lord Auckland to appeal to Pitt for support,[34] and on 23 January he set out for England, while Hamilton appealed to Grenville and Cook wrote to Evan Nepean, an influential civil servant at the Home Office, to declare that Fitzwilliam was trying to wrest control of Ireland out of the hands of the Crown and vest it in the Whig aristocracy—an ingenious argument reminiscent of Fitzwilliam's supposed role in the India Bill crisis of 1783.[35] Pitt, anxious both to protect the old government's servants in Ireland and to assert the authority of the Cabinet as a whole over the apparent attempt of the Whigs to impose their party regime there, responded to the pressure by writing in strong terms to Fitzwilliam. Beresford, he wrote, far from being satisfied with Fitzwilliam's proposals, considered himself as 'forcibly turned out', and his removal, 'though your Lordship at different times expressed apprehensions of Mr Beresford's supposed influence and power (from ideas which I always conceived to be mistaken)' was never 'to my recollection . . . hinted at even in the most distant manner . . . much less . . . without his consent'. If Beresford's removal had been in Fitzwilliam's mind it should have been brought up on 15 November, when both Pitt and Grenville would have objected to it on the principle that it would be inconsistent with the spirit of the coalition. Pitt added that Toler was dissatisfied with his removal, objected to the offices proposed for both the Ponsonbys and to the arrangement for the Duke of Leinster, and declared that all these steps were

in contradiction to the ideas which I thought were fully understood among us. . . . On most of these points I should have written to your lordship sooner [he concluded] but the state of public business has really not left me the time of doing so; and it is not without very deep regret that I feel myself under the necessity of interrupting your attention by considerations of this sort while there are so many others of a different nature to which all our minds ought to be directed.

The rebuke in Pitt's last sentence stung Fitzwilliam into an equally sharp reply.[36] It was precisely to serve those greater ends of national security, he wrote, that changes in the Irish administration were necessary: the monopoly of power in the hands of the Protestant minority caused widespread popular disaffection, but hitherto the mass of the Catholic population had resisted the blandishments of the Jacobins. The removal of those men identified with the old system was an essential prerequisite to that change of policy which alone could preserve the Anglo-Irish connexion. In Ireland the Lord Lieutenant's power to act would be judged by his power to make official arrangements with the support of the Cabinet, and in particular by his power to remove Beresford as the man identified with the old regime. On his arrival he discovered that his 'apprehensions of his [Beresford's] power and influence' had been 'too well founded: I found them incompatible with mine'. If Beresford was to remain, he could not: 'and after the receipt of this, you will be prepared to decide between Mr Beresford and me and that the matter is come to this issue is well known *here'*. As for the question being raised without notice, Fitzwilliam claimed that he had mentioned to Pitt his intention to remove Beresford, and that Pitt 'made *no* objection, nor, indeed, any reply', upon which he had taken it to be within his discretion to do so. If, now, Pitt refused to accept his advice, he should recall him : 'These are not times for the fate of the empire to be trifled with. . . . I will deliver over the country in the best state I can to any person, who possesses more of your confidence.' To both Pitt and Fitzwilliam the squabble over Irish places was now inextricably entangled with the deepest questions of Anglo-Irish relations, and to Fitzwilliam Pitt's argument that the Irish question was a distraction from the more pressing needs of the war sounded strangely: it was Fitzwilliam above all who had urged upon a seemingly reluctant Cabinet in June 1794 Burke's policy of total war against the revolution. His mission in Ireland was merely a part of that policy, and the selfish interests of the Beresford clique should not be allowed to take precedence over it. Both sides had now passed the point of mutual understanding.

Official arrangements were not, of course, the only or the major questions which Fitzwilliam was pressing upon the Cabinet. They were merely the means to the greater end of Irish conciliation, which was to be approached in the first instance by further concession to the political claims of the Catholic community. The Irish Parliament was due to meet on 22 January, and from his conversations with Grattan in England Fitzwilliam was in no doubt that it was intended to bring forward a Catholic relief Bill. He understood that his instructions forbade him from taking up a position in favour of the Bill without specific instructions from the Cabinet, but he believed that if the Irish Parliament showed itself strongly in its favour he was authorised not to oppose its passage. However, to speed the Cabinet's decision was his primary aim, and according to the terms of the agreement of 15 November, he set about collecting information which would lead the Ministers to a firm decision. It must be appreciated that the character of the proposed Bill was not revolutionary. The Act passed at the instigation of Pitt's and Westmorland's government in 1793 had gone a good deal of the way towards conciliation by admitting to the parliamentary franchise Catholics otherwise qualified for the vote and allowing Catholics to hold commissions below the rank of general on the staff. The only substantial political discrimination remaining was the exclusion of Catholics from membership of Parliament (through the oaths and declaration against transubstantiation which had to be taken by members) and from holding civil and higher military offices (through the Test Act). These restrictions, as Fitzwilliam indicated to Portland on 10 February, in practice affected only a very small minority of the Catholic population. Burke had calculated that in the present state of electoral interests no more than three Catholic members were likely to be elected to the Commons and only one peer was likely to take a seat in the Lords. Fitzwilliam urged the vastly more significant effect which such concessions would have upon the spirit and loyalty of the whole Catholic population. Only if admitted to full and equal citizenship of the empire, he argued, would the Catholic gentry and men of property be reconciled to the connexion with Britain and use their influence to restrain the disorder now endemic amongst the peasantry. And if the Irish propertied class were so to exert its influence, the need for large garrisons of British troops to hold Ireland in subjection would be ended and they would be freed for use against the French. Coupled with the proposal for Catholic emancipation was Fitzwilliam's scheme for the establishment of a native force of yeomanry, officered by the Catholic gentry and working harmoniously with the Castle.[37]

Fitzwilliam's reports of the state of Ireland, transmitted regularly to London, therefore stressed the growing spirit of insurrection in Ireland, particularly in the Catholic areas, and urged the need for a stronger system of police. Within a week of his arrival he wrote that 'not one day has passed since my arrival without intelligence being received of violences committed in Westmeath, Meath, Longford and Cavan : Defenderism is there in its greatest force'. And he complained that 'I find the texture of government very weak'; the state of the local magistracy and the central machinery for law and order were alike chaotic. The outrages amongst the peasantry, he reported on the 15th, were not the result of political disaffection but 'merely the outrages of banditti'; the need was to encourage the Catholics of wealth and influence to come forward more zealously in the cause of law and order by removing the political discrimination which rankled with them. 'No time is to be lost,' he wrote; 'the business will presently be at hand, and the first step I take is of infinite importance.'[38]

Fitzwilliam set himself to force urgent action upon what he knew would be an unwilling Cabinet. On 10 January he reported that he found the Catholics already agitating the relief question, though he assured Portland that he would do his best to halt the progress of any measure until he had instructions from London. On the 15th he wrote that he had received an address of welcome from the Catholics of Dublin, and remarked that though he had 'endeavoured to keep clear of any engagement whatever', nevertheless 'there is nothing in my answer that they can construe into a rejection of what they are *all* looking forward to, the repeal of the remaining restrictive and penal laws'. He added:

I shall not do my duty if I do not distinctly state it as my opinion that *not to grant cheerfully* on the part of government all the Catholics wish will not only be exceedingly impolitick, but perhaps *dangerous*. . . . If I receive no very peremptory directions to the contrary, I shall acquiesce with a good grace, in order to avoid the manifest ill effect of a doubt or the appearance of hesitation; for in my opinion even *the appearance of hesitation* may be mischievous to a degree beyond all calculation.

He urged that Pitt should be consulted immediately and, apparently confident that with Portland's backing he would succeed in swaying the Minister's opinion, he began to give encouragement to the Catholic leaders in Dublin. A few days later he noted in a memorandum of an interview with Lord Mountnorris, who asked what the government's line would be on the Catholic question:

I told him, were the question not to be agitated, that under the pressure of other critical business I should not have thought it expedient to introduce so important a subject; but that if it was brought forward by the Catholics themselves, as petitioners, the matter of the petition being as I supposed, it would be proper; undoubtedly I should be for granting it; the Ministers in England were of this opinion.

Despite the omission of any reference to the question in his speech at the opening of the parliamentary session, it was now well understood in Ireland that his attitude towards a relief Bill was favourable, and though he had as yet given no public pledge on it he was moving into a position in which it would be difficult to prevent the Bill from passing the Irish Commons.[39] The game was a dangerous one, and Pitt was unlikely to agree to play it. Fitzwilliam was allowing his assessment of the urgency of the situation to override his sense of reality. No British Cabinet in the eighteenth century could lightly decide to reverse the traditional policy of controlling Ireland through the Protestant monopoly. Any Cabinet that wished to do so would have George III to reckon with. The king, on seeing Fitz-william's letters on 5 February, at once declared his uncompromising opposition to any further Catholic relief and in particular to the admission of Catholics to Parliament. It would amount, he protested, to 'the total change of the principles of government which have been followed by every administration in that kingdom since the abdication of James II', and he firmly pronounced the question to be 'beyond the decision of any Cabinet of Ministers'. Fitzwilliam, he declared, was 'venturing to condemn the labours of ages' by advocating ideas which 'every friend to the Protestant religion must feel diametrically contrary to those he has imbibed from his earliest youth'. Six years later Pitt was to show that the king's rigidity on the Catholic question need not deter him from urging emancipation upon him; but in February 1795 Pitt himself was not yet convinced of its necessity. When, therefore, the Cabinet at last met on 7 February to consider Fitzwilliam's despatches the Ministers temporised. They declared the need for more information from Ireland, particularly as to the likely effects on 'the present ecclesiastical establishment and the present constitution of the House of Commons'. In the meantime the Lord Lieutenant was to use every effort to defer the introduction of the measure and was told not to give even the appearance of encouragement to its promoters.[40]

Portland's despatch containing these instructions arrived too late. Fitzwilliam had already written that the Catholics were pressing the relief Bill, and advised that the question must be 'finally and conclusively settled' by the lifting of all restrictions on the Catholics, saving only the ecclesiastical offices and the Crown itself. Two days later, on 12 February, Grattan formally asked leave in the Irish Commons to introduce his Bill, holding back only the details at Fitzwilliam's request until approval could come from London. Reporting this to Portland, Fitzwilliam declared:

I think myself fully authorised to decide for myself upon the subject, but still, considering the extent proposed, I am desirous to have the mode considered in England . . . whilst I hope it is still within my reach to have it limited or modified.

He also requested the confirmation of the proposals to appoint George Ponsonby and Curran as Attorney and Solicitor General. When Portland's despatch, accompanied by a letter from Pitt complaining about his official appointments, arrived on the 14th, he realised that the Cabinet was not prepared to give him the backing he had expected. His reaction was characteristic, but unwise. As in the autumn of 1794 he had threatened to break up the coalition unless his appointment were settled immediately, now again he threatened resignation if the Cabinet did not approve all the measures and arrangements he had proposed. He declared that the lower orders in Ireland were in a state of virtual rebellion and that the only hope lay in conciliating the Catholic gentry by conceding their civil rights. 'These are not times for the fate of the empire to be trifled with.'[41]

This time, however, Fitzwilliam could not count on Portland's support. In both private and official letters on the 16th,[42] the duke expressed fears that the concessions proposed would 'produce such a change in the present constitution of the House of Commons as will overturn that, and with it the present ecclesiastical establishment'. To Fitzwilliam's astonishment, the man to whom he had so long looked as his leader, and whose own policies and measures, Fitzwilliam believed, he had been attempting to carry out in Ireland, now addressed him in terms more appropriate to the most extreme Protestant view. His language seemed to contradict every principle upon which the two men had for long been agreed. Portland, however, was suffering the agonies of a man whose natural response to a crisis—to hope that if he did nothing it would go away—had met the rock of intractable reality. It was Fitzwilliam who stood in the way.

On the 18th, in a covering letter to his despatch of the 16th, which had been before the Cabinet for approval, Portland declared himself 'too much hurt and grieved' by Fitzwilliam's ultimatum 'to be able to sit down and write such an answer to it as every feeling of my heart tells me it is entitled to'. He assured Fitzwilliam that his advice would carry 'the most decisive weight' with the Ministers, but urged patience and understanding of their difficulties.[43] Two days later he transmitted a formal instruction from the Cabinet to 'inform you in the plainest and most direct terms that we rely upon your zeal and influence to take the most effectual means in your power to prevent any further proceeding being had on that Bill until his Majesty's pleasure shall be signified to you with regard to your future conduct respecting it'. And on the next day, when the Cabinet met again to consider the question, Portland actually advised that Fitzwilliam should be recalled. The notification of this decision, Portland wrote, was the most painful task I ever undertook; [but it was] my opinion, and I call it mine, because I chose to be the first to give it, and I was, I believe, the only member of the Cabinet who gave it decidedly, that the true interest of government . . . requires that you should not continue to administer that of Ireland. . . . There appears such a concurrence in the views, such a deference to the suggestions and wishes, and such an acquiescence in the prejudices of Grattan and the Ponsonbys that there seems to me no other way of rescuing you and English government from the annihilation which is impending over it.

He referred again to 'the inordinate desire of George Ponsonby' as the reason for Fitzwilliam's downfall, and asked :

Do you feel that the government of Ireland is really in your hands? . . . Let me implore you to make it your own desire to come away from Ireland. . . . I write to you in the agony of my soul, impelled by the sense of my friendship and attachment to you and of my duty to the public.

The official letter of recall was despatched on the 23rd, accompanied by personal letters from Portland, Mansfield, Spencer, Windham and Tom Grenville, all urging him to accept the king's 'particular wish' —acceded to by George III out of sympathy for Portland—that he should resume his former seat in the Cabinet.[44]

If any injury has been done to *you*, if any blow has been aimed at your political character and reputation [Portland wrote], it is I who have attempted it; revenge yourself on me, renounce me, but assist in saving your country—I will retire, I will make any expiation or atonement that can satisfy you—you are younger, more active, more able than I am, you can do more good. If my . . . renunciation of the world will restore you to the public service, God forbid I should hesitate a moment.

Portland's melodramatic pleas did nothing to cushion the shock of the disclosure that it was he, and apparently he almost alone, who had counselled Fitzwilliam's removal from office. That advice had been given before Portland's letters ordering Fitzwilliam to hold back on the Catholic question had had time even to reach Dublin, much less to call forth a reply. And the suggestion that Fitzwilliam had been a mere puppet in the hands of Grattan and the Ponsonbys —the very men whom Portland had hastily summoned to London in August 1794, to confer with himself and Fitzwilliam on the measures to be adopted in Ireland—seemed to Fitzwilliam an unforgettable insult. He had believed himself to be carrying out in Ireland policies originating with Portland, policies whose achievement Portland had repeatedly stressed were his chief inducement for taking office under Pitt's Premiership. Instead of his advocate and shield in the Cabinet, Portland had been his betrayer. Normally the most generous, lasting and affectionate of friends, Fitzwilliam resolved that he would never speak to Portland again. To him alone he attributed the responsibility for a catastrophe which Fitzwilliam never ceased to believe was not merely his own personal tragedy but a blow at the vital interests of the empire and a betrayal of Whig principles. His recall, he wrote to the Duke of Devonshire,

is a subject of the greatest pain and mortification to me, because it must be the cause of the most complete separation between the Duke of Portland and myself. Either I have been the most wild, rash, unfaithful servant to the Crown and to England, or he has abandoned in the most shameful manner his friend, and his friend's character, for pursuing generally a system of measures that has been the perpetual theme of his conversation, and the subject of his recommendation for years back. It is a painful, a trying task to submit to a separation from a man I have loved so long and so much; but I must submit to it, for I will not abandon my character to the disgraceful imputations that must attach upon it if I do not justify it by charging him with the most shameful dereliction of his friend that ever was experienced by a faithful and a tried one.[45]

Isolation and abandonment by his friends now seemed to Fitz-william to be his fate. 'Here I am,' he wrote to James Adair, 'abandoned, deserted and given up—an object of the general calumny of administration, for they must abuse me to justify themselves.' Adair, hoping to bridge the gulf that had opened up between Fitz-william and Portland, cautiously replied with a hope that 'when the strength of those feelings which I must confess have but too naturally arisen, from the late occurrences, shall have a little sub-sided, your most ancient and respectable friendships may again be renewed'. He assured Fitzwilliam that Portland 'has on every occa-sion expressed in the warmest terms his own undiminished affection and esteem for you, and the deep concern he feels in this most lamentable occasion, which is most plainly visible, and exceeds anything I have before observed in him, in a knowledge of more than twenty years'. It was not only sympathy for Portland, how-ever, that led many in the political world to condemn Fitzwilliam for the crisis. Even Adair suggested that 'it is absolutely impossible that all parties can be *wholly* free from some *degree of blame* and Fox, though asserting his confidence 'that Fitzwilliam will turn out to be as much in the right in all its points, as he is clearly so in my judgement, with respect to . . . the Catholic Bill', confessed that he found the whole affair 'very unintelligible'. On the other side, Fitzwilliam's recall was the occasion for less restrained feelings. The king had already commended Portland's handling of his correspondence with Fitzwilliam, and approved of his 'very feeling and upright declaration' in the closet on the subject. He now repeated his approbation of the Home Secretary's 'very dignified, honourable, and I may add conscientious part . . . on the ill advised conduct adopted in Ireland', and attributed Fitzwilliam's attitude to 'an high spirit and the viewing a favourite object in but one view'. Buckingham was openly delighted at the news, and wrote magnanimously to Grenville that it 'relieves my mind from recollections that have given me the severest pain. I have dismissed from it every part of those unpleasant impressions, and remember nothing that has passed for four months save the declarations of your affection to me'.[46]

Fitzwilliam was never to forget those four months, and the need to justify his case before the public arose not merely from the wish to vindicate his policies and his reputation but also from the importance of assuring himself that he had acted consistently with his lifelong principles. When his old friend Carlisle wrote on 27 February to warn him that it was 'a *very* general opinion on this side the water that your advisers have been hasty and precipitate, that they have hurried you to the adoption of measures which could not have had the previous approbation of Ministers here', Fitzwilliam drew up a reply in the form of a long and considered justification of all his actions since his arrival in Dublin. Declaring that Carlisle must have received his information from 'the very persons who have grossly betrayed and unfeelingly abandoned me', he asserted that the removals of Beresford, Cook and Hamilton were necessary because he could place no confidence in them. Beresford, indeed, was 'a person labouring under the universal heavy suspicions, and subjecting my government to all the opprobrium and unpopularity attendant upon his maladministration'. It was, he argued, the official removals and not the Catholic Bill which explained his recall. The Catholic Bill, he pointed out, was much less extensive than the measure of 1793, and had met with no significant opposition from

any Protestant body. The Cabinet had in any case left the decision
on the subject to 'my judgement and discretion' and his decision to
give Grattan's Bill his backing was taken in order 'to gain credit and
strength to the administration'. He had originally intended to secure
the postponement of the Bill for one session to give time for consultations and full discussion, but found on arrival that Grattan had
decided as long ago as July 1794 to bring it forward at the first
opportunity. Even then, however, he had persuaded Grattan to do
no more than seek leave to introduce a Bill, without disclosing its
terms, and had referred the whole matter to London for a decision.
It would thus have been possible to amend the Bill without causing
a public outcry. Pitt, however, worked upon by 'secret, unavowed,
insidious informations', had determined to use the Bill as a means to
get rid of the Whig administration in Ireland, putting the personal
interests of his friends there before the needs of the country and
breaking the terms of his agreement with Portland at the outset of
the coalition. The accusation that Fitzwilliam had acted in breach
of instructions was merely a screen for the true cause of his dismissal, the resentment of the Protestant ascendancy at their loss of
power. Finally Fitzwilliam appealed to the unprecedented support
which his administration had received from all sections in Ireland,
the unanimous grant by the Irish Commons of 'the largest supplies
that have ever been demanded', and his success in promoting internal
pacification and providing for external defence. Instead of co-operating in this great task the Cabinet were 'cavilling with me on petty
arrangements, and the jobs of intriguing individuals, and . . . abandoning and betraying me'. He concluded by authorising Carlisle to
show his letter to 'as many persons as you shall think proper'. He
himself sent copies to Burke and other friends.[47]

Carlisle showed the letter to the king, who frostily remarked that
he 'cannot help wishing Earl Fitzwilliam may have regained a little
more temper when he returns than appears in his letter' and suggested 'the propriety of trying to set an honourable man right,
whose heart certainly has prevented him from attending to the false
reasoning that prevails in the whole statement'.[48] Meanwhile the
London ministerial newspapers were attributing Fitzwilliam's recall
solely to the Catholic issue, and repeating the accusation that he
had exceeded his instructions in giving support to Catholic expectations. Fitzwilliam thereupon decided to set out his case in detail.
The second letter to Carlisle was dated 23 March, and its general

tenor was the attempt to show 'that the Catholic question entered for nothing into the real cause of my recall' and that he had acted throughout in conformity with the agreement of 15 November. He stressed how his repeated requests for instructions on the Catholic Bill had been ignored by the Cabinet for almost a month, while Ministers had responded almost immediately to the dismissals of Beresford and his associates. It was the threat of a 'change of system' in the Irish administration which had alerted Pitt, and Beresford's visit to London which had resulted in the decision to dismiss him. Fitzwilliam recalled that he had challenged Pitt to choose between him and Beresford; the choice had been made. Portland, meanwhile, had been deceived into changing 'all his former opinions respecting the politics of this country' and in consequence had been made Pitt's instrument, calling for Fitzwilliam's replacement only a day after he had written to Ireland to ask for further information on the Catholic Bill. The conclusion was inescapable:

Let my friends . . . no longer suffer the Catholic question to be mentioned as entering in the most distant degree into the causes of my recall. Let them listen no longer to that terrifying enumeration of evils and miseries to result to the empire from a measure which my enemies assert to have considered either as originating with myself exclusively, or as hurried on by me rashly, precipitately, or without consent or consultation. . . . Had Mr B[eresford] never been dismissed, we never should have heard of them.

Behind even this, however, there lurked a much more sinister explanation of the crisis. The whole affair, Fitzwilliam now claimed, had been deliberately engineered by Pitt to enable him to wriggle out of the terms imposed by the Whigs for the coalition in 1794. Portland's stipulation for the control of the Irish government had been an inescapable condition of Whig consent to the junction: Pitt had now successfully wrested it from them and given Ireland back to the old corrupt faction that had governed it since 1783.[49] Fitzwilliam's case deserves attention, though his accusations that Pitt had plotted his downfall from the start seemed to verge on the paranoiac. The youthful Canning, infatuated with Pitt, called Fitzwilliam's letter to Carlisle an 'idle, intemperate publication', while Auckland remarked that it contained 'passages . . . so extravagant that they have an appearance of insanity'.[50] Yet Fitzwilliam was right to put his Lord Lieutenancy into the context of the Pitt–Portland

coalition of 1794 and to see it not merely as a personal episode but
as a vital incident in the working out of the relationship between the
two parties. Pitt was hardly such a Machiavellian as to have pre-
arranged a crisis which brought Ireland, as one of Burke's Irish
friends remarked, to 'the brink of a civil war'.[51] He may have been
innocent of the more sinister designs which Fitzwilliam, in an agony
of self-justification, felt obliged to attribute to him, but he was not
innocent of responsibility for the crisis. At a moment when Ireland
needed statesmanship Pitt offered only expedients. He allowed his
eagerness for the Portland coalition to override the precautions he
should have taken to see that all areas of policy disagreement should
be fully explained beforehand. He seems to have paid little attention
to what Portland, as well as Fitzwilliam, repeatedly stated to have
been the Whig *sine qua non* for a junction, the handing over to
them of the Irish administration. Pitt could hardly plead ignorance
of the implications of this for Irish office-holders, since Irish politics
were notoriously dominated by patronage and factious self-interest.
He knew also of Fitzwilliam's relationship to the Ponsonbys, of his
enthusiastic adoption of Burke's hopes for Irish Catholic emancipation, and of his staunchly Whig temperament. Fitzwilliam's political
career so far was that of a man utterly committed to Whig ideals and
yet totally inexperienced in practical administration. The times might
have called for justice for Ireland, but the Irish situation also called
for a man of wide experience and political skill. In accepting Portland's insistence upon a Whig government for Ireland and Fitzwilliam
as his nominee for the post Pitt took a risk which was hardly even a
calculated one. And when the enormity of that risk showed itself, in
November 1794, Pitt accepted a compromise which lacked precision
on the most vital questions of all, and left Fitzwilliam with the sincere impression that more was left to his personal discretion than
Pitt or the rest of the Cabinet, let alone the king, could ever accept.

In his government of Ireland Fitzwilliam conceived a policy
which he honestly believed would provide a basis for a permanent
future relationship between the two kingdoms as well as a
solution for the immediate crisis of the revolutionary war. What
he did not appreciate was the strength of the forces opposed
to him and the weakness of Portland's character. Without
strong support in the Cabinet, Fitzwilliam's Irish policies were
doomed. In relying upon Portland, both as the originator of those
policies and as their advocate at home, he put his trust in a

shadow. Indeed, Portland's only decisive act throughout the crisis was to propose Fitzwilliam's recall. If he had had confidence in his own judgement and his own policies, he might at least have considered persuading Fitzwilliam to stay in Ireland, as the only man likely to soothe the disappointment of the Catholics and the Irish Whigs at the Cabinet's refusal of Grattan's Bill. The only condition which Fitzwilliam had made for his continuance in office was not that the Catholic Bill should be accepted, amended or not, by the Cabinet. It was that he should have full responsibility for the appointment or dismissal of members of the Irish administration, and particularly that Beresford and his friends should not be included in it. Such a stipulation may well have betrayed Fitzwilliam's lack of 'coalition-mindedness'[52] but it met with an equal determination on the other side not to give up power and influence. Portland's inability to stand firm on the issue on which he should have supported his colleague most energetically—the Lord Lieutenant's right to decide the membership of his own government—settled Fitzwilliam's fate. Portland could not stand up to Pitt and the Grenvilles in a battle over Irish patronage. To this extent Fitzwilliam was correct in claiming that the Catholic question was not the primary reason for his recall, and there was a good deal of justice in his claim that it was Portland who had let him down.

His contemporaries were divided in their judgements on the causes of his recall. His former friends were more distressed by the breach between him and Portland than concerned to attribute blame to either, while the supporters of Pitt and the old government naturally condemned him. His two 'Letters to Lord Carlisle' found their way into print, though in an unauthorised and to some extent inaccurate form.[53] His attacks on Portland and the other Whig members of the Cabinet greatly distressed his friends, while his assertions that Pitt had deliberately ruined his prospects of success did not convert his enemies. Loughborough spoke for many when he condemned the publication of the letters as 'the most violent breach of public and private confidence',[54] though Fitzwilliam later declared on his honour that they were not printed at his direction or with his knowledge. He had intended the letters to be a semi-public justification, to be circulated only amongst his friends. Whether published or not, the letters dismayed old Whig friends by their asperity towards Portland. Tom Grenville echoed the feelings of many when he wrote that he was

distressed for the Duke of Portland, Lord Spencer and our common
friends in the Cabinet that you can for a moment imagine them to have
taken too weak an interest in your credit and support. . . . What is there
more in this than such a difference of opinion as among manly and
independent minds cannot but at some times arise. . .; where is the
accusation, where is the shadow of any thing like a question which
touches upon your credit, honour or character? . . . Hurt and afflicted as
I am at the present distresses of your mind, at the very agony of soul in
which I have seen the Duke of Portland suffer all that one man can
suffer for another, at the anxiety and despondency of all your friends, I
do yet retain a confident and sanguine expectation that the good affections and friendships of so many days and years will weather out this
bitter storm.

Fitzwilliam, however, was inflexible. 'Think not,' he had written
to Burke on 9 March, 'that I have been deficient in point of temper:
I trust I have been firm, but not obstinate. I do not know, since the
commencement of my difficulties, that there is much or anything to
correct in my conduct. . . . I have not been rash and passionate.'
After returning to England he went for a few days to Lord John
Cavendish's house at Billing. From there he replied to Tom Grenville
that

after six days' absence from the scene which might have inflamed my
mind and misled my judgement, in the quiet, calm, sober repose of
Billing I remain of the same opinion that I had formed in Dublin Castle
respecting the usage I have received. . . . He [Portland] has been
bewildered, and in his confusion has been led into irretrievable error;
but that error is of a nature never, I fear, to be got over: he has been
induced to abandon his principles, and give up his friend, his firm, his
steady his staunch supporter. . . . [He] suffered himself to be the dupe of
cunning and design, has been made the instrument of his own and my
disgrace—a disgrace of a nature most gratifying to our common enemies.

He declared himself resolved

to separate myself altogether from every sort of intercourse with the
man with whom I have passed so many years of my life in the most
intimate, cordial, unsuspecting friendship.

And he described his own distress when, encountering Portland's
son, Lord Titchfield, when out hunting, he had judged it necessary
to cut him.[55]

The breach with Portland affected all Whig society. Even Lady
Rockingham, who declared with a grim inevitability her lack of

surprise at Fitzwilliam's failure to find a working relationship with Pitt, expressed her feelings of dismay at the personal consequences. Writing of Fitzwilliam's experience with Pitt and his friends, she remarked that 'he had not been long enough in their school to have learned their mother tongue nor likely to have been a very apt scholar', but she was distressed that

two friends who I love so much and who loved each other so well are no longer united. . . . I dare not think upon it, and yet I can think of nothing else; but am for ever saying to myself—This cannot be, and it must not be.

Portland, too, sought a reconciliation. He wrote at the end of May 1795 to send Fitzwilliam news of Titchfield's engagement, pleading 'the remembrance of happy times and a fond attachment to the old unbroken habits of my life'. Fitzwilliam drafted, but probably did not send, a long reply which confessed his continued private 'emotions of joy and sincere satisfaction for your sake', and declared that it had been his first impulse to rush to Burlington House with his congratulations, but that he dared not risk an interview on such a subject. He sent a less effusive letter on Titchfield's marriage in August.[56]

Fitzwilliam left Ireland on 25 March, his carriage attended by silent crowds and passing through Dublin streets draped with mourning. The Irish capital, Grattan wrote, was silent and unhappy, but the Irish people had found a unity never known before: 'Never was a time in which the opposition here were more completely backed by the nation, Protestant and Catholic united'.[57] The consequences of Fitzwilliam's return were awaited with foreboding, for it was widely anticipated that grief would give way to protest and disaffection. Fitzwilliam was aware of the possible consequences, and more than ever determined to make it clear that the responsibility for what might come was not to be placed upon his shoulders. On his return to England he decided to compose a memorial to be presented to the king, which would absolve him from the charge that his conduct of affairs had endangered the peace of Ireland or the security of the nation. Burke, who was charged with the drafting of a text, wanted, in characteristic fashion, to make it an apologia for Whig policies in Ireland and, as he wrote to Fitzwilliam, not 'a mere defence' but 'a charge on your enemies'. 'He works with a warmth and assiduity that belongs so particularly to his generous and friendly temper,' wrote Lord Milton, 'but I must own amongst us he prances at that unbridled rate that we want your hand to shorten his stroke now and then.' A suitable—and abbreviated—text was agreed upon, and Fitzwilliam went to the levée on 22 April to present it.[58] The king was at his most gracious and inscrutable, seemed, thought Fitzwilliam, impressed by his arguments of the slight effect which the admission of Catholics to Parliament would have, and was insistent that no slur was cast on Fitzwilliam's character by the episode. Writing afterwards to Pitt, however, the king dismissed the memorial as 'rather a panegyric on himself than any pointed attack on Ministry' and remarked, 'I cannot say much information is to be obtained from it'. Secure in the constitutional support which the royal prejudices on the Catholic question had received in confidential advice from the Archbishop of Canterbury and Fitzgibbon, George III felt no need to disclose his hand either to Fitzwilliam or to Pitt. The question was closed, and Fitzwilliam's attitude represented no more than a 'little momentary warmth'.[59]

Fitzwilliam had not closed the question, however. Not only did he take no pains to hide his resentment against his former colleagues in the Cabinet, excepting Windham, the only one whom he felt to have made any sincere effort to avert the breach,[60] but he now pursued the justification of his mission into the House of Lords. On 24 April he rose in the House to demand an investigation into his conduct in Ireland and the reasons for his recall, declaring that Ministers had tried 'to throw all the blame from their own shoulders, and . . . to fix the load on his'. Grenville blandly replied that 'the mere fact of a nobleman being removed from being Lord Lieutenant of Ireland' implied no personal censure, nor did it call for any statement or investigation on the part of the Cabinet. Moira and Norfolk, still in opposition, spoke in Fitzwilliam's support, and Norfolk declared his intention to move for a committee of enquiry. The debate on Norfolk's motion took place on 8 May, but, predictably, nothing new emerged. The ministerial speakers took refuge behind the principle that dismissals and appointments were the sole prerogative of the Crown. Grenville went so far as to pronounce that if a precedent were established for parliamentary enquiry into the removal of Ministers it would be a short step to 'enquiring whether or not their successors were well chosen, and advising as to their appointment'—steps repugnant to the eighteenth-century doctrine of the separation of powers. The pill was sugared by tributes paid

from all sides to Fitzwilliam's personal and public reputation, though
his friends declared that these arguments were mere evasions, since
this was an exceptional case in which Parliament might claim the
right to enquire into the manner in which the prerogative had been
exercised. Even as an exploration of eighteenth-century constitutionalism, however, the debate lacked substance. Fitzwilliam's chief
supporters, Norfolk, Moira and Lauderdale, were mainly anxious to
use the issue to attack Pitt's government and his previous record as
Minister. Norfolk introduced his motion with a survey of politics
since 1782 and a comparison of Pitt's government with the 'system
of court oppression' practised in pre-revolutionary France—a comparison Fitzwilliam must have heard with mixed feelings. The debate
was further impeded by a long and rambling defence by Westmorland of *his* record as Viceroy and of his supporters in Ireland. Fitzwilliam's vigorous defence of his character and his Irish policy fell
into the sparsely occupied middle ground between the partisans of
government and those of opposition, each intent upon their own
political advantage. The debate foreshadowed the political isolation
which Fitzwilliam was to experience for the next few years, and
showed that unless he was prepared to commit himself again to the
Foxite opposition—a step which, in his view, was prevented by
their Jacobin principles at home and antagonism to the war with
France—there was no political group of any substance with which
he could align himself. The division was on party lines, Carlisle,
Mansfield and Spencer voting against the motion, while only twenty-
one peers and four proxy votes supported it. The protest which Fitzwilliam had prepared for the *Journals* was, however, a personal one.
It declared that Fitzwilliam had

acted faithfully, zealously, affectionately, dutifully and diligently
towards his sovereign; that he has acted with an enlightened regard to
the true interests of the nation, which under His Majesty's authority he
was appointed to govern. That he stands upon the merit of his measures
and the prudence of his arrangements: that by them confidence was
recovered to government.

The protest ended with a plea for the abandonment of religious
prejudices and for a union of all religions and property 'in one bond
of common interest, and in one common effort against our common
enemies, the known enemies of all religion, all law, all order, all
property'.[61] It was on these grounds that Fitzwilliam would have

wished to be judged, and on these grounds that his efforts would be
vindicated by the future history of Ireland. Fitzwilliam failed because
he had not the patience or the political skill to accommodate his
means to his ends, but at least he had attempted to realise a vision
of what the Anglo-Irish connexion might become in the hands of
men whom, perhaps mistakenly, he had seen as the only instruments
for the purpose. If the sordid realities of Irish politics defeated him,
it was none the less an honourable defeat. He had set out, in Burke's
phrase, with the belief that 'your ancient and illustrious family . . .
your posterity, your stake in the country, the interests of your
religion, your king and your country, all call on you loudly to do
something out of the common road'.[62] His mission became a conflict
between a long-term, imaginative statesmanship which might have
opened up a new road for Ireland and short-term practical expediency which was all that Pitt's Cabinet could encompass in the midst
of an increasingly desperate war. If Fitzwilliam was wrong, he was
wrong for the right reasons. It was more than could be said for Pitt.
As Fitzwilliam wrote to William Ponsonby shortly after the debates
in both Houses on his recall, 'the suspicion of much duplicity on the
part of Pitt sticks to his coat—this is all we can expect from it at
present: it will, however, be one of the catalogue of charges that,
accumulating one upon another, will one day or other become too
numerous and heavy for even his good luck to stand under'.[63] Pitt's
downfall was indeed ultimately to come from the Irish Catholic
question, though in a way that would have astonished Fitzwilliam
could he have foreseen it in 1795.

Only one further episode remained to complete the story of Fitzwilliam's Irish mission. The dismissals of Beresford and his colleagues
had been attributed by Fitzwilliam not only to the need to have
new men to administer new policies but to suspicions of corruption
and malversation on the part of the old. In his first 'Letter to Lord
Carlisle' Fitzwilliam had referred to Beresford's 'maladministration'
and his determination 'not to cloud the dawn of my administration,
by leaving in such power and authority, so much imputed malversation'. Beresford's departure had been followed by the setting up of a
parliamentary enquiry into the affairs of the Dublin Wide Streets
Commissioners, with the administration of whose funds Beresford
was concerned. The enquiry was allowed to drag, and at the end of
the session it was dropped without any evidence damaging to Beresford having come out. Allegations by Grattan of further irregu-

PLATE III

Fitzwilliam in later life, by Sir Thomas Lawrence (Wentworth Woodhouse)

PLATE IV

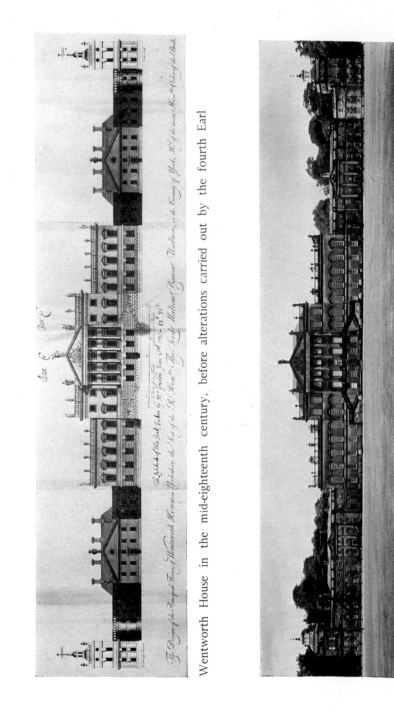

Wentworth House in the mid-eighteenth century, before alterations carried out by the fourth Earl

Wentworth Woodhouse today

larities in Beresford's management of the customs were also unsupported.[64] Beresford now sent to Fitzwilliam a complaint that his reputation had been unjustly defamed. 'Direct and specific charges I could fairly have met and refuted,' Beresford wrote, 'but crooked and undefined insinuations against private character, through the pretext of official discussion, your lordship must allow, are the weapons of a libeller.' He demanded satisfaction. Fitzwilliam, who had privately written to Burke describing Beresford as 'an old rotten stinking jobber', declared his readiness to meet him, and arrangements were made for a duel. Rumours evidently leaked out, and Fitzwilliam was 'obliged to quit the house . . . hastily in the morning, for fear of an arrest by the police'. His intended second, Moira, was so closely watched that he was unable to leave home, and Lord George Cavendish came forward in his place. It was from Cavendish's house that they set out for Marylebone fields early in the morning of Sunday 28 June. Cavendish called upon Beresford to say that Fitzwilliam was ready, and the two seconds—Sir George Montgomery acting for Beresford—consulted on the possibility of a settlement by an apology from Fitzwilliam. On arrival at the chosen spot in Marylebone fields, however, Fitzwilliam's proposed written apology failed to satisfy his antagonist. By this time a crowd of about fifty people had assembled, and the principals and their seconds moved away to another field near Paddington. Montgomery paced out the ground while the duellists made ready : he dropped his gloves on the ground to mark their positions, and Beresford took his place, waiting for Fitzwilliam to reach his mark. As he was but two paces from it a magistrate, warned by the report of an intended meeting somewhere in the district, ran on to the field and called on him by name to keep the peace. Fitzwilliam turned, 'much agitated', was arrested, and gave up his pistol. He turned to Beresford and said, 'Now Mr Beresford, that we have been prevented from finishing this business in the manner I wished, I have no scruple to make an apology'. He said, Beresford remarked, 'as much as it was possible for him to say', and assured him that the letters to Carlisle were 'never meant for publication . . . for the press but only to be shown to . . . friends . . . [and] that the expressions which he used arose from impressions he had received from those he conversed with, and were not intended to injure or relate to my private character'. Beresford declared himself satisfied and they shook hands, Fitzwilliam exclaiming 'Now, thank God, there is a complete end to my

H

Irish administration', and hoping that 'whenever they met it might
be on the footing of friends'. It was a satisfactory ending to what
might have been a tragic affair. Beresford paid tribute to Fitzwilliam's demeanour. 'On the whole,' he wrote, 'Lord Fitzwilliam
acted like a gentleman, seemed conscious that he had done what was
not warrantable, and, as far as I could conjecture, was unwilling
to fire at me.'[65] Fitzwilliam expressed to Burke the hope 'that I may
now be permitted to be at rest, and that the curtain may be dropped
upon the scene of my Irish administration'. As Burke remarked in
reply to the news of the duel, 'if we lived in times of justice it is
not Lord F. that ought to have been called to account for the
words—but the other for the acts'. However, what mattered was
'that a virtuous man has escaped with life and honour—and that his
reputation for spirit and humanity, and true dignity must stand
higher than ever, if higher it could stand'.[66]

Notes
[1] Fitzwilliam's viceroyalty has been examined, with rather differing
conclusions, by Lord Ashbourne, *Pitt: some Chapters of his Life and
Times* (1898), pp. 180–229; J. Holland Rose, *Pitt and Napoleon* (1912),
pp. 20–36; T. H. D. Mahoney, *Edmund Burke and Ireland* (Cambridge,
Mass., 1960), pp. 217–71; E. M. Johnston, *Great Britain and Ireland* (1963),
pp. 104–16; F. O'Gorman, *The Whig Pary and the French Revolution*
(1967), pp. 218–32; R. B. McDowell, 'The Fitzwilliam episode', *Irish
Historical Studies*, XVI (1966), pp. 115–30. The episode is also dealt with
in W. E. H. Lecky, *A History of Ireland in the Eighteenth Century*, ch.
VII (1913 edn., III, pp. 238–324). Lecky's detailed account is highly sympathetic towards Fitzwilliam.
[2] R. Burke junior to Fitzwilliam, 6 October 1792 (*Corresp. of E. Burke*,
VII, p. 245); *Diaries of Sylvester Douglas, Lord Glenbervie* (ed. F.
Bickley, 1928), I, p. 36. Pitt wrote to Lord Westmorland, the Lord
Lieutenant, on 18 November 1792 that a legislative union of the two
kingdoms would, by making the Irish a minority in Parliament, provide
a safe ground for concessions to them (Salomon, *Pitt*, p. 599).
[3] Fitzwilliam to Lady Rockingham, 31 August 1794: Ramsden MSS, I,
f. 100.
[4] *Corresp. of E. Burke*, VII, pp. 235–46.
[5] Portland to Spencer, 2 February 1789 (Althorp MSS, second Earl
Spencer, misc. box 8). Fitzwilliam was among those mentioned by
rumour for the viceroyalty in 1789 (*The Star*, 6 January, 1789); Mansfield
to Windham, 12 October 1794 (*Windham Papers*, I, pp. 259–60); Fitzwilliam to Portland, 23 June 1794 (Portland MSS, PWF 3765).
[6] William Brabazon Ponsonby (1744–1806), eldest son of John Ponsonby, second son of the first Earl of Bessborough, MP in Irish House of
Commons 1764–1801, and U.K. Parliament 1801–6; 1806 created Baron

Ponsonby of Imokilly. His wife, Louisa, daughter of Viscount Moles-worth, became Fitzwilliam's second wife in 1823. George Ponsonby (1755–1817), third son of John Ponsonby, MP in Irish House of Commons 1776–1801, U.K. Parliament 1801–17, Chancellor of the Exchequer in Portland's Irish administration (1782), Lord Chancellor of Ireland under the 'Talents' (1806–7), leader of the Whig party in the House of Commons 1807–17.

[7] Fitzwilliam accepted the Lieutenancy on 10 August (Portland to Adair, 4 and 12 August 1794: B.M. Add. MS 50829; Portland to Fitzwilliam, 14 August: F 31d). Lord Grenville suggested to his brother Tom on 29 August that no change could happen in Ireland until the new year: *Court and Cabinets*, II, p. 277.

[8] Fitzwilliam to Grattan, 23 August 1794: *Memoirs of the Life and Times of Henry Grattan*, ed. H. Grattan (1849), IV, p. 173.

[9] Portland to Fitzwilliam, 14 August 1794 (F 31d); Rev. W. King to Lady Rockingham, n.d. (Ramsden MSS, I, f. 120).

[10] J. Adair to Portland, 5 August 1794 (Portland MSS); Portland to Fitzwilliam, 17 October 1792 (F 31a) and 11 September 1794 (F 31d), to Windham, 8 October (*Windham Papers*, I, p. 256). Portland also wrote to Adair on 4 August that Ireland 'was *one of my great inducements* for accepting the situation I now hold' (B.M. Add. MS 50829).

[11] W. Ponsonby's 'Report of the original proposition of the Duke of Portland in June 1794', enclosed in Ponsonby to Fitzwilliam, 4 May 1795: F 29a.

[12] Buckingham to Grenville, 8 July and 20 September 1794: *Fortescue MSS*, II, pp. 597, 634. For Buckingham's resentment, see his letter to Tom Grenville, 24 November 1794 (B.M. Add. MS 42058, ff. 11–12). For the reception of the Irish commissioners in London in 1789 see *The Star*, 28 February–13 March.

[13] For the negotiations with Tom Grenville see *Fortescue MSS*, II, p. 619; *Court and Cabinets*, II, pp. 277, 282–3, 298; T. Grenville to Fitzwilliam, 11 November (N 46); Buckingham to T. Grenville, 24 November 1794 (B.M. Add. MS 42058, ff. 11–12).

[14] Burke to Portland, 9 September 1794, and to Fitzwilliam, 14 September (*Corresp. of E. Burke*, VIII, pp. 9–12); T. O'Beirne to Portland, 23 August, and to Fitzwilliam, 1 September (N); Fitzwilliam to Portland, 8 September and [8 October] 1794 (Portland MSS, PWF 3772, 3774); Portland to Fitzwilliam, 11 October 1794 (F 31d); O'Beirne to Portland, 25 August 1794 (N); Fitzwilliam to Windham, 11 October 1794 (*Windham Papers*, I, pp. 257–9).

[15] Portland to Fitzwilliam, 11 October (F 31d); Windham to Fitzwilliam [12 October 1794] (F 31i); Portland to Fitzwilliam, 14 October (F 31d); Pitt to Windham, 16 October (*Windham Papers*, I, p. 275).

[16] Burke to Windham, 16 October 1794 (two letters) and to Lough-borough, [19 October], Windham, 20 October and Fitzwilliam, 21 October: *Corresp. of E. Burke*, VIII, pp. 34–57. Richard died on 2 August 1794.

17 Grattan to McCan, 27 October 1794 (*Grattan*, IV, pp. 178–9): Fitzwilliam to Lady Fitzwilliam [16 October] and [n.d.] (N, x512/8, 14, 29
and 9).

18 *Grattan*, IV, p. 178; Burke to Fitzwilliam, 7 November 1794 (*Corresp.
of E. Burke*, VIII, pp. 74–5); Fitzwilliam to Lady Fitzwilliam, [8 Novem-
ber] and [n.d.] (N, x512/9 and 13).

19 Fitzwilliam's memorandum is in F 29b, headed 'Heads of a conversation at Pitt's, November 15 1794—shown to him after the conversation
—shown afterwards to Grattan and the Ponsonbys'. Grenville's memorandum is printed in *Fortescue MSS*, III, pp. 35–8.

20 The office of Secretary of State in Ireland was a sinecure, previously
held by John Hely-Hutchinson, Provost of Trinity College, who died in
1794.

21 John Beresford (1738–1805), second son of Marcus, Earl of Tyrone,
MP for Waterford 1761–1805, First Commissioner of the Revenue from
1780, Privy Councillor (G.B.) from 1786. An extremely able civil servant
and member of one of the most influential families in Ireland, for many
years he was known as 'the uncrowned king of Ireland'. His brothers and
numerous sons held many of the highest posts in the Irish Church,
administration and army.

22 Fitzwilliam to Pitt, 14 February 1795: F 5.

23 *Grattan*, IV, p. 177; *Parl. Register*, LIII, pp. 274–7.

24 The meeting at Pitt's on 15 November 1794 was clearly not a
Cabinet meeting, as Dr E. M. Johnston described it (*Great Britain and
Ireland*, p. 110).

25 Dr W. Drennan to S. McTier, 28 February 1795: *The Drennan
Letters*, ed. D. A. Chart (Belfast 1931), p. 224.

26 Fitzwilliam to Burke, 18 November: *Corresp. of E. Burke*, VIII, p. 78.

27 The French invaded Holland over the frozen rivers in December
1794 and forced the British troops there to retreat across the Waal. The
French entered Amsterdam on 20 January and the Stadholder of Holland
was deposed on 27 February. The Dutch fleet was now available to help
a possible French invasion across the Channel.

28 Letters from T. L. O'Beirne (?1784–1823, Bishop of Ossory 1795 and
Meath 1798), to Portland, *c.* 19 August 1794 (Portland MSS, PWF 7245)
and 23 August (N); to Fitzwilliam, 20 August, 6 September and 1 November (F 29a), 1 September, 25 November and 15 December (N): Memorandum, N 48.

29 Fitzwilliam to Portland, 7 and 8 January 1795 (F 5); Portland to
Fitzwilliam, 13 January (F 31e). The king wrote to Portland on the 13th:
'As I trust the promotions . . . have been thoroughly weighed and
thought necessary I consent to them' (Portland MSS, PWF 4076).

30 Fitzwilliam to Portland, 15 January, 23 January, 24 January (F 5);
McDowell, 'The Fitzwilliam episode', p. 123.

31 Holland Rose stressed this fact to counter Fitzwilliam's complaints
about the delay in answering his despatches, but Mahoney (pp. 396–7)
has established that Fitzwilliam's important letter of 15 January must
have arrived in London on the 27th, the day on which Portland also

acknowledged receipt of Fitzwilliam's of the 22nd. It therefore took Portland a week to reply to the letter of 15 January.

[32] Portland to Fitzwilliam, 2 February: F 31f. The objections were solely on the grounds of protocol, and Wolfe's character. Portland said that no objections had been raised by 'any of our colleagues' to the proposal to place Wolfe on the bench.

[33] Fitzwilliam to Pitt, 7 February: F 5.

[34] Beresford to Auckland, 9 January 1795 (*Corresp. of Rt. Hon. John Beresford*, ed. W. Beresford, II (1854), pp. 49–52). Auckland received the letter on the 15th, conferred immediately with George Rose and went to see Pitt on the 16th, as did Westmorland, who had heard of Beresford's dismissal on the 13th. Beresford appealed to Pitt in writing on 8 February (*ibid.*, pp. 53–8, 69–70).

[35] Lord Grenville to Fitzwilliam, 28 January (B. M. Grenville MSS, unnumbered); Cook to Nepean, 27 January (Chatham Papers, P.R.O. 8/30/327). Cook also enlisted Buckingham's aid (*Court and Cabinets*, II, pp. 329–30 and 330–3).

[36] Pitt to Fitzwilliam, 9 February (F 31f); Fitzwilliam to Pitt, 14 February (F 5).

[37] Burke to Fitzwilliam, [c. 26 September 1794] (*Corresp. of E. Burke*, VIII, pp. 21–2); Fitzwilliam to Portland, 10 February 1795 (F 5). The admission of Catholic forty-shilling freeholders to the franchise did not, of course, give any substantial political power to the Catholics as such; it merely strengthened the electoral influence of the greater Protestant landlords.

[38] Fitzwilliam to Portland, 10 and 15 January 1795 (F 5). Fitzwilliam's plan for a Catholic yeomanry alarmed the king as much as the thought of Catholic emancipation: it would be, he wrote to Pitt, a 'Roman Catholic police corps . . . which would keep the Protestant interest under awe' (Stanhope, *Pitt*, II, pp. xxiii–xxv). Portland echoed the king's objections to Fitzwilliam on 16 February (F 31f).

[39] Letters in F 5; memorandum, F 6. Fitzwilliam drafted some notes for his speech (F 30a) which included the following passage: '. . . On this subject ['the necessity of uniting all descriptions of his Majesty's people in interest and affection'] I have nothing particular to command from his Majesty: the whole is left wholly to your own wisdom and good temper and I have only to assure you of his Majesty's most cheerful concurrence in every measure which your wisdom and comprehensive patriotism shall point out for this salutary purpose.' In the speech as delivered, the words from 'on this subject' to 'good temper' were omitted. (*Annual Register*, 1795, State Papers, pp. 157–9). The king approved this in draft as 'calculated for the occasion' (to Portland, 13 January 1795: Portland MSS, PWF 4076).

[40] George III to Pitt, 6 February 1795 (Stanhope, *Pitt*, II, pp. xxiii–xxv); Portland to Fitzwilliam, 8 February 1795 (F 31f). The king's memorandum is in Chatham papers, P.R.O. 8/30/103 and is printed in *Eng. Hist. Docs*, XI, pp. 158–9.

41 Fitzwilliam to Portland, 10, 12 and 14 February; to Pitt, 14 February: F 5.

42 The private letter is in F 31f, the official one in F 31e.

43 F 31f. The letter was received by Fitzwilliam on the 25th.

44 Letters from Portland, 20 and 23 February, from Grenville, Mansfield and Spencer, 23 February and Windham 24 February: F 31f. Pitt's request to the King that Fitzwilliam be offered the seat in the Cabinet (22 February) is in *Later Corresp. of George III*, II, No. 1208.

45 Fitzwilliam to Devonshire, 28 February 1795: Chatsworth MSS, 1281. Grattan made similar accusations against Portland: to Burke, 14 March 1795 (*Corresp. of E. Burke*, VIII, pp. 196–7), and Lord John Cavendish accused the Duke of being dominated by 'persons much more artful than himself' (18 March; Grey MSS).

46 Fitzwilliam to J. Adair, 9 March 1795 (B.M. Add. MS 50830) and Adair's reply, 14 March (F 32–13); Fox to Lord Holland, 6 March 1795 (*Memorials and Corresp. of C. J. Fox*, III, p. 100); George III to Portland, 21 February and 5 March 1795 (*Later Corresp. of George III*, II, Nos. 1205, 1211); Buckingham to Grenville, 11 March, (*Fortescue MSS*, III, p. 34).

47 Carlisle to Fitzwilliam, 27 February (F 31i; copy in *Carlisle MSS*, pp. 703–4); Fitzwilliam to Carlisle, 6 March (*ibid*., pp. 704–11). Fitzwilliam sent Burke a copy of his letter to Carlisle on 9 March (*Corresp. of E. Burke*, VIII, pp. 180–1).

48 George III to Carlisle, 22 March: *Carlisle MSS*, p. 713. Loughborough averred that Fitzwilliam was mistaken in arguing that Grattan's Bill proposed merely a minor extension of the 1793 Act, which had in fact gone as far as was possible towards Catholic emancipation within the bounds of the existing constitution (*ibid*., p. 712).

49 *Ibid*., pp. 713–21. Carlisle's reply of 17 April is in F 31i. 'The truth is,' Fitzwilliam wrote to Burke on 21 March, 'that Mr Pitt had determined from the day that we kissed hands in July not to keep faith with us in any one of the terms and propositions he had made' (*Corresp. of E. Burke*, VIII, pp. 211–12).

50 D. Marshall, *Rise of George Canning* (1938), pp. 99–100; Auckland to Lord Henry Spencer, 2 April 1795: *Journals and Corresp. of Lord Auckland*, III (1862), p. 295.

51 Rev. T. Hussey to Burke, [27 February 1795]: *Corresp. of E. Burke*, VIII, p. 162.

52 McDowell, 'The Fitzwilliam episode', p. 117.

53 The letters were published in Dublin and London under the title *Letter from a Venerated Nobleman—to the Earl of Carlisle* (1795). Lord Milton stated to Fitzwilliam that the version published in Dublin had been 'stolen' and that it was reprinted in London by the editor of *The Sun*, without authorisation. Debrett asked Fitzwilliam and Milton for a correct text but was refused (Milton to Fitzwilliam [7 April 1795]: F 48).

54 Loughborough to Carlisle, 20 April 1795: *Carlisle MSS*, p. 728.

55 T. Grenville to Fitzwilliam, 22 March 1795 (F 31i); Fitzwilliam to Burke, 9 March (*Corresp. of E. Burke*, VIII, pp. 180-2); to Grenville, 3 April (B.M. Add. MS 41855, ff. 62-4).

56 Lady Rockingham to Fitzwilliam, 25 March 1795 (F 128h). Portland wrote to her on 8 March to express his 'exquisite anguish' and his unalterable 'attachment and affection' for Fitzwilliam (Ramsden MSS, I, f. 114). Portland's letter to Fitzwilliam on 30 May and the draft reply (same date) are in F 128e.

57 Grattan to Fitzwilliam, 28 March and 15 April 1795 (F 30a); *Morning Chronicle*, 31 March.

58 Burke to Fitzwilliam [12 April] (*Corresp. of E. Burke*, VIII, pp. 227-30); Milton to Fitzwilliam [7 April] (F 48). Burke's draft (F 116c) was considered too long and a much shorter version was submitted to the king (F 30a, misdated 22 May: printed in *Later Corresp. of George III*, II, pp. 336-40).

59 Fitzwilliam to Grattan, 25 April 1795 (*Grattan*, IV, pp. 208-12); George III to Pitt, 29 April 1795 (*Later Corresp. of George III*, II, 1243). For the king's consultations with Loughborough, Kenyon, the Archbishop of Canterbury, Fitzgibbon and others on the question whether the coronation oath forbade his assent to any Bill for Catholic emancipation see Mahoney, p. 269, H.M.C., *Kenyon MSS*, p. 542, and *Later Corresp. of George III*, II, pp. 317-21.

60 Leaving the closet on 22 April, he met Spencer and Windham in the antechamber and, he wrote to Grattan (25 April, *loc. cit.*), though he received Windham with 'decent openness', he cut Spencer, whose '*shame was upon his countenance, and I did nothing to wipe it off—it was on its proper place*'.

61 *Parl. Register*, XL (II), pp. 427-8, 463-94, 501-2. Spencer wrote to Pelham that he was relieved that the debate had 'passed off better than I could have contemplated . . . you will see that we were as discreet as possible on the subject' (16 May: B.M. Add. MS 33101, f. 188). The vote was 83 (and 17 proxies) against 21 (and 4 proxies). The Archbishop of Canterbury and eleven bishops voted in the majority. Portland spoke only very briefly at the end of the debate and did not vote (the debate had been postponed for over a week because he was ill). A similar motion was proposed on the same day in the Commons by Joseph Jekyll, and supported by Fox and Grey. It was lost by 188-49. The debate was also notable for a disastrous speech by Canning (Marshall, *Rise of George Canning*, pp. 83-4) and a maiden speech by Sylvester Douglas (*Glenbervie Diary*, I, pp. 49-50). The anxieties of the day brought on one of Fitzwilliam's attacks of migraine, which incapacitated him for several days afterwards. Fitzwilliam had the protest printed and circulated in both kingdoms.

62 Burke to Fitzwilliam [c. 22 November 1794]: *Corresp. of E. Burke*, VIII, p. 80.

63 Fitzwilliam to W. Ponsonby, 24 May 1795: Grey MSS.

64 Grattan sent Fitzwilliam an account of the proceedings of the Committee of Enquiry on 27 May 1795 (F 30a). Burke censured the Ponsonbys

for not pressing the enquiry energetically enough and allowing it to peter
out at the end of the session: 'They drew off the dogs just as they were
on the haunches of this fat buck', he remarked (5 July 1795: *Corresp. of
E. Burke*, VIII, pp. 285–7).

65 Beresford to Fitzwilliam, 22 June 1795 (F 30b) and reply, 23 and 28
June (*Beresford Corresp.*, II, pp. 113–14, 111; Fitzwilliam to Burke, 4 March
(*Corresp. of E. Burke*, VIII, pp. 169–72). Accounts of the duel are found
in B.M. Add. MS 33101, f. 189 (Portland to Pelham, 28 June); *Beresford
Corresp.*, II, pp. 114–20 (Beresford to Buckingham and to M. Beresford,
28 June); *Corresp. of E. Burke*, VIII, pp. 277–8 (Lord John Cavendish to
Burke [28 June]).

66 Fitzwilliam to Burke [30 June 1795]; Burke to Lord John Cavendish,
1 July 1795: *ibid.*, pp. 278–9, 281.

CHAPTER EIGHT

A man of principle
1795–1801

Fitzwilliam's return from Ireland did not result in any change of political principles, but it altered his political alignment. 'I stand unconnected with any political party', he wrote to James Adair in September 1795.[1] Divided from Pitt and Portland by resentment, mistrust and a conviction of their duplicity towards him and the cause of Irish Whiggism, he could no more bring himself to join Fox and the rump of opposition while they advocated peace with France and domestic reform. For six years he maintained an independent position, devoting himself to the maintenance of those fundamental principles which he had set out in 1793 and which he saw as the basis of his political creed—the upholding of the aristocratic and monarchial constitution, within the limits allowed by the rights of Parliament and people, and the pursuit of the war and repression of internal disaffection as the twin threats to that traditional order. In the House of Lords and in south Yorkshire he appointed himself a guardian of constitutional liberty against both the Crown and the Jacobins. He played a leading part in organising regiments of yeomanry cavalry in the West Riding in the summer of 1794, principally in order to put down the Jacobin threat to law, order and property, and as colonel-commandant of the regiments he personally led forces to quell disorders in Rotherham and Sheffield in the following summer.[2] In Parliament he gave his approval to the 'Two Bills' of December 1795, thus marking his continued separation from the opposition, who fought them bitterly at every stage as destructive of constitutional liberties. From the beginning of the 1795–6 session, indeed, Fitzwilliam made it clear that he would not swerve from support of authority—even Pitt's authority—against sedition.

At the opening of Parliament on 29 October the king's carriage was stoned and jostled by a crowd calling for peace and bread. The king himself was struck by a stone, and on the way back to

Buckingham House his private carriage was mobbed in the park, the
crowd beating on the carriage with sticks and trying to force open
the door. Cries of 'No king' were alleged to have been heard. A mob
of several thousands crowded round Buckingham House for some
time, while others smashed the windows and damaged the body of
the state coach at St James's Palace. These events followed shortly
after a tumultous meeting organised by the London Corresponding
Society in Copenhagen Fields to demonstrate for reform. The meeting, said to have been attended by 200,000, approved a 'Remonstrance to the King' which reminded him of 'the favours conferred
by this country in transplanting your princely house from the
poverty and obscurity of Hanover, to the dignity and opulence of
the then (but not now) most respectable sovereignty in Europe'. The
remonstrance demanded reform, peace and the removal of Ministers
as the only measures 'by which the country can be saved, or the
attachment of the people secured'. The 'Two Bills', against treasonable practices and seditious meetings, were a direct consequence of
this meeting and the attack on the king. They were opposed not
only by the Corresponding Society itself, whose operations would be
virtually suppressed by them, but also by the Whig Club, with the
support of over a hundred petitions and remonstrances from London,
Westminster, Middlesex, several other counties and 'almost every
town of note in the kingdom'.[3] Fitzwilliam's strong support of the
Bills thus marked his position as separated by a yet unbridgeable
gulf from Fox and his friends. The opposition, he wrote to George
Ponsonby in October, were advocating 'the most desperate system
of universal subversion' and no one could trust them:

With my disinclination to the Ministry, with the affections I shall ever
bear to the most conspicuous part of Opposition, I must . . . agree with
my neighbours in thinking that before Opposition can be Ministers they
must give to the public, security . . . for the maintenance of things as
they are.[4]

Fitzwilliam's adherence to his principles might also carry him
against the measures or policy of the government, especially on the
question of war or peace. Fitzwilliam suspected that the Cabinet was
bent on a negotiated peace with the new Directory in France, whose
establishment might hold out the prospect of a more settled, though
republican, order across the Channel.[5] Though he travelled up to
vote for the address at the opening of the session, therefore, as he

wrote to Burke, he gave only 'a silent vote . . . reserving to myself
the right of explaining the words of that address according to the
interpretation I think the words liable to'. His support was limited to
the maintenance of order and the British constitution, and did not
extend to the approval of the government's conduct of the war or to
any peace settlement which fell short of a Bourbon restoration in
France.[6] Since, as he recognised, this placed him almost alone in the
House of Lords, he resolved to attend only when matters affecting
these principles arose, and he returned to Milton shortly after the
debate on the address. He was summoned back again early in
December when Pitt announced that the government was preparing
to consider overtures from the French. Burke urged him to protest
against 'this shameful and ruinous business'. Fitzwilliam responded
immediately. Burke's summons, he wrote, 'came most opportunely
to decide a wavering mind to do the thing that was right'. In the
debate on 14 December he emphasised once again that the war was
'of a nature different from all common wars', and had been begun

not from any of the ordinary motives of policy and ambition in which
wars generally originate. It was expressly undertaken . . . to restore
order to France, and effect the destruction of the abominable system that
prevailed in that country. Upon this understanding it was that he had
separated from some of those with whom he had long acted in politics,
and . . . upon this understanding he had filled that situation, which he
some time since held in His Majesty's Cabinet.

There could be no peace while the present French regime existed : 'It
was still a pure democracy, containing the seeds of dissension and
anarchy and affording no security for religion, property or order'.

His speech found no support. He wrote afterwards to Burke, 'One
feeble voice can do no good : the satisfaction of doing that which is
right was therefore my only motive, and the recollection of having
done so will be my only recompense'. On the same day he voted for
the third reading of the Seditious Meetings Bill, reflecting with bitterness on the irony of the government's pressing the Bill on the one
hand while on the other opening the door to French emissaries
bringing its principles to England.

Are they to range at large [he wrote], in every town and every house,
preaching their doctrines and perhaps even buying proselytes? — are
Englishmen to be sent to Paris to be witnesses of the successful result of
audacious usurpation, and of the elevation of Tom Paine from a stay-

maker to a fine gentleman, from an exciseman to a sovereign, as the reward of the Rights of Man and the Age of Reason.[7]

Fitzwilliam's political standpoint at this time is clearly defined in his letters to friends such as Burke and to his members or candidates for his seats in the Commons. The first, and basic, principle was resistance to all reform, both as dangerous in the present state of affairs and as an interference with the established constitution. Writing to Georgiana in July 1798 on the vacancy of a seat at Higham Ferrers, he avowed that 'nothing will induce me to bring in a person who will not act decidedly against . . . a parliamentary reform in England'. The second principle was support of the war against republican France until the Bourbon monarchy could be restored; but he would be prepared to return a member whose opinion was different, provided that he would not vote against the principle. Thirdly, he was uncompromisingly determined not to rejoin Pitt's administration or to give it any general support on issues which did not involve the war or reform. On the other hand he was equally inflexible that he could not join Fox and the Whig opposition so long as they remained committed to both peace and reform. He declared to James Adair on 12 September 1795 that he would actively support the government on the war and

on all occasions where they support establishment against innovation, monarchy and aristocracy against the inroads of sans-culottism; but beyond these points I profess no friendship or goodwill towards an administration from which I have received such gross ill-treatment.

As for the opposition, 'I don't know that they would wish for the appearance of connexion with me, and I am sure I should but little wish it with them, till such time as all the leaven of sans-culottism is worked out of their composition'.[8]

Fitzwilliam was now the chief exponent in politics of Burke's principles. The link became explicit when, on the opening of a vacancy for Peterborough in 1796, Fitzwilliam wrote to Burke to offer it to his friend French Laurence and to define the terms of the relationship he wished to establish between patron and member.[9] He avowed himself to be 'the inveterate enemy of all innovation' and 'though a friend to popular privileges on ordinary occasions, and having no dislike to the check on public men by popular discussion . . . I had rather see a bad Minister go uncorrected than a good constitution stabbed in its vitals'. As for his political position, under no circumstances whatever will I be in connexion with Mr Pitt. It is sufficient for a man's life to have been duped once. I hesitate no less to say that I will never hold communication with the Duke of Portland until he has made that *amende honorable* to those . . . whose weight and consideration in Ireland he has made subservient to his own purposes and views in this country.

He went so far as to say

my inclinations, my private attachments, the habits of my life, all combine to make me anxious to see the moment when I may be able to give the members of opposition honourable assistance. . . . But in stating this it certainly is not in my contemplation to become again an active member of an opposition. Those days are over—circumstances have happened that make me think that I can be no more usefully so . . . but, in one word, should circumstances ever present to me the opportunity of doing essential injury to Mr Pitt's power, or of rendering effectual service to Mr Fox, I will not fail to seize it.

Once established in the seat for Peterborough, Laurence became Fitzwilliam's chief political confidant. He began at once to take an interest in Fitzwilliam's son, the young Lord Milton, who was soon to follow the family path to Eton. Milton's education was an unusual one for a young nobleman of his day. His parents introduced him not only to the standard classical literature and Roman history which underlay all gentlemanly studies at that time, but also to more modern studies. Milton proved to be less interested in the arts than his father—the war-time interruption of continental travel denied him the early aesthetic stimulus it had given to Fitzwilliam—but he grew up to take a serious-minded interest in political and economic questions. Laurence, an academic and scholarly lawyer, seems quickly to have understood Milton's bent, for he made the unusual but very suitably Whiggish proposal that he should take the young boy through a detailed study of English constitutional history. 'My great object,' he wrote, 'is to drag him, if I can, through the Rolls of Parliament which have never been explored by an historian and for want of which help . . . all who have written on the subject of our constitution have been egregiously misled in very important particulars.' 'Nothing can be more acceptable to Lady F. and myself,' Fitzwilliam wrote. 'He is growing up in awkward times; God only knows what rank in society he has to fill; but it is our duty to proceed with him, and fit him to fill that rank to which he was born : whosoever lends a hand towards that end will do a most acceptable service to

us.'[10] What Milton's education in fact owed to Laurence it is difficult
to say; but the older man's interest in the boy helped to endear
Laurence to Fitzwilliam in a personal as well as a political sense, and
to strengthen still further the link with Burke weakened in 1794 by
Richard's death.

This was forcibly illustrated by the events of October–December
1796, when Lord Malmesbury set out for France to discuss a peace
negotiation with the Directory. At the opening of the new Parliament on 6 October Fitzwilliam moved an amendment to the address
in the Lords, criticising the step. Both administration and opposition
speakers welcomed Malmesbury's mission so that Fitzwilliam's
was the only voice raised against it—'the solo you played in
the grand orchestra', as Burke described it. The unanimity of both
sides in Parliament arose, Fitzwilliam declared, 'not from Opposition
concurring in the measures of Government but from Government
abandoning their own measures to adopt those of Opposition—the
regular order of things seems subverted'. His protest, based on a
draft by Burke, was a strongly expressed attack on the futility of
seeking peace with 'a species of power, with whose very existence
all fair and equitable accommodation is incompatible'. Such a peace
would be dishonourable in view of the principles adopted in declarations by the government against any peace except 'through the
ancient and legitimate government long established in France', and
dangerous in its example of encouragement to the principles of
popular revolution. The protest concluded with an affirmation that

having acted throughout the course of this awful and momentous crisis
upon the principles herein expressed, and after having on the present
occasion, . . . fully reconsidered and jealously examined their soundness
and validity . . . conscientiously adhering to, and firmly abiding by them,
I thus solemnly record them, in justification of my own conduct, and in
discharge of the duty I owe to my king and country.

The protest, remarked the *Annual Register*, 'breathes the genuine
spirit first roused, and perhaps, still actuated to a greater extent than
was acknowledged by the British government'. Burke assured Fitzwilliam that his arguments were 'relished by the public' and given
greater force by 'your personal weight and character'. The speech
also prepared the way, as Laurence wrote, for Burke's new publication, the *Two Letters on a Regicide Peace*, which appeared on 20
October and which Burke described to Fitzwilliam as 'my poor
attempt to second what you have done'.[11]

Fitzwilliam welcomed Burke's pamphlet. He unhesitatingly attributed the dispirited mood of the country not to the defeats of our
allies on the continent nor to the effects of the war on trade and the
consequences of the bad harvests and high prices of the past two
years, but to the government's reluctance to treat the war as an
ideological conflict. If ministers had been sincere in adopting that
principle, he declared, the public would have rallied, 'but that is all
now over, not for want of spirit in the people, but of principle in
our government'. 'You have roused a spirit in the country,' he
assured Burke, 'which does not act only because those who ought
to make use of it choose to keep it under.' 'They [the public],' he
declared to Laurence, 'never would have been in this mood if those
who lead them had not led them astray.' Pitt was deliberately holding out the terror of invasion and the dislike of taxes to frighten
the country into accepting a peace which at heart the public
detested: and he attributed the Minister's desire for peace to his
fear of Ireland, where the disaffection of both north and south,
Protestants and Catholics, had rendered the government powerless
to resist rebellion. Ireland could no longer be held down in time of
war; the landing of a few thousand French troops there would be
decisive. It was for this reason, Fitzwilliam was convinced, that the
cause for which he believed the war should be fought was now
being abandoned. He thus linked the humiliating peace negotiation
on which Pitt had now embarked with the repudiation of his Irish
policy of 1795. In his view the war could be successful and popular
only if Ireland were conciliated and the enthusiasm of the public in
England enlisted for a crusade for the monarchical and aristocratic
principle. Rather than relieve Irish discontent by the 'change of
system' Fitzwilliam had advocated in 1795, and then continue the
war with the support of the united force and loyalty of the two
kingdoms, Pitt preferred to submit to a humiliating peace with
jacobin France.

Every other political consideration [Fitzwilliam wrote], continental connexions, balance of power in Europe—the existence of civil society itself
—is to be sacrificed, rather than give up their system in Ireland. . . . Had
it been permitted to me to have gratified them [the Catholics] in the
little they looked for, Ireland would not have been what it now is, a
millstone upon the neck of England.

Malmesbury's mission, however, failed to establish satisfactory
grounds for a negotiation, and he returned to London on 20

December. The immediate danger of a Jacobin peace was past. The incident had nevertheless emphasised Fitzwilliam's political position and placed him more emphatically before the public eye as the major representative of the Burkean attitude to the war. Laurence reported that Addington, the Speaker, had told him after Fitzwilliam's speech that he considered him to be 'a man of high integrity; no person could say that his lordship had abandoned his principles'. He assured Fitzwilliam of 'the very just veneration in which your name is held by all parties' and declared that his speech had been warmly received in the City by the trading community.[12]

If, however, Fitzwilliam's response to the peace negotiation sharpened his differences with Ministers, it also emphasised his isolation and lack of sympathy with the opposition. Fox naturally welcomed Pitt's initiative, since he had always deplored the war and the associated repression of political sentiment at home as dangerous to the historic cause of liberty. In addressing his constituents at the Westminster anniversary dinner on 10 October Fox declared both for peace and for an end to the suppression of radicalism at home. The cases of Muir and Palmer, transported to Botany Bay in 1794 for advocating reform in Scotland, had stirred Fox to violent protest at the time of the Pitt–Portland coalition, so hardening the conservative Whigs' determination to separate from him. In his speech on the address Fitzwilliam had referred to the possibility of the release of the 'seditious convicts at Botany Bay' as a humiliating consequence of peace with France. Fox, in contrast, declared that they had been unjustly punished 'for a mere discussion of political opinions' and repeated his abhorrence of their sentence. He also emphasised his detestation of the 'Two Acts' of December 1795. Nothing could have pointed more clearly the continuing gulf between Fitzwilliam and the Foxites, and Laurence despaired of any way out of the dilemma, short of divine intervention.[13]

The government of this country must be in the hands of either Mr Pitt or Mr Fox [he wrote]: such is our unfortunate situation: and between the specious treachery of the one and the undisguised violence of the other nothing apparently but the merciful interposition of Him who brings good out of evil by His own mysterious ways can save us.

Fitzwilliam returned to the House of Lords on 30 December to speak in the debate on Malmesbury's recall and to move an amendment representing once again 'the dangerous principles advanced by the French Republic, the necessity of a perseverance in the contest, and the impropriety of courting any negotiation of peace with France in its present state'. His speech and amendment, he told Burke, were designed 'to recall the House of Lords to their principles and their senses' by asserting that the principle on which the war was begun and on which the coalition of 1794 was founded was 'the destruction of the system in France' rather than, as Spencer declared in reply, merely to secure British interests and restore peace to the Continent. The denial of Fitzwilliam's assertions not only by Grenville but by the old Portland Whig Ministers was, Fitzwilliam wrote, 'heartbreaking'; but it also symbolised yet again his political division from his former associates. He could not, he told Laurence on 1 January, accept that

the motives of our joining with Administration were common motives, perhaps those of getting as many good places as we could. . . . Perhaps . . . I may discover at last that to be President of the Council, or Lord Lieutenant of Ireland, was the only inducement to my breaking through all the habits of my life, and to my separating from the friendships of my infancy.

His awareness of this isolation led him to discourage Laurence, an inveterate and long-winded speaker in the House, from moving resolutions on the principle of the war which could only demonstrate a lack of support from either side. He felt, as he wrote to his Yorkshire friend Stephen Croft in April 1797, that he was 'the most isolated individual in politics in the king's dominions . . . a person who approves of nothing doing and therefore of no set of men whatever'. Ministers had abandoned the principles 'upon the strength of which they induced me to join with them', while opposition was 'more hostile ten times in my opinion, and more decided to act upon principles contrary to my views, than the Ministry'. His mood was one of hopelessness. 'Feeling a most complete inability to do any good, I must leave all to chance.'[14]

Yet a way back was beginning to prepare itself, even in December 1796. That way could lead only towards Fox, for Fitzwilliam's resentment against Pitt and Portland over Ireland was implacable. Fox's advocacy of peace and reform were serious obstacles to full association with opposition, but on other questions Fitzwilliam was prepared to co-operate against the Ministry, and any point which tended to suggest improper or unconstitutional action by Ministers

was particularly acceptable. In early December such an issue arose
with the disclosure in Pitt's budget speech that £1,200,000 had been
lent to the Austrian emperor without parliamentary sanction.[15]
Laurence reported that Pitt spoke of the loan 'as an irregular act,
which he ventured from a grave necessity, and meant to justify from
the circumstances'. Fox immediately rose to condemn the measure,
'talked of stopping the votes of the supplies on account of it, and
declared that if the House would not take it up, the people ought'.
He gave notice of a motion of censure on Ministers for acting without parliamentary authority, and wrote to Fitzwilliam to urge his
support :

Notwithstanding our difference of opinion on the subject of the war,
and, as I fear, upon many points respecting the internal state of the
country, yet I can not help hoping that you must think as I do upon
Pitt's audacious defiance of the constitution. . . . I own that if before
. . . I make my motion I knew your opinion to be favourable for us it
would be a great satisfaction to me.

Fitzwilliam at once took the point. Writing on 11 December to
Laurence he avowed his complete support for Fox's principle :

The House of Commons had better at once surrender up formally their
right to dispose of, to control, to superintend the public purse, if they are
no longer thought worthy to be consulted or even to be communicated
with about great and important measures of expense.

He drew Fox's distinction between a vote of credit to cover extra
expenditure incurred in war-time during a parliamentary recess and
applying money to new purposes without the House's consent while
Parliament was sitting. The amount and fitness of the loan were not,
in Fitzwilliam's view, in question—'had five times the sum been
demanded . . . I would have given it'—but the House had not been
asked to authorise any loan to the emperor, and indeed had almost,
by implication, forbidden any such proceeding. Pitt was guilty of
'a proud, arrogant assumption of power, that . . . if it passes
unnoticed, it is a dangerous infraction upon a most material constitutional principle and usage'. Laurence consulted Burke and found
him less disposed to rush into a censure of Pitt and more inclined to
excuse him on the grounds of necessity. He was accordingly per-
plexed how to act between Fitzwilliam's eagerness to support almost
any censure on Pitt and Burke's warning that Fox was merely play-

ing politics. He suggested that Pitt's action was tactically excusable, on the grounds that his professed desire for peace talks with France would have seemed insincere if he had disclosed a large subsidy to one of our Continental allies to continue the war. Fitzwilliam, however, was not interested in excuses, and stated bluntly his view that 'Whether it is within the letter of the law and the constitution to make such an use of the vote of credit I don't pretend to know: but I am sure it is contrary to the spirit and *practice* of the constitution to give Parliament *the go-by* in money transactions'. He added:

It is far from my wish to pull down the authority of the Crown in these times, but if the Crown begins by infringing the rights of the Commons, in my opinion it will give rise to a collision between the two, which I fear will not end advantageously for the Crown.

If Ministers rode rough-shod over the constitutional rights of the Commons the result would only favour the Jacobins. Laurence, in an agony of indecision which a careful study of precedents failed to resolve, voted at length in the minority—his 'first serious vote', as he wrote to Fitzwilliam, and one in which his patron's standpoint 'formed me to the true impartiality of a judge'. He went down to the House prepared to abstain if the course of the debate had swayed his judgement contrary to Fitzwilliam's. Happily, the ministerial defence seemed vague and unconvincing, and 'I walked out among the minority with as much satisfaction to my own mind, as I ever shall give a vote'. He was disappointed only at not having had the opportunity to speak.[16]

Burke was no less gratified by Laurence's discretion than Fitzwilliam, whose eagerness in attacking the government was alarming his political mentor. 'I see that his mind grows to be ulcerated and inflamed,' Burke warned Laurence, 'and that little is wanting to make him again precipitate himself into the Fox connexion.' He warned that any overt attempt to dissuade him from doing so might have the contrary effect, and urged Laurence to treat him with delicacy. Laurence therefore used some tact and a great deal of flattery to ask his instructions how to vote on Pitt's next motion for a vote of credit, which Fox intended to oppose:

Your opinion upon all subjects—I speak most sincerely from the very bottom of my heart—is so correct, wise and upright that I should be very inattentive to my own benefit and improvement, independently of every feeling of gratitude, if I were not desirous of consulting it whenever I have an opportunity.

He pledged himself that 'I never will go against your opinion where I know it, and upon all important business I shall seek to know it'. Fitzwilliam repeated that his objection had been to Pitt's previous method of proceeding, and not to lending money to the emperor by proper constitutional means. He wished to 'give to the Crown the amplest means of assisting our allies, and supporting that common cause in which we are engaged' and declared that the prosecution of the war, subject only to proper constitutional forms, was uppermost in his mind. The affair passed off quietly in the end, the opposition choosing not to divide the House, and the final collapse of the peace negotiations about the same time restored both Fitzwilliam's and Laurence's composure. Congratulating himself that they had been shown to be right on the impossibility of compromising with the revolution, Fitzwilliam concluded: 'One good thing we know, we are still at war'. And, his parliamentary attendance concluded by his speech on the failure of the peace negotiations on 30 December, he retired to Milton. 'I have no thoughts of going up to town,' he wrote in February 1797:

. . . were I of calibre to call the attention of our House, I would repeat my efforts again and again; but that not being the case, I should lose even the little attention I can attract by too frequent repetition. Who calls for me, what is the ground to be taken, on which I should be seconded by a single individual?[17]

Fitzwilliam could not, however, expect to lead a life entirely retired from active politics as long as Ireland continued to feature in them. 'My mind is always trembling for the fate of Ireland,' he wrote to William Ponsonby in November 1796. 'In my mind there is no hope of salvation but by you and Grattan . . . still holding out your assistance and protection for the oppressed.'[18] Only by giving the Irish people the hope of reform through constitutional channels could the designs of the revolutionaries be defeated. Yet parliamentary reform was still a bugbear that he could not overcome. On 4 November the Irish Whig Club, with Grattan in the chair, had set up a committee on the state of the representation, and its report, presented on 2 December, declared a reform of Parliament and Catholic emancipation to be essential 'to establish public satisfaction and tranquillity'.[19] Three days later Fitzwilliam wrote to urge restraint. Certainly the present system was unjust:

Its being so completely aristocratical leaves the lower orders *without protection;* and in that example we may learn what tyrants we aristocrats can be when there is no check whatever on the selfish bent of the human mind—Happy the country where there is such an alloy of democracy as brings the overbearing inclinations of the great to a fellow feeling for the low : as makes it necessary that the one should court the other; this alone will secure to the lowest an equitable share of protection from their superiors, and renders the latter the most useful part of society, even to the former.

Nevertheless, he wrote, 'I tremble when I see ancient arrangements meddled with : there is no ascertaining, when once the dyke is cut, how far the waters will flow'. Fitzwilliam's words expressed the fundamental character of his Whig ideals. As always, the difficulty was to choose between practicable alternatives, and his advice to his friends in Ireland—to restrict themselves to debates in Parliament—was hardly likely to produce effective results. William Ponsonby pointed out that Parliament had lost all the confidence of the people and that it was corrupted by government to such an extent that it was completely at the Castle's disposal. Several of Fitzwilliam's correspondents now warned him that defenderism and other signs of disaffection were spreading rapidly throughout Ireland. 'It seems,' one wrote, 'as if the present government really wishes to drive the people into rebellion by the arbitrary and oppressive measures they pursue. There is not an unprejudiced person in any part of the kingdom that don't attribute these disturbances to your removal.'[20]

The dominance of Ireland in Fitzwilliam's mind during these months constantly confirmed his antipathy to the present Ministers, whom he blamed again and again for the situation that had arisen. Thus he inclined more and more towards opposition as Fox and his friends took up Irish questions in Parliament. Burke and Laurence were correspondingly alarmed lest Fox's renewed interest in Irish affairs should draw Fitzwilliam over. Laurence, who had been having conversations with John Keogh, the agent of the Irish Catholics, sent Fitzwilliam a long report full of disturbing news about the extent of disaffection among the Catholic community and urged that it would be preferable for Grattan and the Ponsonbys to raise the Irish question in the Dublin Parliament rather than have it brought up at Westminster. When Whitbread announced for February 1797 a motion of censure on the government for the failure to intercept the

French invasion ships off Bantry Bay in December 1796, Laurence
suggested to Fitzwilliam that he might join in the censure on the
mismanagement of the Irish administration but vote against the
proposed enquiry on the grounds that he could not support a
measure tending to the replacement of the Ministry by the current
opposition, with their 'views of indefinite changes in the form of
Parliament or the prerogatives of the Crown'. Fitzwilliam agreed
that the motion 'offers but a choice of evils', but suggested that any
danger of radical reform was remote, whereas 'the fate of Ireland is
really at hand. . . . Our first business is to save Ireland from imminent and immediate danger and it will be only the second to guard
England against future mischief'.[21] Laurence consulted Burke, remarking that 'I am afraid that I shall be wished to go a little beyond my
own opinions', though he reflected that 'whatever I do, or do not, I
shall feel myself a little the stronger, as I have this day paid my
own election bills of nearly £500 at Peterborough'. Burke reassured
Laurence that though the question was a delicate one there was
little prospect in fact of Whitbread's motion being carried, and
Fitzwilliam's opinion should therefore turn the scale. 'I don't like
that all his members should be found voting against him,' he
remarked. Fitzwilliam's attitude, however, was hardening. Not only
did he suggest that Laurence should speak in the debate, but he
betrayed an increasing sympathy towards opposition in general.
Though not wishing for a change of Ministry, on the grounds that it
might 'lead to a change in the constitution', he avowed an inclination towards 'reform in the abuses of executive government', and
declared:

I differ with you on another point, which is that this administration is
the only one fit to carry on the war. I see not the slightest difference
between them and any others for that purpose: they profess now to
carry it on, as a measure of dire necessity. Mr Fox would carry it on for
the same reason, and peace would be made by him more to advantage,
because, made by him, there would be virtually a saving of the country's
honour—made by Mr Pitt, the country is *beat* into it; made by Mr Fox
it is a measure of choice.

This almost open avowal of complete support for Fox horrified
Laurence, who replied that Fox could not, consistently with his
declarations on the subject, honourably conduct the war on his
present principles, nor would a peace made by him be more
honourable to the country than one made by Pitt. As for reforms,

Fox would not stop short of 'a virtual democracy' and 'I cannot accede to a general proposition on this subject'. Finally he appealed to Burke's name:

Burke thinks that I might vote (he says not a word about speaking) on either side without dishonour. Let me request of your lordship calmly and seriously to review the whole subject; and I will abide by your decision. Yet I will plainly confess that it seems to me a conduct something like what I suggested, while it would give opportunity for conciliating Ireland, would be best calculated to keep a check over the two contending parties . . . and might in time bring them to a better sense of their duty.[22]

Laurence did not vote for Whitbread's motion, nor was he the only one of Fitzwilliam's members to resist his patron's leanings towards opposition. James Adair, still trying to bridge the gap between Fitzwilliam and Portland, actually voted for the government. Replying afterwards to Fitzwilliam's demand for an explanation, he declared that he thought the Ministers' explanations satisfactory, and that in the present state of Ireland and the war it would be unwise to help weaken the government's authority. He stoutly declared his 'firm persuasion, that the support of administration, *during the continuance of the war*, is essential to the safety of both kingdoms'. None of Fitzwilliam's members voted for Whitbread's motion, leaving him, as he despondently remarked in a letter to one of his Yorkshire friends, 'an individual, taking occasionally my own line, but standing aloof: I have nothing to do with the making or unmaking of Ministers'. He nevertheless remained a determined advocate of the policy of a change of men as well as measures in Ireland. A 'total change of system', he wrote to Burke on 9 December 1796, alone would cure the country's troubles: Portland must be made to bestir himself by 'the most vehement incitement of persons about him, never quitting him, and increasingly urging, and goading him on . . . to assert his own opinions and act upon them, against the authority of Mr Pitt'.[23]

The hope of detaching Portland and Windham from the Cabinet over the Irish question, and of using the issue to reconstitute the governments of both kingdoms, now came to the front of Fitzwilliam's mind. In March 1797 attempts were being made to find a 'third party' strong enough to provide the basis of a government independent of both Pitt and Fox. Sixteen members of the Commons, led by Sir John Sinclair, the Scottish agriculturist, and John

Pollexfen Bastard, MP for Devon and an archetypal independent, together with a number of peers,[24] revived the scheme which several of them had promoted in 1788 for an 'armed neutrality'. Burke and Laurence disapproved of both the plan and its framers. 'They are a body without sense and without principle, and can come to nothing,' Burke warned Laurence. The only realistic alternative to the present government, he thought, would be a Foxite one in which neither Portland nor Fitzwilliam, if included, could play any principal part 'as long as he [Fitzwilliam] holds the maxims, and is animated by the sentiments for which, as a statesman, we value him'. Laurence agreed. He would welcome an effective 'third force' pressure group, he wrote in March, not as the nucleus of a new administration but to hold the balance between Ministers and opposition, 'to support the Minister stoutly, if he would do his duty, or transfer that support to opposition, if they would be candidates for power on fair terms. . . . But there is not the remotest chance of such a party'. The new group, now of some thirty or forty, had approached him, but he 'neither agreed nor dissented'. In general he felt it unrealistic to expect that any stable government could be formed against both Pitt and Fox, nor was it clear what alternative policies such a third party would adopt. His suspicion was that they were merely anxious 'to save Mr Pitt' by relieving him of the necessity to make peace.

Fitzwilliam, however, welcomed the possibility of forming a new arrangement which might displace Pitt and establish a government for both England and Ireland founded upon Whig principles, and including Fox. In conjunction with Laurence he now drew up a 'Memorial on the state of Ireland', advocating Catholic emancipation and the dismissal of the anti-Catholic members of the Dublin administration. These measures, he argued, would even now reconcile the loyal Catholic population to the British Crown and isolate the radicals and Jacobins of the north. Fitzwilliam hoped that the leading Whig proprietors of Irish estates would join him in presenting the memorial to the king. These lords included not only Devonshire and Bessborough but also Moira and Hertford, the friends of the Prince of Wales and men involved in the 'third party' discussions now going on in London. The implications were obvious: if the Irish 'change of system' which Fitzwilliam advocated could be made the major element in the third party's programme, Fitzwilliam would give the scheme his backing. Burke saw the danger, and tried to pour cold water on the memorial. Moira and Hertford, he wrote, were 'men of ambition . . . very irregular in their ideas; and . . . full of ambition and designs, of which self is the centre'. Laurence withdrew his support for the scheme as a result of Burke's disapproval and after a conversation with Moira in which, he alleged, Moira avowed that his interest was solely to gain popularity in order to preserve his estate in case of a rebellion in Ireland. Fitzwilliam nevertheless gave his co-operation to Moira's move in the Lords on 21 March for an address to the king 'imploring His Majesty's paternal and beneficent intervention, to remedy the discontents which unhappily prevailed in his Majesty's kingdom in Ireland' and putting forward the same proposals, in order 'to impress the people with confidence in the government'. Fitzwilliam spoke in support, but the motion was inevitably lost by seventy-two votes to twenty. Fitzwilliam's memorial was now superfluous, and he retired to Milton, as Laurence reported, 'very melancholy as to the situation of things here'.[25]

His spirits were to be revived in May, when the 'third party' scheme blazed up again. Now additional hope of success seemed to be offered by evidence of a change of attitude by Windham and Portland. Burke wrote to Windham on 30 March to say that 'the [Irish] government is losing the hearts of the people, if it has not quite lost them, by the falsehood of its maxims, and their total ignorance in the art of governing'. Windham's response breathed a deep despondency not only over Ireland but over the war situation and the lack of spirit in the country. Portland too seemed to be wavering, and early in May the Duke commissioned William Baldwin, Fitzwilliam's legal advisor and member for Malton, to speak to Burke about a possible reconciliation with Fitzwilliam. Laurence reported that Windham seemed ready to consider a new arrangement for Ireland, based on the dismissal of Fitzgibbon and the Beresfords, and that he appeared 'more and more reconciled to the necessity of taking in the Ponsonbys'. Laurence suggested that Fitzwilliam might write to George or William Ponsonby to sound their views about a new coalition in Ireland, and to suggest the discreet dropping of their advocacy of parliamentary reform in order to smooth the path.[26]

Fitzwilliam arrived in town on 15 May, his mind still affected by Burke's discouragement. 'Upon a consideration of the great turn of affairs, and of the new aspect of things,' he wrote to Burke on his arrival, 'my own mind gives much to your way of thinking.' The next few days' events changed his attitude completely. On the following day he met his old friend Carlisle, apparently by chance, in the street, and after a brief conversation they agreed to meet again on the 17th. Carlisle, who was reported to be associated with the 'third party' scheme, began by asking Fitzwilliam's opinion of the Irish situation. He replied that Catholic emancipation alone 'would avail nothing . . . the only hope of parrying the evil that threatened us was in a change of *men*. . . . *Grattan and the Ponsonbys* must be made the government of the country'. Carlisle replied that this could be done only if the government in London were also changed, and asked Fitzwilliam what his attitude would be to that. He replied only that, at all costs, there must be a 'change of system' in Ireland. Burke was horrified. 'I am astonished to find [Lord Fitzwilliam] approving as he does, in a short letter to me, my ideas upon the subject of a coalition,' he wrote, 'and yet proposing a plan in direct opposition to it.' Such a Ministry would be 'Jacobinical' and under the entire domination of Fox; it would, of course, destroy all that Burke had worked for since 1790.[27]

Fitzwilliam wrote to William Ponsonby on 20 May to report his conversation with Carlisle and to tell him of Laurence's contacts with Windham. There would be no difficulties about the removal of Fitzgibbon and Beresford, he thought, but 'the bitter pill is the *admissions*', and parliamentary reform might be a possible stumbling block. The Ponsonbys, he suggested, should weigh carefully whether they were prepared to serve in a government that would remain responsible to a Cabinet under Pitt, and suggested that

Pitt will use all his art to baffle these attempts . . . but he may be driven to admit that your assistance is indispensable; it is to bring things to the point of that admission that I am working—that once effected, I do not see how it is possible . . . that the government of Ireland should not be fully and completely in your hands. Indeed . . . from that moment you become the arbiters of this government, as well as that—I know not how an administration can exist here, to which you refuse your confidence.

His advice, in sum, amounted to a suggestion that Grattan and the Ponsonby brothers should accept office if it were offered as 'expressly the wishes of his Majesty'.

Ponsonby consulted Grattan and his brother, and replied on the 29th that the concession of both parliamentary reform and Catholic emancipation would be a *sine qua non* in any negotiation.[28] As for a new arrangement,

There is but one person from whom such a proposal could come to us and be complied with, and even then it must be through you and the result of your own discreet and personal communication. I should pay no attention to anything coming through the *usual and ordinary channel* of such communications with this country. As to the support that might be looked for from us, I shall give no answer. I feel no disposition to give any confidence to Ministers and must beg to decline saying anything upon the subject.

Ponsonby's douche of cold water merely confirmed what had now become clear in London—that the coalition scheme was impracticable. Portland told Sir Gilbert Elliot that

He was determined for one to resist all attempts to turn out the Ministry or make any considerable change in it; that he thought it more than ever their duty to stay in . . . that Pitt was of the same opinion, and that, in short, they were *all* of that mind.

Windham too declared on 10 June 'that they could not with safety to the country commit the powers of government to Opposition, and that there was no intention to change'. By 15 June Moira recognised that the negotiation was 'completely extinct'. 'Opposition are too unpopular to have anything left to hope for,' concluded Lady Holland.[29]

The episode nevertheless showed that Fitzwilliam remained eager for a reunion with Fox, and it was this aspect of the affair which most alarmed Burke. When Fitzwilliam rode over to Eton on 30 May to see Milton he called at Beaconsfield, where Burke was in the last stages of his fatal illness. It was their last meeting, and one which Burke found disturbing. 'It is not easy for me to describe to you the state of [Lord Fitzwilliam's] mind,' he wrote to Laurence. The situation in which Fitzwilliam found himself was 'enough to perplex a very clear understanding, such as in truth his understanding naturally is'; but his ability to see the situation clearly was clouded by 'his own passions' and 'a strong predilection to Mr Fox . . . and a still stronger with regard to Mr William Ponsonby'. Fitzwilliam was also 'influenced, too much so in my

opinion, though very naturally and very excusably, by a rooted
animosity against Mr Pitt, and . . . an incurable suspicion of his
sincerity'. Fitzwilliam's Irish friends were not under his guidance
or control, and in the matter of parliamentary reform in particular
they were acting contrary to all his principles; still, Fitzwilliam
was so infatuated that 'I plainly perceive that if he was consulted,
he would advise to throw everything into their hands. . . . I have
entered into a very great detail with him, perhaps into too great a
detail upon all these points . . . yet I am afraid that I have poured
too much into a mind in itself over-anxious and over-full'.[30]

The collapse of the 'third party' scheme resolved Burke's fears,
and Fitzwilliam returned temporarily to his independent course.
Such, indeed, was Burke's last message to him, through the faithful
Laurence, who stayed at his bedside to the end in the early hours of
9 July.

'Inform Lord Fitzwilliam from me [he said] that it is my dying advice
and request to him, steadily to pursue that course in which he now is.
He can take no other that will not be unworthy of him.' . . . As I
remember, this was almost if not quite the last thing which he said on
public affairs.

Burke's voice came as a reminder to Fitzwilliam of the stand he
had taken two years earlier, to be the man of principle, following
the line he believed to be right, and independent of party politics. It
was a voice strong enough to recall to Fitzwilliam's mind the long
Whig tradition for which Burke had come to stand and which lay
at the root of his own political life. Echoes of Burke's own words
to him at the time of Rockingham's death must have passed
through his mind as he read Laurence's letter.

You have his place to fill and his example to follow; and you are the
only man in the world to whom this would not be a work of the greatest
difficulty. . . . It is only going on in your own course and inclining with
the best of your ordinary dispositions. You are Lord Rockingham in
every thing. . . .

Memories of almost a lifetime's affection and trust, with hardly an
interruption, could not fail to impress Fitzwilliam's sensitive feelings:

The loss is irreparable [he wrote to Laurence] in every point of view:
with him is gone all true philosophy, all publick virtue; there is nothing
left but factious schemes and time-serving manoeuvres, contending one

with the other, which shall do most mischief—not one English sentiment, not one statesmanlike idea—this is the publick loss. The private one is of everything that was warm, zealous, partial, where once he had placed his affections; for my own part, I feel it is the loss, not of a friend, but of a father; of one to whom I looked up for advice and instruction; and who gave them with the interest and fidelity of a parent.

And Laurence assured him that 'indeed he most cordially loved you with all the affection of which (far above the affection of ordinary men) his great mind and soul were capable'.[31] Burke's death therefore strengthened for a time rather than diminished his influence over Fitzwilliam's mind. It had gone too deep ever completely to be forgotten. But in day-to-day matters his advice and his warning voice were no longer available, and though Laurence for a time seemed to inherit his role of political advisor, Burke's death also removed another obstacle from the path of reconciliation with Fox. Fitzwilliam's headstrong and impatient temperament had needed the curb of Burke's influence, and though in recent years Burke had too often been incapable of giving consistent and sober counsel, at moments of crisis it was to his wisdom that Fitzwilliam had instinctively turned. For the present there was no one to supply that want. For the future it must lead more or less directly to a reunion with Fox, as a means of supplying the need for political guidance and personal affection.

Laurence's project for collecting Burke's pamphlets and correspondence and publishing those parts which were thought proper for the public eye helped to perpetuate his influence.

What you have in contemplation [Fitzwilliam wrote] cannot be the work of a day: it will require time, for it will be the most interesting and most instructive compilation ever given to the world. . . . It will prove that . . . the motives of his conduct were not the occasional passion of the moment, but arose out of one regular, well digested, organised system of principles . . . which seemed to have prepared him for every occurrence which could arise in human policy.

The reading of Burke's correspondence and writings was bound to confirm his principles in Fitzwilliam's mind. They contained, he told Laurence, 'a body of ethicks, of morality, of universal and national policy that will please, will instruct and mend a world'. Fitzwilliam was also anxious, however, to exclude from the publication of Burke's writings passages containing attacks on individuals,

particularly his old friends, and he declined to supply Laurence with
the authorised text of the 'Observations on the Conduct of the
Minority' on the grounds that it was throughout an indictment of
Fox's conduct. He also worked through the mass of Burke's correspondence with Rockingham from 1766 to 1782 and declared that it
set out 'the principles upon which the great body of Opposition acted
at that time'.[32] In these ways Burke's death helped to revive and
confirm in Fitzwilliam's mind the Whig heritage on which his
political creed was founded; but it was more the Whiggism of
Burke's opposition days before 1782 than the more conservative
creed of 1790–4 that rose uppermost in his mind.

The shaky position of the Ministry in the spring of 1797 was
reflected in a revival of public agitation. From all quarters of the
kingdom, from 'almost every county, city and town of note in
England and Ireland',[33] addresses for the removal of Ministers poured
in. The country's mood was deeply depressed. The suspension of cash
payments by the Bank of England in February, the naval mutinies in
April and May, the government's financial difficulties and the continued
distress due to interruptions of trade and shortage of food brought
home the difficulties of waging war alone against the continually
growing power of the French Republic. By the summer of 1797 the
whole of northern and central Italy was under French domination,
Austria was negotiating for peace, and England stood alone facing the
threat of French, Dutch and Spanish naval power against a disaffected
Ireland. Despite Abercromby's successes in the West Indies and the
triumphs of Jervis and Duncan against the Spanish and Dutch fleets,
there seemed little hope of a successful revival of the anti-French
crusade of 1793. In June, therefore, Lord Malmesbury again set out
for France, this time to Lille, to face a French government strengthened by the conquests and supported by the growing popularity and
influence of Bonaparte. As the meeting of Parliament approached,
Fitzwilliam confessed his despondency to Laurence. It was, he wrote,

disgusting in the greatest degree to find one set of our [news]papers,
replete with the *triumphs of the true Republicans*—and another set,
pouring forth abject prayers that we may be admitted to peace with
these audacious subverters of everything like order or establishment. . . .
There is nothing wanting, but the ability to do it as it ought to be done,
that stands in the way of my going up to read my miserable countrymen
a severe lecture upon their conduct.

He was inclined to think, however, 'whether this may not be a line of conduct better adapted to the calibre of my abilities—rather to keep quietly within my shell than to put forth with very weak means, against the strong current of the tide'. As long as both government and opposition vied with each other for peace his own efforts seemed not worth making. Laurence, replying on the day Malmesbury's expulsion was known, thought his failure might create an advantageous climate: 'Your lordship's steady and sturdy old English principles are wanted', he wrote. 'They have ever been reverenced when seen, they may now be followed.' He urged Fitzwilliam to move a strong amendment and follow it up with a forcible protest, 'done in your own easy, clean, spirited and vigorous style', and he offered to move a similar amendment to the address in the Commons. Fitzwilliam contented himself with the reflection that he had already 'left my last will and testament in the journals of our House'. His views on the war were, indeed, well enough known and it would have become tiresome to repeat them at every opportunity. He did declare his intention to support the government's newly increased taxes, writing to Laurence that 'I have not protested against a peace with Jacobin France to blink the unpopularity that may attend the means of fighting with her. . . . It is sufficient that *no* peace is, for me to feel it incumbent upon me to offer myself up, to bear my share . . . of obloquy and unpopularity'. He would come up to town to support the Assessed Taxes Bill, though for no other purpose. He nevertheless censured the government's measures for home defence, and particularly Dundas's Bill to allow the militia, enlisted for home service only, to be sent to the Channel Islands. Though he was willing 'to submit to any degree of unpopularity in conjunction with the Ministry . . . in pursuit of what is right—when they choose to act abominably, they shall meet with my reproof'.[34]

The opposition, meanwhile, had declared their intention of giving up regular attendance in a Parliament where they could achieve nothing. The failure of Grey's motion for reform on 26 May had resulted in the secession of most of the Foxites from the two Houses. At the Whig Club on 6 December Fox nevertheless declared his continued adherence to the cause of peace with France and internal reform. 'He seems,' Laurence wrote, 'to have settled the object of his ambition to figure in feathers and satin as an English Director under the protection of the *Great Nation*, as the robbers and murderers of France now call their own sanguinary faction.' Writing in January

1798 to his Yorkshire friend Stephen Croft about the proposed
county meeting to address for removal of Ministers, Fitzwilliam
declared that though he had 'many grounds of quarrel and many
subjects of heavy complaint' against the administration, yet 'if Mr
Pitt is removed . . . Mr Fox or his immediate connexions must be
the Ministers of the country'. His objections to the Foxites, he
averred, were not mainly due to their advocacy of a French peace,
since he did not believe that even they could negotiate a treaty
satisfactory to themselves with 'imperious France'; his true objection
was that 'they will change our representation' in such a way that
'will truly frenchify us: for my part I have nothing less at heart
than to be *frenchified*. . . . With all my predilections for the persons
(and certainly they are strong) I never will lend an aiding hand to
turn my country adrift upon the uncertain waves of unknown seas'.[35]

It was in this state of mind that Fitzwilliam received the unexpected offer in February 1798 of the Lord Lieutenancy of the West
Riding. When he had refused the office from Shelburne in 1782 it
it had been given to Lord Surrey, who was now, as eleventh Duke
of Norfolk, one of the leading members of the Foxite opposition in
the Lords. On Fox's birthday, 24 January, Norfolk had taken the
chair at a banquet at the Crown and Anchor tavern in London, and
had proposed the toast of 'Our sovereign—the Majesty of the
People'.[36] The king at once instructed Portland to dismiss him from
the Lord Lieutenancy and Colonelcy of the West Riding militia, and,
according to William Baldwin, whom Portland approached as an
intermediary, signified that Fitzwilliam would be 'the only proper
person to succeed him'. Portland assured Baldwin of his own wish
that Fitzwilliam would accept, but expressed his fear that he would
refuse to entertain an offer through Portland himself as the responsible Minister. He asked Baldwin to sound Fitzwilliam's views.
Baldwin tried to persuade Fitzwilliam that the offer came as 'the
pure original wish and desire of the sovereign, springing from him
only', and that the circumstances of Norfolk's dismissal implied the
royal approval of Fitzwilliam's views on internal policies. And he
suggested that the Lieutenancy was 'an office not at all connected
with Ministers but with the county'. Laurence was also called in and
wrote on the following day at Pitt's request, pointing out that it was
not intended to suggest 'any appearance of an obligation derogating
from your known opinions of difference from them' [the Ministers].

Fitzwilliam remained suspicious. If, he assured Laurence, 'the pro-

posal is really his Majesty's sentiment . . . I am all obedience'; but
if it was 'only a little coquetting . . . I must decline receiving any
[offer] of a public nature'. He demanded that the offer must be
officially stated 'as originating with his Majesty himself: if a word
is left doubtful, if a syllable leaves it liable to the construction of
being made in consequence of the advice and suggestion of any of
his Ministers, I shall decline the apparent honour intended me by
his Majesty but the real service to them'. Portland and Pitt both
assured Laurence that they understood Fitzwilliam's scruples and
they tried, within constitutional limits, to respect them. They authorised Laurence to transmit the king's 'royal pleasure, that your lordship should take upon yourself the government of the West Riding
of Yorkshire', though Pitt stipulated that no form of words or
procedure should be open to the construction that the king was
giving his approval to 'your lordship's former conduct in opposition
to the sentiments of your then colleagues on the Irish question or
implying any want of confidence in his present Ministers'. In the
end Fitzwilliam received the offer of the Lord Lieutenancy in an
audience with the king on 14 February and accepted it: 'the business
ended exactly as I could have wished', he assured Laurence, and
though the Prince of Wales, on whom Fitzwilliam called the following morning, disapproved of his accepting anything during Pitt's
administration, he nevertheless received him kindly. Fitzwilliam
also called on Norfolk, where he was 'well received, and everything
perfectly right'. 'Being now in the gears,' he wrote to Charlotte, 'I
must put my shoulder to the work, and do the business in the best
way I can.' His acceptance of the office nevertheless again emphasised
his differences with Fox, who had written to Lauderdale on 4 February that Norfolk's toast provided an excellent 'line of demarcation
for us, to distinguish the two parties in the country; for it is
impossible to support the Revolution and the Brunswick succession
upon any other principle'.[37]

Fitzwilliam's new duties absorbed a great deal of his time for the
next twenty-one years. He always found it more congenial, as he
had written to Portland in June 1794 when resisting the duke's pleas
to come into the Cabinet, to 'work without doors',[38] and for the
past sixteen years he had tried to play in south Yorkshire the role
that Rockingham had filled with such distinction. The innate
paternalism of the Whig aristocratic creed was instinctively to Fitzwilliam's liking, and his local position was always, to him, the first

I

responsibility he owed to the nation in return for the rank and property birth had bestowed on him. It was in this spirit of public service that he entered on the new era of his life, though the novelty lay in the office he now formally held rather than in the continuing concern for local interests that he had always felt.

Fitzwilliam's activity in helping to suppress radical demonstrations and disturbances in south Yorkshire since 1792 was undoubtedly the principal reason for his being offered the Lord Lieutenancy. He had been keeping a close eye on events in Sheffield since December 1791, and his awareness of popular agitation in south Yorkshire lay behind much of his increasingly conservative thinking since that time. The arrival in Sheffield in 1793 of Henry Redhead Yorke, whom Fitzwilliam contemptuously described as 'the vagabond demagogue', had revived popular agitation for reform. At a monster meeting on 7 April 1794 Yorke attacked the government as 'a corrupt, crazy, and wicked administration', and advocated direct action by the people rather than peaceful but hitherto ineffective petitioning of Parliament. As a result Yorke and Joseph Gales, proprietor of the radical *Sheffield Register*, were arrested and tried for libel and conspiracy. These and the other treason trials of 1794 drew attention to reports of preparations for armed rebellion, and Fitzwilliam, who had received evidence in the summer of 1793 of parties of young journeymen drilling secretly on the moors, became convinced that plans were laid for an insurrection. He believed that the 'better sorts' and almost all the lower orders were well affected, and reported that distributors of radical handbills were frequently subjected to drenchings under the village pump, but during the summer of 1794 he encouraged the precautionary raising and arming of local troops of Volunteer yeomanry for use against local disaffection. He himself took an active role as Colonel and Chairman of the General Committee of the West Riding Yeomanry cavalry. The very existence of these forces was usually enough to cow the local reformers, and though there was a serious riot in Sheffield in August 1795 it seemed to be provoked by complaints from the regular troops stationed there about their pay rather than by political agitation. Fitzwilliam hurried down at the head of the Yeomanry to face a crowd sympathetic to the soldiers. The Riot Act was read and, the crowd refusing to disperse, the Volunteers opened fire. Two persons were killed and several injured; Fitzwilliam expressed his satisfaction that the incident produced no repercussions, despite the popular grievances about the high price of bread. He thought that the success of the operation would have a good effect by showing the readiness of the Volunteers to act in the cause of law and order, and hoped that 'in the manner in which it has ended . . . it will be productive of good, and tend much to the future quiet of the place'.[39]

The treason trials of 1794–5 and the 'Two Acts' of 1795 helped to stem the progress of radical politics in south Yorkshire, but as Lord Lieutenant after 1798 Fitzwilliam continued to keep a close watch. In the autumn of 1800 the situation deteriorated again. The grievances of the people were now mainly concerned with high food prices, the result of bad harvests allied to the economic dislocations of the war, especially since 1797, when severe price inflation set in. The farmers, corn millers and merchants were accused of profiteering at the expense of the poor, and in September 1800 Fitzwilliam hurried to Sheffield with a force of local Yeomanry cavalry to head off a party of demonstrators on their way to attack a corn mill at Attercliffe. A confrontation followed. Fitzwilliam addressed the crowd, urging that displays of violence could do nothing to increase the deficient supply of corn, and after the arrest of one hothead who refused to lay down his bludgeon, the reading of the Riot Act and patrols by the troops, the crowds dispersed peaceably. The danger had been the greater in that most of the Sheffield Volunteers were thought to be unreliable and sympathetic to the mob, some of whom were their own friends, wives and children 'calling out for bread'. Fitzwilliam's assessment of the situation, however, was a calm one. The disturbances were wholly due to food prices and shortages, he wrote; against a Jacobinical mob the Volunteers would remain dependable.[40]

Others were less cool-headed. In October 1800 reports flooded in of popular disaffection throughout the West Riding, from Tickhill in the south-east to Leeds, Bradford and Huddersfield in the west.[41] Nightly meetings in secretly guarded locations on the moors were reported, together with rumours about the purchase of pikes and drilling of squads of armed men. Even the establishment in Bradford of a group of the harmless if eccentric sect of New Jerusalemites, who believed in the identity of their leader, Richard Brothers, as the Messiah, gave rise to alarming speculations amongst Fitzwilliam's correspondents. In the manufacturing area round Leeds and Huddersfield the stagnation of trade, giving rise to unemployment and short-time working, added to the distress of the industrial craftsmen and

to the alarm of the propertied gentry and middle class. In March
1801 the Leeds magistrates reported widespread combinations among
the lower orders, illegal oath-taking ceremonies for subversive purposes, and preparations for an armed insurrection to overthrow the
constitution. Only the presence of regular troops, it was reported,
kept the situation under control. These fears were grossly exaggerated, but Fitzwilliam, though sceptical of the wilder rumours,
was genuinely alarmed by reports like those of the proceedings of
the 'Friends of Liberty' near Keighley, who were meeting on the
moors in April

to expose fraud and every species of hereditary government, to lessen
the oppression of taxes, to propose plans for the education of helpless
infancy and the comfortable support of the aged and distressed, . . . to
promote universal peace, civilisation and commerce, to break the chains
of political superstition, to raise degraded man to his proper rank

and to ask 'have we a fair and impartial representation in the
Commons House of Parliament?' Petitioning Parliament was useless,
it was declared, because it consisted of 'a majority of mercenary
hirelings, government pimps, corn dealers, placemen, pensioners,
parasites, etc, and yourselves starving for bread—no, let them exist
not one day longer, we are the sovereignty . . .' This echo of the
radical second part of Paine's *Rights of Man* brought Fitzwilliam up
to the area, and the volunteers were put on one hour's notice. Others,
however, reassuringly declared that the disaffected were a small
minority and that the people in general were 'strongly . . . attached
to the present order of things'. There was, Fitzwilliam reported to
the Home Office, an active, well organised and disciplined leadership
at work, but the mass of the people were concerned only with high
food prices and not with politics. The coming of peace and the
reopening of the Baltic market for cloth were expected to quieten
the situation. He asked for reinforcements of the regular troops in
the area as a precaution, but avoided provocative action which might
worsen the situation. During the summer of 1801 the alarms
diminished, and the negotiation of the treaty of Amiens satisfied the
more respectable elements who had subscribed to several petitions
for peace from West Riding towns in the early weeks of the year.[42]
After 1802 alarms arose mainly from the industrial activities of
trade unions and Luddites rather than from signs of political dis-

affection, which hardly reappeared until the second decade of the century.

Against this background of local activity in the cause of order and the established constitution Fitzwilliam continued to act a conservative role in national politics. Other pressures, however, were pulling him towards the opposition, providing their commitment to parliamentary reform could be kept below the surface. And there was one issue which at this period of his political career was apt to predominate over all others—that of Ireland—which drew him inexorably towards his former friends. The Irish rebellion of 1798 and its aftermath reinforced the call of old friendship, which now began to draw Fitzwilliam back to Fox.

Fitzwilliam's continuing interest in Ireland stemmed not only from his political and family connexions and the policies of his viceroyalty but also from his position as a major Irish landowner. His estate, inherited from Rockingham, covered 66,000 acres, the greater part of the cultivated area of County Wicklow. In 1812 Edward Wakefield praised it as one of the best-run estates in the kingdom, and declared that it 'exhibits an appearance that would do honour to any part of Europe'.[43] Fitzwilliam had continued Rockingham's policy of enlightened and benevolent landlordism under his uncle's steward, William Wainwright, a Yorkshireman who was trained in the estate office at Wentworth and who became one of Fitzwilliam's most trusted servants. The estate also conferred considerable electoral influence. Under the Irish representative system county voters were, for various reasons, almost entirely and universally under the political domination of their landlords. The independence which conventionally distinguished county electorates in England was quite uncharacteristic of their Irish counterparts. Fitzwilliam, accordingly, had virtually complete political sway in the county. In 1815 he was landlord over 834 of the 1,676 registered voters, and this gave him virtual control of both seats for County Wicklow throughout the period 1782–1832. He nevertheless always made it a condition that the candidates he proposed should be men of independent property in the county, and acceptable both to his tenantry and to the other major landowners there, and he always declared that he claimed only one of his tenants' votes and that they were free to dispose of the other as they wished. Nevertheless, as Wainwright wrote in 1783, the county was generally regarded as 'no more than a borough of your lordship's'. Even the reaction after the regency crisis in 1789 did not shake his control, though there was a sharp contest in which Fitzwilliam's influence over both seats was put to the test, and Fitzwilliam's first proposal to put up Henry Grattan had to be dropped. In the 1790s both members, William Hoare Hume and Nicholas Westby, were elected through his influence, and when Westby died in 1800 Fitzwilliam was able to secure George Ponsonby's return in a contest against Lord Carysfort's son, Lord Proby, by 695 votes to 622.[44]

Fitzwilliam's Irish estates were not valued only for their political influence. Wainwright's annual remittances to England between 1782 and 1785 amounted from about £8,000 to £10,000, and from 1790 to the end of 1793 he was regularly sending over some £16,000 (English) per year. His methods were no doubt much like those of other Irish stewards: 'I have used every means', he wrote in May 1786, '(except that of selling the tenants' half-starved cattle) to make up this remittance'. In January 1798, as the disorders in the countryside were boiling into rebellion, he was celebrated in verses circulated among the insurgents:

> Bad luck to William Wainwright and his confederesees—
> It is for their bad actions their hearts weel make to bleed—
> To see them conviscated all on that counting day—
> And all our Irish soldiers the blody thieves will slay.

Even Fitzwilliam's liberal sympathies hardly sufficed to make the lot of the Irish peasant a less than cruel one. Nevertheless, there was no question that the state of the common people aroused strong feelings in him.

We may have in our mouth Liberty and free constitution [he wrote to Burke] but in the practice in Ireland it is a state of most odious oppression and abject slavery for the great body of the people—there are there two laws and two constitutions, one for the rich, and one for the poor. Can it be a matter of surprise, or a cause of complaint, that there is no attachment, no zeal for the safety of such a country?

Much as he abhorred rebellion and its accompanying atrocities on both sides, he found in the state of the Irish people ample cause for the growth of hatred towards their British governors and oppressors.[45]

From 1796 Wainwright's letters from Malton, the headquarters of the estate, began to reflect the crescendo of violence in Ireland. At the end of 1796 he was busy organising yeomanry corps in the four parts of the estate, at Shillelagh, Newtown, Rathdrum and Wicklow, and, on Fitzwilliam's orders, he was trying to encourage both Protestant and Catholic enrolment. A fifth of his own yeomanry troop in Shillelagh were Catholics, he reported, but it was difficult to enlist Catholics as privates in the infantry corps: he knew of only two out of fifty in the Newtown troop, and none at Rathdrum or Wicklow. Fitzwilliam subscribed to the expenses of these forces, which were used for the first time in December 1797 to escort Wainwright on his way from Malton to Dublin with the rents through country now infested by robbers. 'This is a fresh way of travelling and a very unpleasant one,' he wrote. In January 1798 he passed on reports of over a thousand men parading with guns, pikes and scythes, and three weeks later he reported that timber was being cut to make pikestaves. In March he sent news of outrages committed by marauders on some tenants, who had had their cowsheds burnt or machinery broken. By the end of May the whole county was in 'such a ferment as I am not able to describe occasioned by militia and yeomanry endeavouring to disarm the inhabitants of pikes and other offensive weapons, prepared for the destruction of the Protestants'. The operation had succeeded, but 'this could not be accomplished until flogging became general. Some have even stood one hundred lashes before they would confess where the offensive weapons were concealed—scarcely one Catholic but what are concerned'. Several tenants had absconded owing large sums of rent, and their deserted houses were immediately burned. 'The petty schoolmasters to a man are implicated,' he averred, 'and from them our misfortunes have been completed.'

The Irish rebellion broke into the open towards the end of May 1798. The first major attack by the rebels, on Naas, near Dublin, was repulsed on the 24th, but it was followed by others on Rathfarnham, Wexford, Tallanghill and Kildare. The garrison of Wexford was overrun by a force of 15,000 and the town surrendered on the 30th. For three weeks the uprising raged, until the rebels' main force was routed on 21 June at Vinegar Hill. Wainwright was there with his Shillelagh troop. His first engagement was on 28 May, when half his cavalry troop with two companies of infantry and two detachments of militia engaged a crowd armed with pikes and fowling pieces. 'No quarters were given them,' he wrote, 'except to about six, who have since been shot . . . we are in a complete state of rebellion, and the inhabitants seeking refuge without knowing a place of safety.' Marching a few days later towards Vinegar Hill, he found the countryside 'burned and destroyed and the greater part of the Protestant inhabitants put to death'. Thirty-nine rebels were shot in one day at Carnew; 'The last week has been a scene of confusion; we have been for the most part on horseback, and God only knows what will be the event'. A few days later the rebels overran part of County Wicklow and burnt down the house at Malton, Wainwright escaping just in time with the estate records and papers. On the 16th he reported that rebels were 'committing great depredations' on the estate. The destruction was almost total:

The rebels burnt the houses of the Protestants and the army those of the Catholics [he wrote after Vinegar Hill]. The cabins left standing are deserted and such of their inhabitants as are not with the rebel army are hiding in breaks of furze on the hills. . . . The peaceable and loyal inhabitants as well as the disaffected have been plundered . . . what the rebels left has been taken by the army and it seems we shall have a scarcity of provisions before the new potatoes come in. Malton is a dreadful place to see, the conflagration was very great.

Fitzwilliam's estate was 'the seat of war and rebellion in this part of the county', and 'the country is ruined, what the rebels do not destroy is laid hold of by the soldiers, whose outrages . . . in spite of their officers are boundless'. Even Vinegar Hill did not put an end to the rebellion in County Wicklow. On 7 August Wainwright reported that the rebels still held most of the country between Tinehaley and Rathdrum and that not a single Protestant was left in the former place. 'I fear it will take years before the Protestants and Catholics can again be reconciled to each other,' he wrote. 'God only knows when tranquillity can be so far restored that any tenant (except a Catholic) may with safety occupy [his farms]'. By 19 August, however, the county was quieter, and Wainwright was supplying timber on credit to tenants who were rebuilding their homes. Over 160 houses were destroyed in the Carnew area of the estate alone. 'I must crave your lordship's forbearance as to my accounts up to Lady Day last,' he confessed, 'for it has not been in my power to write one scrawl on the subject, neither do I yet know under whose roof I can retire for the purpose, being in the store of a malthouse at present where a great many others lodge with myself.' Neither was it surprising that in September he should report that 'no money can be had amongst your lordship's tenantry . . .

those that have their rents are not inclinable to pay at present and were their cattle distrained we should not find any buyers'. His Yorkshire phlegm and orderly habits of business were not entirely destroyed by his experiences.[46]

Fitzwilliam's emotions on receiving Wainwright's reports were a compound of anger and dismay. The spread of disaffection amongst his own tenantry was a bitter blow, and he unhesitatingly blamed it on the repressive and unimaginative policies of the government. He constantly stressed that, in his view, the rebellious and Jacobinical mood of the Catholic south dated from after his recall in March 1795 and, more precisely, from events in County Armagh in the summer of that year, when a massacre of Catholics was alleged finally to have alienated the Catholic community from the British government. Fitzwilliam stressed also the declaration of the State prisoners in Dublin in July 1798 to the effect that the Society of United Irishmen had been aiming solely at parliamentary reform until 1796, when, in order to attract French help, they adopted the design of a republic and a separation from Britain. The declaration also asserted that the society had 'made but little way amongst the Catholics . . . until the recall of Lord Fitzwilliam', but that his recall had presented the opportunity for certain leading conspirators to persuade the Catholics to join the disaffected Presbyterians. It was from this time, Fitzwilliam declared, that the origin of the rebellion should be dated. Now the Irish 'have become most inveterate rebels . . . [and] Ireland will never be tranquillised till the people give credit to a fundamental change of system'. In Fitzwilliam's eyes the rebellion was the final though deplorable vindication of his viceroyalty.[47]

He had no hesitation, therefore, in deciding what line to take in the proceedings on Ireland which followed the rebellion. The general policies of government should be condemned, as well as the atrocities committed by the government's troops, though no support, naturally, was to be given to the motives or activities of the rebels themselves. In both Houses of Parliament Fitzwilliam and his friends supported the opposition's attacks on the government's responsibility for the rebellion. On 14 June Sheridan moved in the Commons for a committee of enquiry into the causes of the uprisings. Laurence and Sir William Milner spoke in support of the motion, which was lost by 43 to 159. Baldwin as well as Laurence and Milner voted in the minority. The following day the Duke of Leinster made a similar

I*

proposal in the Lords, and Fitzwilliam himself spoke in support,
voted in the minority, and signed the opposition protest. On 19 June
the Commons debated the proposal to authorise the sending of
English militia regiments to Ireland, the opposition speakers resisting
it on the grounds that it was improper to use the militia as if it were
part of the standing army, rather than in its original and constitutional role as protector of the liberties of the people against the
Ministers.[48] On 22 June Lord George Cavendish moved five resolutions criticising the government's Irish policies and censuring the
Irish administration, and Fox moved for the ending of the policy of
repression by force and torture, and the removal of those Ministers
who were responsible for it. Fitzwilliam supported similar motions
by Bessborough and Bedford in the Lords on 27 June and signed the
latter's protest.[49] His members in the Commons were forced to
recognise that all this implied a change in their political situation.
Baldwin, who sat for Malton, and who had voted on Fitzwilliam's
orders for Sheridan's motion for the enquiry on 14 June, wrote
on the following day to say that, his own views being on the contrary
side, he had voted only because Fitzwilliam had insisted, and asked
to resign his seat. Adair, of Higham Ferrers, had spoken against the
opposition motions on 22 June. Only Laurence and Sir William
Milner were found consistently supporting Fitzwilliam's line throughout the Commons debates—the latter as a consistent Foxite, the
former no doubt wishing to avert Fitzwilliam's rushing directly into
opposition.[50] Nevertheless, despite Laurence's restraining influence
the Irish rebellion in effect completed the progress back to opposition that Fitzwilliam would have been prepared to make in 1795
but for the war and the reform question.

Fitzwilliam's hostility towards the government's Irish Union proposals in 1799–1800 followed naturally from his disapproval of their
policies since 1795, and was unaffected by the possibility that the
Union might enable the policy of Catholic conciliation, to which
he remained pledged, to be more safely adopted. The Union scheme,
he believed, would split the higher orders of Catholics, on whose
loyalty the government must be dependent to keep the lower orders
in check. After the defeat of the first proposals in the Irish Commons on 23 January he wrote, 'the measure cannot be carried but
by the length of the sword. It cannot be an Union of consent on the
part of Ireland'. He took the lead against the Union resolutions
introduced by Grenville on 19 March 1799, declaring not merely an

opposition to the proposed details but a total hostility to the discussion of the scheme as long as Ireland remained in a state of turmoil and incipient rebellion. What, he asked, was to be offered to the Catholics of Ireland in return for their acceptance of the Union? Vague hints as to the possibility of emancipation, thrown out by government spokesmen, were insufficient. He entered a plea for emancipation in any case, on grounds of common sense. 'Did anyone at this time of day believe,' he asked, 'that the family of the Stuarts would be supported by the Catholics?' A year later, when the proposed Articles of Union were debated in the Lords, he declared that no one wished more cordially for a complete union between the two kingdoms, but it must be one that would unite and not divide the two peoples. The present Bill, he asserted, destroyed the Irish constitution in return only for promises of British investment in Ireland which would not take place. He also supported Holland's motion for Catholic emancipation in both kingdoms before a Union, declaring that the penal Acts were 'framed against a particular description of persons which now ceased to exist: they were directed against superstition, bigotry and disloyalty; and therefore should not affect the liberal, the well-meaning, and the loyal Catholics of the present day'.[51]

Though opposition in the British Parliament to the Union Bill was slight and ineffective, Fitzwilliam had maintained a consistent position and had found himself acting more and more with men like Moira and Fox's nephew, Holland. By the end of 1799 Fox was writing that though he himself had no wish to take any further part in public affairs, 'among those who still continue to think it worth while to resist Ministers there are two who have from me every degree of good will and affection; I mean Fitzwilliam and my nephew'. The reunion was not yet complete. When Fox returned to the Commons in February 1800 to urge peace once more, Fitzwilliam still disapproved of his arguments. He believed that the true interests of the country demanded a continuation of the war at least until the French would accept the *status quo ante bellum*. Yet he repeated his criticism of the administration's measures; 'if I incite to war, I am not bound to approve the unwise conduct of it. . . . I must therefore reprobate the want of wisdom and of enlightened policy, which entails a continuation of war . . . as much as those who declaim the loudest upon the subject.' Though he declared to Laurence that his mind was 'no other than you have always known it always to be',

the avowal of these views represented the beginning of a shift of
position. Criticism of the government's handling of the war began to
take prominence over his continuing support for the principle behind
it, and by the late summer of 1800 he was changing his attitude
from one of doctrinaire principle to one of practical expediency.[52]
On the news of an approaching peace between France and Austria,
Britain's last Continental ally, he asked whether Britain was

> to continue to act upon the principle that no peace can be had or main-
> tained with France under a government produced by the revolution,
> without such danger to the constitution and existence of Great Britain,
> as no circumstances whatever can justify the risk of the measure? It
> would be running a great length, to suppose this position to have no
> length of tether. . . . I am ready to confess that I do not see how war
> without Continental alliances can tend to produce a counter-revolutionary
> system in France, or any change whatever in the form of government, or
> in the government itself. . . . By arms nothing, then, can *now* be effected.
> . . . To carry on a war for the purpose of ruining France by finance is
> as ridiculous as the attempt by arms is desperate and impossible without
> alliances.

Thus although he maintained that his mind was unaltered on the
general principle of a peace with revolutionary France, he now
maintained that this was a consideration subordinate to the major
question of the practicability of continuing the war. And, he thought,
France under the control of Bonaparte was less likely to propagate
revolutions than in the days of the Jacobins:

> He may continue the use of revolutionary jargon, but he will check all
> revolutionary practices. He may gratify his lust of glory by subjugating
> kingdoms and nations, but he will subvert the orders of things in them
> no more than is necessary for his first purpose.

To this not unpenetrating analysis he added his belief that the British
people were now less attracted by revolutionary doctrines:

> The truth really is that they are become odious. The people have seen
> that, after all, revolutions are but a lottery for power, [and that after-
> wards] the people . . . are left worse than they were found, having been
> fleeced of everything valuable. From the result of the consideration,
> then, I am inclined to think peace desirable.

He told Laurence that he supported the continuance of the war only
because Bonaparte's ambitions in Europe made a satisfactory settle-

ment impossible. He professed no public opposition to a peace which might leave France with a republican constitution, and by the end of 1800 Fox was beginning to hope that the long-awaited reunion of old friends was approaching. He suggested that Grey might cultivate Laurence, 'notwithstanding his tediousness', and when Wyvill set about organising a county meeting in Yorkshire to petition for peace and the removal of Ministers, Fox agreed to approach Fitzwilliam for his support. He cautioned Grey that Fitzwilliam was 'strangely prepossessed against Wyvill', and that 'anything in favour of reform it would be impossible to propose to him'. That question should therefore be kept in the background, but there was good hope of Fitzwilliam's co-operation in a move to rally the public against the war and the Ministry.[53]

Fitzwilliam came to town at the end of January 1801 to concert with Grey and Bedford an amendment to the address for the first debate of the United Kingdom Parliament on 2 February, and he agreed to move it in the Lords. 'It gives me great pleasure,' Fox assured him on the eve of the debate, 'to see all those I love in open and declared opposition to this most detestable government.' Fitzwilliam's language in the debate was remarkable:

He had not the least hesitation in saying that he thought it the duty of that House to pause, and to inquire why we were to go to war, before they pledged themselves to support his Majesty's Ministers in it. . . . It had been his lot, perhaps, more than any other individual, to urge that House to the maintenance of the principles upon which the war against the revolution had been founded. . . . But he must own that the thing was hopeless. . . . France was now, in fact, established into a monarchy under republican forms, and under a new ruler. . . . The die was cast— he must submit.

No clearer avowal could have been made that Fitzwilliam was now, to all intents and purposes, a member of Fox's opposition.[54] His solitary stand of nearly six years was over. During that time he had laboured for the principles he believed in—justice for Ireland, through a change of policy and a change of men; persistence, so long as practicable, in the war against republican France and Jacobin doctrines all over Europe; and resistance at home to all reform so long as reform was inextricably compounded with the danger of subversion. These principles had kept him loyal to Burke's doctrines and Burke's memory, despite his almost paranoiac distrust of Pitt, his unforgiving attitude to Portland, and the deep and instinctive pull

towards his old attachment to Charles Fox. The Irish rebellion had
been the decisive event, while the establishment of the Consulate in
France had softened his doctrinaire resistance to the idea of peace
without a Bourbon restoration. Only parliamentary reform divided
him from Fox, and the approach of a peace with the new France
and the revived hope of Pitt's collapse over the Catholic question
made that possibility too seem less terrifying. His old Whig instincts
triumphed in the years of the Union debates, and from February
1801 he was Fox's friend again—a second political reunion that was
to last till Fox's death.

Notes
¹ Fitzwilliam to Adair, 13 September 1795: B.M. Add. MS 50829.
² I intend to give a fuller account of Fitzwilliam's activities in support
of the 'Cause of Order' in Yorkshire on another occasion.
³ *Parl. Register*, XLIV, pp. 2–10; *Annual Register*, 1796, p. 40.
⁴ Fitzwilliam to George Ponsonby, 6 October 1795: F 30a.
⁵ The Directory was set up under the constitution of 23 June 1795 and
came into being at the end of October: *Annual Register*, 1795.
⁶ Fitzwilliam to Burke [31 October 1795]: *Corresp. of E. Burke*, VIII,
p. 336. He wrote to Baldwin on 24 September 1795 that his vote for the
address was intended to express his support for the principle of the war
only, 'and will not involve an approbation of the management': N.
⁷ Burke to Fitzwilliam, 9 December 1795, and reply, 17 December
(*Corresp. of E. Burke*, VIII, pp. 357–8, 361–2); *Parl, Register*, XLIV, pp.
183–5.
⁸ Fitzwilliam to the Duchess of Devonshire, 29 July [1795] (Chatsworth MSS, 1298. 1); to Adair, 12 September 1795 (B.M. Add. MS 50829).
Adair's reply, 26 September (F 32), avowed his wish to give the government general support, partly because of the unlikelihood of there being
a better one, and partly from the 'strong partiality I cannot help still
feeling for the Duke of Portland'.
⁹ Fitzwilliam to Burke, 30 August 1796: *Corresp. of E. Burke*, IX, pp.
74–6. French Laurence (1757–1809) D.C.L. 1787, Regius Professor of Civil
Law at Oxford 1796, Judge of the Court of Admiralty of the Cinque Ports,
was a notable civil lawyer and a recognised authority on international
and maritime law, with a large practice in the ecclesiastical and
Admiralty courts. He had helped Burke in the preparation of the case
against Warren Hastings and was a counsel for the managers of the
impeachment. He was also a political pamphleteer, wrote ballads for
Fox at Westminster in 1784 and contributed to *The Rolliad*. He was one
of Burke's literary executors, with Fitzwilliam, and with Dr Walker King
was co-editor of Burke's *Works* (1803 and 1808) (D.N.B.). Laurence's reply
to the offer (6 September) is in F 32c.
¹⁰ Laurence to Fitzwilliam, 23 September 1796 (F 32–31) and reply, 26
September (N).

11 Burke to Fitzwilliam, 30 October 1796, and Laurence to Burke, 14 October (*Corresp. of E. Burke*, IX, pp. 101, 99); Fitzwilliam to W. Ponsonby, Sunday 9 [?] [1796] (Grey MSS); *Journals of the House of Lords*, XLI, pp. 15–17; *Annual Register*, 1797 (published 1800), p. 110; *Letters on a Regicide Peace* (Burke, *Works* (1808), VIII). The protest was published in *The Times*, 11 October.

12 Fitzwilliam to Laurence, 10 November (N, x515/153) and to Burke, 10 November 1796 (*Corresp. of E. Burke* (ed. Fitzwilliam and Bourke, 1844), IV, pp. 355–9); Laurence to Burke, 14 October 1796 (*Corresp. of E. Burke*, IX, p. 95); to Fitzwilliam, 26 October (F 32c).

13 *Morning Chronicle*, 11 October 1796; Laurence to Fitzwilliam, 26 October 1796 (F 32c).

14 *Parl. Register*, XLVIII, pp. 39–42; Fitzwilliam to Burke [1 January 1797] (*Corresp of E. Burke*, IX, pp. 218–20); Fitzwilliam to Laurence [1 January 1797] (N, x515/3) and 'Sunday' [January 1797]; Laurence to Fitzwilliam, 31 December 1796 and 8 January 1797; Fitzwilliam to S. Croft, 2 April 1797 (N).

15 The emperor was Britain's only remaining ally, but over half a million pounds had already been given in subsidies in 1794 and 1795, and many in Parliament thought him unreliable and concerned only with his own interests. There had been much opposition therefore to a proposal for a loan in January and February 1795 (*Annual Register*, 1795, State Papers, p. 104).

16 Laurence to Fitzwilliam, 9, 12 and 15 December 1796 (N); Fox to Fitzwilliam, 10 December (N, x516/32/1); [13 December] (N, x515/152); Fitzwilliam to Laurence, 11 December (N); Burke to Laurence, [13 December 1796], [14 December 1796] and 16 December (*Corresp. of E. Burke*, IX, pp. 173–5, 179).

17 Burke to Laurence, 16 December 1796 (*Corresp. of E. Burke*, IX, pp. 178–80); Laurence to Fitzwilliam, 17 December 1796 (N), and reply [18th] (N, x512/33); Fitzwilliam to Laurence [December 1796] and [14 February 1797] (N, x515/135 and 133).

18 Fitzwilliam to W. Ponsonby, 28 November 1796: Grey MSS.

19 *Dublin Evening Post*, 3 December 1796.

20 Fitzwilliam to Burke, 5 December 1796 (*Corresp. of E. Burke*, IX, pp. 144–6); W. Ponsonby to Fitzwilliam, 7 December 1796; Gregory to Fitzwilliam, 18 September 1795 (F 30a). The 'Defenders' were a Catholic organisation, formed for defence against the Orangemen who were organised to disarm Catholics, and who were responsible for many outrages in doing so.

21 Laurence to Fitzwilliam, 7 December 1796 and 21 February 1797 (N); *Parl. Register*, XLVI, p. 220 (2 November 1796), XLVI, pp. 749–56 (3 March). Lionel Damer, Laurence, Lord Milton, and Sir William Milner voted in the minority (*ibid.*, p. 778); Fitzwilliam to Laurence, two drafts, one headed 'Thursday', the other 'Sunday' [February 1797]: N, x515/148. Fitzwilliam refers to Erskine's seconding Grey's motion for parliamentary reform on 26 May 1797, proposing universal householder suffrage in the boroughs (*Parl. Register*, XLVII, pp. 593–4).

[22] Laurence to Burke, 20 February 1797, and reply [c. 20 February] (*Corresp. of E. Burke*, IX, pp. 248–51); Fitzwilliam to Laurence [22 February 1797] (N, x515/4), and reply, 24 February 1797 (N).

[23] J. Adair to Fitzwilliam. 4 March 1797 (F 32/22); Fitzwilliam to R. Sykes, March 1797 (N) and to Burke, 9 December 1796 and 14 December 1796 (*Corresp. of E. Burke*, IX, pp. 156–8, 175–6).

[24] For an account of the affair see A. Aspinall, *Later Corresp. of George III*, II, pp. xxv–xxix.

[25] Burke to Laurence, 5 March, 12 May 1797, [ante 22 March]; Laurence to Burke, 7 and 28 March (*Corresp. of E. Burke*, IX, pp. 271, 275–6, 291–4, 337). Memorandum, F 30f; Laurence to Burke [March 1797] and 22 March 1797 (*Epistolary Corresp. of Burke and F. Laurence* (1827), pp. 158, 163–6); *Parl. Register*, XLVIII, p. 115. A similar motion by Fox in the House of Commons was lost by 220–84. Lord Grenville declared that Moira's motion was concerted with Fitzwilliam (*Court and Cabinets*, II, p. 365). The Prince had written to Pitt on 8 February to advocate concessions to Ireland and to offer his own services as Lord Lieutenant (A. Aspinall, *Corresp. of George, Prince of Wales*, III (1965), pp. 313–6). Pitt's rebuff is in *ibid.*, p. 320.

[26] Burke to Windham, 30 March 1797, and reply, 25 April; to Laurence, 12 May : *Corresp. of E. Burke*, IX, pp. 299–302, 312–4, 333; Laurence to Fitzwilliam, 16 May and [19 May] 1797 (N).

[27] Fitzwilliam to Burke, 15 May 1797 (*Corresp. of E. Burke*, IX, pp. 340–1); *The Times*, 13 March 1797; Laurence to Burke, Burke to Laurence, 18 May (*Corresp. of E. Burke*, IX, pp. 349–55).

[28] Fitzwilliam to W. Ponsonby, 20 May 1799 (Grey MSS); Ponsonby to Fitzwilliam, 29 May 1797 : F 30/141.

[29] Aspinall, *op. cit; Journal of Elizabeth, Lady Holland* (1908), I, pp. 148–9. Fox, who had been to see the king on 24 May to say that he did not wish his situation to be a stumbling block, deplored Bedford's statement that no alternative administration could be formed without him; *Memorials and Corresp. of C. J. Fox*, III, p. 271.

[30] Burke to Laurence, 1 June 1797 : *Corresp. of E. Burke*, IX, pp. 364–6.

[31] Laurence to Fitzwilliam, 9 July 1797 (*ibid.*, pp. 373–4); *supra*, p. 35; Fitzwilliam to Laurence [11 July 1797], Laurence to Fitzwilliam, 13 July (N).

[32] Fitzwilliam to Laurence, Sunday [30 July 1797] and [c. 9–10 August 1797] (N).

[33] *Annual Register*, 1797, p. 249; appendix to Chronicle, pp. 84–9.

[34] Fitzwilliam to Laurence [16 September 1797], [December 1797], [January 1798] (N, x515/44); Laurence to Fitzwilliam, 20 September (N).

[35] Laurence to Fitzwilliam [7 December 1797] (N); Fitzwilliam to S. Croft, 25 January 1798 (N).

[36] *Annual Register*, 1798, Chronicle, p. 5.

[37] Baldwin's 'Memorandum of the offer of the Lord Lieutenancy of the West Riding to Lord Fitzwilliam' (F 32h); Baldwin to Fitzwilliam, 1 February 1798, and reply 2 February; Laurence to Fitzwilliam, 2 February 1798, and reply 2 February; Portland to Laurence, 3 February; Laurence

to Fitzwilliam [3 February] and 8 February; Fitzwilliam to Laurence [16 February] and to Charlotte [15 February—two letters] (N 53 and x512); Fox to Lauderdale, 4 February 1798: *Memorials and Corresp. of C. J. Fox*, III, p. 276. Fox provocatively repeated Norfolk's toast at the Whig Club dinner on 1 May and was struck out of the Privy Council by George III. The offer to Fitzwilliam was of course proposed to the king by Pitt (31 January) (*Later Corresp. of George III*, III, p. 16).

38 Fitzwilliam to Portland, 23 June 1794: Portland MSS, PWF 3765.

39 Fitzwilliam to Portland [25 May 1794] (Portland MSS, PWF 3760); W. Lunn to Rev. H. Hunter, 10 August 1793 (F 44b); Fitzwilliam to Burke, 9 August [1795] (*Corresp. of E. Burke*, VIII, p. 298); also correspondence in F 44e. On Yorke's activities in Sheffield see J. Taylor, 'The Sheffield Constitutional Society', *Trans. Hunter Archaeological Soc.*, V (1940), pp. 136–42. For Fitzwilliam's activity in the West Riding see Militia and Yeomanry corresp. (Y 17) in Wentworth Woodhouse MSS, Sheffield.

40 Fitzwilliam to Portland, 3, 8 and 10 September 1800; F 44d.

41 For the following section see correspondence in F 45a.

42 Petitions and reports of meetings, 1801, F 45b.

43 E. Wakefield, *An Account of Ireland, Statistical and Political* (1812), I, p. 283. I am also indebted to Dr P. J. Jupp's unpublished Ph.D. thesis on 'The Parliamentary representation of Ireland, 1800–20' (University of Reading, 1966) for some details.

44 Wainwright to Fitzwilliam, 30 September 1783 (F 89a); Portland to Fitzwilliam, 13 October 1789 (F 115a).

45 Wainwright to Fitzwilliam, 20 May 1786 (F 89b–79); Verses enclosed in Wainwright to Fitzwilliam, 21 January 1798 (F 89–194); Fitzwilliam to E. Burke, 27 November [1796]: *Corresp. of E. Burke*, IX, pp. 136–8.

46 Wainwright's letters to Fitzwilliam, 1797–8, F 89. Wainwright calculated Fitzwilliam's losses on the estate at £2,902 but Fitzwilliam instructed him to withdraw the claim for government compensation.

47 'Memorial of the State Prisoners in Ireland', 29 July 1798. A copy, marked 'belongs to Lord Moira', in F 32g; Fitzwilliam to Devonshire, 30 August 1798, says that the mass of the people were loyal until the spring of 1797, but now 'there is not a sound part in the whole' (Chatsworth MSS, 1445). Fitzwilliam to Laurence, 21 September and 14 October 1798: N.

48 *Parl. Register*, LI, pp. 396–8, 398–401, 406–8. The debates were not reported as the gallery was cleared of strangers beforehand. Five-sixths of Fitzwilliam's first West Yorkshire Militia volunteered for service in Ireland. Fitzwilliam refused to associate himself with the offer: 'I cannot lend myself as a firebrand or bayonet of Lord C[ornwallis]' against the miserable and helpless, nor as the instrument to chastise those who resist, even by force, such oppression', he wrote to Laurence [25 June 1798]: N. At the beginning of September he travelled to Dublin intending to put himself at the head of his Yeomanry corps in County Wicklow, but after only a few hours in Ireland he re-embarked for England (*Beresford Corresp.*, II, p. 184; Laurence to Fitzwilliam, 21 September (N).

⁴⁹ *Parl. Register*, pp. 447–50, 487–93. Again the speeches were un-reported. The session ended on 29 June. Fitzwilliam told Laurence [25 June] that he hoped for the Prince of Wales's support on the 27th in the Lords (N).

⁵⁰ Baldwin to Fitzwilliam, 15 June 1798: N. Milner had declared in the summer of 1794 that he could not follow Fitzwilliam in supporting the war, but Fitzwilliam refused to allow him to resign his seat: Milner to Fitzwilliam [25 September 1794]: N.

⁵¹ Fitzwilliam to Laurence, [29 January 1799] (N, x512/31); *Parl. Register*, LIII, pp. 274–7, LVI, pp. 502–3, 538, 418–9.

⁵² Fox to O'Bryen, [6 December 1799] (B.M. Add. MS 51467, ff. 36–7); Fitzwilliam to Laurence, [February 1800] (N, x512/30). On 11 June 1799, in the debate on the Russian subsidy, Fitzwilliam moved an amendment to declare that the real object of the war was to be the deliverance of Europe, not 'from the tyranny of the French Republic', but 'from the French Republic'—thus placing the emphasis on the overthrow of the Republic itself rather than on its power over other countries. (*Parl. Register*, LIII, pp. 689–90).

⁵³ Fitzwilliam to Laurence, 2 August and 26 October 1800; Laurence to Fitzwilliam, 4 November (N); Fox to Grey, 'Thursday' [January 1801: misdated 1800], 'Sunday' [January 1801: misdated 1800] and 'Friday' [January 1801: misdated 7 November 1800]: *Memorials and Corresp. of C. J. Fox*, III, pp. 296, 308, 305.

⁵⁴ Fox to Fitzwilliam, 1 February 1801: N. Fitzwilliam told Laurence [January 1801] that his amendment had been 're-cast by Grey' (N). His speech is in *Parl. Register*, LIX, pp. 17–20.

CHAPTER NINE

Old friends and new: opposition and office 1801–7

Fitzwilliam's return to regular opposition in the first weeks of 1801 was based on political calculations. He had not given up his belief that no secure or lasting peace could be established until France returned to an ordered constitution, nor was he prepared to embrace reform at home. There was, however, a greater prospect than for some years of destroying Pitt's government, which was already weakened by internal dissensions over war and peace and now further threatened by the political consequences of the Irish Union. This possibility outweighed the more distant prospect of disagreement with Fox over France and reform. In any case, the ministerial crisis of February 1801 pushed these questions into the background.

The Minister's resignation became publicly known on 7 February. Pitt had failed to persuade the king to agree to Catholic emancipation and the repeal of the Test Act in both kingdoms as a consequence of the Union, and for this and other reasons he offered his resignation on 4 February. Spencer, Grenville, Dundas, Windham and several other colleagues followed suit. Fox's immediate reaction was that it was all 'a notorious juggle', and indeed the crisis seemed to offer little hope to opposition. Pitt not only recommended the known anti-Catholic Henry Addington to the king as his successor but expressed a strong wish that his friends would stay in office and support the new Minister, while the ostensible issue on which he resigned was one on which the Whig party was already pledged. 'Opposition are cut out, as emancipation is one of their questions,' Georgiana remarked; by taking Addington the king 'has shut his door on opposition'. Nevertheless, the resignations of Grenville, Spencer and Windham held out a prospect of a new party alignment. All three were strongly pledged to Catholic emancipation—Spencer, as his sister Georgiana recorded, resigned 'because his strongest principles went to emancipation and not yielding in the Cabinet'. Gren-

ville's resignation was equally significant, since his attitude towards
a negotiated peace was also markedly similar to Fitzwilliam's. The
possibility of a 'New Opposition' based on common attitudes to
foreign policy and Ireland was in the air, and Fitzwilliam was
anxious to have the Catholic question brought forward in both
Houses in order to test the extent of possible agreement. Grenville
too recognised that since he and his colleagues had resigned over the
Catholic question they must support emancipation if the opposition
were to bring it forward.[1]

In the midst of these calculations the king's relapse into illness
offered further encouragement to the Whigs. Fitzwilliam urged Fox
to come up to town and lodged him at Grosvenor Square, where on
28 February there was a party conference to discuss the possibility
of a regency. Malmesbury reported that Fitzwilliam, Fox, Lansdowne
and Carlisle had made an offer of their services to the prince, and
Carlisle wrote on the 26th to urge him to accept the 1788 regency
scheme as a basis for negotiation and not to insist on the 'question
of right'. Though the king's recovery thwarted these plans, the crisis
had helped to bring together again both wings of the Whig party.
As late as the end of March, Fitzwilliam still thought that the old
party divisions would be reconstituted, and that the king must
eventually choose between Pitt and opposition: 'the idea of an
Addington administration is the joke of every party,' he wrote.[2] It
was an accurate prophecy in the long run, but Fox's more doubting
view was the more realistic for the time being. He refused to be
infected by Fitzwilliam's optimism or Holland's eagerness, and
declared his own reluctance to re-engage in the old battles:

Do not fancy [he had written to Fitzwilliam on 1 February] . . . that
there is anything more I abhor than the thought of having anything ever
to do with public affairs. As to being at the *head* of them nothing would
ever induce me to undertake it.

Even on the Catholic question he regarded the prospect of a debate
without enthusiasm, and though he declared it to be the only issue
in politics he cared much about, he thought its importance would
be mainly symbolic; its purpose would be only 'to have the names
of all the respectable men in both countries pledged in its favour
and the first talents engaged in its support'. He doubted whether on
tactical grounds it would enjoy much favour in the party, and
he pointed out to Holland that nothing could be accomplished with-

out strong public backing.[3] All that was done was to raise the question on 25 March when Grey's motion on the state of the nation was discussed in the Commons.[4] Grey asked whether there had been any engagement with the Irish Catholics in return for their support of the Union, and whether it had been the king's refusal to allow a Bill for emancipation which had led to the ministers' resignations. Pitt evaded the issue, repeating his view that the question of concessions to the Catholics was one of expediency and not of right, and that to grant emancipation without a Union would have been a 'rash and destructive' step. The Union accomplished, it would have been possible to settle a 'comprehensive and extensive system'; but 'although I wished to submit the question of the Catholics to Parliament, there were such opinions stated as made me feel it impossible, with propriety, to bring the measure forward as a Minister'. He sheltered behind the constitutional argument that for Parliament to enquire into the relations between the Crown and Ministers would shake the foundations of the balanced constitution. As for emancipation now, he declared that 'if any attempt to press it, so as to endanger the public tranquillity, should be made, or to pervert the affection of any part of his Majesty's subjects, we should take our full share in resisting such attempts . . . with firmness and resolution'. As he had adopted the policy of concessions on grounds of expediency, he had now abandoned it on the same grounds.

Fox rose after midnight to wind up for the opposition in a long speech. Referring to Fitzwilliam, he remarked:

. . . Though I am eager to avow my partialities for that noble person, it is not from private friendship or personal regards that I call upon any candid man to deny, if he is able, . . . that the system introduced by that noble lord would not, if then adopted, have prevented those dreadful scenes of havoc, murder and devastation, which have ever since desolated that wretched country.

No evidence, he asserted, had ever been produced to show that any approaches were made by the Irish to France, nor any proposal for separation and independence avowed, 'until every petition for peaceful redress of grievances was spurned and rejected'. Now, Fox declared, Pitt had succeeded in again rousing the spirit of discontent among the Irish: 'the measure which was to be the remedy becomes the source of all distempers'. He concluded with a declaration that the Catholic claims were based on rights, not expediency:

and the government which does not acknowledge these rights, the rights of man in the strictest sense of the word, (notwithstanding the constant clamour against, and abuse of, that phrase) not as theories and speculations, but as active and living principles is not, and cannot be a legitimate government. . . . Change your system towards that country. . . . Let impartiality, justice, and clemency, take place of prejudice, oppression, and vengeance, and you will not want the aid of martial law, or the terror of military execution.

The debate ended in the early hours of the 26th with a majority of 291–105 against Grey's motion. It marked, to a great degree, the end of Fitzwilliam's intimate involvement with the Irish question. He always remained a supporter of emancipation and an opponent of Irish coercion, but the Union had created a new political relationship between the countries, and as Fitzwilliam's viceroyalty faded into history its consequences began to seem more remote from the situation with which the politicians had to deal. Until the emergence of O'Connell's movement in the 1820s British statesmen needed to pay less attention to the conciliation of Ireland. Their possession of Irish votes in the Imperial parliament depended less upon their attention to Irish interests, in the wider sense of that term, than upon their ability to gratify the personal wants of Protestant Irish patrons and members.

Foreign affairs rather than Ireland provided the main political preoccupations of the next few months. Addington's first task was to secure peace with France. Negotiations were begun within a week of his full assumption of office and the preliminary articles were signed on 1 October. The terms were widely condemned as humiliating. Grenville wrote to Spencer that he considered them 'inadequate to any reasonable expectation, and of a nature to leave the country . . . in a state of . . . extreme insecurity'. Laurence and Fitzwilliam naturally shared this view. Bonaparte, wrote Laurence, 'is to give nothing, but to receive back everything which he had lost'. The treaty was

both absolutely and relatively considered, . . . worse than any which this country ever made after the most unsuccessful war. . . . [It] abandons . . . all the great and momentous objects of our long and arduous contest . . . [and] having tacitly confirmed the French Republic in the quiet possession of a more extensive, well-compacted, and formidable empire, than any European power has seen for ten centuries, puts her in a condition of beginning again the struggle with us for the dominion of the seas, whenever she may think most opportune.

The preliminary treaty, he declared, 'surpasses all that my imagination could have conceived, of weakness and pusillanimity'; it was a 'prostration of Great Britain at the feet of France'. He offered to take the lead in opposing it when it came before the House. Fitzwilliam heartily agreed with Laurence's strictures. 'English humiliation has reached its acme,' he wrote. He too would come up to the meeting of Parliament to declare his opposition. Tom Grenville remarked that Fitzwilliam was 'determined to oppose the peace even if he should be single'. Both Laurence and Fitzwilliam were, however, depressed that Fox, while condemning the terms of the treaty as a complete triumph for Bonaparte, publicly rejoiced that peace was made. At the Whig Club on 12 October he delivered a speech which Laurence described as 'a splenetick triumph in the present humiliation of the country', and an endorsement of 'the fashion of French politicks. . . . How can an honest man act in concert with any political connexion that now exists?', he asked. Fitzwilliam confessed that if the treaty was

a great trial of patience, what passed at the Whig Club is no less so: I cannot bear to think of either. I stand up a little for English dignity and I look for English feeling: I find none of the first in the one, nor of the latter in the other.[5]

Fitzwilliam declared his views in the Lords' debate on the preliminary treaty on 3 November, after Grenville had denounced the terms at length as humiliating and disgraceful. Referring to his past declarations against peace, he denied that he was unwilling to agree to any peace made with republican France, but asserted that the present terms provided no more than 'a hollow and precarious truce'. He argued that even the propositions made at Lille in 1797 had been more advantageous, in the circumstances, than these. Now it appeared that 'for the two islands of Trinidad and Ceylon, this country had been nine years engaged in war, and had wasted some hundred millions of money, and the lives of thousands of her subjects'. Finally he referred again to his continuing anxieties lest the peace should allow 'the letting loose of corresponding societies, and giving an opportunity of dispersing the pernicious principles of the French Republic to the seditious and disaffected'. Eventually, when the definitive treaty was brought before Parliament in May 1802, Fitzwilliam was one of the sixteen opposition peers who voted against it.[6] Windham and Tom Grenville maintained similar arguments in the Commons. The debates on the treaty thus brought together those former friends of Pitt who disapproved of the treaty and the conservative Whigs of the Fitzwilliam–Windham school, while emphasising the gulf which still existed between them and the Foxites. Only occasionally could the various groups excluded from the Ministry co-operate fully with each other.

One issue on which the new peacetime government could be challenged by all the opposition was the state of the civil list debts. One of Addington's first tasks was to bring before the House the arrears incurred by the civil list during the war years. This raised an old Whig constitutional issue on which Fox and Burke had collaborated in 1780–2—the need to keep a close parliamentary watch upon the 'influence of the Crown' through the limitation of civil list expenditure. Burke's Act of 1782 had been a landmark in the process of parliamentary control, and it had established provisions designed to prevent the civil list from running into arrears. Despite these provisions, during the inflationary war years it had been allowed to run into debt to a total of nearly a million pounds.[7] In the Commons Fox argued that the grant of the sum in arrears amounted to an endorsement of Ministers' disregard of parliamentary control, while in the Upper House Fitzwilliam led for the opposition by declaring that Ministers must have disobeyed Burke's Act. The opposition was, of course, ineffective. Only three other peers were prepared to risk the sovereign's personal displeasure by supporting Fitzwilliam's motion for an enquiry, and it was lost by a majority of fifty-six. Other constitutional issues were found, however, in the Militia Bill of May 1802, when Fitzwilliam argued against the proposed augmentation of the militia on the ground of opposition to standing armies as well as for the liberal reason that the militia system was socially unequal and was in effect 'a levy on the poor'.[8]

Fitzwilliam's efforts did not immediately produce a united and rejuvenated opposition. Fox was still inclined to despondency, and in March declared that he would not seek election to the next Parliament.[9] Between December 1801 and March 1802 Addington had tried to strengthen himself by approaching various members of the minority, particularly Grey, Tierney and Moira, and the prospect naturally tended to weaken their cohesion. The negotiations came to nothing, but efforts to energise the conservative wing of opposition were equally unavailing. Fitzwilliam's members Laurence and William Elliot, his new colleague at Peterborough and another disciple of Burke,[10] set themselves to promote a vigorous parliamentary campaign against the Ministry, but were unable to carry the Grenvilles with them. Laurence also had hopes of attracting support from Charles Grey, who had married one of Lady Fitzwilliam's Ponsonby nieces in 1794 and who, wrote Laurence, had begun to abandon 'his more obnoxious doctrines of former times'. Fitzwilliam invited Grey to call at Milton on his way to town for the meeting of Parliament, but the debates on the Treaty of Amiens in March 1802 confirmed the alignment of Fitzwilliam with the Grenvilles and Windham, while Fox's flirtation with Bonaparte during the succeeding months made a junction still more remote.[11]

The division was accentuated by the efforts of the conservative opposition to put the case against the peace before the public. In December 1801 Windham, Elliot, Laurence and Tom Grenville proposed a scheme to support a new paper, a weekly *Political Register*, to be run by William Cobbett and to 'contain all genuine State Papers and other sound information, as well as political essays'. Cobbett required a guarantee of £600 to finance the first six months' publication, whose purpose was to attack Addington's administration and the peace treaty. The list of subscribers reads like a roll-call of the new opposition: in addition to the original projectors, Fitzwilliam promised a subscription of £100 and to take twelve copies for free distribution, while Spencer, Buckingham, Grenville and Temple were all shareholders. By early February, Laurence reported, the venture was thriving, with 800 copies a week being sold.[12] Through the summer it continued to attack Addington's peace terms, giving prominence to the efforts of Laurence, Elliot and Windham in its reports of parliamentary debates and publishing a series of attacks on the peace terms by Cobbett himself. Inevitably Cobbett soon began to take a sharp tone towards Fox, whose public declaration of pleasure at Windham's defeat in the Norwich election in June drew upon him the epithet 'the friend of Fitzgerald and O'Connor'. Fox's visit to France in August and September drew down Cobbett's wrath in a way which distressed Fitzwilliam. At the beginning of September the *Register* depicted Fox as he 'crawls to the feet' of Bonaparte and 'bows his grey head to the earth before him, and gathers up the crumbs that fall from his table'. In the next issue but one, Cobbett published a letter to Fox which began:

Sir—I have never till now thought you a person of any political

importance. . . . I have never, till now, been able to persuade myself,
that it was possible for you ever to have any considerable weight in the
councils of this nation. . . .

Cobbett went on to assert that Fox's true object in visiting Paris was
'*to make yourself Minister of this country by his* [Bonaparte's] *means*'.
Fitzwilliam declared to Laurence that he had been 'greatly hurt' by
Cobbett's 'violent invective against Charles Fox', and described the
letter as 'a farrago of calumny. With the old private friendship that
has so long subsisted between Charles and me,' he added, 'I cannot
be the dispenser of libels against him.' He withdrew his support from
the paper, and asked that the twelve copies for whose distribution he
paid should in future be sent to Grosvenor Square, where, no doubt,
they were burnt. Both Fitzwilliam and Laurence nevertheless deplored
Fox's visits to the First Consul's court, on the grounds, as Laurence
remarked, that it

will place a new bar in the way of his obtaining power or recovering the
lost confidence of his country. He neither knows how to be, nor how to
cease to be, a public man : and there is a considerable party in the House
of Commons which neither knows how to act with him, nor how to
quit him.

The task of reconstituting a united opposition to Addington was still
a long and difficult prospect.[13]

The elections in the summer of 1802 provided the first opportunity
to secure a strong support 'out of doors' for the new opposition.
Fitzwilliam's electoral influence was maintained without difficulty.
In the West Riding the peace terms, popular at first, became less so
when trade failed to revive, and it was reported that Wilberforce
and Lascelles were losing support in the industrial areas. Opinion
amongst the Yorkshire clothiers was now beginning to take a direction which would carry the Wentworth interest back to favour in
1806 and 1807. The spread of combinations among certain classes of
workmen, particularly the shearmen or cloth dressers who were
becoming nationally organised, was noted by Fitzwilliam in September 1802. Their grievances were concerned with new capitalistic
trends in the industry and the accompanying tendency by the masters
to defy the old Elizabethan statutes which protected the 'domestic
system' and the status of the craft worker.[14] Fitzwilliam's first
reaction was of disfavour towards a system of combination which
tended to limit the freedom of others to enter a trade, though he

remarked that he had reservations about the Combination Acts in principle.[15] In course of time, however, the industrial situation in the West Riding was to provide a basis for a new offensive by Fitzwilliam's supporters and for the recapture of one of the seats in 1806.

Elsewhere Fitzwilliam's seats gave little trouble. Furthermore, all Fitzwilliam's members were now more fully in accord with his political attitude. Of the men who had veered towards Portland after 1795, Adair was dead, and Baldwin no longer occupied one of Fitzwilliam's seats. Francis Foljambe, Fitzwilliam's friend and candidate for Yorkshire in 1784, had taken over Higham Ferrers. Laurence and Elliot, staunch collaborators in their patron's political activities, shared Peterborough. At Malton Charles Lawrence Dundas, Fitzwilliam's nephew, and a local gentleman, Bryan Cooke, were also devoted followers, while another Dundas—Laurence—was safely seated with Sir William Milner, a devoted Foxite, at York. From Ireland two supporters, George Ponsonby and William Hoare Hume, represented County Wicklow. Fitzwilliam commanded a more substantial, united and influential squadron in the Commons than for many years past.

The approach of the new parliamentary session saw renewed negotiations amongst the parties, as the events of the summer and autumn seemed to disclose the ambitious designs of Bonaparte. In August he had annexed Elba, in September Piedmont was incorporated into France, and in October Switzerland was invaded and forced to accept a French constitution. The last stroke was too much even for Fox's admiration of Bonaparte, while to Grenville and Fitzwilliam it seemed a vindication of their criticisms of the peace. 'It is our fixed policy', Laurence declared, 'to submit to humiliation rather than contend with difficulties . . . There can be no confederacy on the continent which can have the most remote chance of shaking the enormous power of the French Republic.'[16] The news of continued French aggrandisement since February 1802, when the Italian Republic had been constituted with Bonaparte at its head, had energised the Grenvilles and Fitzwilliam's section of the Whigs to co-operate more closely in and out of Parliament. Fitzwilliam, Carlisle, Windham and Elliot were foremost in urging action on the Grenvilles, but, though Tom Grenville was eager enough, his brothers were more cautious. Lord Grenville still hoped that, by cautious moderation, they might persuade Pitt to change his attitude and come out against the new Ministry, despite his pledge to the king

not to oppose it. He was also aware of the dangers in making the
'new opposition' appear to the public as alarmists and war-mongers.
When Carlisle wrote to Tom Grenville in late August to urge discussions about tactics in Parliament, he met with little encouragement. Tom thought the public indisposed towards any active opposition and towards any renewal of war, and feared that most of their
friends would prefer not to attend Parliament in the present state of
public opinion. Even the prospect of renewed war in the autumn
failed to unite the new opposition. There were personal difficulties
too. Grenville insisted that if war did come only Pitt could be Prime
Minister. Buckingham in his turn pointed out the difficulties in face
of any coalition which included members of the present Cabinet,
who were pledged against the Catholic claims and for peace. The
'Stowe congress' of November 1802, attended by the leading members of the Grenville party and Spencer, was therefore indecisive.
The new opposition proposed no amendment to the address at the
end of November, and for the time being Fox and the old opposition
were left in possession of the field.

Fitzwilliam deplored the Grenvilles' timidity, especially since it
appeared to stem from their attachment to Pitt, for whom Fitzwilliam always continued to feel a deep mistrust and dislike. He
wrote to Laurence on 10 November to urge that greater efforts should
be made to rouse the public and Laurence replied with an assurance
that he, Windham and Elliot were in full agreement, though perhaps
less disposed to hang back from a possible coalition with Pitt.

It is most essential [he wrote] . . . to recall men if possible from parties
of persons, to parties of principles, and . . . to make the greatest men of
publick talents feel their interest as well as their duty impel them to
commit everything in this cause [of resistance to French ambition]. . . .
Our future conduct towards parties and individuals must be guided by
their conduct towards their country, with little or no retrospect beyond
that which they may render inevitable.

He thought the Grenvilles seemed inclined to draw towards Pitt but
not necessarily 'more unwilling than ourselves to connect themselves
with Mr Fox if he would take the part which is yet open to him. . . .
We are for keeping aloof from either till the sincerity of both is
sufficently tried'. Fox for his part, always 'a friend to coalitions',
expressed no malice towards Pitt, and wrote to his friend Denis
O'Bryen that 'neither he [Pitt] nor anybody else can do *much* in the

House of Commons, unless there is a hope of his returning to power'. As to the foreign situation, although he believed that 'peace . . . is the grand object', he declared that it was a question how long the French would leave Britain a choice of peace or war. For the time being the Foxites supported the Ministry on the address, and, like the new opposition, decided to wait upon events abroad. Not until the spring of 1803 did the political situation begin to resolve itself.[17]

By April 1803 affairs at home and in Europe were coming to a crisis. Pitt, a semi-recluse at Walmer, nursing his gout and his grudges against Addington's budgets, was becoming increasingly frustrated by the Minister's failure to consult him and by the political restraint which his pledges to Addington and the king imposed upon him. Canning worked on his resentments, while Grenville urged the claims of his country in face of the Cabinet's supineness. At the end of March, Grenville went to Walmer to urge the formation of a broad based administration, to be led by Pitt and including the new opposition and selected members of the old—Moira and Grey in particular, Fox, he believed, being disinclined to office. Fox, using the Whig Club and other convivial gatherings rather than the House of Commons as his platform, was being studiously moderate on the foreign issue, and at one of a series of dinners given by the Prince of Wales for the old opposition in March 'pronounced the highest eulogium' on Pitt. This moderation pleased Fitzwilliam who, Grey reported to Fox in March 1803, was

full of indignation against Bonaparte, and of fears for the situation of the country; but consoled by thinking that he may now agree with both you and me. . . . He spoke of you particularly with the warmest affection. I fully participate in all your feelings about him, and nothing would make me so happy as any event . . . that could bring us to act cordially together.[18]

Rumours buzzed through the town of ministerial and opposition negotiations. Those of Pitt's friends who, as Laurence put it, 'think with us as far as sometimes to talk a little more confidentially with us', wished for 'something like a public call upon him to return to Parliament and to office'; Addington, wishing to forestall the apparently approaching coalition of Pitt with his opponents, sent Melville to Walmer to offer a reconstruction of the Cabinet with Pitt and Addington serving under the nominal premiership of Chatham. Pitt's immediate and contemptuous rebuff left Addington no other resource

but a coalition with Grey and the old opposition, but Grey, Laurence
reported, would not treat except upon 'some plan of comprehensive
arrangement'. Grenville and Spencer too might insist upon a complete dissolution of the present administration and 'specific assurances relative to the principles of the new government in foreign
and domestic policy'. Windham, Laurence reported, would support
such an arrangement only if Fitzwilliam was included in it. The
other members of a new Cabinet under Pitt might be Spencer, Windham, Chatham, Camden, Melville, Moira and Grey. The last, Laurence
remarked, 'would be likely to connect himself personally with your
Lordship rather than with any of the others'. At Windham's request,
he put the scheme before Fitzwilliam for consideration, declaring
that he had told Windham that 'considering your present retired
and insulated situation, I was convinced that no motive whatever
but a sense of public duty . . . could induce you to engage in any
arrangement of such a kind', and suggesting that 'the humiliation
and peril, into which we are now plunged' might operate 'against
your remonstrances, as a call too imperious to be disobeyed'.[19]

Fitzwilliam's reply has not survived. Its terms, however, may be
guessed at. Laurence afterwards referred to 'the principle, which you
have so clearly and forcibly stated, and which alone I should think
admissible for any public man whom I love and esteem', as being
too strong for some of the parties to the proposal. They, he thought,
would have accepted a compromise which placed some of the
present Ministers in office again in 'inefficient' Cabinet situations.[20]
No doubt Fitzwilliam had insisted, not only upon a clear declaration
of British intentions in Europe, but upon the exclusion from the
Cabinet of any minister responsible for the humiliating peace and
foreign policy of the past two years. Discussions came to nothing at
an early stage, but Fitzwilliam's position was clearly assuming a
central importance. Windham was looking to him for support and
even leadership, while Grey's attachment seemed to open up the
possibility that Fitzwilliam might become the centre of a reunion
of old Whig connexions. Fox too wrote towards the end of April
to remark that although 'I must always . . . keep one point in view,
upon which I fear we much differ, I mean peace . . . whether we
agree or not, I should like you to know all my thoughts upon
political matters'. Fitzwilliam was also in communication with the
Grenvilles through Tom Grenville, with the Prince of Wales, whose
strength in the Commons, Fox wrote, was 'greater . . . than I had

supposed' and who was working for a union of opposition groups, and also with the activists led by Canning who were urging measures in Parliament to force a confrontation between Pitt and Addington. The outbreak of hostilities on 18 May, however, saved Addington for the time being. Pitt refused to undertake the outright opposition which Grenville and Canning urged upon him now that the country was at war, and the 'union of talents' which the new opposition had been working for was indefinitely postponed—to be only partially obtained and then after Pitt's death. On 23 May, the failure of the opposition's plan of unity became manifest in the Commons as Pitt, in one of his finest speeches, defended the government and supported the war. Fox's equally brilliant attack on Addington on the 24th resulted in a minority division of only 67, and Pitt retired to Walmer to organise the local volunteers against the French invasion.[21]

The outbreak of war once again energised Fitzwilliam's efforts to infuse determination and purpose into British policy. He threw himself into a joint scheme with Canning and the Grenvilles for a vote of censure on the government's handling of the negotiations with France by a series of resolutions to be moved by himself in the Lords and by Colonel Patten in the Commons. The resolutions were agreed in a series of meetings between Fitzwilliam, Tom and Lord Grenville, and Canning, and were moved by Fitzwilliam on 2 June and by Patten on the 3rd. The Lords' debate went on until 4.30 a.m. when the resolutions were rejected by ninety-six to fourteen; despite this large majority, the division, declared Grenville, was 'much the greatest blow the Doctor and his gallipots have yet received'. In the Commons, Tom Grenville made an effective two-hour speech, but Pitt, playing his own hand, moved the order of the day against the motion and found himself supported by only fifty-eight votes. The government won the final division by 277 to 36, Fox and his friends abstaining because, speaker Abbot noted, 'he thought the Ministers blameable in their conduct, but would not give a vote that should tend to remove them, because he thought them more pacific than any other Ministers who would succeed them'. He and his friends left the House before the division, in which the minority consisted substantially of the Grenville–Fitzwilliam alliance.[22]

The divisions of 3–4 June ended all realistic hopes of an early resolution of the political crisis. Pitt, chagrined by the ignominious division on his motion, retreated into neutrality again. His conduct, wrote Tom Grenville, had hurt his public reputation, antagonised the

king, and strengthened Addington by showing the extent of the
Crown's influence in the Ministry's favour. His speech in the debate
had also confirmed the breach between himself and Addington, who
noted that his motion was 'an act of direct hostility . . . and from
that time his opposition was never relaxed when it could be shown'.
The king, Abbot noted on the next day—the royal birthday—was 'in
high spirits'. The natural alliance, however, was one which would
unite Pitt, Grenville, Spencer, Windham and Fitzwilliam. All were
committed to Catholic emancipation and the vigorous prosecution
of the war, and Fitzwilliam's contacts with Fox and Grey held out
the hope of their co-operation, or at any rate support, so long at
least as the possibility of peace negotiations with France remained
remote. Fox himself wrote in June to O'Bryen to deprecate any attack
on the Grenvilles:

When the court is in direct and bitter hostility to them, and when more-
over Pitt and they seem to be every day getting further distant from each
other, is *this* the moment for us to attack them? . . . I can not help
thinking that among the different corps of the enemy, these G's are
those who have preserved most of something like a title to reputation.

Fox's conclusion was that his political friends 'ought to contend that
there is not the smallest reason for distinguishing any one of these
gangs as at all more set upon even than another [and that] you are
quite right in your system of doing *nothing*. It is as wise as it is
agreeable'. He nevertheless concluded that, though he was far from
wishing for a coalition at present, 'neither would I throw unnecessary impediments in the way of any future one with any persons
who are capable of acting in *real* oppositions'.[23]

Before the first session of the new Parliament ended, Addington
presented his various opponents with another issue on which they
could co-operate. This was Yorke's scheme to recruit an army of
reserve of 50,000 men by ballot of all males between 18 and 45,
serving for four years for home defence. The Bill met with Pitt's
approval but incurred the instant opposition of Windham, Yorke's
predecessor as Secretary-at-War and a Colonel of Volunteers. Windham argued that the new force would not only be insufficient, but
would be liable to all the defects of the existing militia system, and
in particular that by allowing paid substitutes it would attract
recruits away from the regular army, which was available for
offensive as well as defensive operations. Elliot, too, opposed the

Bill. A month later, the government introduced a further measure, the Military Service Bill, to provide machinery for the compulsory enrolment by Lords Lieutenant of all able-bodied males between the ages of 17 and 55, to be called out in case of need. On this occasion, Windham objected to the tardiness of the government's measures and censured the feebleness of their entire defence strategy. Pitt, however, again supported the Bill, while Fox, making his first appearance in the House for several weeks, also declared his approval of it. Though he disliked the war, he said, he did not wish to oppose the necessary measures for carrying it on effectively and for defending Britain against invasion. Both Fox and Windham called on the government to invite the voluntary service of all loyal subjects; but when they did, the resulting deluge of enthusiastic offers considerably embarrassed them. Stocks of arms were inadequate, it was impossible to train the volunteers effectively, and the only impressive thing about the new forces was their numbers. Fox described the volunteer system as 'theatrical, ostentatious foppery'. In August recruitment had to be stopped. Public confidence in the Ministry's competence was severely shaken, while its opponents in Parliament were able to push home further accusations of incapacity for the task of running the war. Laurence thought that the consequence was a closer accord between Pitt, Fox, and Windham, representing the three main political groups outside the ministry. 'Some of the friends of the Minister', he informed Fitzwilliam, 'privately told me that such another day [as 18 July] would crush them.'

Laurence was now trying to bring Fox, Windham and Carlton House into accord.

In the course of these transactions [he wrote], I have received some intimations from Carlton House . . . There are in that quarter many flattering complaints of your Lordship, as not affording His Royal Highness sufficient opportunities of showing how highly he values your Lordship's advice. . . . It is requested, that you will consider what opinion you would give, should any occasion arise to demand it under the present circumstances of the country.[24]

Fitzwilliam had been out of touch with political events for six weeks owing to the claims of Lieutenancy business in the West Riding. Laurence's letter, he wrote, 'gives me the first insight into subjects that before involved me in much perplexity'. He did not share the views of Addington's opponents on the question of defence policy.

K

He thought the enrolment of large numbers of untrained men, without adequate provision for officering the corps, would be hazardous. 'All the higher orders,' he wrote, 'particularly when you get into the manufacturing district, tremble at the thought of arms being put into the hands of the people indiscriminately . . . having none in authority over them, at least, not such as ought to be.' *His* policy was to encourage recruitment into the existing volunteer regiments where 'we are sure at least of having proper commanders'. Nevertheless, he rejoiced at the signs Laurence reported of closer co-operation between Windham, Fox and Pitt: 'It is that sort of junction', he wrote, 'which I feel to be necessary for the security of the country in these times, and in all for the maintenance of the Constitution in its true spirit'. As regards Laurence's hints about Carlton House, his lack of assiduity in paying court there was not from any intention to avoid it, but solely because of his urgent preoccupations in Yorkshire. 'I know my duty whenever the occasion arises,' he assured Laurence.[25]

Once again Fitzwilliam's position in politics assumed great importance. His friendship for Fox and his political agreement with the Grenvilles and Windham marked him out as the possible keystone of a new political grouping which would be sufficiently powerful and widely-based to provide a viable alternative to Addington. The raising of the Irish question in the summer of 1803 increased his significance. Robert Emmet's rebellion and the murder of Lord Chief Justice Kilwarden in Dublin had again focused English eyes in that quarter, and when the new session opened in November Fitzwilliam tried to have the Catholic question brought up again in Parliament. Fox was cautious, wishing to consult Grattan and George Ponsonby before taking any step, and he feared a lack of support at Carlton House because of Sheridan's influence. He thought the Prince's attitude crucial. 'My opinion is as strong as yours,' he told Fitzwilliam, 'and if I thought I had Carlton House as much with me on this point as I once thought I had, I would not wait for other opinions. . . . His name would smooth all. It would not only be the additional force he would bring, but the effect his name would have in promoting zeal and unanimity among us.' The Irish Whigs, however, advised against bringing up the Catholic question again at present. The Grenvilles were also against trying the question, fearing that it might strengthen the government, and Grey argued that weak support in Parliament would do more harm than good to the Catholic cause.

The issue again failed to consolidate old and new oppositions, while the French question still held them apart. Tom Grenville even thought for a time that Addington would win Fox over by trying to negotiate a peace at any price. Fitzwilliam confessed his feeling to Lady Rockingham on 6 December:[26]

My heart goes completely with your wishes; its bent is to agree on all subjects with Charles Fox: but our opinions have been terribly at variance. New occurrences and change of circumstances will, I hope, bring us together again—but still I am anti-Gallican: I ask not, what sort of Government prevail, but under none, can I submit patiently to the strange assumption of power over independent nations, daily making by France. Here is the root of my present opinions: I am sure, it is the growth of good Whig soil.

In January 1804, while Parliament was in recess, discussion among the opposition groups reached a climax. Grenville urged Pitt to make up his mind formally to oppose the government, and at a meeting at Stowe in mid-January the Grenvilles and Spencer conferred on the possible means of making him do so. Buckingham suspected that Pitt intended merely to use the Grenvilles to make the running against Addington and then to step in at the critical moment, posing as the king's protector from opposition. Tom Grenville however assured Fitzwilliam that there was now better hope of a united opposition, followed by a new and comprehensive administration, than since the formation of the current government. Grenville's letter, Fitzwilliam told Laurence,

gives me spirits, it gives me hopes, that there exists the possibility of a comprehensive system of opposition, on general grounds . . . I feel the importance of such an occurrence, as the only means of rescuing the constitution from its present degraded state.

When, however, Grenville wrote to Pitt to urge a 'declared and regular opposition', and said that he had given Fox the assurance that the Grenvilles were ready to co-operate in the formation of a ministry of *all* talents, Pitt rejected the plan, as Fox had foretold. The Grenvilles thereupon made approaches to the Foxite opposition for a junction. Fitzwilliam eagerly welcomed the plan. Windham, renewing contact with Fox for the first time in twelve years, had a conversation with him on 3 February, and a month later drew up a paragraph for a newspaper announcing an agreement for co-operation between Grenville, Windham and Fox. Grey, however, though considering an alliance with the Grenvilles the most natural one in the present circumstances, feared that they were too unpopular in the country and too small a group in Parliament to be a sufficient basis for overthrowing the Ministry against the wishes of the Court. He would agree to a junction only if there were some assurances that the Grenvilles would consider a peace 'on reasonable terms' and that 'the strength of the Union . . . would be such as to afford a reasonable hope of rescuing the country from the hands of an administration by which it has been disgraced and must be ruined'. He feared that a junction with them would 'make only what at best would be called a strong opposition', which it would need 'great activity and unremitting perseverance' to convert into a new administration. Fox and Fitzwilliam alike believed, for their different reasons, that a junction with the Grenvilles now offered the only realistic prospect of a satisfactory alternative to Addington's weakness or Pitt's ambition.[27]

Pitt's adherence to a coalition of 'all the talents' was now doubted by most of the Whigs. Grey thought that 'he cannot make up his mind to an open war with the Court, and still cherishes a secret hope of being applied to in their distress'. In the circumstances Grey felt it impossible to expect Fox to serve *under* Pitt, and proposed to Whitbread that Fitzwilliam might take the Treasury and nominal premiership, with Pitt and Fox serving under him as their fathers had served under Devonshire in 1757.[28] Meanwhile, rumours of a recurrence of the king's illness complicated the situation, and made it more necessary than ever to cultivate the support of Carlton House. On 9 March, Fitzwilliam raised in the Lords the question of the king's capacity to carry out his royal functions, declaring 'from an authority on which he thought he could rely' that there was substantial doubt about it. Though the Lord Chancellor, Eldon, declared that the king was fully competent to transact his normal business, the affair helped to draw the opposition groups together, and they resumed their attacks, opposing the Bill to allow 10,000 Irish militiamen to serve in England and on 23 April mustering in strength on Fox's proposal for an enquiry into the state of the country's defences. Their division of 204 against the government's 256 included all the prince's friends as well as the main body of Pitt's, Fox's and the Grenville followings. The prince now declared outright for opposition. It was the decisive blow to Addington. The Cabinet decided to resign and Addington opened negotiations with Pitt, who saw the king on 7 May. Pitt was not disposed to press the king, still visibly weakened by the effects of his illness, to allow him to form the comprehensive administration insisted on by his allies. At a meeting of Fox's friends at Carlton House on 7 May, however, it was agreed, despite Fox's offer to retire, that no one would accept office if he were excluded. On the following day Fitzwilliam, Spencer, Windham and the Grenvilles took a similar resolution. Pitt was therefore compelled, as Fitzwilliam forecast, to 'patch up his administration by the first threads and tatters he lays his fingers on'.[29] Once again Fitzwilliam's prospects of Cabinet office were dashed. He had been nominated by Pitt as Foreign Secretary of State in the proposed 'broad bottomed' Ministry, as an earnest of his agreement to the 'hard line' policy towards France. Fitzwilliam regretted the failure of the scheme only on public grounds. He was never to overcome his distaste for high office.

Towards the end of May, as Pitt was 'eking out his government with Roses and Dundases', the King's health again gave rise to alarm.[30] The prince invited Fitzwilliam, Carlisle and Buckingham to dinner at Carlton House on 29 May. Afterwards he took each one aside, starting with Fitzwilliam. He disclosed his fears for his father's health, declared his conviction that a regency would have to be created, and said that he wished to have them, with Fox, Grey, Windham and the two other Grenville brothers, as his advisers. After their interviews with the prince, Fitzwilliam and Buckingham conferred until 1.30 in the morning. Fitzwilliam urged Buckingham to press Lord Grenville to come up so that they could take the prince under their direction and prevent his falling into other hands. Fitzwilliam also said that he was prepared to agree to a regency under the plan of 1788, at any rate as a temporary measure, to allay any scruples Grenville might have. The conference, Buckingham wrote, was 'very satisfactory'.[31] The prince's attempts to obtain fuller information about his father's condition were rebuffed, however, and the new Ministers again stoutly declared that the king was fully competent to transact state affairs. The prince's annoyance was increased when the king refused his application for a military command, and by the king's making new arrangement for Princess Charlotte's upbringing at Windsor without her father's knowledge. The prince now resumed his old political connexions. Despite approaches by Pitt to Moira, the chief of the prince's friends, in the

autumn of 1804, the prince and his group now supported the
opposition.

The events of the winter and spring of 1803–4 thus created a new
political alliance between the groups previously identified with Fox
and with Grenville, while the Prince of Wales and his friends hovered
rather uncertainly at their head. Fitzwilliam had played a leading
part in bringing this junction about, and he remained an important
member of the new grouping. Grenville's greater administrative
experience made him their natural political leader in the Lords, while
in the Commons Fox, Grey and Windham took the leading parts.
The alliance was not yet, however, a cordial union, and Fitzwilliam's
role once against was that of a supporter in the country and a conciliator and mediator, helping to keep personal relationships among
the various groups smooth and harmonious. He retained his dislike
of high departmental responsibilities and he did not thrust himself
forward into the party's central councils, but his influence was felt
at Carlton House and among the political leaders, and his views were
important in formulating opposition policy. The continuing preoccupation of the leading Whigs with Ireland and the Catholic
question was particularly significant and helped to keep Fitzwilliam
in the forefront.

As the session of 1804–5 approached, the Catholic Committee in
Dublin began to agitate the question of emancipation and Grenville
wrote to inform Fitzwilliam in November that he intended to raise
it early in the session. 'You have long known my opinion on the
subject,' Grenville wrote, 'and certainly it will be a matter of some
personal satisfaction to me to have an opportunity of delivering it
in public.'[32] In the event, it was 10 May 1805 before the Catholic
petition was presented in both Houses. In the meantime Fitzwilliam
set about providing a seat at Westminster for Grattan, so that the
most distinguished of the Irish Whig parliamentarians could add his
weight to the discussion. After an unsuccessful application to Lord
Dundas, his brother-in-law, for one of the seats at Richmond, where
a recent enclosure had antagonised several electors and Dundas's
legal arrangements were incomplete, Fitzwilliam accepted Charles
Lawrence Dundas's offer to resign one of the seats at Malton. Grattan's début at Westminster was a triumphant one, and, Holland
recorded, 'From this period he became a favourite of the House:
they not only admired his orations, but revered the man'.[33] The
opposition's motion was lost, however, the Prince's members voting

with the majority. The lukewarmness of several of the party and the prince's growing hostility towards the question made it a dangerous one for them to press, and it was dropped with some thankfulness. Grenville declared on 27 May that the opposition was still disunited, and that he found only Spencer in general agreement with him. Nor would he co-operate in any measure which implied a censure on Pitt's first administration. He deplored his inability to influence the party in any degree, and declined to see himself as its leader.[34]

Pitt's second administration was nevertheless unsuccessful. Lacking the strength of talent of his first Ministry, harrassed by a strong if still incompletely united opposition and wracked by ill health, Pitt was forced into further dependence on Addington's support. In January 1805 'the Doctor' and his friends re-entered office, Addington going to the Lords as Viscount Sidmouth and replacing Portland, who was now seriously ill, as Lord President of the Council. The union was short-lived and unhappy. In February the publication of the Tenth Report of the Commissioners of Naval Enquiry incriminated Dundas (now Viscount Melville) in financial irregularities committed during Pitt's first administration, and the Sidmouth group deserted the Minister in his attempt to protect his old friend. In early July they resigned. Pitt's administration was now the feeblest shadow of the firm government that had been hoped for in 1804. Fox thought that Pitt would try to carry on alone, relying on the king's and the public's distaste for 'storming the Cabinet . . . aristocratical faction, interested coalitions, etc. etc.' to rally support amongst the independents. The public, however, Fox believed, wished for a comprehensive administration and would blame Pitt for the lack of one. The possibility of an alliance with Sidmouth was in Fox's mind, as tending to suggest that Pitt was contending against 'all the men of influence in the country'. He urged his friends to be studiously moderate in their speeches, and to avoid the mistakes of 1784 when Whig overconfidence and intransigence had raised the public clamour against them. Tom Grenville, however, considered that Pitt had no serious intention of broadening his administration, and since the opposition parties all stuck to their demand for 'no exclusions' he had little real alternative. In June, Pitt did send Lord Camden to Grenville to propose a government 'on the most extended plan', but when Grenville repeated his determination not to desert Fox the negotiation languished. During the summer further rumours of approaches from Pitt continued to circulate, and in August Fox urged Fitzwilliam to come to Stowe, where a meeting of opposition leaders was planned to coincide with a visit from the Prince of Wales. It was important, Fox suggested, that if Pitt did make any approaches the opposition should have agreed on a suitable answer, since Pitt's motive would be not to create a new Ministry but to throw the onus for a failure to do so on to them. When Pitt visited Weymouth in September, however, the king refused to consider any changes.[35]

Foreign affairs still plagued the opposition. The Grenvilles were as uncompromising as ever on the question of peace with France, while Fox remained a reluctant supporter of the war and hoped for a negotiation with Napoleon. The new and old oppositions similarly differed on their attitudes towards Pitt, the Grenvilles hankering for a reunion with him while many of Fox's friends regarded such a possibility with extreme distaste. Fox, whose lifelong creed was that 'Without coalitions *nothing* can be done against the Crown, with them God knows how little!' was determinedly civil towards both Pitt and Sidmouth, and tried to restrain his friends from taking any line with regard to the war that might offend Grenville. The latter, however, remained suspicious that he and Fox differed too much over the war for fruitful co-operation to be possible for long.[36] In this mood of uncertainty the politics of 1805 moved haltingly into the last weeks of Pitt's life.

Fitzwilliam's political activity was interrupted in the summer of 1805 by a serious illness. For several weeks through August and September he was confined to Milton House, where, his son told Laurence, he was 'extremely nervous and weak'. Fox became anxious about his friend's health. 'What you say of the value of his life,' he wrote to Windham, 'is true in every respect, but I feel in this case so much on the account of private friendship and affection that all other considerations are absorbed in this. Our acquaintance is now of forty-nine years' standing and our friendship uninterrupted, cultivated constantly on his side by kindnesses and obligations of the most essential nature.' Portland too was seriously ill at this time and, Laurence wrote, he seemed 'during the remainder of his life . . . doomed to linger under a painful disease, which admits of no cure, and now very little palliative . . . but from opiates'. Laurence suggested that a private reconciliation with Fitzwilliam might afford the duke 'the most sincere delight,' and despite his own weakness Fitzwilliam managed to write a few lines 'with his own hand', Milton reported, 'a thing he has not done for some weeks'.[37] The personal hostility which the Lord Lieutenancy had aroused in Fitzwilliam was now buried. Portland in fact recovered from this phase of his illness, and after enduring with great courage the dreaded surgery of 'cutting for the stone' in the days before anaesthetics, returned to political life to help engineer the downfall of Fitzwilliam and his colleagues in the Ministry of 1806–7 and to become nominal Prime Minister once more in the reconstituted Pittite Cabinet of 1807–9.

Fitzwilliam made a gradual recovery, and by early November was fit enough to return to some degree of political activity. His spirits were revived also by Milton's engagement early in December to his cousin Mary Dundas. The young heir was not yet twenty, a rather awkward, ungainly young man, and as Georgiana unkindly wrote to her mother 'both clever and amiable but so odd in person, and so unlike other people it was a great chance against him ever finding any woman who liked him for himself'. Milton's serious and earnest nature would hardly appeal to Georgiana's taste; his cousin Mary, however, was a childhood friend, and, Georgiana continued, 'he is so steady there is no fear of his finding out in a few years that he likes many better than her'.[38] Milton's parents were overjoyed at the engagement, which cemented still further the bond with the relatives of Fitzwilliam's favourite sister, while they would hardly have shared Georgiana's reservations about Milton's future. Fitzwilliam's relationship with his son was always close, affectionate and trusting on both sides, and for the rest of his life the two worked closely together in political, family and estate matters. If Milton, like his father, never quite attained the political distinction which his family and friends hoped for him, he too became a conscientious, influential and respected figure in Whig politics, and filled with some credit the responsibilities to his country and his order handed on to him by his father's example.

Milton's engagement was swiftly followed by less welcome news. Milton himself became seriously ill of a fever, and there was anxiety about his recovery for some weeks. As the political crisis following Pitt's illness and death developed in January 1806 Fitzwilliam was prevented from playing any part in it by his refusal to leave his wife and son in order to travel to London. 'My own crazy frame,' he wrote to Grenville, in any case was 'not quite . . . equal to a long sitting in the House.' Despite rumours that Fitzwilliam was to become First Lord of the Treasury in the new Cabinet and that the

K*

king had spoken of him 'with great warmth and esteem', Fitz-william's role had to be a more unobtrusive one. Writing however to Grenville on 27 January, he expressed his 'heartfelt satisfaction' at the news that Grenville and Fox had agreed to form a full union and to co-operate wholly in a new administration. 'I assure you,' he wrote, 'it has been the anxious object of my wishes very, very long.' The coming to power at last of a truly broad based administration in January 1806 was to Fitzwilliam the crowning moment of his political life. Fully united again with Fox, yet assured by the presence of the Grenville group that the new government's domestic and foreign policies would be those he could approve of, Fitzwilliam felt that the political prospect was brighter than for twelve years back. Fox had assured Tom Grenville that though he wished for peace in principle, he was satisfied that it was unattainable on any satisfactory terms for the present. As to the question of continental alliances, it was to be regarded as speculative in present circum-stances.[39]

Pitt died in the early hours of 23 January. The news shocked the nation, and not least Lord Grenville, who retired, overcome with grief, to Dropmore. Even Fox and Grey were obviously affected: they 'have shown more feeling than any of his [Pitt's] quondam friends', Georgiana wrote, and Fox said that 'it appeared as if there was something missing in the world'. Grenville was anxious lest the old Foxite rancour against Pitt should break out in Parliament and prevent the cordial union of talents that had now been agreed upon. He begged his brother to ask Fox to agree to the proposed motion for a public funeral to honour the dead statesman, saying that no one could confer on him so great an obligation as to support it. Fox felt it impossible to contradict a lifetime's political hostility by sup-porting the motion, and Grey and Windham also opposed it. Gren-ville nevertheless assured Fitzwilliam on the 26th that when he saw the king on the following day he would insist on no exclusions. The king asked only for a day or two to consider Grenville's proposed Cabinet list, and on 3 February, after some negotiation, he agreed to it.[40] Fitzwilliam, who had been proposed for the Irish viceroyalty in the first plans of the new administration, now resumed his former office of Lord President of the Council on Fox's entreaty. 'It is really of more importance than I can explain without a very long letter that you should not object to this,' Fox wrote. 'It is of importance to the public cause, it is also of very great importance to me personally.' Fitzwilliam replied that he would have preferred the Privy Seal, 'as having least official duty and confinement, but if becoming a responsible party by being of the Cabinet without office would answer the purpose, I should prefer that very much indeed'. To Laurence, he confided his view that

with respect to office, it was the wish of my heart and my determination to have none, nor could I see any advantage to those I was attached to, that I should. Charles Fox however . . . desires me to accept as of *personal* importance to him—on this consideration I submitted.[41]

Fitzwilliam was not prepared to submit to *every* solicitation of Fox's however, nor was his wish not to hold office absolute. On 2 February, Fox wrote to ask whether he would be willing to give up the Lieutenancy of the West Riding so that it could be restored to the Duke of Norfolk.[42] Even Fox, for once, was rebuffed. The Lord Lieutenancy was now Fitzwilliam's main sphere of activity and his most valued office. Here he had found his natural and congenial role, and here his public activity was to remain concentrated for another thirteen years.

Fitzwilliam was something of a sleeping partner in the 'Talents' Ministry. Lacking enthusiasm for high office in itself, he was doubly glad to be able to leave the direction of policy in the hands of friends whom he knew he could trust and with whose views he was generally in agreement. Grenville, Fox, Windham and Grey all represented, in various ways, different aspects of his principles. Sidmouth, whose inclusion in the Cabinet had deprived Fitzwilliam of his wished-for office of Privy Seal, was a different matter, but his faction was relatively weakly represented. Fitzwilliam, with all his friends, disliked his presence but had to accept its necessity. Fox, however, welcomed Sidmouth's participation in the Ministry in order to prevent the strengthening of the opposition. 'It will stop up all the earths,' was his reported comment to Holland. He recognised, however, that Sidmouth's presence would prevent the Cabinet's bringing forward the Catholic question for the time being, and he urged his pro-Catholic supporters—Holland and Fitzwilliam in particular—to be patient on this score. He told Holland that his primary aims were to make peace and to abolish the slave trade: 'Two such glorious things', he told his nephew, 'I can't give them up, even to you'. Meanwhile, he urged the Catholic leaders to leave the religious question undisturbed until a new Parliament could be elected, under the auspices of a favourable administration.[43]

The abolition of the slave trade was the measure now closest to
Fox's heart. He had given his immediate support to Wilberforce's
campaign from its beginning in 1787, and in 1792 he had declared
that he would prefer abolition to any other political good that could
be achieved. Hitherto, despite Pitt's personal support, Wilberforce's
repeated motions had lacked the backing of government, and had
therefore been insufficiently supported to overcome the resistance of
West Indian interests and conservative gentlemen unwilling to risk
the possible economic consequences. Now both Grenville and Fox
insisted that the full weight of administration should be put behind
the measure. Fitzwilliam was one of those who had previously
opposed abolition, at first largely on commercial grounds, and since
the massacre in San Domingo in 1791 because of the fear that it
might lead to an uprising of freed slaves and the destruction of the
West Indian economy. In 1792 the slave trade question had been one
of the two major issues on which Fox had identified a difference
between himself and Fitzwilliam, and neither had changed his views.
Fitzwilliam, however, was disinclined to resist the determination of
his colleagues. When Grenville introduced a resolution on 24 June
that would commit Parliament to take measures for abolition early
in the next session, Fitzwilliam felt it necessary to define his attitude.
He confessed that he still 'felt rather alarmed at the consequences the
resolutions might produce' but he added that 'he could not help
feeling disposed to support them'.[44]

In the next session, as the abolition Bill moved towards its com-
pletion, Fitzwilliam took no part in the debates, while Grenville's
warning to the other anti-abolitionist peers that the government
would tolerate no obstruction on the measure had its effect. On 25
March 1807 the Slave Trade Abolition Bill passed its final stage in
Parliament, and the first part of Wilberforce's life's work was
achieved. The measure was significant for Fitzwilliam mainly in
regard to the electoral position in Yorkshire. In the 1807 election,
the slave trade was to be one of the major issues which placed Wilberforce beyond hope of successful attack by either of his rivals in
the county, and Milton, fighting on his father's interest, was able to
use his own support for abolition and the West Indian interests of
the third candidate, Henry Lascelles, to swing abolitionist and non-
conformist votes away from what would otherwise have been a
natural political coalition between his opponents.

Fox did not live to see the triumph of his last liberal cause. In

March 1806 symptoms of his fatal illness, attributed to dropsy, began to appear. His decline was rapid. A constitution never wholly robust and weakened by youthful dissipation and persistent neglect was ill-equipped to resist such a disabling and progressive disease. By the end of July he had to give up all business, and in August he was twice tapped and large quantities of fluid removed from his body. At the beginning of September he was taken to the Devonshires' elegant villa at Chiswick, where a cot was put up for him in one of the smaller of the rooms designed over eighty years before as a theatre for the display of the classical virtues and the imitation of Roman civilisation. It was a peculiarly appropriate place for the tragic scene now approaching. The association between Burlington's Palladian movement in architecture, and the classical revival of which it was a part, and Whig political thinking was clear and explicit. Both looked to the ancient Roman qualities of order, liberty and republican spirit. Both worshipped moderation, sense and style. Both were founded on the belief that a society based on and protected by a powerful but responsible aristocratic order offered the strongest guarantee of peace and harmony to all its members. As Fox spent his last days listening to readings from the eighth *Aeneid*, in which the blessings of a simple domestic peace are eulogised as the culmination of martial triumphs, Chiswick became the last resting place of eighteenth-century Whiggism. Fitzwilliam was irresistibly drawn to the scene. He hastened to be with the friend to whom he had given his deepest and longest affection for nearly fifty years.

Fox's death on 13 September, together with that of Pitt only a few months previously, ended a phase of eighteenth-century political life. It also closed an epoch for Fitzwilliam. Despite the separation of 1794–1801, Fox was always at the focus of Fitzwilliam's political career. Fitzwilliam himself, now 58 years old, had many years yet to live, but none of them surpassed the political enthusiasms of his youth, when he had taken over the leadership of Whig interests in the north, or sat with Fox at Brooks's Club planning the opposition political campaigns against Pitt in the 1780s. The death of Fox, followed in a few months by the coming of age of Lord Milton, symbolised the end of the old and the beginning of the new era. Fitz-william's political hopes were now centred in his son, and his own role became more than ever that of counsellor, conciliator and adviser to the younger, more vigorous men whose political enthusiasm was still fresh. In Fitzwilliam men like Grey, Althorp and,

later, Russell found a living reminder of historic Whiggism and the
survival of its ideals into the nineteenth century. This was not, however, to be an entirely passive influence, and on many occasions
during the next fifteen years Fitzwilliam's attitude was to be a significant element in moulding Whig political strategy.

Fox's death was followed by a reconstruction of the Cabinet.
Howick Grey [now Lord] was Fox's natural successor as Leader of
the Commons, and after a series of difficult negotiations he also
took the foreign secretaryship. Fitzwilliam offered to resign the Lord
Presidency of the Council to Sidmouth in order to bring Holland into
the Cabinet as Lord Privy Seal, assuring his colleagues that 'I look
upon it as a release' and that he derived 'the greatest satisfaction in
making room for Lord Holland'. He retained, however, his seat in
the Cabinet without office, Grenville declaring that this was 'a condition to which we all attach the highest importance'. Howick wrote
that nothing could have reconciled him to Fitzwilliam's resignation

but the knowledge that it was really more agreeable to yourself, and
that it seemed to afford the means of preventing the present administration from breaking up; and even that would not have done so, had it
not been settled that you are to retain a seat in the Cabinet.[45]

Fitzwilliam welcomed his release from official responsibility. To
mark his generosity, the Ministers agreed that he should be offered
the revived Marquessate of Rockingham. 'It is probably a point about
which he is not very solicitous,' Howick wrote to Grenville; 'but it
would be a peculiar gratification to me to have the title . . . offered
to him.' Howick valued and respected Fitzwilliam through family
connexion, shared affection for Fox's memory and common veneration for historic whiggism. Transmitting the offer of the marquessate
on 25 September, he wrote that it

would be particularly gratifying to myself as marking at this moment a
just respect for the principles and character of the party first united
under the Marquess of Rockingham, and so long supported by Fox, and
not as one upon which I suppose you to be personally solicitous.

Fitzwilliam's reply was characteristic. The question he wrote,
'requires, not the decision of a Cabinet, but of an individual . . . ;
for notwithstanding you may state the case as a matter of party
consideration, if it really is so, I must assume upon the party, and
take upon myself to decide for them . . . '. For himself, he felt that

Rockingham's memory might have been honoured by reviving his title in 1782 or 1783: then,

it would have been considered as honourable to his memory and would have been gratifying to the numerous body of persons who had long been attached to his person, and who continued to adhere to his principles: for myself I can speak, that to have succeeded him as his representative and heir in his rank in the peerage, would have been in my view of the thing a great distinction, and would have formed the pride of my life. But not only the lapse of time, twenty-four long years, take away from all its effect; it is no longer the anxious desire that the name of so much virtue should not be obliterated; that it should ever be present to the world: a variety of intervening circumstances have altered the very nature of the thing, and under existing ones I must become myself a bar to the revival of his title—would it be for his honour—can I by any stretch of the imagination, bring myself to conceive, that I am reviving his dignity in the peerage when I am placing it at the tail of a Marquess of Sligo etc. etc. . . . All my feelings forbid it.

The refusal marked not only Fitzwilliam's own indifference to personal distinctions, but the keen sense he always felt of the responsibilities which the Rockingham inheritance had placed on him. Though his refusal was framed as a personal one, it rather represented his feelings about the failure of Whiggism in the past quarter of a century to uphold and maintain the legacy of his uncle's political career.[46]

Nevertheless, 1806 was like 1782 in one respect—that after many years in the wilderness of fruitless opposition, it marked the return to power of a largely Whig administration. The parallel was to became even more direct in 1807 when for the second time this period of Whig dominance was to be ended by the personal activity of the sovereign. In the meantime, as before, the government pursued those liberal political objectives which were associated with the name of Whiggism and, also as in 1782–3, under the patronage of the heir to the throne. The prince was deeply distressed by Fox's death, which occurred while he was visiting Doncaster races, on another northern tour. 'He has lost all appetite and even taste for wine,' Fitzwilliam reported. '. . . He . . . has never recovered his spirits since.' The prince was, indeed, too unwell to attend Fox's funeral, at which Fitzwilliam was a pall-bearer. He returned to the north in the autumn, visiting Wentworth at the beginning of November and confiding in Fitzwilliam his anxieties about the state of Europe, the Westminster election and, above all, his matrimonial troubles.[47]

The prince's marriage in 1795 to Caroline Matilda of Brunswick
had been a disaster from the start. He had contracted the marriage
only in order to secure a final settlement from his father. His bride
offended all his fastidious feelings by her coarse manners and
unattractive appearance, and the royal couple soon separated, to go
their equally indecorous and profligate ways. Now, largely in order
to ensure the princess's exclusion from the upbringing of their
daughter Princess Charlotte, the prince urged the Ministers to undertake the ironically named 'delicate investigation' into allegations of
his wife's immoral conduct. The Cabinet appointed a committee of
four to look into the charges, and on 14 July their report was submitted to the king, exonerating the princess from the specific charges
of immorality, but censuring her indiscreet behaviour. At the same
time, the Pittite opposition naturally took up the princess's case, and
on 2 October Spencer Perceval drew up a long defence of her conduct which was clearly intended to be a public justification of her
and an attack upon her husband. The prince, as Fitzwilliam told
Howick, was in a state of great agitation about this document. 'We
all know,' Fitzwilliam wrote, 'that there is not a man more alive to
public opinion, of more sensitiveness on that score than he is.' The
Cabinet's delay in dealing with the question agitated the prince still
further, and Fitzwilliam wrote on his behalf to both Howick and
Grenville to urge that the matter should be dealt with before the
meeting of Parliament, so that opposition might not be able to make
capital out of it when the Houses met. 'The princess,' he pointed
out, 'appears a woman suffering under the effects of calumny,
debarred from exculpation, and virtually oppressed by power,' while
the prince was suspected of 'having brought against an innocent
woman the most base charges, founded upon fabricated perjuries
. . . from motives the most disgraceful, and with views the most
dangerous.' It was neither just to the prince nor judicious for the
government's own political interests to allow this opinion to continue. The withholding of the report from the public would tend to
confirm the view that it was discreditable to the prince. Whatever
its conclusions (Fitzwilliam had not read it), the prince's interests
could best be served by publicity, and he urged on grounds of 'bare
humanity' to the prince himself that immediate steps should be
taken. Grenville's reply was, however, cautious. It was important
both for the prince's sake and for the government's interests not to
take a false step, and Perceval's defence alone was so voluminous that

it would take some time for every Cabinet Minister to study it. On 25 November Howick wrote to tell Fitzwilliam that a Cabinet was shortly to be held to discuss the matter, 'and that it is much desired, and particularly by the prince, that you should be present'. After a series of meetings the Cabinet eventually determined, with Fitzwilliam present, that the government should endorse the report of the committee and that no further steps should be taken. The outcome of the affair was unsatisfactory from the prince's point of view, despite the committee's conclusion that he had behaved entirely properly in reporting to the king the allegations made against his wife. It was difficult, however, to see what else the Ministers could have done in the face of lack of clear evidence to support the charges.[48]

If the affair left the prince dissatisfied with the attitude of the Ministers, the events of the next three months did little to appease him. By early December 1806 disorder was again breaking out in Ireland. 'We are I fear,' Howick wrote on 8 December, 'upon the point of being reduced to the choice of urging the Catholic question, and the other measures connected with it, or resorting to the use of force, a system which we have so much condemned.' Fitzwilliam, drawing on his personal experiences, replied that 'one administration after another has lost the confidence of Ireland, and ours I fear will do so too; we shall do nothing till the hour of necessity is come, and then what we shall do will be done too late for any advantageous effect'.[49] The difficulty, however, was not so much a question of timing, or even of lack of goodwill on the part of the British and Irish administrations. With Bedford as Lord Lieutenant and Fitzwilliam's friend William Elliot as chief Secretary, the Castle was favourable to the Catholic claims, while Grenville and most of the British Ministers (except the Sidmouth group) were committed to the cause. Bedford, in fact, insisted as stoutly as Fitzwilliam had done in 1795 that his government was committed to conciliation. The difficulty lay, of course, with the king, who remained as inflexibly opposed to Catholic emancipation as in 1795 and 1801. The Cabinet's solution to the dilemma was bound to be an unsatisfactory one. They had to try to appease Catholic opinion in Ireland (and satisfy their own Lord Lieutenant) with the appearance of concessions, while avoiding the political crisis at home that would result from their advocating the substance. And the knowledge that English public opinion remained anti-Catholic placed the trump cards in the king's hands. It was a dilemma that inexorably destroyed the Ministry during the next three months.

Fitzwilliam was prevented by a recurrence of illness from regular attendance at Cabinet meetings, even during the political crisis between the Ministry and the king in March 1807. His attitude, however, was never in doubt. The Cabinet's scheme, incomplete though it was from the point of view of an ultimate solution of the Catholic question, had his unwavering support. The proposal put forward was not only less than a half-measure, but clouded in ambiguity from the start. In 1793 all military ranks in the Irish army below that of general on the staff had been opened to Catholics. The provision did not, however, hold good outside Ireland, so that a Catholic officer of an Irish regiment serving outside that kingdom would become liable to the penalties of the law. This was, of course, a mere technicality. The Cabinet however selected this supposed grievance of the Irish Catholics for remedy, and proposed that the provisions of the 1793 act should be extended to all Catholics in the united British and Irish army created by the Act of Union. One writer has remarked that it was a 'typically Whig idea of meeting the agrarian and economic grievances of the almost barbarous peasants of the west of Ireland with the boon of extending to Irish gentlemen the privilege of safely exercising military commissions in England'.[50] This misinterprets the Whig attitude as formulated by Fitzwilliam in 1795 and still at the root of the new proposal. As in 1795, the Whig policy was to harness the Catholic gentry in Ireland to the support of the anti-French cause, and so to reconcile the Irish propertied class to the British crown and constitution that it would exert over the mass of the Irish peasantry that strong social and political discipline that was maintained over their counterparts in Britain. The means, however, were pitifully inadequate to the end, and even as a counter to the threat of an Irish rebellion—the grounds on which the Cabinet principally urged it to the king—it was a meagre offering to Catholic ambitions. The king and the Sidmouth group reluctantly accepted the proposal on the grounds that it merely extended the concession of 1793 to the remainder of his Majesty's dominions. The Irish were unlikely to be satisfied with this, and the Catholic representatives in Dublin asked whether the intention was also to extend the act of 1793 to allow Catholics to become generals on the staff. Elliot gave what might be interpreted as an assurance that it was, which caused a rift in the Cabinet between the Whigs and Grenvilles on one hand, and Sidmouth and his friend Ellenborough on the other. Howick, in the meantime, seems to have failed to explain to the king the precise scope and intention of the Bill, and the king, whether through advancing years and weakening of the brain,[51] or, more likely, through a determination to play his Ministers at what seemed their own underhand game,[52] did not seek a full explanation until after it had been introduced into the Commons. Six days later George notified Grenville of his objection to the measure as it now stood and demanded its withdrawal. By a majority of four to three—Holland, Howick and Windham being in favour of resignation—the Cabinet, in Spencer's and Fitzwilliam's absence, agreed to withdraw the Bill, but declared that they reserved the right to declare in Parliament their support for the principles behind it. This, as Sheridan remarked, amounted not merely to the act of banging their heads against a brick wall, but to the building of a wall for the express purpose of banging their heads against it. The king demanded a pledge that the Ministers would never again propose any Catholic concessions to him, and their refusal inevitably implied their departure from office.

The Ministry's downfall was not, however, merely the result of George's intransigence. The demand for the pledge in fact was unnecessary if it were intended to force them to resign, for the Cabinet was already breaking up under the strain. Bedford had declared that he could not continue as Lord Lieutenant if the Bill was withdrawn, while Spencer, who as Home Secretary was responsible in the Cabinet for Irish affairs, declared the same purpose. In consequence, as Howick informed Fitzwilliam on 17 March, 'even if the King had not determined the matter for us, I think we should at all events have found ourselves compelled to come to that resolution [of resigning] at last'.[53] In any case Sidmouth and his friends had already left the Ministry, while Portland, emerging as the potential leader of the old Pittite group, had written to the king on 12 March virtually offering to form a new Ministry pledged to resist all Catholic claims.[54]

Fitzwilliam, receiving Howick's letter on the 18th, confessed himself taken by surprise at the outcome of events. He thought that the king's consent to the Bill had been distinctly given: but in the circumstances he expressed his satisfaction that the result was to be the resignation of the Ministers: 'Consistent with their characters and principles, it must be so, there can be no other honourable conclusion, if all that has been introduced, is not carried to the last letter.' If in fact Fitzwilliam and Spencer had been able to attend the Cabinet meeting on 15 March at which it was agreed by four votes to three to drop the Bill, it seems likely that the minority view that the government ought rather to resign would have prevailed—which might, in the long run, have been the more satisfactory course. Now, Fitzwilliam, though having no office to resign, asked Grenville to seek the king's permission 'no longer to attend the meetings of his confidential servants'. Grenville, obdurate to the last, insisted that the Ministry was not going to resign, but would force the king to turn them out. This, however, was a mere point of protocol. Grenville's observation that 'the current of public opinion is so strongly in our favour in consequence of the extreme moderation of our conduct, that I very much doubt whether they can form a government' was unrealistic to say the least, and on 25 March Portland took office as Prime Minister.[55]

Fitzwilliam was the last casualty of the Talents' suicide. On 31 December, Howick had proposed to Grenville that Fitzwilliam should be offered the Garter. On 1 January Grenville wrote to make the offer, which Fitzwilliam accepted. Now, before going to the levée to take leave of the king, Fitzwilliam asked whether the proposal had been agreed to. It was a point, he declared, 'I am far from considering as personal to myself, but as one that possibly may throw a considerable degree of light upon other more important matters'. Grenville in reply confessed : 'I must take shame to myself for my negligence about the Garters, which I had omitted to mention to the king till after he had determined on changing his government'. Not unexpectedly, the nomination was now 'received with only a silent bow'.[56] The refusal, like the offer itself, might be thought symbolic. In the era after Fox's death the Whig party again looked back to its Rockinghamite traditions. It was important to Howick, Fox's successor as the party's leading statesman, that he should receive the support of the old aristocratic Whiggery, now represented by Fitzwilliam as its senior surviving member and lifelong exponent. He had proposed Fitzwilliam for the Garter on the grounds of his public services to the party and his long association with Fox. Personally, as Howick recognised, 'there is no man who cares less about distinctions of this kind', but to honour Fitzwilliam in this way would be a symbolic gesture as well as a mark of the genuine personal esteem which he and all the leading Whigs felt for him. And as the offer marked

Fitzwilliam's status in the post-1806 era as the Whig elder statesman, the king's refusal—natural enough in the political circumstances of 1807—might be taken as equally a reminder that nothing had changed since 1783. As the last period of Fitzwilliam's political life was opening, the incident of the Garter, together with Fitzwilliam's refusal of the Marquessate, symbolised the position of the Whig party in the politics of the early nineteenth century.

Notes
1 Fox to Holland, 8 February 1801 (*Memorials and Corresp. of C. J. Fox*, III, p. 186); Duchess of Devonshire's diary, 7 February 1801 (Chatsworth MSS); Grenville to Buckingham, 2 February (*Court and Cabinets*, III, pp. 128–31).
2 Holland, *Memoirs*, I, p. 177: Colchester, *Diary and Correspondence of Charles Abbot, Lord Colchester* (1861), I, p. 250; Malmesbury, *Diaries*, IV, p. 53: Carlisle to the Prince of Wales, 26 February (*Carlisle MSS*, pp. 731–2; Fitzwilliam to Lady Fitzwilliam [23 March 1801] (N, x516/42). Lansdowne said that the Prince had considered Fitzwilliam for the Irish viceroyalty in a prospective regency administration (Aspinall, *Corresp. of George, Prince of Wales*, IV, p. 185).
3 Fitzwilliam to Lady Fitzwilliam [23 March 1801] (N, x516/42); Fox to Fitzwilliam, 1 February 1801 and 'Thursday' [1801] (N); to Grey, 'Friday' [1801], and to Holland, 19 April 1801 (*Memorials and Corresp. of C. J. Fox*, III, pp. 328–30, 189).
4 *Parl. Register*, LIX, pp. 559–659.
5 Grenville to Spencer, 6 October 1801 (*Fortescue MSS*, VII, p. 53); Laurence to Fitzwilliam, 11 October 1801; Fitzwilliam to Laurence [16 October 1801] (N); T. Grenville to Lord Grenville, 22 October (*Fortescue MSS*, VII, pp. 64–5); Fox to O'Bryen [4 October 1801] (B.M. Add. MS 47566, f. 96); Laurence to Fitzwilliam, 13 October (N).
6 Woodfall's *Parl. Register*, 1801–2, I, pp. 90–1, 176. The reformers who had been imprisoned without trial were released in March 1801. The definitive treaty was signed on 27 March 1802.
7 E. A. Reitan, 'The Civil List in eighteenth century British politics', *Hist. Journal*, IX (1966), pp. 318–37. The actual debt was £990,000.
8 *Parl. Register*, 1801–2, II, pp. 189–200 and 165–6, III, pp. 327–9.
9 Fox to Lauderdale, 26 March 1802 (*Memorials and Corresp. of C. J. Fox*, III, p. 366).
10 Elliot (died 1818) was MP for Portarlington 1801–2, and for Peterborough 1802–18. He set out his principles in a letter to Laurence, 8 December 1801 (N. 59/2). He declared his adherence to Burke's *Reflections*, advocated the repeal of the 'Two Acts' in peacetime and declared his support for Catholic emancipation in the right circumstances and his total hostility to parliamentary reform. He would give neither regular support nor regular opposition to Ministers but would judge according to

their measures. Fitzwilliam approved of this declaration, and Elliot soon became one of his close political confidants.

[11] Laurence to Fitzwilliam, 2 March and 17–20 March 1802; Grey to Fitzwilliam, 23 January 1802 (N).

[12] Laurence to Fitzwilliam [December 1801] (N. x516/33); T. Grenville to Spencer, 5 January [1802] (Althorp MSS, second earl, misc., 46); Fitzwilliam to Laurence [December 1801] (N). *The Porcupine*, previously 'the only paper . . . which took a manly part on the peace', as Laurence remarked, had been bought up by the government and was edited by the now Tory Redhead Yorke (*supra*, p. 244). The 'shareholders' in the new paper guaranteed only to support potential losses to the amount of their 'subscriptions'. For Cobbett's plan, see *Windham Papers*, II, pp. 173–5.

[13] *Cobbett's Annual Register*, II, (1802), pp. 25–6 (issue for 10 July), 279 (4 September), 338–46 (12 September); Fitzwilliam to Laurence, 25 September and Laurence to Fitzwilliam, 25 September (N). Cobbett was soon less dependent on the patronage of his first supporters. In January 1803 he claimed a circulation of 2,000 copies a week—'an instance of success uparalleled in the history of periodical publications' (III, *c*. 1).

[14] R. G. Wilson, *Gentlemen Merchants*: *The Merchant Community in Leeds, 1700–1830* (Manchester, 1971), pp. 90–109.

[15] Fitzwilliam to Laurence, 25 September [1802]: N, x515/6; and see *infra*, p. 348.

[16] Laurence to Fitzwilliam, 25 September 1802: N.

[17] Correspondence in *Fortescue MSS*, VII, pp. 82–131, *passim*, and *Court and Cabinets*, III, pp. 192–216, *passim*; Laurence to Fitzwilliam, 15 November 1802 (N); Fox to O'Bryen, [5] and [17 December 1802] (B.M. Add. MS 47566, ff. 128, 130).

[18] Grenville's narrative, March–April 1803 (*Court and Cabinets*, III, pp 282–90); Laurence to Fitzwilliam, 13 April 1803 (N); Grey to Fox, 19 March (Grey MSS).

[19] Laurence to Fitzwilliam, 26 March, 13 and 15 April 1803 (N); Grey to Fox, 3 August 1803 (Grey MSS).

[20] Laurence to Fitzwilliam, 23 April 1803 (N).

[21] Fox to Fitzwilliam, 22 April [1803] (*ibid.*); T. Grenville to Buckingham, March, and to Lord Grenville, 1 and 8 April (*Fortescue MSS*, VII, pp. 151–4); Marshall, *Rise of George Canning*, pp. 231–2; *Parl. Hist.*, XXXVI, 1387–1408, 1437–91.

[22] T. Grenville to Lord Grenville [28 May 1803] (*Fortescue MSS*, VII, pp. 169–70); *Parl. Hist.*, XXXVI, 1533–73; Colchester, *Diary*, I, pp. 425–6; Grenville to Buckingham, 14 June (*Court and Cabinets*, III, p. 303).

[23] T. Grenville to Buckingham, 7 June (*ibid.*, p. 304); G. Pellew, *Life of Sidmouth*, II, p. 140; Colchester, *Diary*, I, p. 427; Fox to O'Bryen [26 June 1803] (B.M. Add. MS 47566, f. 139).

[24] Colchester, *Diary*, I, p. 429; *Parl. Hist.*, XXXVI, 1606–46; *Parl. Debates*, I, 1738; P. Ziegler, *Addington* (1965), pp. 201–2; Laurence to Fitzwilliam, 11 August 1803 (N).

[25] Fitzwilliam to Laurence, 14 August [1803]: N, x515/45.

26 Fox to Fitzwilliam, [29 November 1803]; Fitzpatrick to Fitzwilliam, 23 December 1803 (N); T. Grenville to Buckingham, 25 November 1803 (*Court and Cabinets*, III, pp. 333–4); Fitzwilliam to Lady Rockingham, 6 December [1803] (R 164/33).

27 Buckingham to Lord Grenville [14 January 1804] (*Fortescue MSS*, VII, pp. 207–8); T. Grenville to Fitzwilliam, 28 January 1804 (N); Fitzwilliam to Laurence, 30 January (N. x515/42); Grenville to Pitt, 31 January 1804, and reply, 4 February (*Fortescue MSS*, VII, pp. 211–14); Fox to O'Bryen [29 January], (B.M. Add MS 47566, f. 180); *Windham Papers*, II, pp. 230–1; G. M. Trevelyan, *Lord Grey of the Reform Bill*, 2nd edn., 1929, pp. 133–4; Grey to Fox, 2 and 9 February 1804 (Grey MSS).

28 Grey to Whitbread, 4 and 11 April [1804] : Whitbread MSS.

29 *Parl. Debs.*, I, 807–9; R. Hunter and I. MacAlpine, *George III and the Mad Business*, pp. 131–8; Colchester, *Diary*, I, pp. 499–501, 506–7; *Court and Cabinets*, III, p. 350; Fitzwilliam to Lady Fitzwilliam, Tuesday [May 1804] (N).

30 Stanhope, *Pitt*, IV, p. 177; W. Elliot to Lady Spencer, 17 May 1804 (Althorp MSS, second earl, misc., 54); Grenville to Buckingham, 21 May (*Court and Cabinets*, III, p. 355).

31 Buckingham to Grenville, 30 May 1804 (*Fortescue MSS*, VII, pp. 224–6); T. Grenville to Spencer, 6 June (*Althorp MSS*, second earl, misc., 55).

32 Grenville to Fitzwilliam, 14 November 1804; B.M., Grenville MSS, unnumbered.

33 Lord Dundas to C. L. Dundas, 9 March 1805 and C. L. Dundas to Fitzwilliam, 11 March (N); Holland, *Memoirs*, I, pp. 198–202.

34 Grenville to Buckingham, 27 May 1805; *Court and Cabinets*, III, p. 421.

35 Fox to O'Bryen [7 July 1805] (B.M. Add. MS 47566, ff. 213–5); T. Grenville to Spencer, 21 July and 25 June 1805 (Althorp MSS, second earl, misc., 59); Fox to Fitzwilliam, 1 August [1805] (N).

36 Fox to O'Bryen [7 August 1805] : B.M. Add. MS 47566, f. 219.

37 Milton to Laurence, 3 September 1805; Laurence to Fitzwilliam, 28 August 1805 (N); Fox to Windham, 6 September (*Windham Papers*, II, p. 268).

38 Georgiana to Lady Spencer [6 December 1805] : Chatsworth MSS.

39 Fitzwilliam to Grenville, 20 January [1806] (*Fortescue MSS*, VII, p. 328); Dorchester to Fitzwilliam, 7 and 28 January 1806; Fitzwilliam to Grenville, 27 January 1806 (N); T. Grenville to Buckingham, 12 January (*Court and Cabinets*, IV, pp. 10–12).

40 Georgiana to Hartington, 22 January 1806 (Chatsworth MSS, 1844); Grenville to T. Grenville, 24 January 1806 (*Fortescue MSS*, VII, pp. 335–6); to Fitzwilliam, 26 January (B.M., Grenville MSS).

41 Colonel Macmahon to the Duke of Northumberland, 31 January 1806 (*Corresp. of George, Prince of Wales*, V, p. 315); Fox to Fitzwilliam, 29 January 1806, and reply, 29th (N); Fitzwilliam to Laurence, 30th (N, x515/5).

42 Fox to Fitzwilliam, 2 February 1806 (N).

43 Holland, *Memoirs*, I, pp. 209–10, 250, 213.

44 *Parl. Debs.*, VII, 809.

45 Grenville to Fitzwilliam, 22 September 1806; Howick to Fitzwilliam, 23 September (F 64a); *Windham Papers*, II, pp. 316–20; Fitzwilliam to Grenville, 24 September (B.M., Grenville MSS: incorrect version in *Fortescue MSS*, VIII, pp. 355–6).

46 Howick to Grenville, 24 September 1806 (*Fortescue MSS*, VIII, p. 354); to Fitzwilliam, 25 September (F 64a); Fitzwilliam to Howick, 27 September (Grey MSS). Rockingham had been the only marquess in the British peerage at his death. The Prince of Wales accepted Fitzwilliam's reasons for the refusal as 'quite unanswerable' (*Corresp. of George, Prince of Wales*, V, p. 462).

47 Fitzwilliam to Grenville, 24 September 1806 (B.M., Grenville MSS).

48 Fitzwilliam to Howick, 7 November [1806] (Grey MSS) and to Grenville, 6 November (*Fortescue MSS*, VIII, pp. 427–8); Grenville to Fitzwilliam, 8 November (*ibid.*, p. 431); Howick to Fitzwilliam, 25 November (F 64a); Cabinet minute, 23 December (*Windham Papers*, II, pp. 322–5).

49 Howick to Fitzwilliam, 8 December 1806 (F 64/29), and reply, 12 December (Grey MSS).

50 A. F. Fremantle, *England in the Nineteenth Century*, II (1930), p. 185.

51 As suggested in *ibid.*, p. 187. For an account of the crisis see M. Roberts, *The Whig Party: 1807–12* (2nd ed., 1965), pp. 7–34.

52 *Ibid.*, pp. 22–3.

53 Howick to Fitzwilliam, 17 March 1807 (F 64/33). Grenville told Spencer on 16 March that if the Ministers at the Cabinet on the 15th had known of his attitude they would have decided for resignation (*ibid.*).

54 Portland to the king, 12 March 1807: *Later Corresp. of George III*, IV, pp. 525–8.

55 Fitzwilliam to Grenville, 18 March (*Fortescue MSS*, VIII, p. 100): Grenville to Earl Fortescue, 18 March (Fortescue MSS at Barnstaple), and to Fitzwilliam, 18 March (F 64a).

56 Howick to Grenville, 31 December 1806; Grenville to Fitzwilliam, 1 January 1807; Fitzwilliam to Grenville, 3 April 1807; reply, 5 April (*Fortescue MSS*, VIII, pp. 490–1, IX, pp. 2, 130–1, 134).

CHAPTER TEN

An elder statesman
1807—18

The collapse of the 'Talents' administration and the formation of an anti-Catholic government under Portland was rapidly followed by a dissolution of Parliament. The Ministers clearly needed to strengthen themselves in the Commons, which had been elected only six months previously under the influence of their predecessors, while the issue on which the change of government had occurred gave them the opportunity to capitalise on the national anti-popery prejudices. The elections presented a particular challenge to Fitzwilliam's political interests, which had been strengthened by government support in 1806, and resulted in one of the most spectacular contests in the unreformed electoral system.

In the autumn of 1806 the opportunity had at last arisen to reap the benefits of the changing political circumstances in Yorkshire. Ten years previously the retirement of Henry Duncombe from the representation of the county had found Fitzwilliam's friends hesitant and uncertain. Walter Fawkes, a wealthy landed gentleman from the Leeds area and a moderate reformer, had made tentative soundings and had canvassed Fitzwilliam's support. Fitzwilliam had assured him of his good will, but cautiously declared that it had always been his wish 'to follow the sense of the county'. Sinclair made efforts to whip up support for Fawkes against Henry Lascelles, a supporter of Pitt and younger son of Fitzwilliam's chief Yorkshire rival, the Earl of Harewood, but when Lascelles let it be known that he was ready to stand a poll, Fawkes withdrew—'so Pitt has got the county by purchase', Sinclair remarked.[1]

For ten years, Lascelles and Wilberforce remained in possession. By 1806, however, the situation had changed. The interest of government was now to a large extent behind Fitzwilliam, who as Lord Lieutenant could expect to wield some additional influence in the county. Furthermore, popular opinion in the West Riding clothing districts became bitterly hostile to Lascelles, who had openly allied himself with the new capitalists like Benjamin Gott, who were trying to dismantle the mainly Tudor legislation which protected the interests of the 'domestic' clothier against the larger units now coming into the industry. In March 1806 Parliament set up a committee of enquiry to examine demands for the repeal of the old statutes, with Lascelles and Wilberforce among the members. Lascelles was reported to have treated the witnesses representing the domestic clothiers with some contempt, and his attitude aroused bitter resentment in the textile districts. In October 1806, when the 'Talents' dissolved Parliament to strengthen their numbers in the Commons, Yorkshire was one of the places to which they looked for an advantage. Grenville urged that no opposition should be offered to Wilberforce, but he agreed that Lascelles as a 'decided political enemy' could not expect any favour from the friends of the new administration. Fawkes was persuaded to come forward, met with an enthusiastic reception in the West Riding manufacturing district, and declared his determination to contest the election. Lascelles, who was taken by surprise, resigned his seat.[2]

The Whig victory in Yorkshire was short-lived, however. Fawkes himself, though a worthy and liberal-minded man, had no taste for the laborious duties of a county member, which, he soon discovered, involved him in all kinds of wearisome business on behalf of his commercial and industrial constituents. And though wealthy, he had not the resources to resist a serious challenge from Harewood House if a poll were threatened. Within a few hours of the news of the dissolution in April 1807, Fitzwilliam received a letter bearing the news of Fawkes's decision to withdraw. 'A more vexatious event,' Fitzwilliam wrote to Laurence, 'could not have been imagined.' With no opportunity for consultations, he had to decide at once 'whether after having so lately rescued the county out of hands so hostile to us, we should suffer it to fall back again, without a struggle, into the same hands, or should take the tremendous step of entering into a contest, such as must be that of the county of York'. Only one course was feasible. In the urgency of the moment it was impossible to look far for another candidate; but Milton was about to come of age, had been in Parliament since October 1806 as member for Malton, and was prepared to fight the battle for his family interest.

Whatever may be the inconveniences attending such an undertaking

[Fitzwilliam wrote], and I don't under-rate them (for I look for a diminu-
tion of income of not less than £4,000 or £5,000) still we felt ourselves
forced into the undertaking, to save the dishonourable appearance of
shrinking under the cry [of 'no Popery'] Ministers have endeavoured to
raise against us.

The whole resources of the Wentworth fortune were mobilised in
Milton's support, while it was rumoured that Lord Harewood too
had declared his readiness 'to spend in it his whole Barbadoes
property'.[3] For over five weeks a political contest such as had never
before been seen was fought across the length and breadth of Yorkshire. Every nerve and sinew, physical, psychological and financial,
was at full stretch on both sides, while the county was in a fever
of excitement and upheaval as the rival candidates and their friends
and agents sought out voters, harangued the crowds, opened the
inns, and distributed propaganda in newspapers, pamphlets, broad-
sheets, ballads and handbills. A correspondent in the *York Herald*
alleged that on Milton's side 'a greater number of canvassing agents
were employed, a greater activity exerted, and a greater profusion
of expense incurred, than have been before known in the history of
election contests'. Committees and subcommittees were set up to
manage the various branches of electoral organisation—canvassing,
propaganda, transport, the engagement and supervision of inns,
polling arrangements, and the thousand and one intricacies of political
management. 'Go where you will,' *The Times* remarked, 'you run
against one of his lordship's agents. He seems not only to have an
agent or two to every village, but one to every coach.' The *York
Herald* reported on the day after the close of the poll:

Nothing since the days of the revolution has ever presented to the world
such a scene as has been for fifteen days and nights passing within this
great county. Repose or rest have been unknown in it, except it was seen
in a messenger, totally worn out, asleep upon his post-horse, or on his
carriage. Every day the roads, in every direction, to and from every
remote corner of the county have been covered with vehicles loaded with
voters; and barouches, curricles, gigs, flying waggons, military cars with
eight horses to them, crowded sometimes with forty voters, have been
scouring the country, leaving not the smallest chance for the *quiet* traveller
to urge his humble journey, or find a chair at an inn to sit down upon.[4]

The Yorkshire election involved many issues and interests. Fitzwilliam wrote:

We are contending against a most formidable confederacy. A strong Tory party, acting in conjunction with the whole corps of merchants, Tories like themselves, who have been in possession of the county for twenty-five years; this formidable phalanx is supported by every exertion of the Ministry, and the king: the king has more influence in Yorkshire than can be conceived; half his corps of janissaries are great landed proprietors in Yorkshire—all this influence is upon the stretch. . . . Add to all this the High Churchmen, and no Popery—fortunately Yorkshiremen have their wits pretty much about them. They are not easily catch'd; the cry goes for nothing in the county, though the Party do all they can to inflame the people's minds on that topic. . . . But I look for victory, and trust we shall triumph over this host of enemies.

The Catholic question was in fact of lesser importance than the economic rivalry of clothiers and merchants. Over three-quarters of Milton's votes—7,625 out of 11,177—came from the West Riding, against less than half of Wilberforce's and sixty per cent of Lascelles's. In the main clothing districts, Milton polled even more strongly in comparison with his rivals. Wilberforce calculated that Milton received the votes of 1,081 clothiers, against 331 for himself and 273 for Lascelles. In the south of the Riding, where the Wentworth influence was strongest, Milton gained the support not only of Wentworth tenants but also of the craftsmen and small manufacturers of Sheffield and Rotherham. Milton's victory represented to some degree 'the triumph of a coalition between aristocratic influence and an industrial "middle class" of small independent masters and craftsmen over the merchant clothiers and the upper and middling gentry of the rural areas'.[5] Even so it was a narrow victory, in doubt until almost the last. The final margin after fifteen days' polling was Milton 11,177, Lascelles 10,990. Wilberforce, revered by the independent freeholders as the man who abolished the slave trade and for his twenty-three years as the diligent servant of the county's interests, came top of the poll with 11,806 votes, many of them cast at the individual's own expense and all costs paid by public subscriptions or private contributions from all over the country. Over £60,000 was raised in a fortnight, but Wilberforce's total chargeable expenses were no more than half that sum. In contrast, the battle cost Harewood and Fitzwilliam each over £90,000; Harewood's accounts totalled more than £93,600, Fitzwilliam's over £5,000 more.[6]

The result of the Yorkshire contest was widely hailed at the time as a Whig victory, despite the fact that it was largely due to the

fortuitous circumstances of Milton being able to take advantage of
the economic grievances among the clothiers. It was, the Whig election manager William Adam declared, 'the most splendid and the
most useful contest of election which has ever taken place in this
country'. For Milton himself it was something of a personal triumph.
Though young and inexperienced he had spoken stoutly and with
credit before the public. Laurence proudly professed himself surprised and astonished at 'Milton's judgement as well as eloquence',
and remarked that 'he seems destined to be a prodigy through life'.
The Times, too, approved of him:

> To see a young nobleman of the eighteenth-century abstain from the
> fashionable dissipation, enter at an early age into married life and give
> his mind to politics is a pleasing spectacle. . . . It is highly desirable that
> a promising young peer should be a member of the House of Commons
> before he takes his hereditary seat in the other House. He thus acquaints
> himself with the popular feelings. . . . The independent freeholders of a
> county . . . are perhaps the best *superiors* that he can have. . . .

Without a father willing to spend £100,000, of course, Milton would
not have achieved the position of member for Yorkshire at the age
of only 21. Nevertheless, his personal qualities—seriousness, diligence,
and enthusiasm for the Whig cause—enabled him to fill it with credit
to his family and his party. From now on Milton became the family's
spokesman in Parliament, where he helped to strengthen the moderate
liberal element in the opposition ranks.[7]
    The decision to set up Milton for the county had unexpected
repercussions in his former constituency of Malton.[8] He had been
returned for one of the seats in this quiet but prosperous market
town in October 1806, six months before his twenty-first birthday.
The town was largely within Fitzwilliam's estate, and over 450 of the
500 voters were directly or indirectly tenants on the family property.
In an age when tenants naturally expected to give their landlords
political allegiance, few people saw anything unusual or improper
in Malton accepting its parliamentary representatives at Fitzwilliam's
nomination. On his side, Fitzwilliam performed the duties of a landlord with an admitted benevolence and conscientious attention to
the town's interests. His candidates were expected to pay their own
expenses, to make a 'present' of £100 to some local institution or
good cause at every election, and to distribute the customary small
sums and free entertainments to the people of the town in a way

suitable to the rank and status of the individuals concerned. During almost the whole of the eighteenth century these attentions and the grateful deference of the voters created an atmosphere of peaceful goodwill which was broken only by the noisy and alcoholic celebrations at every election.

Towards the end of the century, however, unrest began to arise amongst the professional and middle-class element in the town, who were beginning to resent the servile status of a pocket constituency and whose outlook was less deferential towards the landed aristocracy and its privileges. In 1789 *The Times* noted that some of the leading townspeople were opposed to Burke's political views, and in 1805, when Grattan was put forward, the agent advised that an extra allowance should be given to the voters and the young men of the town. In 1807 Fitzwilliam's preoccupation with the county election added a further inducement to his rivals in the area to act. On Milton's twenty-first birthday, as the town was ringing with 'bells and every demonstration of public joy', two candidates were unexpectedly produced. One was a local gentleman, Isaac Leatham, who had laid the foundation of his interest in 1800 by bringing cheap corn to the market at a time of severe scarcity and high prices, while Fitzwilliam had provided only 'nourishing soup' prepared in the brewing vessels at the lodge and sold at a penny a quart and salt fish procured from Hull. Leatham's derisive slogan of 'salt fish and taties' was a timely reminder that Fitzwilliam's charity had on this occasion been outmatched by his competitor. The other candidate was a stranger to the town, Charles Winn-Allanson, Lord Headley in the Irish peerage, whose family was established near Ripon and who, it was rumoured, was sent to Malton by Sir Mark Sykes, an old enemy of the Wentworth interest, to prevent his candidature against Sykes at York. Headley, ominously, was to become a member of Wilberforce's county committee, and he quickly made clear the High Church grounds on which he stood by raising the 'no Popery' cry. He also declared that he had brought £10,000 with him and could fetch another £10,000 if necessary. On the other side Colonel Bryan Cooke, the previous member, was joined by one of Fitzwilliam's nephews, Robert Lawrence Dundas. At the end of the first day's poll, with Cooke trailing a poor fourth, Leatham (running third) agreed to stand down and to ask his remaining supporters to vote for Headley. On the second day the poll closed, with Headley second, forty-four votes ahead of Cooke. The Wentworth monopoly at

Malton was broken for the first time since the family had acquired the borough in 1713.

Fitzwilliam's reaction was quick and ruthless. Two thirds of the voters had voted either wholly for the 'independent' candidates, or for one of them and one of Fitzwilliam's, and even some who had voted on Fitzwilliam's side were alleged to have used their influence against him. Most of these were tenants or under-tenants on the estate. Strict instructions were now issued that all tenants who had voted against orders were to be discharged, and that any whose own tenants had similarly voted should discharge them, on pain of being turned off themselves. The tolls levied by the estate on barge traffic on the river Derwent were increased for all owners who had voted against the recommended candidates, and other measures were taken against the businesses of those who had been disaffected. Lord Carlisle, at nearby Castle Howard, agreed to call in his bills from George Parker, his apothecary, one of the leaders of the 'independent' party, declaring that he should 'blister and clyster no more of my family or tenants', and other tradesmen found their customers calling in their accounts. These draconian measures were soon effective. Evidence was also quickly gathered to contest Headley's return on grounds of bribery and treating, while his solicitor and agent was induced to give evidence that Headley had bought off Leatham by offering him £500 to pay his expenses. With this and the usual collection of tales of electoral bribery and drunkenness, the petition against Headley was successful in the Commons. The ensuing by-election in April 1808 vindicated Fitzwilliam's punitive measures, the electorate, as Carlisle remarked, consisting of 'some having begun to be ashamed of their ingratitude, but more having taken alarm at the power you can exercise to their great inconvenience'. Cooke stood again as Fitzwilliam's candidate, while the 'independents' put up a local gentleman, Major Robert Bower, Headley and Sir Mark Skyes agreeing to subscribe to his expenses. Cooke's election was a foregone conclusion, only eighty-two voters carrying their defiance to the last, and most of the Fitzwilliam tenants returning to their old allegiance. The regenerate were rewarded with remission of their notices to quit, though surcharged with a 25 per cent increase in rents as a reminder. The river tolls were restored to their former level, and only a few individuals were excepted from the amnesty.

One sequel remained. In one of his speeches Bower had asserted that Fitzwilliam was not only a tyrannical landlord, but a trafficker in borough interest—that one of the seats at Malton had at one time been offered for sale. Fitzwilliam demanded that Bower withdrew the allegation, which was certainly false, and, on his refusal, sent him a challenge. When the principals met, however, at 4.30 a.m. on Doncaster racecourse, Bower agreed to an investigation of the story, and later published a full retraction. Once again Fitzwilliam's courage in defending his reputation was not to be put to the final test, and once again he emerged from the ordeal with credit.

The contests at Malton in 1807 and 1808 proved to be an isolated episode in the borough's history. The episode was a warning that even the most liberal and well-intentioned of landlords, as Fitzwilliam certainly was, could no longer expect the unhesitating obedience of his tenants in elections; but it also showed that the landlords still had it in their power, if they cared to use it, to enforce their political influence.

Not all Fitzwilliam's electoral battles in 1807 met with such success. In York city Sir William Milner, still holding the seat gained in 1790 after Galway's retirement, was a popular and respected member, a lifelong Foxite with a reputation for 'insuperable honesty and disposition to plain dealing'. His position was considered absolutely secure, even among the venal and unreliable electorate of this notoriously corrupt constituency. The second seat had been won for the Whig interest in 1802, when the reformer Richard Slater Milnes retired and Lawrence Dundas, Fitzwilliam's nephew, was returned as Milner's colleague, a 'man with good Whig blood in his veins', as Sinclair described him (while his own vessels were full of Milner's claret). At first the two members maintained separate interests and separate committees as a tactical measure, 'so as to keep up the semblance of contesting parties, to please the rabble and buoy them up with the hopes and chances of future contests', as Sinclair put it, but the apparent unanimity of their politics made it impossible to carry on this subterfuge. The result was to raise up a clamour for an opposition candidate so that the voters could profit from a contest, and in 1807 Sir Mark Sykes presented himself on the powerful cry of 'no Popery'. 'There is a very anxious and violent Tory Party in the towns and many Methodists who are to a man our enemies.' wrote one of Fitzwilliam's supporters. The alliance of the High Church cathedral interest and the Methodists resulted in the loss of one of Fitzwilliam's seats, Sykes coming second to Milner after a six days' poll.[9]

The third Yorkshire borough in which Fitzwilliam maintained an interest was Hull. Here, however, the position had always been precarious. Lord Burford's victory in 1790 was partly due to his local connexions, but he retired in 1796, ostensibly in disgust at Pitt's seeking peace negotiations with France. In 1802 Fitzwilliam was elected as High Steward of the borough, and one optimistic supporter declared that 'the Rockingham interest *never* stood on so *firm a foundation* as at present'. Hull politics were notoriously unstable, however, and Fitzwilliam's attempt in 1802 to win a seat for W. J. Denison failed at the polls. Samuel Thornton and John Staniforth, both Tories, were elected by large majorities. The unanimity of the town corporation, Trinity House and the Dock Company plus the weight of the government interest were too strong to be overcome, and it was small consolation that the irate populace had prevented Thornton from making his speech of thanks, 'demolished the chair prepared for him, and would have torn him to pieces, if he had not escaped privately'.[10]

In 1806, the situation was altered by the change of administration. Government interest was powerful at Hull, and Fitzwilliam immediately began to demand a share in local patronage for his friends, to the chagrin of the sitting members. Armed with this advantage, and with the support of some of the Trinity House, Denison was now successful. Thornton was the losing candidate, despite the humiliation of having to ask Fitzwilliam for 'the favour of your good offices with your Lordship's friends at this place' and 'the general good wishes of his Majesty's government'. 'We have obtained a signal victory', Richard Sykes claimed, 'without giving any liquor, any ribbons, or having made any canvass'. And, he added with the prudence of the true electioneer, 'Your Lordship has never been mentioned on this occasion'. It was, Fitzwilliam wrote (perhaps a little disingenuously) to Grenville, 'an extraordinary event . . . it happened without my interference, or even knowledge . . .; but the populace would have a third man, and Denison as a favourite of theirs was put up'. 'The election was gained,' wrote Daniel Sykes, 'by the unaccountable eagerness of the lower class of voters together with some dexterity in taking advantage of it.' The seat was kept in 1807, though Denison withdrew before the poll, having found that his agents had been too unguardedly distributing money to the voters, but Lord Mahon was prevailed on to stand in his place and Thornton was again defeated.[11]

L

Elsewhere, the elections passed off uneventfully for Fitzwilliam's
candidates. Higham Ferrers, the safest of all his seats, was given as a
refuge to Windham, who had been driven out of Norfolk by a petition
'Amidst so many defeats and doubtful contests,' Windham wrote
from the constituency, 'it may be some satisfaction to know that no
accident has happened here, but that every thing has proceeded in
its regular course.' At Peterborough, Laurence and Elliot were quietly
re-elected, and in the county of Northamptonshire Spencer's son Lord
Althorp, who came top of the poll in 1806, attributing his victory to
the solid support of Fitzwilliam's tenants, was also rechosen without
a contest. The 1807 election, called in order to deplete the strength
of the Grenville–Whig alliance in the Commons, in fact did little to
do so. As with Fitzwilliam's seats, so with the party's fortunes in
general, a few disappointments and losses did little to weaken the
numerical strength of the party's forces in the new Parliament. The
opposition were not far wrong in claiming from 200 to 220 seats in
the new House, though attendance at divisions was of course somewhat less. The ineffectiveness of the Whigs in opposition between
1807 and 1812 was due less to their numbers than to the deficiencies
of their leadership and the lack of a positive and distinctive programme on which they were all agreed.[12]

At the outset of their opposition, even before the formal handing
over of offices, Grenville was writing to Howick of his

great repugnance to any course of very active opposition—having been
most unaffectedly disinclined to take upon me the task in which I have
been engaged, and feeling so much pleasure in an honourable release, I
could not easily bring myself to struggle much to get my chains on again.

He objected to any course of vigorous activity designed to compel
the king to change his Ministers. He saw no prospect of the king
being forced to do so by a mere parliamentary struggle, and less of
subsequently being able to carry on a government in face of hostility
from the court. He deprecated the tendency 'of all oppositions that
I have seen in this country . . . that the eagerness of those who were
least qualified to decide has always run away with the judgement of
those who are supposed to direct'. In face of this disinclination on
the part of the retiring Prime Minister to become leader of the
opposition the Whig coalition was doomed to impotence from the
start. Howick also was only too ready to sacrifice public duty to
private ease, and his repeated reluctance to leave Northumberland—

usually on the grounds that his wife was either pregnant or had recently been pregnant—became the despair of all those who wished for an active campaign. Fitzwilliam, nine years older than Grenville and sixteen years older than Howick, though always willing to obey a summons to a major debate, had for some years regarded himself rather as a counsellor from a distance and the representative of Whiggism in Yorkshire than as an active leader in the House of Lords or in party assemblies in London. In any case, the effects of his illness had not yet worn off. 'I doubt whether I shall be stout enough for a campaign,' he warned Howick at the beginning of April; . . . still there hangs about me a nervous feebleness, that is more fit for the quiet of the country than the bustle of London'. In the frequent absences of its three senior members, therefore, it is not surprising that the history of the party for the next ten years and more was one of internal dissension and external weakness. The impression of quarrelsomeness and irresponsibility which the party gave to the independents in the Commons made it impossible to attract enough support to overturn the equally feeble governments of Portland and Perceval, even in face of such scandals as those of the Duke of York and Mrs Clarke or the Walcheren expedition. These circumstances together made calculations of the party's voting strength in the two Houses almost irrelevant. Howick's optimistic forecast of 250 supporters in the Commons and his hopeful predictions of strength in the Lords proved a poor guide to the party's prospects, which were further damaged by the death of Howick's father and his removal to the Lords as second Earl Grey in November 1807.[13] Grenville accurately described the event as a calamity for the party.

It proved difficult to fill Grey's place as leader in the Commons. Tom Grenville refused to consider the post and Whitbread, perhaps the only leading debater in the party who wanted it, was unacceptable because of his radical views on reform and because his ambition, like Sheridan's once, was perhaps too little disguised by conventional Whig diffidence. The choice therefore fell on George Ponsonby, who was little known in England and who at the time was not even a Member of Parliament, but who certainly possessed his full share of diffidence and distaste for the job. Fitzwilliam naturally approved of the choice of the man he had wanted to make the leader of his administration in the Irish House of Commons in 1795. 'I never heard him speak,' Fitzwilliam told Holland, 'but from all report, his

powers of debate are considerable; his manner far from offensive to
the body of his opponents and popular with his own party . . . He
has many qualities that point him out as a desirable leader.' Ponsonby's conciliatory inoffensiveness was not perhaps the best of
qualities for the leader of an offensive opposition, but since the
Whigs were far from that they seem to have got the leader they
deserved. 'I have really and truly no wish for the situation,' Ponsonby
himself declared; 'I am sincerely convinced that I am not qualified
for it, and . . . if our friends can agree upon any other person, I will
act under him, with as much zeal and more pleasure than I shall feel
in taking the lead myself.' His modesty did him credit as a man but
showed up the limitations of the party he was to lead. The main
reason for choosing him was that, as Holland wrote, 'no person is
likely to create so little difficulty in the House', and that 'no feelings
should be excited [in the party] likely to lead to any schism or
separation. . . . We found him most acceptable and least objection-
able to all branches of the opposition'.[14] Ponsonby's task was primarily to keep the party together—or more passively, to prevent its
disintegration—and to conciliate rather than to lead. Within the
limits expected of him, and possible in the circumstances, he did his
best.

During the next five years the Whigs had to define their attitude
towards three major issues, the Catholic question, the war, and
reform, and to deal with specific problems arising from each. In at
least two of them it became apparent that the union between the
old Foxites, led by Grey and represented in the Commons by the
more vigorous and radical approach of Whitbread, and the Gren-
villites, few in number in the Commons but important from the
weight of their consideration in the Lords, was a delicate and incomplete one. The Catholic question was their closest bond of union in
principle, but in practice it was perhaps their gravest liability. So
long as George III remained politically active, it would face them
with the dilemma of either giving up all hope of office, or appearing
to desert their principles in order to achieve power, while the hostile
state of public opinion provided no grounds on which to mobilise
popular support against the Crown. After Fox's death, too, the Prince
of Wales was turning against the Catholic claims. Between 1807
and 1811 the Whigs tried to escape from this dilemma by securing
the agreement of the Irish Catholic leaders to some scheme to give
the Crown a veto on the nomination of Catholic bishops in Ireland,

in order to provide 'securities' for the Protestant established religion in case of emancipation.[15] The long and tortuous negotiations ended in failure, not only because no agreement was reached but also because they led to a loss of confidence in the Whigs by the Irish, who considered, not altogether unjustly, that the Whigs were more interested in resolving their own political dilemma than in pressing for justice for Ireland. In any case a new Catholic organisation in Ireland now began to replace the aristocratic leadership of men like Fingall and Kenmare, on whom the Whigs placed their hopes, by a more democratic movement with which they had less sympathy. By 1812, emancipation had become a different issue both in Ireland and in English politics. All that the Whigs achieved by their honourable persistence in upholding the Catholic cause between 1807 and 1812 was their own continued exclusion from power.

The Catholic question at least presented a general principle upon which all shades of Whig opinion could agree. The questions of the war and of reform tended to divide them, largely along existing lines. To Fitzwilliam, belief in the continued prosecution of the war against French ambitions in Europe was axiomatic, and it aligned him still on this issue with the Grenvilles. Grey now so far agreed with this view as to admit that though peace was preferable to war with France in principle, an honourable peace was at present impossible to obtain and that the war was no longer a war of reaction against liberal principles. Grey, Grenville and Fitzwilliam were none the less staunch critics of the way the war was being conducted. On the other hand, the mantle of Fox had perhaps fallen too heavily on men like Holland and Whitbread, who continued to urge Fox's contentions of the 1790s that the present war, like that of pre-1802, was unjust and anti-liberal. Holland, though agreeing that the Whigs ought not to encourage popular clamour for peace, confessed that he was 'a very *peaceable* man and am far from thinking the object unattainable'. It would be wrong, he thought, to suggest to the public or to the French 'that all parties among us were equally warlike'. Whitbread's language on the subject of peace at a dinner at Lord Grenville's on the opening of the session in 1808 was more extreme, and distressed his host, who 'seemed dumbfounded and hardly spoke a word'. Fitzwilliam and Milton, however, acted vigorously to stifle a proposed peace petition from Yorkshire in December 1807; Fitzwilliam reported that Milton's supporters, the manufacturers, were for it because of the damage to their trade, but they were persuaded against it largely on the grounds that it would give encouragement to the enemy. 'The more they cry out,' wrote Fitzwilliam, 'the more they proclaim that exclusion [from continental markets] is their ruin, the more certain will be Bonaparte's adherence to that system.' The only solution to the 'continental system' now enforced by the French against British exports to Europe was, in Fitzwilliam's view, to attempt to exploit the markets in North and South America, and he welcomed the news that the British had enabled the Portuguese royal family to escape to Brazil from Napoleon's conquest of Portugal. 'I trust we shall profit [from the circumstance],' he wrote to Laurence, '. . . for losing in Europe we are, and I fear irrevocably. . . . I fear our European commerce is gone: our hopes must be to open or rather to increase an American one.'[16]

The closure of Europe to British exports was followed by Russia's adherence to the continental system after Tilsit, and the British expedition to Copenhagen to bombard the Danish capital and carry off or destroy the Danish fleet, to prevent its use against Britain. The Copenhagen expedition was justified by Ministers as a necessary act in time of emergency, but it raised a storm of criticism in which the opposition joined. Fitzwilliam put the case against it to Grenville on 6 December.[17] It meant, he wrote, that Britain must now contend against French power, 'not only without an ally, but without the good wishes, without the favourable disposition of any part of Europe or America—the new world as much irritated against us, as the old'. He concluded:

there is an end of national character—no justice, no candour, no fairness, no consideration for the difficult situations of others . . . we call upon others, to approve, to justify, to guarantee the propriety of our acts of violence and injustice. . . . Become robbers and buccaneers, we have not even goodwill or compassion on our side.

Yet, despite the opportunities offered by the government's ill-judged policies abroad and despite their strong disapproval of direct intervention in Spain and Portugal, the opposition leaders determined to abstain from dividing on the address when the Houses met in January 1808. Small wonder that the opposition made a pitiful figure in Parliament throughout the session, or that they found themselves in disarray at the end of it. The leaders were unable to restrain Whitbread from calling on Fox's memory to support his motion for peace at the end of February, and even on the Copenhagen affair their divisions were slack and relatively feeble.[18] On the Peninsular War, too, they were divided three ways. To Whitbread and the pacifists it was naturally an unwelcome extension of a war already bad in principle; to Grenville it was yet another field for the bungling and mismanagement which characterised Portland's war effort, and he consistently opposed the sending of further troops to Spain or Portugal. To Holland, however, the Spanish resistance to Napoleon was a glorious crusade for liberty, and Fitzwilliam, more cautiously, also took an optimistic view of its significance. 'I am, like you,' he wrote to Grey in July, 'in heart about Spain : every day's intelligence gives one more confidence.' He looked to a war of attrition in Spain which would drain Napoleon's strength, while Holland's enthusiasm aroused his liberal zeal. 'These Spaniards are a fine people,' Fitzwilliam wrote, '—by their own energy they will emancipate themselves,' and Napoleon would be forced to throw more and more troops into the peninsula to hold the country down. 'Probably it will turn out the beginning of his downfall,' he prophesied. The only drawback was that success in Spain would be to the advantage of ministers, by distracting attention from the failure of their Baltic policies. Even in December, when the news from Spain was less favourable, Fitzwilliam refused to be downcast. The French had certainly made progress, but at the cost of much hard fighting and without a decisive victory, while

every mile they advance, either their own army must be weakened by the garrison they must leave to keep possession of what they have overrun, or they must run the risk of their own communication being cut off by the mere women of the country. . . . I cannot yet despond—I believe he has yet much to do, and am inclined to think his means not so great as he is accustomed to have.

The only fault in Fitzwilliam's appreciation of the strategic position was his failure to realise the value of Wellesley's base at Lisbon, which he thought was occupied merely to satisfy 'the cry of our Portuguese merchants and manufacturers'. Otherwise, Fitzwilliam was one of the few and the first to appreciate the significance of Napoleon's 'Spanish ulcer'.[19]

Fitzwilliam not only disagreed with Grenville's pessimistic view of the Spanish war, and on this issue leant more towards the Whig point of view. He was more eager than his leader for an active course in Parliament. In January 1809, Grenville wrote in despond-

ency about tactics for the coming session. He disapproved still of the
sending of British troops to Spain, and forecast 'nothing but disgrace
and loss from our efforts'. The great military power of France 'with
the absolute command of all the resources of Europe', seemed to him
irresistible. As to parliamentary tactics, he disliked the 'harrassing
opposition' pursued in the House of Commons in the last session, on
the grounds that 'it produced evil instead of good'. He insisted that
'the state of the country requires that the attention of public men
should appear rather to be directed to the great and broad lines of
policy on which our existence depends, than to the means of gratifying petty animosities, or pursuing inconsiderable triumphs on objects
often scarcely worth the discussion they occasion'. Though disliking
'any thing that had either the appearance or the name of *secession*',
he concluded that he would confine his Parliamentary attendance to
a few occasions of major significance. In no other way, he felt, could
'we in the House of Lords' show disapproval of the tactics of the
radical skirmishers in the Commons.

Fitzwilliam took a less gloomy view. Grenville's wishes as to
attendance in the Lords he confessed 'with respect to myself will suit
my convenience and habits better than any other line of conduct',
but he deprecated any attempt to stifle the activity of opposition in
the Commons. Attacks on particular topics would be 'but the echo
of the public voice', and many members would feel themselves only
to be following the inclinations of their constituents in censuring the
'gross misapplication of means and the irreparable loss of time and
opportunity' by the government in the conduct of the Peninsular
War. As Fitzwilliam appreciated, an opposition that failed to reflect
public criticism of government virtually forfeited the claim to fulfil
any constitutional function. Ponsonby and Lord Henry Petty, the
virtual second-in-command in the Commons, echoed Fitzwilliam's
views and Ponsonby begged Grey to heed them. Fitzwilliam had urged
on Milton, Ponsonby wrote, a more vigorous attitude in the Commons
on the grounds of 'the general dissatisfaction of the country'.[20]
Grey's lassitude, Grenville's obstinacy and Ponsonby's weakness prevailed, however, and again no amendment was offered to the address
in January 1809. Once more the virtual abdication of its nominal
leaders left the opposition to flounder through the session as best it
could, and the result again was to deepen the dissatisfaction within
its ranks.

1809 was also important as a crucial year in the revival of the reform movement in Parliament. This, too, caused havoc among the Whigs. Even in Fox's day, they had never been a party wholly committed to parliamentary reform, and after 1801 the issue had been allowed to slumber. The public was apathetic, the Grenvilles hostile, and no capital was to be gained by taking it up. From 1806, however, a new reform movement began to arise. One of its roots was in the Westminster Committee, once Fox's showplace but now, under Burdett and Francis Place, a seed-bed of democratic radicalism. Another root was fed and nourished by revelations and scandals of corruption and inefficiency in high places, such as the disclosure in 1809 by Gwyllm Lloyd Wardle, a radical backbencher, of the alleged malpractices of the Duke of York's mistress, Mary Anne Clarke, in taking payment for promises of influence to secure commissions and promotion in the army, of which the Duke was Commander-in-Chief. In 1807, too, the Talents had themselves helped to revive the reform question by starting an enquiry into sinecure offices, which resulted in a report in 1809 showing that seventy-six members of Parliament shared sinecures valued at a total of over £150,000. In April 1809 Viscount Folkestone, a radical Whig and associate of Whitbread, proposed a committee of enquiry into corrupt practices in the disposal of offices, and on 4 May John Curwen, member for Carlisle, introduced a Bill to prevent the sale of seats in Parliament. Whitbread himself, acting on the Foxite principle that the interests of the party would best be served by offering leadership to, and taking control of, popular radicalism, associated himself with Burdett and the radicals.

All these events opened a split in the party between the conservatives and moderate reformers on the one hand, and the younger radicals on the other. Wardle, for example, was regarded with distaste as an unprincipled adventurer by the older, more conservative Whigs, and Grey refused to commit the opposition to his support. The younger radicals, however, elected Wardle to the Whig Club. The party leadership was cautiously favourable to moderate economical reform in the field of sinecures and influence—though, as the Grenvilles were collectively perhaps the largest beneficiaries of the spoils system, this was a question not to be too hotly pursued— but to associate with irresponsible demagogues of the Burdett and Wardle type was another matter. Fitzwilliam held to the principles of twenty-five years before in supporting attempts to reduce what he still considered to be the dangerously increasing 'influence of the

L*

Crown' but yet opposing parliamentary reform as an inroad into the fundamentals of the constitution. He refused to acknowledge Burdett's case against the committal of the printer Gale Jones to Newgate by the House of Commons, and accordingly withheld his sympathy from Burdett himself.[21] Milton voted for many of the economical reform motions of the period 1809–12, but he opposed Thomas Brand's very moderate Parliamentary Reform Bill in 1810 in language so conservative that on one occasion he drew calls of 'Hear, hear' from the ministerial benches.[22] Not until 1819 did Milton's ardour begin to warm towards reform as a possible question for the party to take up—by which time the Grenvilles were no longer associated with the Whigs, and public opinion was moving decisively towards it.

Through these years of disheartening internal conflict Fitzwilliam, now the elder statesman of the party, gave his loyalty principally to the conservative leadership. A close bond of affection had now grown up between him and Grey, while Grenville could still appeal to Fitzwilliam's own convictions of the need for consistency and firm principles in political life. In September 1809, for example, when Portland's resignation brought about the need for a ministerial reconstruction and Perceval wrote to Grey and Grenville to offer a negotiation for a junction, Fitzwilliam approved of their instant rejection of the proposal. It amounted, Fitzwilliam wrote, to 'nothing further than an offer to fill vacant offices in the present administration'. It would have been a different matter if the king had summoned Grey and Grenville to confer with him on the formation of a new administration on a broad basis; this, however, was no more than a trap to draw the opposition into association with the pitiful remnant of a discredited government, while their differences from the old Ministers on the war and the Catholic question would have involved them in a dereliction of their principles. Visiting Doncaster races during the negotiations, he took the opportunity to sound Whig opinion in Yorkshire and reported that 'the general cry was "no patchwork"—"the country is lost, if a compromise is made with the remnant of such an administration as the last"—certainly never was an administration sunk lower in public estimation, none ever more despised and deprecated'. Grey's decision not even to travel to London to discuss the offer had been received with 'universal approbation . . . and universal joy'.[23]

Fitzwilliam himself was lobbied by Lord Lonsdale, who called at

Wentworth to inform him of the offer and who, Fitzwilliam believed, came from an audience with the king himself. Lonsdale hinted that Grey might be offered the Treasury, but he also let slip that the king, on approving Perceval's letter, had

added a *prohibition against further communication with him on the subject*, until a definitive arrangement should be submitted for his consideration—Thus, my dear Lord [Fitzwilliam wrote to Grenville] access to the presence is interdicted to you and to Lord Grey, until you have the honour of being introduced by the remnants of this administration, as persons selected by them to fill the vacant offices.

Fitzwilliam's information about Lonsdale's visit and about the public approval of their refusal was welcomed by both Grey and Grenville. It confirmed them in their resolution to refuse Perceval's offer of talks. It showed that the king, above all, was unwilling to modify his attitude to the Catholic question, and to come in or to form a new government without some assurances on that issue would be dishonourable. Fitzwilliam expressed his pleasure:

Taking therefore the whole of the case together, the offensive prohibition from the [royal] presence, the base diabolical intention of attempting to sow the seed of disunion between persons united on principle and friendship, I can hardly express the extent of my joy and satisfaction, that all their mischievous, insidious machinations are defeated.

This was all very well, but while the Whigs were standing on their dignity they were making inevitable the very course against which they complained so bitterly—the formation of a narrow and weak administration in which, they believed, the country could have no confidence. Perceval kissed hands as First Lord of the Treasury on 4 October. As Althorp wrote to Milton, it was an example of

the king being able to keep any administration he likes, for when you come so low as the last administration, the degrees of weakness below it are scarcely perceptible, and yet they might have continued in office God knows how long provided they had not quarrelled among themselves.

Grey, however, was determined never to take office unless he could be allowed to propose a settlement of the Catholic question, and since such a *carte blanche* was not to be expected in the present reign, he was virtually declaring his refusal to take part in any administration under George III. In these circumstances it could

surprise no one that the party should forfeit public sympathy.
Perceval was able to claim that henceforth the administration would
stand on the principle of 'the public sentiment of loyalty and
attachment to the king' and that it would win the support of the
'floating strength' of the House—those independent members whose
support was vital to every government. George Ponsonby expressed
his despondency to Grey in December 1809. It was absurd, he wrote,
even to call the opposition a party: they were merely

a number of members hostile to Government sufficient if they acted
together to overthrow so weak an administration as the present, but
divided as they are by jealousies and distrust of each other, I confess I
look forward to nothing but bickerings and defections among ourselves.[24]

The situation called for some firm leadership from the Lords, but
Grenville too professed himself 'too old, too scrupulous, and in the
present state of the country, much too timid' for 'a daily parliamentary opposition'. In January 1810 Fitzwilliam wrote to Grey to
try to inject a note of decision into their counsels. Ponsonby's
leadership in the Commons was again being challenged, but Fitzwilliam threw his weight once more behind him. He suggested that he
'would better carry the lead, if he felt himself released from the
obligation of courting the good fellowship of one perfectly
determined to hold none with him, nor with the Party, but an
unconditional submission . . . to his dictates'. In Fitzwilliam's view
the party would be strengthened rather than weakened by throwing
off the radical wing and reconstituting itself on the old whig principles. Tom Grenville, writing on his brother's behalf, urged on Fitzwilliam 'the indispensable necessity of immediate and personal
communication' with Grey and Grenville in London. 'They can do
nothing,' he wrote, '. . . until you come and take in these discussions
the part that belongs to you.' Particularly pressing was the question
of the Catholic petition, on which there was tactical disagreement
between Grenville and the rest of the party leaders.[25] Fitzwilliam
failed to heal the breach, and the session of 1810 thus passed off
with little advantage to opposition.

The political situation did not change until the autumn of the
year, when George III suffered a renewal of his illness. The Prince
of Wales had declared to Moira in 1807 his decision to take no
further part in party politics, and since that time the Grey–Grenville
opposition had operated independently of the prince's small squadron

in Parliament. The prince and Grenville disliked each other, and Grey also refused to be on intimate terms with him. The prospect of the king's prolonged incapacity, however, inevitably aroused Whig hopes that a regency or the king's death might carry them into power. No one placed much reliance at any time on the prince's steadfastness to any course. In 1809 he had reserved his position on Perceval's offer to Grey and Grenville, and hints had been dropped that, were the Whigs to consult him and re-adopt him as their leader, he would abandon his 'neutrality' in their favour.[26] On the news of his father's relapse, however, he behaved with ostentatious propriety. He had learnt a good deal since 1788 and, as Fitzwilliam had remarked in 1807, he was morbidly sensitive to public opinion, which for the past few years had shown itself affectionately loyal to George III. He remained at Windsor for some time in semi-seclusion and communicated with neither Ministers nor opposition. As one observer reported, 'all are agreed that he is behaving in a very exemplary manner in all respects'.[27] In mid-December, however, the disclosure of Perceval's regency resolutions, modelled on those of December 1788, altered the situation. The renewal of the pro-posals to give custody of the king's person and supervision of the Household to the queen, assisted by a Council, and the temporary restriction on the regent's power to create peers (except, on this occasion, to reward outstanding military or naval service) and to grant pensions and certain offices, called from the prince a reminder to Perceval of his attitude to Pitt's Regency Bill. The Whigs also took up again their contention of 1788–9, arguing that 'the plainest, the most direct and 'only constitutional mode' of procedure was by a Joint Address of the two Houses to the prince, asking him to assume the powers of regency.[28] The prince instructed his parliamentary followers to assist the Whigs in opposing Perceval's scheme, while the king's advanced age and diminished strength since 1789 might be expected further to increase the opposition's numbers with desertions from the ministerial ranks.

Grenville and his followers, of course, had formerly supported Pitt's plan, while Grey was even more firmly opposed to the restric-tions now than in 1789; but both wings of the opposition, together with Canning and his friends, were prepared to vote against the government once the details of the restrictions came into considera-tion. As Grenville had written to Fitzwilliam at the beginning of the crisis, in such a matter 'we cannot either of us act without

some reference to past times, but be assured that my principal
endeavours will be that even on such points my conduct and
language shall only more strongly indicate the satisfaction I have
derived from your friendship and from that of others with whom I
am connected'. Fitzwilliam assured Grey that 'I am glad that you
declared so distinctly your adherence to former principles'. He came
up to town to attend the Lords' debates, and his and Grenville's votes
helped to defeat the government in the Upper House on the 4th, by
105 to 102.[29] Grenville, however, embarrassed by the re-publication
of one of his speeches in 1789, voted on the other side on a subsequent division and negated the victory. With some modification of
the Household arrangements, the Regency Bill now passed both
Houses and on 6 February the prince was sworn in as regent before
the Privy Council, his powers limited as regards the Household,
peerages and places, for twelve months.

Before the Bill was through both Houses speculation about a
change of Ministers began. The prince called Grenville to a conference at Carlton House on 6 January. He was embarrassed and
indecisive. He could not give his confidence to Perceval's Ministry,
but if he brought in the Whigs he feared that, if his father should
recover and find them in office, he might be responsible for the
king's final relapse or even his death. He wished for a broadly based
administration, and asked Grenville to consult Grey and Moira, the
leader of the prince's party, about its formation. Grey arrived in
town on the 9th, objected to the prince's request for the reinstate-
ment of the Duke of York as Commander-in-Chief and his suggestion
that Canning be included in the new arrangement, and soon reduced
himself to a state of despair over the difficulties in the way of a new
administration. Grenville's own views, expressed in a fifteen-page
letter to Grey, disclosed a wide area of disagreement between the
two leaders, and had to be withdrawn to prevent a complete breach.
On the distribution of offices, too, the two wings of opposition began
to squabble heartily. Whitbread and his friends objected to Grenville's taking the post of First Lord of the Treasury while continuing
to hold the valuable post of Auditor of the Exchequer, which, constitutionally at any rate, would have put Grenville in the position
of being able to audit his own accounts. Grenville, however, would
take no office but the Treasury, or at any rate he would insist on
controlling Treasury patronage. Many devices were considered to
avoid this *impasse*, including, according to Charles Abbot, that of

Fitzwilliam's appointment as First Lord of the Treasury. The prince was said to have offered the post first to Holland, and then to Fitzwilliam, who declined on the grounds that he had determined not to take any office.[30] Grey, however, professed himself satisfied with the suggestion that Grenville should hold both offices but forego the salary of the Auditorship for as long as he did so, and on 22 January the Cabinet was provisionally settled. Fitzwilliam was not named for office, but, as in 1807, it was suggested that he might enter the Cabinet without portfolio. Grey was to be Foreign Secretary, Holland and Ponsonby to hold the other two secretaryships of state, and Whitbread was to have the Admiralty. Tierney, Erskine and Lansdowne also represented the Foxite side of the Opposition in the Cabinet. Fitzwilliam hardly felt, therefore, that his presence was necessary to strengthen the representation of that element in the coalition, and for the last time he refused a Cabinet place. William Elliot, too, despite Grenville's personal entreaties, declined a post.[31]

The proposed administration had not, however, yet taken office. The prince wavered at the critical moment, while a sudden improvement in the king's health at the end of January seemed to suggest that, as in 1789, he would recover in time to prevent the change from coming into effect. At the beginning of February the prince, reportedly influenced by his mother's entreaties to do nothing that might endanger the king's recovery, told both Grenville and Grey that he had decided to make no change in the Ministry. 'I fancy a paroxysm of *fear* seized the Prince,' wrote William Elliot, 'and he last night intimated to Lord Grey and Lord Grenville . . . that his feelings of filial affection so overpowered him that he could not bring himself to the resolution of making at this time a change in the administration.' It was a small consolation indeed to the disappointed Whigs that, at the Privy Council meeting for the swearing-in of the regent, the busts of Charles Fox and the fifth Duke of Bedford were 'ostentatiously displayed at the head of the table', or that the prince chose to be pointedly rude to Perceval as he kissed hands. Yet Grey and Grenville did not reproach the prince for his conduct: indeed, they approved of his decision, so long as the king's early recovery seemed possible and the powers of the regent remained restricted. Fitzwilliam agreed.

I do not regret the [Prince's] determination [he wrote to Grenville]. . . . Under the declarations of the physicians, what system of measures could they [a new Ministry] have adopted, but, during their expected short tenure, to have trodden in the track of their predecessors and successors. . . . To be relieved from undertaking a task, big with so much difficulty and embarrassment, is surely most fortunate, and a great blessing.[32]

He proposed only that it should be made known to the public that the Whig leaders had counselled the prince to keep the present Ministers in office, so that it would seem that he had acted not merely in response to his mother's entreaties but on the political advice of his friends. Fitzwilliam suggested that the Whigs should continue to show him 'every attention. . . . I know of none which I can mark towards him', he added, 'but that of attending the House of Lords when he first goes down, and shall therefore go up for that occasion'.

Fitzwilliam's advice was prudent and statesmanlike, though, bearing in mind that he had refused even the premiership because of his own disinclination for office, it was perhaps easier for him to give it than it was for his more ambitious friends to take it. Nevertheless, hopes that this was to be but a temporary administration nourished Whig hopes of an early resumption of progress towards the promised land. Unfortunately, though the king did not recover and the prince assumed the full regency powers in mid-February 1812, they then found themselves still excluded. Perceval's government was popular with the independents and not too unsuccessful abroad, the prince was naturally indolent and disposed not to make unnecessary changes, and his favourites the Yarmouths were suspected of encouraging him away from his old Whig connexions.[33] There were, in any case, many issues on which the prince and the Whigs were at variance. Ever since becoming regent, the prince had made it his wish to see his brother the Duke of York restored to the office of Commander-in-Chief, and, with some misgivings, the Ministers consented. A section of the younger Whigs, in alliance with the radicals and Wilberforce and the 'Saints', but against the wishes of Grey and to the embarrassment of the Grenvilles, decided to contest the appointment in the Commons, and on 6 June Milton moved the House against it on the same grounds on which he had spoken for the Duke's removal in 1809. The motion was lost by 47 to 296, but the prince was angry that the son of one of his leading Whig friends should censure his brother. On the Spanish war and on the Orders in Council, both strong opposition points against the Ministry, the regent also found himself opposed to his former friends, and the Catholic question now loomed ever larger as a barrier between them.

In the summer of 1811, when the king's condition deteriorated so as to indicate the likelihood of the regency becoming permanent, Fitzwilliam expressed his forebodings. 'If he [the prince] suffers the Ministers to proceed one line farther in their measures for Ireland, I shall look upon [it] . . . as positive proof that he has adopted his father's politicks, and means to keep the Whigs at a distance', he wrote. The consequence for the Whigs would be 'perpetual exclusion. . . . Things will be ten times worse than during the king's government, for now all hope will be at an end'.[34] Fitzwilliam, however, contributed to the difficulty when he pressed his friends to raise the Irish question, which was debated in the Lords at the critical moment of 31 January 1812, only a few days before the regency restrictions were to expire. To Fitzwilliam, there could be no doubt that Fox's memory and his own deep-seated convictions required that he should raise the question. 'Surely the affairs of Ireland cannot pass off without observation,' he wrote to Grenville on 29 December. The Irish government's recent attempt to suppress the (illegal) Catholic Convention epitomised, to Fitzwilliam, the repeated follies of British policy there since the 1790s, and suggested the permanent continuation of the same measures. In the debate, he repeated his diagnosis that the basic cause of Ireland's discontent was the denial of full civil rights to the Catholics. No religious reason existed, he claimed, for that continued denial: 'It was idle to suppose that there was a single particle of religion in the opposition made to the Catholic claims'. The anti-Catholic laws had been political in origin, to ensure the continued exclusion of the Stuarts from the throne and to protect the 'Glorious Revolution'. No such dangers now existed; all that the laws did was to foster division and grievance. The relief granted in 1793 to the lower orders of Catholic voters had not, he pointed out, led to any dangerous consequences; it was now the higher orders who felt the grievance of exclusion from Parliament, from public office and from professional advancement. Echoing his arguments of 1795, he demanded:

Was it not of the greatest importance in the war in which we were engaged that the whole united strength of the empire should be put forth, and that all ranks and classes of his Majesty's subjects should be united in one common bond of union?

The debate went on until 6.30 on the following morning, Grenville winding up with a renewed declaration of his support for full Catholic emancipation and announcing his abandonment of the

'securities' sought after 1807 in the veto. The motion was defeated
by 79 to 162.[35]

Fitzwilliam's instincts were liberal, but his tactics were foolish.
His motion showed that there was a substantial anti-Catholic
majority in the Lords, it produced an explicit statement of intent
from Grenville, the most likely candidate for the premiership if the
prince should resort to the opposition, and it angered the prince,
now moving into an anti-Catholic position, by appearing to indicate
that the Whigs might try to force him. Though there were many
other issues on which the prince saw himself to be in disagreement
with his former allies, the Catholic question seemed at this moment
to be the most intractable one. The prince's wish, insofar as he was
clear that he had one, was for a broad based Ministry that would
protect him from the dominance of any one party—a common and
understandable principle among the later Stuart and Hanoverian
monarchs. It would also enable him, he believed, to play off one
faction against another in order to get his own way. Proposals were
therefore made to Grey and Grenville for a coalition with the existing Ministers, on the basis that concession to the Catholic claims
should be delayed until after the king's death. Grey and Grenville
rejected this compromise. They would accept office only if they
were given authority to carry a relief Bill, and consoled each other
with assurances of the 'total want of confidence in the prince's
steadiness and good faith'. To coalitions in principle, Grey had
written to Holland in October, and 'where circumstances have
occurred to render them useful to the public and honourable to the
parties concerned in them, I am, as you know, no enemy . . . No
man less cherishes permanent resentments either political or personal,
than I do'. Coalitions, however, must be founded on agreements in
principle on 'the great features of . . . policy'. No such agreement was
possible with the present Ministers. A coalition, therefore, seemed
'neither desirable nor practical; and the only question could be as
to the manner of receiving the proposal'. Perceval was consequently
confirmed in office and the Whigs were confirmed in opposition, in
the latter case for eighteen years. Fitzwilliam nevertheless approved.
A coalition on the terms proposed would have been 'disgraceful to
the parties, mischievous to the public'. 'I congratulate you and Lord
G.,' he wrote to Grey, 'that the proposal was made in a shape that
put an end to all doubt, not only to every doubt in your own minds,
but to the possibility of a particle in that of any other person.' He

feared, however, that the Whigs would get the worst of it with the public, and that 'we shall hear of nothing but your overbearing principles and conduct—and the patriotic views of the P[rince]'. He recommended that another issue, that of the Orders in Council, should at once be brought forward 'to mark [the] essential difference between you and his Ministers' and to show that 'the united administration would have been united in office, separate in principle'. Fitzwilliam himself offered to 'go up the first opportunity you give me of giving a vote. I long to give one on that occasion, my proxy won't satisfy me—I feel quite eager to give a vote against the *P.'s own administration*'.[36]

In the spring and summer of 1812 Fitzwilliam helped to bring forward what he believed to be a popular issue for the opposition as well as a necessary question for his Yorkshire interests, the discontents of the commercial and manufacturing community against the Orders in Council, particularly as they affected trade with America.[37] Attempts to make electoral capital out of the distresses of trade were perhaps not unconnected with fears that the new government under Liverpool, appointed after Perceval's assassination in May 1812, would call a general election to strengthen itself in the House. Surely enough, a dissolution was announced in the autumn. Wilberforce retired from Yorkshire, and at first Lascelles declared that he would not be a candidate. J. A. Stuart Wortley, another ministerialist and a near neighbour to Wentworth House on his estate at Wortley Hall, near Barnsley, came forward in his place. At the Cloth Hall in Leeds he declared against parliamentary reform and Catholic emancipation, and announced that his 'sentiments were in unison with Mr Henry Lascelles's more than with Lord Milton's'. Lascelles, however, began to hedge, saying that if he were called on by a large body of electors he might not decline nomination. Until the last moment, therefore, a renewal of the contest of 1807 seemed to threaten, and Milton's electoral managers hurriedly sent out handbills and offered retainers to professional agents in case of a canvass and a poll. Fortunately, the propaganda against the Orders in Council won the support of the clothiers, which was confirmed by Milton's lending the Trustees of the Mixed Cloth Hall in Leeds £1,000 to extend their premises for the sale of cloth produced by the domestic masters. At the election day on 17 October, therefore, Milton found that 'all went on very well . . . much to my satisfaction'. Lascelles was nominated after all and Wortley withdrew.[38]

Elsewhere deaths and retirements necessitated a considerable reshuffle of seats and members. Laurence had died in 1809, and his seat at Peterborough had been filled for three years by the Marquess of Tavistock, who was elected for Bedfordshire in 1812. Now George Ponsonby took the seat, moving over in turn from the Duke of Bedford's borough of Tavistock. Elliot continued as the second member for Peterborough. At Malton there was a complete change, Cooke retiring through ill health and Robert Lawrence Dundas being abroad with his regiment. Here Fitzwilliam returned another nephew, John William Ponsonby, Viscount Duncannon, together with the heir of an influential Yorkshire family, John Charles Ramsden, who was Lady Rockingham's nephew. 'Mr Ramsden being now of age,' Fitzwilliam wrote, 'I have felt it due to Lady Rockingham's memory to make her nephew an offer of the seat.' At York, where Milner's death in 1811 had enabled Fitzwilliam to return another nephew, Lawrence Dundas, Sir Mark Sykes still retained the second seat without a contest. Higham Ferrers, too, had lost its most distinguished representative when Windham died in 1810. Duncannon had then been put into the seat, and on his transfer to Malton Fitzwilliam now offered it to William Plumer, an old and faithful member of the Newcastle and Rockingham parties, who was born in 1736 and had first entered Parliament in 1763. Like Ramsden at Malton, Plumer was a symbol of the Rockingham inheritance, and the offer was received in those terms, as coming from

the heir and representative of the fortunes and the virtues of that nobleman, who, in private life and in his political conduct, was best entitled to the veneration, and the love of all good men of his day—whom I (as one of the humblest of his friends) respected, and adored; and whose name and character will be mentioned with the highest reverence as long as regard shall be had to true honour, and the best qualities of our nature.

Plumer's age and diffident disposition made it unlikely that he would be again an active parliamentarian, and Fitzwilliam seems to have made the offer largely on account of old memories and loyalties, and upon what Plumer called an 'easy, quiet and most honourable plan'. He even assured Plumer that his old attachment to parliamentary reform need be no barrier to his acceptance. Finally, at Hull, where Fitzwilliam's candidate Lord Mahon was not only unpopular but also abroad in Sicily, both seats fell to the Tories.[39]

Fitzwilliam dabbled in two other boroughs in 1812. At Lincoln, where the Monson family had a strong interest, he was consulted by the recently widowed Lady Monson in the search for a candidate. A moderate reformer of the Foxite school, John Nicholas Fazakerley, was recommended by Milton's friend Robert Price and returned. At East Retford, where the Newcastle influence had long been powerful, a rebel party among the voters approached Fitzwilliam for patronage and a candidate. The party was headed by the reform publicist T. H. B. Oldfield, who put himself forward as election manager. Fitzwilliam recommended Mrs Jane Osbaldeston's son George, known as 'Squire Osbaldeston' and a famous sportsman and huntsman of the day. He was elected, though he never cared much for parliamentary life and gave up the seat at the next dissolution. 'I did not consider it an honour at all,' he wrote: 'I thought it a great bore.' The election, however, was more costly than had been suggested, and Osbaldeston's refusal to meet Oldfield's financial demands led to a costly lawsuit in which Oldfield turned informer to allege corrupt practices against his own candidate. It was a distasteful affair, but one which marked the beginning of a political connexion at East Redford, a notoriously corrupt borough, which Fitzwilliam attempted to exploit in later years.[40]

For the most part, Fitzwilliam's interests stood up well to the election of 1812. The elections as a whole, however, were disastrous for the Whigs. 'I fear our party will be sadly cut up in the front row,' Henry Brougham wrote. Tierney, Romilly, Brougham and Horner failed to find seats. 'This has been the most unfortunate general election in my recollection,' Fitzwilliam wrote to Grey, 'because not one occurs to me in which so much talent and character, on the side of opposition, has been lost.' He attributed it to their friends not having 'as many guineas as those of the opposing candidates', though really the outcome can hardly have been unexpected in view of the opposition's sorry record since 1807. The party was more than ever forced back upon the services of its borough proprietors, and Fitzwilliam, as one of their leading electoral patrons, was appealed to on behalf of some of the dispossessed Whig candidates. Lady Bessborough had already asked him, in case George Ponsonby should secure a seat from the Duke of Devonshire at Waterford, if he would return William Lamb for Ponsonby's seat. Lamb was adrift, his seat at Portarlington having been sold to another opposition member, and in fact he failed to find a constituency. Grey wrote to Fitzwilliam on 15 November, assuring him that he realised

that Fitzwilliam's own seats were filled, but asking for his inter-
cession with some of the other Whig borough proprietors on behalf
of Lamb and some others.

In bringing in George Ponsonby and Elliot you contribute so largely to
the common interest [Grey wrote] that perhaps you could better than
any other person get together some of our friends and with the irresistible
plea of your own example, lay before them the necessity, if the party is
to be supported, both of contributing to its immediate strength by the
introduction of efficient members and of preventing the discouragement
which must be the unavoidable consequence of such losses as we have
now sustained. . . . Perhaps by some mutual arrangements after the
meeting of Parliament two or three seats might be opened.

Fitzwilliam, however, disapproved of Lamb's reproachful tone
towards the party leaders, and pointed out in reply that though 'I
certainly have such [electoral] influence, . . . it ought to be known
that influence is not appointment, and in the cases where influence
appears the greatest, a good deal of management is necessary'. Even
Peterborough, where the influence was 'most efficient', could not be
treated as a mere pocket borough to satisfy the ambitions of a young
man. As for the dispositions he had made at the general election,

I am not conscious that there has been anything of capriciousness in a
single instance. . . . Distinguished persons, suitable persons, family connexions, ancient friendships point out the causes, and make up the
mixture of which the selection ought to be composed. In an army,
privates must be found, as well as generals. . . . So must it be in a
Parliamentary party: there must be followers to support the leaders. I
do not mean by this to say that distinguished talents and characters are
not to be looked up to, considered and cherished—the whole course of
my life will demonstrate how much I have ever considered talent and
character, but only that these cannot be considered to the exclusion of
everything else.

Conscious of his own services to the party, Fitzwilliam insisted on a
free hand in the disposal of his electoral patronage.[41]
   The general election made little difference in the strength of the
parties, but if the Ministry was not strengthened, the opening of the
new Parliament found the opposition in the same disarray. Grey
thought the party's difficulties in the Commons 'such as no plan that
we can lay down can remedy', and concluded as usual that 'it is
better that I should remain where I am' [at Howick]:

In the present state of the House of Commons [he wrote to Fitzwilliam] we could not with advantage take up any public question. . . . After so long a warfare in which I have drawn upon myself the implacable enmity of the court, I feel that I have no support from the people. Can I be accused under such circumstances of any desertion of public duty, if I begin at last to wish to withdraw myself from a service in which I meet with such a return?

To Holland also on 3 January Grey confessed his despondency about the difficult issues with which the party had to deal—the Catholic question, the problem of a Regency Act in case the prince should die, with the associated question of the Whigs' relationship with the heiress presumptive, Princess Charlotte, the expiry of the East India Company's charter, the question of peace and the American war. All these provided opportunities for activity, but all were matters on which the party was not unanimous, even as to tactics.[42]

Fitzwilliam's attitude to the questions of the conduct of the war and the terms of peace was still closer to that of the Grenvilles than that of younger Whigs like Holland, whose speech for peace in March 1813 Fitzwilliam declared he had read 'with regret'. Certainly the war was 'not to be perpetuated unless France be reduced to the limits of her ancient monarchy', but he pointed out that to advocate peace which would leave her in possession of any conquered territory would damp the rising nationalist spirit in Europe, and

set up a barrier against the efforts of people striving to shake off the shackles of her despotism, and to vindicate their own independence . . . Let us come to closer quarters in negotiation before we scatter about us such sentiments—they will render France impracticable, the rest of Europe desperate and forlorn.

Grey, however, pointed out in reply that insistence on what amounted to unconditional surrender by France would only tend to prolong French resistance to the allies. 'With all the uncertainty of the success of the next campaign,' Grey wrote, '. . . I should be willing to conclude a peace, which compared with our situation a year ago would be most advantageous, though it may be one to which, with our resources entire, I should not have been willing to submit.' In the meantime, the expression of a willingness to negotiate a settlement on moderate terms would encourage the allies and the French people themselves. Only with respect to the American war which broke out in 1812 did Fitzwilliam censure the government for a too vigorous prosecution of hostilities. Here, however, he was motivated by the traditional Whig friendship towards the United States and by deference to the interests of the Yorkshire manufacturing and commercial interests who suffered from the war. He deplored the apparent desire of the government to achieve 'nothing short of the subjugation of America' and the policy of 'drubbing the Americans into submission'. Opposition to the government on this issue, he felt, would gain popularity for the Whigs.[43]

On the French war, however, Fitzwilliam still adhered to the 'hard line' of the Grenvilles since 1801. Their policy was 'to crush France completely and drive Napoleon from the throne',[44] and they advocated the legitimist cause of the restoration of the Bourbons. On this issue Grey and the Foxites as well as the radicals stood equally firmly for non-intervention in French internal affairs and the right of national self-determination. The disagreement was so fundamental that it nearly shattered the Grey–Grenville coalition in 1815, when Napoleon's return to France from Elba raised the issue in acute form. Grenville at once declared the necessity of 'immediate and vigorous exertion' by Britain to renew the alliances of 1814, resume the war and depose Napoleon again. Though assuring Grey that he had no intention of becoming a supporter of government on this issue, Grenville insisted that he must declare his views even at the cost of a public difference with Grey. Grey, while agreeing that Napoleon was not to be trusted, argued that Britain should not go to war merely to depose him from the French throne. Only a *defensive* war was legitimate. Only if Napoleon made aggressive moves towards Britain would she be justified in taking up arms against him, and if this placed her at a tactical disadvantage she should more than make up for that by having a juster cause to uphold.

Grenville reiterated his views to Fitzwilliam on 30 March 1815. Napoleon, to him, was a military tyrant whose power was based and fed only on military aggression: the choice before Britain was not of war or peace, but whether to fight now or later, at a time of her or of Napoleon's choosing. Fitzwilliam replied that his opinions 'accord completely with those you have expressed'. It gave him 'heartfelt regret' to differ from Grey, 'but my creed is that suspension is certain destruction, immediate activity the only chance of salvation'.[45] Fitzwilliam and William Elliot, who was closely in touch with Grenville, were, indeed, even more dogmatic in their attitude than Grenville himself. Lady Grey wrote on 3 April of Fitz-

william's 'sad infatuation', and at the end of June Grey, looking
back over the episode, declared that Fitzwilliam and Elliot were
'unfortunately the persons most active and efficient in urging Grenville to adopt the part he took; their language was exactly that of
Burke at the beginning of the revolution, and they used it with a
zeal and assiduity that was but too successful'. The question was
indeed one on which, as William Lamb remarked,

the ancient difference about the accursed French revolution, the old
wound. again broke out: the consequence has been old friends have
again taken opposite sides, from which it might be presumed that the
difference was not confined to one subject of policy, but that it diffused
itself generally over every political principle, and was in point of fact.
a general breakup of political connexion and friendship.

Only Waterloo saved the Whigs from that fate and enabled Lamb to
be 'confident . . . that, this subject at rest, we shall again unite, hand
and heart, in the common cause of a well-constituted administration
at home'. Grenville had, in fact, offered some kind of compromise at
the end of March, suggesting that there should be no 'premature
declaration in Parliament', and that they should concur in advocating
only, for the time being, 'immediate and vigorous preparation' and
a close accord with our continental allies. Grey, too, hoped that
circumstances would force Napoleon to be pacific, and believed that
Britain should avoid precipitate action. 'My forbearance with respect
to G[renville],' he told Holland, 'certainly had the effect of preventing his holding any violent language, of keeping back the expression
of his opinions for a long time, [and] of preserving the hope of a
reunion.' If, however, the war had gone on, there would have been
little hope of avoiding a complete breach. The crisis in Europe passed
quickly enough to prevent it. The Whigs agreed at a party meeting
on 6 April not to oppose the Prince Regent's message urging the
strengthening of the army and a closer concert with the allies. Whitbread refused to toe the party line and proposed an amendment, but
was supported by only 37 votes. Grey and Grenville maintained
silence in the Lords until the end of May, when the opposition
moved amendments in both Houses against the renewal of the coalition against France. The Grenvilles and Fitzwilliam's members
supported the government.[46]

The breach was not wholly healed by Waterloo, for the Whigs
still disagreed over the peace terms. Grenville and Fitzwilliam sup-

ported the Bourbon restoration, while the liberal wing argued that
it amounted to the imposition by external force of a regime totally
without support in France itself. These disagreements continued to
plague the Whigs into the 1816 session, when the question was again
broached of an amendment to the address. Fitzwilliam deprecated
any amendment, on the grounds that, whatever its precise subject,
it might imply 'the imputation of dissenting from the address
generally', and thus contesting the peace terms. Tierney argued that
some amendment was wished for by the party in general, and that
it would be impossible to avoid one; it was desirable, therefore, to
find a form of words 'for which all our friends could cordially vote,
and by the adoption of which any discussion which might lead to a
difference of opinion would be at least postponed'. In the event,
when Tierney's mild amendment was proposed in the Commons by
Thomas Brand, Milton opposed it, though speaking against large
military establishments and the continuation of the property tax. In
the Lords no amendment was moved, and Grenville declared his
hearty support of the address. Holland despaired of agreement with
Grenville and Fitzwilliam and feared a continuation of the split on
the question of the army of occupation in France (which was necessary in order to maintain Louis XVIII on the throne). Grey admitted
that Grenville's and Fitzwilliam's opinions were 'very stiff' on the
Bourbons, but thought nothing in the debates precluded future co-
operation, and was encouraged by Milton's tone of hostility towards
the government in the Commons. Grenville in fact was willing to
co-operate in opposing the expense of the maintenance of a large
army and of forces of occupation in France and on 7 February he
produced a draft amendment to that effect which was approved by
both Grey and Fitzwilliam.[47] 'To the principles professed and doctrines laid down I subscribe most distinctly,' Fitzwilliam assured
Grenville, 'and I am decidedly of opinion that present circumstances,
and the complexion of the times call imperiously for such a profession of faith.' He expressed reservations on certain points, and
expressed his view (contrary to that of Grey and the liberals) that
the army of occupation should be seen as necessary to maintain the
Bourbon regime rather than as a force to guarantee the payment of
the French war indemnity. The debate in both Houses passed off
sufficiently well, Elliot striking the only discordant note by arguing
in the Commons (as Fitzwilliam no doubt would have done in the
Lords, had he attended) that the maintenance of the hereditary

succession in France was the best guarantee of a return to a moral order. The debate and division, Grey wrote to Fitzwilliam, gave him

a satisfaction which it would not be easy to express. . . . I look forward with more comfort than I thought I ever should do again to anything in politics to a cordial and vigorous co-operation during the remainder of the session on those points on which we agree; to enforce a system of economy, to reduce unnecessary and expensive and dangerous establishments and to bring back the government to the true principles of the constitution.[48]

On the issues mentioned by Grey, Fitzwilliam had no hesitation in co-operating heartily against the maintenance of large establishments and the continuance in peacetime of the property tax. 'Our first duty to our own country,' he assured Grey in December 1816, 'is to reduce establishments and to retrench expense.' He was even willing to see the army of occupation withdrawn from France in December 1816, on the grounds that the Bourbon regime was now soundly established. With the removal of this divergence of views, he declared, there now remained 'not . . . a shade of difference between our opinions upon the whole subject of our foreign policy'.[49] On the property tax, too, he threw himself ardently into the campaign to rouse the country. Yorkshire and Northamptonshire held county meetings and produced petitions, as did even Higham Ferrers. In March 1816 the property tax was defeated by 238 votes to 201, though as much because of the spontaneous feeling of the middle classes in time of economic depression as because of Whig political organisation. The 1816 session closed on an optimistic note for the Whigs.

The next session, however, was to be less propitious. The government's defeat over the property tax had no political repercussions, and in 1817 the spectre of parliamentary reform reappeared to trouble Whig minds. Here was a far more fundamental issue on which Fitzwilliam was still at variance with many of the party. Back in February 1816, in rejoicing over the end of their disagreements over the peace settlement, and urging co-operation on retrenchment, Grey had mentioned the need 'to bring back the government to the true principles of the Constitution'. His letter went on to declare that opposition could hardly look for much positive success, since after twenty-five years of war the people were now insensitive to the idea of liberty, and had been 'trained to habits of submission', while the country gentlemen cared more about getting patronage for their sons and connexions than for 'the feelings which formerly belonged to their station'. It was easy to see in this despondent language the germ of the argument that parliamentary reform was needed to reconstitute the Commons as an effective check upon government. By the end of 1816, too, continued distress in the manufacturing districts, the recession of trade to the continent, and the prolonged agricultural depression had given rise to renewed popular demands for reform. In December Grey, attempting to define the issues on which the party should operate, mentioned to Fitzwilliam '1 change of foreign policy – 2 reduction of expense – 3 Catholic emancipation' as 'the three great points which I feel myself bound to maintain'. But, he went on, it was impossible to shrink from also facing the issue of parliamentary reform, much as he would prefer to keep silent on it at present. It would be 'forced upon us', and he would be compelled to declare his continued support of a moderate reform, though his views were 'a good deal tempered by the experience of the last twenty-five years' and by no means so far reaching as in his 1797 plan. The only scheme he would now support would be 'one of a much more limited and gradual operation', and he would by no means propose even that as a *sine qua non*, or even as a remedy for the current distress. Nevertheless 'I have the pain of thinking that there must be some difference between us. You will see that I am moderate enough to be denounced by Cobbett, Hunt & Co. as a traitor, though not moderate enough to reconcile your opinion to mine'.[50] Fitzwilliam dismissed the question off-handedly. 'Mr Hunt & Co. have already done its business,' he declared. 'I am not in much alarm upon the subject.' A riot at Sheffield, concerted with the Spa Fields meeting in London, had passed off with feeble support. He thought that the public cared little for the cause, which he believed was supported by a mere gang of demagogues and extremists. As for the view that the Commons did not adequately represent the public, he regarded the defeat of the property tax as 'proof incontestable' that it did.

Others were less secure in their confidence. Grey was alarmed by the general symptoms of 'violent irritation and discontent', and feared that 'Burdett and his adherents' were pushing matters to 'a contest between the Crown and the mob', which would alienate the supporters of moderate reform from the cause in the interests of security. It was partly to counteract this development that he wished to have an amendment to the address which should mention 'a *moderate* reform of Parliament'. The task of framing one which would appeal to all sections of the opposition was difficult. It seemed to be intended, wrote William Elliot, to find a form of words that would satisfy both Burdett and the anti-reformers at the same time —'a very dubious policy', as he remarked. Tierney, Elliot reported, was impressed with the support for parliamentary reform among the lower orders, and wished to see the opposition take the lead of the moderate reformers. Grenville, however, continued 'a decided enemy to parliamentary reform in *any degree*, and entirely concurs with us in thinking that any admission whatever on the subject would be only opening the way to the wildest innovations'. At the meeting held at George Ponsonby's house on 21 January to draw up an amendment Elliot firmly declared that 'no influence of friendship or party connection' could induce him to support even an indirect or ambiguous reference to reform in any public document. His declaration, delivered, Tierney wrote, 'in a state of more than usual alarm', proved to be superfluous. Grey had decided that any official mention of reform would be inadvisable, and urged his friends that it should be left to individuals to give their views on it as they wished. The amendment was concerned only with popular distress and retrenchment, and demanded an enquiry into the general state of the country.[51]

The state of the country was, in itself, however, the cause of new divisions in the opposition's ranks. On 28 January the Prince Regent's carriage was struck by a stone or an airgun pellet on the way back from the opening of Parliament. 'He has been hissed, hooted and pelted,' Fitzwilliam wrote to Milton.

. . . In answer to our professions of loyalty and attachment he has expressed how highly he estimates the proofs of these our feelings, and therefore that he feels no other sentiment on the occasion but deep regret at the violation of the laws and the breach of good order. Minds differently constituted might perhaps under similar circumstances have lamented that they could not show themselves to their subjects without being hiss'd, hooted and pelted.[52]

Despite these sardonic reflections, Fitzwilliam shared the common alarm at the evidence of further disturbances taking place throughout the industrial areas and in London, while public meetings, clubs and societies were demanding parliamentary reform. The government

decided to set up secret committees in each House to investigate
these alleged conspiracies against the constitution. The Whigs were
faced with a dilemma like that of 1793–4, when similar tactics had
been used by Pitt to frighten the alarmist Whigs into a breach with
Fox. Fitzwilliam and Grenville were nominated to the committee in
the Lords, and Milton, Elliot, Lamb and George Ponsonby to that in
the Commons. Predictably, the reports, presented to the Houses on
18 and 19 February, declared that there was no doubt of a traitorous
conspiracy organised in the metropolis and supported in many
industrial areas, for the overthrow of the government and constitution and 'a general plunder and division of property' to the advantage
of the 'lower orders'. The meetings at Spa Fields in November and
December had been designed, the Lords' committee alleged, to promote actual insurrection, while Hampden Clubs, Union Clubs and
Spencean Societies in many parts of the country had helped to spread
disaffection for the same ends. Speeches had been made against the
social order, the distribution of property, religion and morals, frequently followed by 'profane seditious songs and parodies of parts
of the liturgy' in which the assembled crowds had joined. Further
measures, it was declared, must be taken to preserve peace and
order. On the day following the presentation of the Lords' committee's report Sidmouth moved the suspension of Habeas Corpus.
Grey opposed the second reading of the Bill on the 24th, and Holland
and Wellesley voted with him. Fitzwilliam and Grenville voted for
the suspension, but in the Commons the large majority of the party
opposed it, Milton differing from his father in voting with them on
the grounds that insufficient cause had been shown for the measure.[53]
A few days later the Seditious Meetings Bill, to prevent the subversive activities of the clubs and societies, was introduced into the
Commons and it passed through all its stages in both houses by the
end of March.

Fitzwilliam's support for the policy of repression once more
seemed to indicate a split on the lines of the 1790s. When Grey
summoned a meeting of those members who seemed likely to oppose
the suspension Fitzwilliam was not included. 'It is no small mortification to me to think,' he wrote, 'that when you are collecting your
friends about you, I am not one of the summoned: but I feel the
misfortune, that upon all subjects arising out of such circumstances
as have given rise to the present call, there is an original difference
of opinion that keeps us asunder.' He could only hope 'that this will

be the last occasion' and that 'the principles which lead to our difference of opinion are on the wane, that they will die away and be no longer subjects of discussion'; and he stressed that on other issues 'our principles are the same, and we should act together even did not mutual esteem and affection ensure our co-operation'. On the Seditious Meetings Bill, he had written to Charlotte to say that although he approved of the Bill as a temporary measure, 'I shall be sorry indeed should it pass *permanently*—it will operate an essential alteration in the constitution'. Fitzwilliam's alarmism was not, like Grenville's, untempered by fundamental adherence to Whig principles.[54]

Fitzwilliam's support of the suspension of Habeas Corpus was short-lived. It was first weakened by news from Yorkshire early in March that his friends there generally supported Milton's opposition to suspension, on constitutional grounds. A correspondent from Leeds also pointed out that a numerous meeting organised by 'the friends of rational liberty', 'the most respectable and unanimous that ever met in this borough' had met to address the regent on his escape on the 28 January. It's tone reflected the 'genuine spirit of attachment to the best principles of our constitution' which was 'extensively prevalent' throughout the area. The meeting had originated among the local supporters of the Whig interest, but the address was approved of by all parties, despite some purely political opposition from the mayor and corporation. This reassuring news brought Fitzwilliam to the West Riding to make his own investigations, the result of which was a declaration that 'I was led to think nothing beyond ordinary powers [of the law] was called for . . . and therefore (whatever I might have thought before) that the prolongation of the suspension was not then necessary'. His new opinion was confirmed by further news from the Riding three months later. Early in May news reached a Sheffield magistrate of an intended rising in the manufacturing districts of Lancashire, Yorkshire, Derbyshire and Nottinghamshire, timed for early June. Seven alleged leaders of the plot were arrested and sent to London for examination. Information then leaked out of a proposed meeting of delegates from several West Riding towns at Thornhill Edge, near Sheffield, three days before the rising was due to start. The yeomanry were waiting for the delegates on the appointed day, and the eleven who appeared were arrested. Fitzwilliam, who was in London, at once wrote to his Deputy Lieutenant, Sir Francis Wood, to approve

of the vigorous measures that had been taken. He had voted for the
suspension of Habeas Corpus, he wrote, because

to my sorrow I considered the power of arbitrary detention absolutely
necessary considering the temper in which I found the people, and here I
think the case has occurred when mischief may be prevented by the
means which that measure affords—if the principal agitators are kept
out of the way, and restrained from inflaming the minds of the people,
their minds will cool again, and soften down into a state suitable to the
social relations of life.[55]

Matters soon appeared in a different light. Among those arrested
at Thornhill Edge was Oliver, a government agent posing as the
delegate from a revolutionary group in London, who appeared to
have been the moving spirit behind the whole scheme. Suspicion
was aroused when he alone was quickly released, his ten fellow
conspirators being sent to Wakefield for interrogation, and on 14
June a report in the *Leeds Mercury* disclosed the extent of his
activities. Oliver, it was alleged, had appeared in Dewsbury, Wakefield and other parts of the West Riding in April attempting to raise
support for a supposed insurrection in the metropolis. The disclosures, Fitzwilliam wrote to Milton, created a sensation. He did not
believe that Oliver had been sent by the government deliberately to
foster an insurrection, but he was convinced that his activities had
contributed materially to what had happened and that without his
active inducement no activity would have taken place. There was
some rioting near Huddersfield on the 8th, but Fitzwilliam declared
that the episode had proved to him 'the insignificant number of those
disposed to mischief' and

the soundness of all above the few miscreants who are ripe for mischief.
... These circumstances must cause a change in my opinion respecting the
measures necessary for the occasion. I see no cause for the continuance
of greater powers than the ordinary ones, because I see no chance of
disturbance if the people are left to themselves.

He announced to Milton that he would oppose the further suspension
of Habeas Corpus after the expiry of the current Act on 1 July. Fitzwilliam did not attend the Lords' debate on the second Suspension
Bill in June, but Milton, opposing it in the Commons, referred to
the 'trembling hand and aching heart' with which he had opposed
the first Bill because 'it was the only time he had ever had the misfortune to differ from one to whose opinions all his respect was

due'; now, however, 'that difference . . . was removed. . . . That person (Earl Fitzwilliam) had made a strict investigation into the situation of those parts of the country: and the result was, that he was perfectly satisfied that there was no ground for the present measure'.[56]

Fitzwilliam thus found his way back into harmony with Grey and the main body of the Whigs. Grenville, however, declared that Fitzwilliam's information about Oliver did not change his views on the propriety of prolonging the suspension. 'I may possibly be too much of an alarmist,' he confessed, 'but when I consider the character of the times, and the circumstances of the country, I cannot but think that where so much is at hazard it is better to err on the side of too much precaution.' The issue of repression rather than that of reform now determined the alignment of the parties. Whereas at the beginning of 1817 it had seemed that the Grenvilles might carry Fitzwilliam, Elliot and Milton with them against Grey and the liberal Whigs, now Fitzwilliam and his associates aligned themselves firmly with Grey once more, leaving the Grenvilles isolated. By the end of the 1817 session, the junction between the Whigs and the Grenvilles was effectively broken,[57] and it was Fitzwilliam's repudiation of repression which finally drew the line between them. Though still as firm an opponent of parliamentary reform as ever, he remained at heart a Whig of the eighteenth century, who, while advocating the maintenance of an ordered and deferential society, also valued the liberty of the subject and the connexion between the party and the people. Correspondence between Grenville and Fitzwilliam, as between Grenville and Grey, virtually ceased after this time, while the deaths in 1817 and 1818 of Horner, George Ponsonby and William Elliot, all formerly links between the two groups, helped to dissolve the personal ties between them. Politically the cord was broken over the continuation of the Habeas Corpus suspension and the activities of Oliver in Yorkshire in the early summer of 1817. The improvement in the economic situation which set in about the same time removed much of the sting from popular agitation for the time being and, as Elliot agreed in December, contributed 'to the preservation of internal tranquillity'.[58] It contributed also to the reassurance of Fitzwilliam and the consequent isolation of the Grenvilles, who virtually seceded from opposition by placing themselves on a separate bench in the Commons at the beginning of the 1818 session. From this time until their coalition with the

M

Ministry in 1821 they operated as an independent 'third party', increasingly moving towards the government.

The cutting of the tie with the Grenvilles reduced the disparities between the furthest sections of the opposition, but it did nothing to unify the still quarrelsome Whig factions. The death of George Ponsonby in July 1817, despite his ineffectiveness as a party leader, was a further blow to the party. 'We considered his death a public calamity,' Fitzwilliam wrote. The search for his successor again exposed their disunities. Milton was one of the possible candidates, though, like most of the others, an unwilling one. Lady Spencer suggested the role to him at the beginning of July, and begged: 'Let no selfish considerations prevent you from manifesting this virtuous devotion to the common welfare'. Milton professed his inadequacy for the post, while his friend Robert Price warned him that it would ruin his health and that Brougham and his friends would be ungovernable; 'he would often profess to follow you', Price wrote, '[but] . . . try to make you responsible for his mad schemes'. Brougham, now the ablest debater in the opposition ranks, was unacceptable to his colleagues because of what Lady Spencer called 'his total failure in judgement, his entire want of discretion and his absence of all steadiness in political principle'.[59] In the end Tierney was virtually drafted by the rank and file in the Commons, a choice, Fitzwilliam wrote, 'the most proper, and indeed the only one that can with propriety be made'. He found the terms of the request, however, a little ominous. The letter to Tierney used the phrase 'for carrying into effect our views of the constitution', words which, Fitzwilliam wrote, might 'be construed to mean nothing, . . . in the true Burdettite fashion', but which laid open the way for future disagreement as to what meaning they ought to have, and which might be interpreted as an indication that reform was to be a party question. 'Let the object of the party be confined to the single object of resistance to those measures of government, resistance to which has been the cause of that popularity, which has been experienced by the opposition during the present elections,' Fitzwilliam wrote, 'and which if steadily pursued will lead more and more to increase of power and influence.'[60] There was little realistic hope, however, of a strong, united and purposeful opposition while its leaders either continued to profess indifference to politics or tried to avoid commitment on the only positive issues on which there might be any hope of presenting to the public a distinctive political

image. 1817 not only marked the freeing of the Whigs from the
dead weight of Grenvillite conservatism. It also confirmed their continued isolation from general public support and their lack of a real
programme for the future.

Notes

[1] R. Sinclair to Fitzwilliam, 31 May 1796: F 34i. For a detailed account
of the Yorkshire elections of 1806 and 1807 see my article in *Northern
History*, ii (1967), pp. 62–90.

[2] Fitzwilliam to Grenville, 20 October, and reply, 28th (*Fortescue MSS*,
viii, pp. 392–3, 400). The 'State of the Canvass' (E 213a) showed 9,056
promises for Fawkes.

[3] Fawkes to Howick, 23 November [1806] (Grey MSS); E. Baines, *Life
of Edward Baines* (1851), p. 63; Fawkes to Fitzwilliam, 25 April 1807 (F
42a); Fitzwilliam to Laurence, 29 April [1807] (N, x515/2); to Baldwin,
[1 May 1807] (N); Wilberforce, *Life*, iii, p. 315.

[4] *York Herald*, 23 June and 6 June 1807; *The Times*, 5 June.

[5] *Northern History*, loc. cit., pp. 84–5; Fitzwilliam to Grenville, 19 May
1807 (B.M., Grenville MSS); Wilberforce, *Life*, iii, p. 329. On the state of
opinion in the clothing districts see also R. G. Wilson, *Gentlemen
Merchants*, pp. 90–109 and 169–71.

[6] *Northern History*, loc. cit., pp. 86–90.

[7] W. Adam to Fitzwilliam, 13 June 1807 (F 32e); Laurence to Fitzwilliam
[May 1807], F 48/23; *The Times*, 5 June 1807.

[8] For a detailed account of the Malton elections of 1807 and 1808 see
my article 'Earl Fitzwilliam and Malton', *Eng. Hist. Review*, lxxx (1965),
pp. 51–69, where the quotations that follow are to be found. The total
cost to Fitzwilliam of the two elections was over £1,800.

[9] Sinclair to Fitzwilliam, 20 May and 17 May 1802 (F 35g); 26 April
1807 (E 170–1); R. Croft to Fitzwilliam, 4 May 1807 (E 177). The polling
figures were Milner 1454, Sykes 1316, Dundas 967.

[10] 'Letter to several gentlemen of Hull on Lord Burford's retreat, May
1796' and Burford's address to the electors of Hull, 16 May 1796 (F 115e);
T. Scatcherd to Fitzwilliam, 3 March 1802; Denison to Fitzwilliam, 7
July (F 36a).

[11] Grenville to S. Thornton, 28 August 1806 (B.M., Grenville MSS);
Thornton to Fitzwilliam, 20 and 25 October; R. Sykes to Fitzwilliam, '2
o'clock Friday' (E 210); Fitzwilliam to Grenville, 2 November (*Fortescue
MSS*, viii, p. 420); D. Sykes to Fitzwilliam, 13 December, and R. Sykes,
14 December (N); R. Sykes to Fitzwilliam, 28 April (E 171/4) and [4 May
1807] (N); Denison to Milton, 20 April (E 171/2).

[12] Windham to Fitzwilliam, 8 May 1807; Althorp to Fitzwilliam, 16
November 1806 (N); Aspinall, *Corresp. of George, Prince of Wales*, vi, p.
147. Grenville calculated that in the new House the government would
have 360 supporters, opposition 210, doubtful 88. W. H. Fremantle
estimated that the government would divide 280, opposition 150–60
(*Court and Cabinets*, iv, pp. 173, 190).

13 Grenville to Grey, 20 and 23 March 1807; Fitzwilliam to Howick [7 April 1807] (Grey MSS). For the state and activities of the opposition between 1807 and 1812 see M. Roberts, *The Whig Party, 1807–1812*.

14 Grenville to Fitzwilliam, 26 November 1807; Windham to Fitzwilliam, 24 November (F 32e); Fitzwilliam to Holland, 13 December 1807 (B.M. Add. MS 51593, ff. 36–7); Ponsonby to Grey, 9 December 1807 (Grey MSS); Holland to Fitzwilliam [13 December 1807] (F 32e).

15 *Corresp. of George, Prince of Wales*, VI, pp. 16–17, 144–5, 245–6. See M. Roberts, *op. cit.*, ch. I, for a full account of these negotiations.

16 Holland to Fitzwilliam, 16 December 1807 (F 32e); *Corresp. of George, Prince of Wales*, VI, p. 244; Fitzwilliam to Grenville, 6 December 1807 (B.M., Grenville MSS); Fitzwilliam to Laurence, 21 December (N). Milton's speech on the address, 21 January 1808, deplored the warlike tone of the speech and hoped that Ministers would pursue all opportunities of negotiation (*Parl. Deb.*, X, 47).

17 Fitzwilliam to Grenville, 6 December 1807 (B.M., Grenville MSS). The British expedition landed in Denmark on 16 August. The city was bombarded on 4–6 September and capitulated on the 7th (Fremantle, II, pp. 214–16).

18 The opposition divided 108 on Ponsonby's motion on Copenhagen on 3 February, and seventy-three on Whitbread's motion, 8 February (*Parl. Deb.*, X, 310–11, 397).

19 Fitzwilliam to Grey, 22 July and 7 December [1808] (Grey MSS).

20 Grenville to Fitzwilliam, 9 January 1809 (F 32e), and reply, 12th (B.M., Grenville MSS); Ponsonby to Grey, 2 January (Grey MSS).

21 Fitzwilliam to Milton [1810] (N). Milton had declared on 15 March 1809 that though he did not accept all Mrs Clarke's evidence, enough had been disclosed to show that some corruption had been taking place, and that the Duke of York should not remain Commander-in-Chief (*Parl. Deb.*, XIII, 540–5).

22 Milton had declared himself against parliamentary reform but in favour of the correction of abuses such as ministerial interference in elections (11 May 1809: *Parl. Deb.*, XIV, 501). On Brand's motion, 'he thought that any alteration in the constitution would be full of danger' (*ibid.*, XVII, 137–40).

23 Fitzwilliam to Grey, 30 September 1809 (Grey MSS), and to Grenville, 30 September (B.M., Grenville MSS).

24 Grey to Fitzwilliam, 26 September, 1 October, 6 October; Grenville to Fitzwilliam, 29 September, 6 October; Lonsdale to Fitzwilliam, 28 September (F 32d); Fitzwilliam to Grey, 30 September (Grey MSS), to Grenville, 30 September and 1 October (B.M., Grenville MSS); Grey to Grenville, 20 October (*Fortescue* MSS, IX, pp. 329–31); Althorp to Milton, 7 October 1809 (N); Grey to Viscount Ponsonby, 3 November (Grey MSS); Plumer Ward, I, pp. 259, 269; G. Ponsonby to Grey, 9 December (Grey MSS).

25 Grenville to Buckingham, 17 December 1809 (*Court and Cabinets*, IV, pp. 404–6); letters in *Fortescue MSS*, IX, pp. 376–7, 385–6, 425–6,

429–33; Fitzwilliam to Grey, 12 January 1810 (Grey MSS), and reply, 13th; T. Grenville to Fitzwilliam, 12 January 1810 (F 32e).

26 *Corresp. of George, Prince of Wales*, VI, p. 354.

27 R. Ward to Lonsdale, 2 December 1810; Lonsdale MSS.

28 *Corresp. of George, Prince of Wales*, VII, pp. 60–2.

29 Grenville to Fitzwilliam, 10 November 1810 (N), Fitzwilliam to Grey [17 November 1810] and 'Thursday' [January 1811] (Grey MSS); *Parl. Deb.*, XVIII, 747.

30 Colchester, *Diary*, II, p. 307; Plumer Ward, I, p. 333. The prince's offers were said to be evidence that his mind was much occupied with thoughts of Fox.

31 *Corresp. of George, Prince of Wales*, VII, pp. 130–5.

32 Elliot to Fitzwilliam, 2 February 1811 (N); *Corresp. of George, Prince of Wales*, VII, pp. 208–9; Fitzwilliam to Grenville, 3 February 1811 (B.M., Grenville MSS).

33 *Corresp. of George, Prince of Wales*, VIII, pp. 5–11.

34 *Parl. Deb.*, XX, 470; Fitzwilliam to Lady Fitzwilliam, n.d. (N, x515); see also *Fortescue MSS*, X, 141–6.

35 Fitzwilliam to Grenville, 29 December 1811 and 15 January [1812] (B.M., Grenville MSS); *Parl. Deb.*, XXI, 408–12, 477–8. A similar motion in the Commons by Morpeth (4 February) was lost by 229–135. Canning and his friends voted with the government (see *Corresp. of George, Prince of Wales*, VIII, pp. 302–16).

36 *Ibid.*, p. 313; Grey to Holland, 27 October 1811 (copy); Fitzwilliam to Grey, 16 February [1812] (Grey MSS). Plumer Ward, I, p. 421, reports gossip that Fitzwilliam was to be Duke of Rockingham.

37 Fitzwilliam to Grey, *loc. cit.*; *Parl. Deb.*, XXII, 107, 245, 320, 500–1, XXIII, 4, 591, 733. The petition of the Yorkshire clothiers was sent to Fitzwilliam on 24 March 1812 in two boxes, each roll being 40 yards long and with a total of nearly 17,000 signatures (T. W. Tottie to Fitzwilliam, 24 March, J. Gant to Fitzwilliam, 24 March; F 110).

38 Correspondence between Lascelles and Wortley, September–October 1812, vol. in Harewood MSS; Tottie and Richardson to Bowns and Newman, 29 September 1812 (E 213a), and other correspondence in E 213 and G 83; Milton to Fitzwilliam, 17 and 22 October 1812 (N).

39 Fitzwilliam to Mrs Osbaldeston, September [1812] (F 42–29); Plumer to Fitzwilliam, 7 and 14 August 1812 (F 83a); Fitzwilliam to Grenville, 18 September 1812 (B.M., Grenville MSS).

40 Correspondence concerning Lincoln in F 108, F 42a and F 78b; Fitzwilliam to Grey, 23 and 28 August [1812] (Grey MSS); Grey to Fitzwilliam, 25 August 1812 (N); on Retford, J. Parker to Grenville, 3 October 1812, and Mrs J. Osbaldeston to Grenville, 2 October (B.M., Grenville MSS); Mrs Osbaldeston to Fitzwilliam, [2 July] and 3 July 1813; Oldfield to Fitzwilliam, 15 August 1814 and 30 May 1815 (F 83b); other letters in F 41, F 42a. On George Osbaldeston see *Squire Osbaldeston: his Autobiography*, ed. E. D. Cuming (1927 edn), pp. 15, 33–4.

41 Brougham to Milton, Thursday [1812] (N, x525); Fitzwilliam to Grey, 18 November 1812 (Grey MSS); Lady Bessborough to Fitzwilliam,

30 September [1812] (F 127); Grey to Fitzwilliam, 15 November 1812 (N), and to Holland, 21 November 1812 (copy); Fitzwilliam to Grey, 18 November (Grey MSS).

42 Grey to Holland, 25 October, 14 November 1812, 3 January 1813 (copies) (Grey MSS), to Fitzwilliam, 22 November 1812 (N).

43 Fitzwilliam to Grey [4 April 1813] (Grey MSS), and reply, 9 April (N); Fitzwilliam to Grey, 22 October 1814 (Grey MSS).

44 A. Mitchell, *The Whigs in Opposition, 1815-30* (Oxford, 1967), p. 81.

45 Grenville to Grey, 28 March 1815, and reply, 30 March (copy) (Grey MSS); Grenville to Fitzwilliam, 30 March (F 32f); Fitzwilliam to Grenville, 2 April (B.M., Grenville MSS).

46 Lady Grey to Lady Ponsonby, 3 April 1815; Grey to Holland, 26 June (copy) (Grey MSS); Lamb to Fitzwilliam, 30 June (N); Grenville to Grey, 31 March; Grey to Grenville, 1 April, and to Holland, 26 June (copies) (Grey MSS); *Parl. Deb.*, xxx, 349-53, 417-63, xxxi, 316-71, 395, 448. Milton spoke against the opposition's amendment, which was defeated by 92 to 331 (*ibid.*, 446-7).

47 Tierney to Fitzwilliam, 26 January 1816 (N); *Parl. Deb.*, xxxii, 42-5 (1 February); Fitzwilliam to Grey, 3 February 1816; Grey to Lady Holland, 5 February 1816 (copy) (Grey MSS). Grey remarked to Holland on the 7th that Grenville's mind had been 'perverted by his Bourbon mania' but that he would be firm in resisting 'large armies and increased expense' (*ibid.*).

48 Fitzwilliam to Grenville, 9 February 1816 (B.M., Grenville MSS); *Parl. Deb.*, xxii, 763-8; Grey to Fitzwilliam, 25 February 1816 (N).

49 Fitzwilliam to Grey, 17 December 1816 (Grey MSS).

50 Grey to Fitzwilliam, 25 February and 13 December 1816 (N). Writing to Holland on 8 December, Grey added a fourth requirement, 'a moderate and gradual parliamentary reform, not a *sine qua non*, but to be supported' (Grey MSS, copy).

51 Fitzwilliam to Grey, 17 December 1816 (Grey MSS); to Milton [March 1816] (N); Grey to Lady Holland, 6 October 1816; to Holland, 23 November (copies, Grey MSS); Elliot to Fitzwilliam, 20 January 1817 (N); Mitchell, *op. cit.*, pp. 102-3.

52 Fitzwilliam to Milton [29 January 1817]: (N, x515).

53 Mitchell, p. 104. Reports of committees, *Parl. Deb.*, xxxv, 411-19 and 438-47; debates *ibid.*, 491, 573-86, 759. Dudley North said he thought 'it was a trick to split us'. Milton did not vote against the third reading on 28 February. He told Charles Pelham that though he had voted against the Bill, he would support other Bills 'to put down the dangerous clubs, and to quiet the country' (C. Pelham to Lord Yarborough, 28 February 1817, enclosed in Yarborough to Fitzwilliam, 5 March: N).

54 Fitzwilliam to Grey [23 February 1817] (Grey MSS). Grey had written on the 22nd to inform Fitzwilliam on the meeting and to express his 'pain . . . in differing with you on any particular measure' (N); Fitzwilliam to Lady Fitzwilliam, 'Friday night' (N, x515).

55 Sir F. Wood to Milton, 4 March, Fitzwilliam to Sir F. Wood, 26 April (Hickleton MSS, A 4. 19. 5) and 9 June [1817] and other corres-

pondence and notes of interrogations (*ibid.*, A 4. 9); Tottie to Fitzwilliam, 1 March (F 83c).

[56] Fitzwilliam to Grenville, 19 June 1817 (B.M., Grenville MSS); to Milton, 19 June (N); *Parl. Deb.*, XXXVI, 1016 and 1029–30.

[57] Grenville to Fitzwilliam, 23 June 1817 (N); Grey to Holland, 28 January 1818 (copy, Grey MSS): Mitchell, p. 109.

[58] Elliot to Fitzwilliam, 19 December 1817 (N).

[59] Fitzwilliam to Grey, 9 November 1817 (Grey MSS); Price to Milton, 18 October 1817 (G 83); Lady Spencer to Milton, 16 July 1817; Althorp to Milton, 21 March 1818 (N).

[60] Fitzwilliam to Grey, 18 July 1818 (Grey MSS).

CHAPTER ELEVEN

Peterloo and reform: the last years 1819–33

Fitzwilliam's commitment to the 'cause of order' in the years of the French revolutionary wars sprang from a lasting belief in the framework of established society. His opposition to speculative ideas of parliamentary reform was strong and persistent. Yet in 1819 he was dismissed from the Lord Lieutenancy of the West Riding for joining in the censure on the Manchester magistrates for the affair of 'Peterloo', when a crowd assembled to hear a political speech by the radical orator Henry Hunt was ridden down by a troop of yeomanry cavalry. The dismissal appears at first sight ironic. Fitzwilliam himself had commanded a yeomanry troop which had dispersed by equally forcible means at least one gathering at Sheffield in 1795. In 1812 a food riot at Sheffield was similarly broken up by a charge from the Hussars, with Fitzwilliam's approval. He had not changed his views by 1819, and his first reaction to the news from Manchester was appropriately cautious. 'I see they are making much of what has happened in Manchester, in London,' he wrote on 24 August, eight days after the event. 'No doubt much may be said against interfering with a legal meeting . . . but circumstances may arise to call for the intervention of the magistrates even on such occasions, and to be impartial, one must hear what they have to say for themselves.'[1] It was only gradually, as he came to realise the dangers which the Peterloo affair presented to the cause of order and liberty, and even more, the political opportunities it offered to his party, that he decided to take the lead in protesting against the government's involvement in the Manchester affair.

Fitzwilliam's martyrdom in the cause of civil liberties over Peterloo was partly, therefore, a deliberate political one. Only nine days after the incident Grey laid down the party's strategy in a letter to Brougham. It was to condemn Hunt and the firebrand radicals, but to declare that in approving the action of the magistrates the government was following an established policy of suppressing constitutional liberties. In this way the Whigs might persuade 'all moderate and reasonable men' to think of them as 'their natural leaders and protectors', and attract all but extremist support away from the radicals. In September Grey commended the use of county meetings to make clear the identity between Whig policy and the popular liberties and to steal the thunder of the radical orators who claimed to speak for public opinion. This policy would capture the 'middle ground' as a vantage point for a Whig revival. A county meeting in Yorkshire, wrote Walter Fawkes, would be 'a healing measure, and if we identify ourselves with the people . . . it will teach them to look . . . to the enlightened and landed aristocracy of the country'. 'It is of the utmost importance,' Milton wrote to Sir Francis Wood, 'to conciliate the lower orders and to show that we are as jealous of the rights of the subject, when violated in *their* case, as we should be in our own.' Fitzwilliam's patronage of the Yorkshire meeting was in pursuit of this strategy, and his known opposition to reform made it all the more effective. 'Lord Fitzwilliam's known horror of parliamentary reform may save him from the odium which may be cast upon us in obeying the call of Sir F. Burdett, Mr Hunt, etc.,' wrote Lord George Cavendish.[2] His attitude also recalled the fundamental Whig principle of resistance to government based on military power rather than on consent. It was in this sense that they interpreted the true meaning of 1688. Fitzwilliam wrote that he objected not so much to the event of Peterloo as such, as to

the approbation given in the name of the crown to the use, in the first instance, of a military body in the execution of a civil process. . . . Who will engage to restore to the civil authority, powers once exercised by the military? . . . Its primary interference in civil matters has been approved in that quarter [the regent] to which alone it looks for approbation, the effect of which I cannot contemplate without alarm—it is this that I am anxious to meet in the earliest stage, to prevent its assuming the dangerous form of an acknowledged precedent.

During the years of his Lord Lieutenancy of the West Riding he had acted always in conformity with the principle that the military power of the crown should be clearly subordinated to the civil magistrates, and exercised with a due regard to the rights of all the people. In 1802 he had declared that 'It is the pride of this country that the laws of the realm are executed by, and the protection

of the inhabitants left to, civil officers, to men in brown coats.
. . . No military establishments have been kept up for the protection
of the subject'. Firmness in upholding the law was essential, but so
was the freedom of the individual which it was the main function
of the law to uphold.[3]

Fitzwilliam also believed that such revolutionary sentiment as
there was in the country was confined to a small number of demagogues and agitators, and that the mass of the people were loyal. He
deprecated alarmist and exaggerated reports of disaffection that
might be used to justify extraordinary action by the government. In
July 1812, he reported to Sidmouth that 'I am confident the country
is not in that alarming state it has been supposed to be'. In 1816 and
1817, when popular distress was combined with demands for parliamentary reform, Fitzwilliam remained calm. The working people,
he believed, were motivated by the sufferings of unemployment, low
wages and high prices rather than by radical propaganda, and he
maintained the opinions he had expressed in 1802 against the Combination Laws as constitutionally unsound and socially unjust. *Every*
class, he believed, had the same legal right to make the most of its
industry, workmen as well as employers. His attitude towards
popular disturbances was thus conditioned by a sense of the dangers
inherent in over-reaction and by a conviction that actual disorder
was the work of only a small minority whose influence was increased
by official repression. He was ordered to his post in the West Riding
by Sidmouth on 7 July 1819, in response to alarming reports of
public meetings in the Leeds area, but he reported after a fortnight's
investigations that the tone of the meetings was 'manifestly humble,
and much lowered'. The people around Leeds, he declared, were
suffering cruelly from unemployment,

but I am told that . . . they bear their hard lot with wonderful patience
and resignation. . . . Bad as these men [the agitators] may be and inde-
fatigable in propagating their doctrines, their mischievous spirit does not
pervade the mass of the people in the West Riding: on the contrary,
from all I can collect, I report with confidence to your Lordship that
the peace, tranquillity and good order of the realm will not be disturbed
by these people.

And he repeated on the 31st that 'there is no cause for suspecting
any disposition of the people of this Riding to turbulence or commotion', and that any discontent that was present 'has nothing to

do with constitutional considerations but arises out of improvements in the art of manufacture, which diminished the calls for their
exertions and industry'. He added his advice 'that no step that could
in any way convey a suspicion or jealousy of the people's views and
wishes, should be adopted, but that on the contrary we should
prove to them by our own demeanour our opinion of their good
disposition and our confidence in their good conduct'.[4]

Fitzwilliam's approach to the Peterloo incident in September and
October 1819 had its roots, therefore in two sources. The first lay in
a lifelong conviction that the function of the Whig party was to
protect the people's liberties from a potentially despotic government, and to preserve the civil foundation of government against
military power. 'If we do not set this matter to rights,' Fitzwilliam
wrote on 5 October, 'the military are henceforward the governing
power in the British Empire.' The second was a calculation of party
advantage that might be gained from the exploitation of the blunder
at Peterloo. The plan for a county meeting at York was carefully
designed to avoid an outright condemnation of magistrates and
yeomanry for supposed atrocities reported in the radical press. 'We
deprecate prejudging,' Fitzwilliam informed Holland on 18 September '—no expressions of yeomanry cutting and slashing, no
breasts of the mother sliced off, nor babes knocked on head in their
mother's arms—no horrid massacres—no exaggerations—but we
shall call for meeting of Parliament for enquiry.' The requisition for
the meeting, drafted by Fitzwilliam, referred to events at Manchester
'which, not hitherto satisfactorily explained, appear to affect
important rights of the people and essential principles of the constitution'. Its purpose was to prevent 'any invasion of the acknowledged rights of the people (if such shall appear to have occurred)'.[5]
At the county meeting on 14 October Milton, in his father's presence,
used deliberately moderate language and contended for no more
than that there was a *prima facie* case for an enquiry. County
meetings in this period were not, of course, regarded as opportunities for the spontaneous expression of popular feeling, so much as
opportunities for the governing class to demonstrate its leadership
of the people. The Yorkshire meeting was thus primarily intended
as a contest between the Whigs and the radicals for popular favour.
'It is reported that the radicals will flock in, in vast bodies,' Fitzwilliam wrote shortly before the meeting, '. . . but . . . I doubt their
lead of the lower orders, when the latter see the higher orders take

up their cause; I have some little proof that the mass desire no better than to be directed by us.' He reported that the meeting was 'well attended by the higher orders' and 'the resolutions carried with general approbation'. Only one speaker, a radical journalist named Joseph Mitchell, attempted to raise the cry of reform, only to be silenced by accusations that he was a government spy and an associate of Oliver.[6] The resolutions (drafted by Fitzwilliam) affirmed the right of public assembly, condemned unlawful interference with it, sympathised with the distresses of the lower orders, and demanded an inquiry into the events at Manchester. In this way the Whigs attempted to stand forth as the true champions of the people's rights.

It was an embarrassing incident for the government. That the Lord Lieutenant of the neighbouring industrial and, some believed, equally disaffected, area should join in even an implied censure of the Manchester magistrates who, however clumsily, had been trying to do their duty in difficult circumstances, presented them with a dilemma. To take action against Fitzwilliam might further identify the government with repression of liberties, but to take no notice, as Liverpool remarked, 'would be ascribed to nothing but timidity, and would discourage our best friends'. On 21 October Sidmouth despatched Fitzwilliam's dismissal. Plumer Ward told the Home Secretary that the step had 'given great satisfaction to our own friends, as indicating proper vigour on the part of the government'. Yet this course played into the Whigs' hands. It presented them with a martyr, not to the radical demagoguery of Hunt and Burdett, but to constitutional Whiggism of the most moderate kind; and it seemed to confirm the Whig contention that the Ministry was seeking a confrontation between armed reaction and extreme radicalism. Robert Price wrote to Milton that the dismissal was a public proof of the lengths the government was prepared to go, and that 'your father's character, his well-known caution, even the fears he has entertained at different times of popular commotions, will now be of service to us'. Holland made the same point: 'It is an open indication of the temper and designs of Ministers,' he declared. 'They have . . . overshot their mark. . . . By attempting to affix the stigma of Jacobinism on you they must convince many moderate men that it is their intention to exact implicit servitude or to charge disaffection on every person of weight and character in the country.' Their persecution of Fitzwilliam might 'reclaim some who are misled by the radicals themselves, and thereby lead them to look up with confidence to the exertions, as well as with respect to the character of public men of rank and consideration'. Fitzwilliam replied:

If you should suffer no pain but that which would be your portion by participating [in] mine, on account of my dismission, you are a fortunate man, you will live and die without a pang—whether the Ministers intended me good or not, is not the question, they have done me a great good, they have released me from all the perplexities and difficulties that surrounded me under existing circumstances.

His dismissal had clarified the issues which the county meetings might have left confused, and presented the Whigs with the opportunity to distinguish themselves from the radicals.[7]

Fitzwilliam's role in the Peterloo affair brought him the acclamations of many of his party. Even before the Yorkshire meeting, his championship of the cause led Brougham, organising a meeting on the same pattern in Cumberland and Westmorland, to write to Milton of 'the veneration we all feel for your most excellent father —and I assure you it is a considerable triumph for me', he added, 'who have for years been telling the ultras etc. that he was the firmest friend the constitution had and as bold as honest'. After his dismissal, tributes poured in. As William Lamb wrote, 'you are no doubt overwhelmed at this moment with those demonstrations of regard, esteem and affection which your character both public and private at once conciliates and commands'. J. R. G. Graham penned an eloquent and emotional panegyric:

I mourn for the lost honour and liberty of my country, which must indeed be prostrate, before the last champion of its chivalry and rights can be insulted with impunity by a worthless government. I mourn for myself and for my countrymen; I cannot grieve for you. Your name is far beyond the reach of every enemy; though tyrants may impose silence, it will live in the heart of every honest man who knows you.[8]

Fitzwilliam was 'the Father of the People, the Nestor in our day of Freedom, the champion of constitutional rights, the enemy unto death not less of slavery than of anarchy'. At a dinner at the liberal Duke of Sussex's house, the duke paid tribute to Fitzwilliam and proposed his health with a long speech in his praise. 'I don't expect it [the toast] will be drunk at Carlton House today,' Fitzwilliam remarked.[9]

His sacrifice of office on this occasion thus greatly increased his influence in the Whig party, and added point to the party's strategy in the debates on the government's repressive measures—the famous 'Six Acts'—which were introduced in the earliest days of the new session, in November and December. 'It is a great grudge I owe to the radicals for a wicked and foolish abuse of great and constitutional rights,' Fitzwilliam wrote to Sir Francis Wood as the Bills were making their way through Parliament, 'that they have furnished to those who wished to find it, plausible pretext for paring those rights down to the quick. Will any [public] meeting ever be permitted to express an opinion adverse to the existing Administration, when *one* time-serving magistrate may dissolve it at his pleasure —the death blow is given to that right, which never can be exercised efficaciously or in my opinion *constitutionally*, but when exercised *en masse*.' While supporting the strengthening of the law against already illegal acts, such as in the Training Prevention Bill, Fitzwilliam and the opposition vehemently opposed further restraints on public meetings, the right of the individual to bear arms, and the freedom of the press. Yet, despite this advocacy of popular rights and constitutional liberties, Fitzwilliam could not yet accept the view of the younger and more eager reformers in the party that the Whigs could defeat the radical challenge only by taking up the cause of parliamentary reform. Grey, who believed fundamentally in the necessity for Whig championship of reform, realised that Fitzwilliam's martyrdom had strengthened the party's obligations to him and made it more difficult to take up the issue as a party question. Writing to Holland on 24 October to discuss the party's future strategy, he struck a note of despondency. Clearly it was impossible to co-operate with either the government in repressing reform or with the radicals in 'putting down the government', but the question was how to arrive at 'a course of policy, founded upon Whig principles, and adapted, according to the best of our judgement, to the difficult circumstances of the times'. It was easy enough to agree in outline on 'economy, retrenchment, enquiry into the abuses of power, a salutary principle of reform applied to the corruptions of the government and the parliament, and a resistance to wild and impracticable theories, which are equally incompatible with the British constitution, and with any settled government. But the details of a regular project founded on these principles will I fear be found very difficult'. In the distressed state of the people a moderate policy would have little public appeal, and would still leave the radicals in possession of the field. Yet to unite the party in favour of that extensive reform which alone would acquire public support was impossible.

I can easily make up my mind [Grey confessed] to a separation . . . with the violent reformers of our party; but I do not know how I could bear (not to speak of its effect on the public interest) a break with some of those who have a tendency at least to the opposite extreme, and particularly after his conduct on this occasion, with Fitzwilliam. Yet I am afraid there is nothing so hopeless as the idea of gaining his acquiescence in *any* measure of parliamentary reform.

He concluded that the most probable outcome was 'the dissolution of the party or at least my relinquishing forever the part I have hitherto had in conducting it'. 'I never felt quite broken-hearted about politics till now', he confessed in December 1819.[10]

Grey's despondency irritated Lambton, his son-in-law and a leading advocate of parliamentary reform. Lambton identified Fitzwilliam as the primary cause of the difficulty. 'Your anxiety to remain with your friends is quite natural,' he wrote to Grey early in January, but 'I wish Lord Fitzwilliam had been as keen to stand by you at other times.' When Grey rebuked him for the remark, he explained his meaning more fully:

I often have objected to the course of Lord Fitzwilliam's public life as having been most detrimental to the public interests from the weight which his support gave to the government in times of alarm, and from his determined hostility to reform. I often gave that opinion, not being then personally acquainted with him. Since that, through your means, I have been introduced into his society, and have become sensible of what no man in his senses who knows him can deny, his most venerable, amiable and virtuous character. But all that introduction and perception, although it made me constantly waive all reference to his political sentiments in favour of his private character, could not erase from my mind the feeling which I had conscientiously imbibed from a consideration of the effects produced in the country by his secession and Mr Burke's [in 1794]. It was in this spirit alone that I made the observation which has offended you: at the same time admitting to the fullest degree his honour, his virtues and his disinterestedness in the public service.[11]

Lambton was right to the extent that it was chiefly from anxiety not to drive Fitzwilliam and his members out of the party that Grey withheld his endorsement of a reform programme in 1820. Party unity, to Grey, was more important than any single political issue, and in his well-known letter to Lambton on 3 January 1820 he warned his son-in-law that reform must remain an 'open' question in the party. Individuals could be free to advocate moderate reform measures, but it could not be a party question.[12] The Grenvilles had already, to all intents and purposes, seceded from the Whig coalition. To drive Fitzwilliam and the rest of the old aristocracy into their arms would further weaken the Whigs as contenders for office. The Whigs therefore failed to exploit the Peterloo affair to the full in 1819 or 1820. In the long run, however, as the Manchester 'massacre' passed into the popular folk-memory of English history, it came to be a milestone on the road that led to the Reform Act of 1832, marking the beginning of the process by which the Whigs gradually became the party of reform. The argument, accepted by Grey, 'that it will be impossible for any party, looking to the support of public opinion, to succeed' without a direct commitment to reform proved invincible in the long run, despite Fitzwilliam's continued reluctance to face it.[13]

The year 1819 marked the opening of Lord John Russell's campaign to secure reform by the piecemeal disfranchisement of corrupt boroughs and the transfer of their seats to new towns. This campaign had as its objective not merely the purification of the electoral system, but the commitment of the Whigs as a party to the principle of reform. In this respect, its outstanding success was Milton's conversion to reform and his father's grudging acquiescence in his personal support of the measure. In December 1819 Russell proposed that the corrupt Cornish borough of Grampound be totally disfranchised, instead of having its own electorate or its boundaries enlarged, as had been done in previous cases of this kind, and that its seats be given to Leeds. Milton at once consulted Thomas Tottie, his father's agent at Leeds, about the franchise qualification to be proposed, and particularly about the likely effects of giving the vote to the resident householders in the borough. Tottie supported the proposal on the grounds that although such an electorate might be no less venal than at Grampound, to give rights of representation to the industrial towns would provide a periodical safety valve for the discontents aroused in those districts by fluctuations in trade, which would otherwise result in dangerous extra-parliamentary agitation. The episode marked the beginning of a movement in Milton's mind towards the acceptance of some measure of reform. William Lamb,

however, was alerting Fitzwilliam to the dangers of tampering even
on so small a scale with the representative structure. The total disfranchisement of a borough and the transfer of its seats to a previously unrepresented place, he wrote, 'is not only new, but is an
admission of some of the main principles of the reformers, and
cannot be considered as anything less, than the commencement of
a reformation in the present system of the representation'. Lamb
pointed out that, while Russell was ostensibly restricting himself to
individual cases of corruption, Lambton had given notice of a far
more sweeping proposal to revive the schemes of 1793 and 1797,
involving triennial parliaments, household suffrage and the large-
scale disfranchisement of rotten boroughs. It was important, Lamb
urged, that the party should know whether its leaders were about to
pledge themselves to such sweeping measures, and he urged Fitzwilliam to communicate with Grey about it.[14]

These speculations were interrupted by the death of George III
on 29 January 1820. The old king had lived in deep seclusion for the
past ten years. He was now blind as well as occasionally deranged,
consoling himself by playing the harpsichord and holding imaginary
conversations in heaven with Handel. Yet his death and the accession
of the Prince Regent as George IV had more than a personal significance. To many it marked the end of a long era in British politics.
The king whose accession sixty years before had been identified by
former Whig politicians with new and dangerous tendencies to exalt
the prerogative and to diminish constitutional liberties, had long
ago become identified with the preservation of old constitutional
traditions against radical Jacobinism. No one in 1820 believed that
the royal prerogative was now a threat to the constitution. Fitzwilliam had lived through all these years, from the days when he
was a boy of 12 at Eton to become the most generally respected of
whig elder statesmen at the age of 72. By 1820 his eighteenth-
century Whiggism, though venerated by many as a treasured link
with sound tradition, was hampering the ability of his party to
adapt to the needs of the new society that had grown up in those
six decades as a result of rapid economic and technological development at home and years of bitter warfare in Europe. George IV was
no more aware of, or in sympathy with, these new developments
than his father, who never travelled further north than Worcester
and who never visited the new industrial complexes which were
now the only environment millions of his subjects knew. Politics

were passing out of the age of kingly supremacy. George IV's Ministers, in general, treated him with less respect and attention than they had given to his father. He was compelled to accept measures both he and his father disliked. He found it impossible to exert that influence over both politicians and general elections which had provided George III, on occasion, with support for his authority against unwelcome Ministers or measures. The post-war period had already seen the beginnings of new forces developing in political life, as the growing commercial, industrial and professional middle-class began to organise for the protection of its economic and social interests. Its instruments were newspapers, public meetings and organisations like the Political Unions which were formed in the 1820s. The old party cries against 'influence of the Crown', and the old struggles of aristocratic groups contending for power and local territorial influence seemed more and more irrelevant to the real issues of the day. The roaring furnaces of Sheffield and Rotherham, the clattering looms of Bolton and Huddersfield, the smoking chimneys of Birmingham and Wolverhampton had little or nothing to do with the political manoeuvrings of owners of country mansions and broad acres. If the aristocratic influence was to survive and to maintain its supremacy, it must adapt to the new conditions and recognise the needs of the new social forces. Ultimately, the Whig party was to succeed, for a time, in doing so. In transforming itself during the 1820s into the party of progress and reform, it captured the respectable and still fundamentally deferential middle-class forces from the dangerous arms of radicalism, and ensured its survival down to the 1880s as the major party in British politics. The Reform Act of 1832 was its primary instrument. The gradual adoption of reform during the 1820s was therefore the crucial element in its survival and adaptation for the future.

It was Milton, rather than his father, who began to see this in the early months of the new reign. Fitzwilliam met the new era in a mood of some despondency. The times seemed out of joint, the new reign offered no prospect of the Whigs being called to office by the man who had once been the key to their hopes, and the old Foxite cause of civil and religious liberty seemed as hopeless as ever. He had no personal respect for the new monarch. A long acquaintance had confirmed Fitzwilliam's view that George was an untrustworthy libertine, on whose promises no reliance could be placed. At least the old king had symbolised qualities of moral rectitude and constitutional stability, and despite their differences on political issues Fitzwilliam had been able to identify in fundamentals with the principles he stood for. He even felt, as he wrote to Holland, 'much disposed to pay a mark of respect to the old king, by attending his funeral, but my heart fails me, now the time is come'. He also took the initiative in suggesting to his old Tory rival Lord Harewood that Yorkshire should follow 'immemorial usage' in sending up an address of congratulation on the new king's accession.[15] The new reign, however, opened with a scandal which helped further to discredit the king and, through him, the institution of the monarchy itself. The vindictive persecution of Queen Caroline—admittedly poor stuff for a martyr to any worthwhile principle, but a wronged woman none the less—aroused popular passion, showed George IV in the worst possible light, and offered proof, which was to be significant for the Whig party, of the need for reform of political institutions. It was in attending to the proceedings against her, and following out their political consequences in the country, that Milton and the Whigs found a further impetus towards a policy for the future.

The relations between George and his wife had remained hostile throughout the regency, and had inevitably become entangled in party politics. The prince demanded that his Ministers should support his vendetta against her, while her cause had been taken up by the London populace to express their contempt for her husband. Fitzwilliam reported in 1813 that the Prince Regent had been 'hooted and hissed from Carlton House to Buckingham House and back again—insulted by language no less', while the princess, appearing incognito at Covent Garden, set the House in an uproar of applause, with cries for the playing of 'God save the King—the Protector of innocence'. The opposition naturally looked to take advantage of this popular feeling, and after 1809 Brougham became the queen's confidential adviser in order to exploit the situation for party ends. A few days after the king's death, Brougham sent for her to return to England—she had lived abroad since 1814—to claim her rights as queen. The new king, on the other hand, had taken immediate steps to try to divorce her, and had already decided that her name should be omitted from the liturgy. The Ministers, anxious to avoid a damaging public scandal that would play into the opposition's hands, urged the king not to take divorce proceedings, but warned Brougham that if the queen set foot in England they would introduce a parliamentary Bill of Pains and Penalties against her. Brougham was willing enough to settle with Ministers if he himself were given a silk gown, which would give him precedence at the Bar and add immeasurably to his income. The negotiations broke down, however, Brougham, for his own purposes, deciding to change his tactics, and on 6 June the queen arrived in London. The Bill against her, containing a divorce clause, was introduced into the Lords on 5 July.[16]

The attitude of the Whig party leaders to the queen's trial, as it came to be called, was ambivalent. Glad enough to embarrass George IV and the Ministers, they found it difficult to swallow the championship of a loose and immoral woman whose cause, they felt, did them no credit. They were also deeply suspicious that Brougham, whose conduct had been shifty to say the least, would embroil them in an unwholesome scandal merely for his own ambitious purposes, and they feared that they would be swept along by a popular frenzy they could not control into measures verging on revolution. Grey took the line that the Whigs should be neutral on the queen's business, and warned Brougham that he would not have the party's political support in defending her in the Lords. Holland wrote that he regarded the whole business as 'degrading . . . to all concerned, and disgusting and tiresome I think to the bystanders'.[17] Fitzwilliam shared these views. He was no stranger to the queen's affairs. In 1814 he had agreed to act, if necessary, as a trustee to administer the parliamentary grant then made to her. In 1820, soon after her arrival, the queen approached him to ask if he would represent her, with Lord Sefton, in negotiations with nominees of the Cabinet. Fitzwilliam's upright character and widely-known reputation no doubt offered great advantages to the queen's dubious cause. He declined, however, to undertake the task, and a fortnight later again rebuffed her suggestion that he might peruse various statements and communications on her behalf. His excuse was that, as a member of the House of Lords, it would be his duty 'to sit, virtually, in judgement upon her Majesty's cause, in which case he ought (if he may use the expression) to go into court with the impartial mind of a juror, who knows nothing of the case, but from the evidence adduced at the trial'. He later wrote to Sir Francis Wood that the exclusion of her name from the liturgy had prejudiced his mind against her before her arrival, and 'I would not go near her; and when I went to the opening of her trial, I went with a mind prejudged against her case'. It was only the weakness of the Ministers' evidence against her that converted him to a conviction of her innocence.[18]

Fitzwilliam found the whole proceeding distasteful and politically dangerous. 'The House of Lords is to be rolled in the kennel for the preservation of Ministers,' he wrote to Milton, '. . . will it not end in the overthrow of the constitution?' He had written to Grey in July of his despair at the Cabinet's scheme:

We are to dethrone a queen, and dissolve her marriage with the king, for the crime of disgusting intimacy with a menial servant, for bestowing on him marks of favour, etc. etc. But if these be crimes in a queen, that call down upon her the vengeance of the nation, what is the nation to do in the case of a king, guilty of similar crimes—is Liverpool bold enough to tell us, that he will dethrone from his hereditary throne a king, *not charged with attempts to overthrow the liberties of the country*, but guilty of the crimes alleged against the queen?

The whole affair, he felt, would discredit the monarchy and with it the established constitution. There was, however, party advantage to be gained. In early November, when it seemed that the Bill would pass the Lords but only by a small majority, he wrote that 'a worse state of things for Ministers cannot be devised. I consider it as their destruction'. As over Peterloo a year earlier, he advocated the bringing into play of public opinion by organising a public meeting at York. 'The eyes of the public are fixed upon Yorkshire,' he wrote to Milton, 'and, [if] the Bill [should be] passed, Yorkshire must be put in motion.' 'There never was an occasion,' he assured Sir Francis Wood, 'when there was so fair a prospect of unanimity. . . . I look forward to a general concurrence of sentiment of Whig and Tory.' He hoped that, if the proposed meeting and petition were restricted to a request for the Bill's rejection, it might be possible to secure the co-operation of Tory interests, which would not, of course, support a petition for the dismissal of Ministers. He set about writing to contacts in Yorkshire to try to secure Tory support, and suggested that Huntingdonshire too might be set in motion.[19] When, however, on 10 November, Liverpool announced that the Bill would be dropped, the idea of county meetings became less attractive. On the one hand, there now seemed no point in meeting merely on the queen's business, and some Whig friends in Yorkshire urged that the primary purpose should now be to agitate for parliamentary reform. Fawkes was pledged not to support anything less, and Sir George Cayley, another leading supporter of reform, demanded that

the Whigs should pledge themselves to bring in a Reform Bill if
they achieved office. Fitzwilliam's correspondents advised, therefore,
against a meeting. The danger was that the Whigs might be
embroiled with popular clamour on behalf of the queen herself, and
lose the potential alliance with Tory interests against the Ministry.
Henry Gally Knight wrote to Milton on 5 December that though he
was convinced of the queen's guilt, he deeply regretted

that oil should have been poured into the popular flame—that the higher
orders should have coalesced with the lower orders when the latter were
violent, and mistaken—that royal authority should have been dangerously
shaken by the censures and the insults which have been insinuated
against the person of the king—that morality should have sustained so
severe a shock by the attempt to represent as of little importance actions
destructive of all delicacy and almost certainly leading to crime.

County meetings, he argued, 'would not tend to allay, but to increase
the popular ferment'. Fitzwilliam was influenced by both arguments.
'We think and talk of nothing but the queen,' he wrote to Lady Ponsonby. '. . . I don't believe it [the government] can last, this odious
persecution has made king and Ministers so unpopular.' A county
meeting, however, he wrote to Grey on 6 December, would 'produce
the reverse of its object, and instead of placing the higher as leaders
of the lower orders, the result will be, that they will be at variance
—nothing will satisfy the latter, but addresses to the queen, declaratory of innocence, etc. etc. to which the former will not subscribe'.
Four days later he added that the proposal to introduce reform into
the business would have defeated its original object: 'at last we are
out of the scrape', he declared, and with the quiet dropping of the
Bill against the queen the uproar died down for the moment.[20]
    The affair, had, however, raised in acute form the question of the
Whigs' attitude to parliamentary reform. The dropping of the Bill,
owing to the narrowness of the government's majority in the Lords
on the third reading, gave rise to speculations that the Ministry was
about to fall and that the Whigs would be sent for. Grey hurriedly
cast about for advice on whether the reform question should be
made a *sine qua non* in a Whig government's programme, and, if so,
what precise degree of reform would satisfy its advocates and the
public. To Holland, he declared his perplexity. 'I have turned it in my
mind over and over again,' he wrote, 'and I am now at last obliged to
confess that I have not yet brought myself to any satisfactory con-

clusion.' The party was not agreed on the principle, 'some of our most valuable friends and supporters objecting to it *in toto*', much less on any detailed scheme; it seemed certain that any proposal mild enough to be accepted by the bulk of the party would not satisfy the public. The first effect of adopting the measure would be to divide the party and jeopardise a Whig government's chances of carrying Catholic emancipation, dismantling the repressive legislation of 1819, reducing establishments, and carrying out other desirable projects. Grey saw only a dilemma; a Whig administration 'could only stand upon public confidence and opinion' but that support would not be forthcoming except upon terms that would divide the party and make it impossible to form a Whig government. His inclination was to adopt reform on an extensive plan, and to give up the chance of forming a government in consequence.

Before he could do so, he had to try to win over Fitzwilliam. On the same day as his letter to Holland, he wrote to appeal to him: 'I cannot sleep when I think of the tremendously difficult questions which I should have to decide' in case of being called upon by the king, he wrote. It was clear that the king would employ the Whigs only in the last extremity, and that he would get rid of them at the first opportunity. 'The security against this,' he wrote, 'must be popular confidence; and can that confidence *now* be obtained or preserved without some concession of the principle of reform? . . . Your known opinions bear no inconsiderable part in the difficulty which I feel on this subject,' he concluded. 'Do you still feel it quite impossible to admit any modification of them?'[21]

Fitzwilliam replied to Grey's appeal with a firm restatement of his old opinions against reform. 'I am obliged to say frankly,' he wrote, 'that hitherto the parliamentary reform has never been placed before me in a manner that has in the least degree weakened my objection, or lessened my apprehension of the extreme danger, that would in my opinion inevitably attend its admission.' His objections in general were threefold. First, the advocates of reform in principle were not agreed on what specific measures were necessary. Second, reform once embarked on would never be final for there could never be agreement that constitutional perfection had been reached. Third, the present system had its advantages. 'Are we quite sure,' he asked, 'that the theoretic systems will be better for the purpose of good and free government, than the existing, undefined, indescribable mode of election, loose and various as it is?' This very variety was a safeguard, for 'what is to become of property, if power is to be deposited in the hands of numbers exclusively?' Even the current campaign against corrupt boroughs met with his disapproval, for

if it be meant that every borough where corruption prevails is to [be] swept out of the list of places sending representatives, I venture to say that in every borough where there is no leading predominant interest, corruption carries the day—and are we to say, that the right of election is to be wrested out of the hands of the general mass of the lower orders who make this corrupt use of their right—half the great towns will be disfranchised, and that rank of population deprived of that support in Parliament, which such representatives are always ready to give them— I should have to cry for the good city of York, whose corrupt elections, in the course of 1819 and 1820, have extracted from my purse £25,000. But if we are to do away [with] corruption, we must seek it where it is to be found, in towers of strength, as well as in the mud walls of weakness—we must not listen to these cries, they cannot, they will not be proceeded on with fairness and equity—and were they so, it would prove most mischievous—the lower orders would be positively deprived of those elections, which they carry, and would be left without protectors —sore though I may be of that right of election, still they shall find in me a strenuous and determined defender, because I think it useful to them to have a share in the government of the country. . . . Grieved as I am, that there should be a difference between you and me . . . I am bound to avow my pertinacity in my old opinions—I feel them too important to give up even to the warmest friendship.

Fitzwilliam's arguments were neither new nor original. They echoed the Burke of the 1780s. But they sounded in Grey's ears the death-knell of Whig hopes. 'He is very unhappy about dear Lord Fitzwilliam,' Lady Grey wrote to her mother, 'and really on his account alone I think he was inclined to risk the loss of all public favour.' In the end, Grey contented himself with a declaration at the Northumberland county meeting at Morpeth of his continued adherence to the principle of reform, avoiding any pledge as to time or circumstances. Whig hopes of office blazed up suddenly on 12 December when Canning resigned from the government, and in January Fitzwilliam urged Grey to come up to town for the meeting of Parliament. Contrary to Whig expectations, however, the government had crushing majorities on all the divisions on the queen's business, the country gentlemen rallying to administration's support on the understanding that the affair was now at rest, and alarmed by Whig flirtations with the radicals out of doors. The opposition was in quarrelsome disarray, while the reformers in the country were alienated by their refusal to adopt the question. Lambton again urged that the only remedy was to adopt reform: 'It is actual insanity to think that we have any chance of turning the Ministers out while the House of Commons is constituted as it is,' he wrote to Grey, 'and we are, therefore, losing our character daily in the eyes of the country by shirking the question, for the sake of keeping those in our ranks who are adverse to reform.' Fitzwilliam was prepared to agree that the conduct of the House of Commons on the queen's business showed that the House for the first time, he believed, no longer represented the decided tone of public opinion. Parliamentary reform, however, remained 'a dangerous experiment —certain destruction in the hands of the vain and presumptuous fabricators of constitutions'. He took refuge in despondency. 'I feel the constitution is on the wane,' he wrote to Sir Francis Wood, 'its spirit being gone, it cannot last—whether despotism or anarchy will be the first upshot I know not, but if the constitution is not now maintained in its true spirit both will ensue.'[22]

If Fitzwilliam was obdurate against reform, even in these circumstances, Milton was ready to be more flexible. He now set himself to persuade his father into a more accommodating frame of mind, and to try to reach an understanding with the moderate reformers which would unite the party in support of some measure to satisfy public demand. In March 1821, meetings were again proposed in several counties to censure the government's conduct of the queen's business and to petition for reform. In Yorkshire Wyvill and his friends drew up a requisition which laid stress on the deficiencies of the House of Commons as a representative of the people. Fitzwilliam refused to give his countenance to a county meeting 'for the loose indefinite purpose of rendering the House a more *effectual representation* or even a more *faithful* one unless the means of doing so be specially defined, in which case, approving the means, I may concur in petitioning for the object'. He would support only some precise and specific plan which was clearly limited in its scope. Milton therefore set himself to try to reach some agreement with the reformers. Writing a week later to Sir George Cayley, the Yorkshire baronet, reformer and aeronautical pioneer, Milton expressed the cautious hope that 'the points upon which we agree are much more important than those upon which there exists a difference or, rather, shades of difference between us'. His own love of liberty,

Milton declared, was so deep that he was even 'willing and ready
to abolish all the game laws at one stroke of the pen', which was a
proof that 'I am not a mere theoretical admirer of liberty, but that
I am willing to carry it into practice even in cases where it would
appear most injurious to what some modern reformers call the
privileged orders'. His attitude towards reform, however, was practical rather than theoretical. He had never subscribed to the view
that the House of Commons was unrepresentative of public opinion
in general,

for though I have voted almost uniformly in a minority, I must candidly
confess that, upon the best and most impartial consideration I was
capable of, it appeared to me that the *country* was quite as much against
my opinions as *Parliament*. . . . This conviction of the consent between
the House of Commons and the people made me an opponent of parliamentary reform, and so I should have continued if recent circumstances
had not satisfied me that that consent is not as perfect as I had previously
thought it.

The queen's business had convinced him that Parliament no longer
adequately represented public opinion; the cause of this defect must
be sought either in the system itself, which made it impossible for
the constituent body to elect good representatives, or in the corruption of the representatives once elected. Rockingham had once
declared, forty years before, that it was not the mode of election, but
the corruption of men when once elected to Parliament, that was
responsible for the evils of the system. In the intervening period the
Whigs had accordingly concentrated their efforts on diminishing
the 'influence of the Crown' as the primary agent in distorting the
representative nature of Parliament. Now, however, Milton admitted
that the electoral system might in some respects be at fault, though
he regarded the extreme reformers' view that it was fundamentally
unsound as 'very unphilosophical'. His own view was founded upon
a series of careful analyses of divisions in the Commons, which had
convinced him that 'the evil originates in the numerous small
boroughs, which from their nature, are liable either to be corrupted,
or to be drawn within the influence of government by means of the
immense patronage which Ministers have at their disposal'. He proposed, therefore, that the reformers should concentrate on a limited
plan to remedy this particular defect, laying aside for the moment
all other schemes and proposals in the interest of unity. His plan
was that, first, the right of election should be extended to a number

of 'those communities known to the law and the constitution which have either lost or never enjoyed the elective franchise, an improvement founded upon the principles of the constitution and sanctioned by ancient usage', and secondly 'to remove the obstacles which, as the law now stands, render the conviction of corrupt boroughs so difficult as to be almost impossible', leaving the disfranchisement of such constituencies to the individual investigation of Parliament in each separate case. If the reformers would limit themselves to some such step—in this case, virtually to the support of Russell's campaign for new machinery to enable corrupt electorates to be disfranchised and their seats transferred to manufacturing towns—Milton held out the hope that his father would 'depart so far from his old opinions and caution on this subject as to give a hope that if certain modifications . . . were adopted in the requisition . . . he might attend a meeting convened in consequence'.[23]

Milton had already made a public declaration of his change of sentiment on reform. On 2 March 1821, when Lord John Russell's Bill to disfranchise Grampound and transfer its two seats to Leeds was in committee, Milton spoke to approve the Bill on the grounds that it 'was founded on constitutional principles'. He declared his support for Russell's original proposal to make the Leeds electorate a popular one, with a 'scot and lot' householder franchise without any further property qualification, against the efforts of ministerialists to impose a minimum £20 rateable value qualification, and he declared that the Bill might be considered as 'the first of a series for extending the elective franchise'. The Bill was eventually amended by the Lords so as not to give the two seats to Leeds but to add to the Yorkshire county representation. Russell had by then abandoned the sponsorship of the Bill, but Milton took the lead in proposing acquiescence in the Lords' amendments in order to show that Parliament was not insensitive to public opinion, and to establish at least the principle of total disfranchisement for gross corruption. He deplored the loss of the opportunity to give the seats to Leeds, but declared his hope that in future measures of the kind it would be possible to strengthen the representation of business rather than landed interests which, he declared, would benefit from the present Bill.[24]

Milton's attitude to the destination of Grampound's lost seats was no doubt influenced to some degree by a careful appreciation of the effects it might have on his father's interest in Yorkshire. Leeds was the centre of rising middle-class political aspirations in the county, and the headquarters of the opposition to Milton's re-election in 1818.[25] He was nevertheless sincere in wishing to see the new commercial and industrial interests better represented in the House, and he hoped that the Whig party might win the leadership of this up and coming political force. On 17 April he avowed in the Commons his total change of opinion on the principle of reform. The occasion was Lambton's motion for extensive reform of Parliament by the adoption of triennial parliaments, equal electoral districts, and the enfranchisement of copyholders, leaseholders and householders.[26] Though Milton declared that he could not support such a radical scheme, he announced his conversion to reform in principle. Hitherto he had resisted it because he had believed that the House of Commons, with all its imperfections, did adequately represent the people. However, 'a better acquaintance with the practices of Parliament, a closer investigation of some of its leading peculiarities, and perhaps a greater maturity of judgement, had induced him to alter the opinions which he had entertained at his outset in public life. He had seen the House of Commons acting in complete and avowed opposition to the sense and wishes of the people'. He quoted Burke's respectable authority for the view that the people were 'perfect judges' of whether the House did or did not adequately represent their interests : and 'from all the enquiries which he had made, from all the consideration which he had given to the state of the country, his conviction was, and it was a conviction most absolute, that the great mass of the middling classes of the community desired, and earnestly desired, reform in Parliament'. At the county meetings he had attended, freeholders and yeomanry were unanimous 'that reform alone could save the country. . . . In truth he now believed that which, until within the last two years he had not believed, that the country desired a change of men as well as a change of measures'. He urged the appointment of a committee on the state of the representation; otherwise, the House 'would fall into such disrepute as would completely disqualify it from the exercise of its functions'.

Milton's conversion was received with joy by the Yorkshire reformers. Edward Baines's whig *Leeds Mercury* saluted him as 'a representative so wise and patriotic, who can burst the bonds of interest, prejudice and party, to espouse the cause of truth', and expressed the hope 'that the Whig nobility generally will follow the laudable example of his lordship'.[27] Though Milton henceforward appeared on the reformers' side in the Commons lobbies, however, his father was still obdurate, and the question produced the biggest crisis of their relationship in March 1822. In 1821, Fitzwilliam was still anxious to restrict county meetings to censuring the government's handling of the queen's affairs. He and Milton attended the Huntingdonshire meeting—'the first of its kind ever held in this county' as The Times reported—on 31 March 1821, at which the Whig leaders in the county proposed resolutions calling for the queen's restoration to her rights and privileges. J. B. Rooper, who was to be a Whig candidate for the county in 1830 and member in 1832, referred to the fact that seventy Members of Parliament shared between them £150,000 per annum of public money and said that, though he was not an advocate of radical reform, the House needed to be made more representative of the people. Milton made a long speech, concentrating on the queen's affairs and on 'the present abuses of the state', particularly high taxation, and concluding with 'an eloquent appeal in favour of the rising liberties of Italy'. In his father's presence he avoided any mention of parliamentary reform, and the meeting agreed to Milton's presenting a petition to the Commons which did not mention the subject.[28] The tide of support was rising, however, as the severe agricultural depression of the early 'twenties hit the pockets of the landed interest. In January 1822 Grey began to speculate apprehensively on a possible junction between the radicals and the Tories. 'Burdett, you know,' he wrote to Fitzwilliam, 'calls himself a reforming Tory, and the most violent language I hear reported, next to the radicals, is that of the Tory country gentlemen who are deficient in their rents.'[29] The continued subservience of Parliament towards Ministers in the 1822 session seemed further proof of its deficiencies as a representative of public interests, and in the spring Milton presented his father with a list of the English parliamentary boroughs and the political alignment of their representatives which was designed to hammer the point home. The analysis showed that whereas the boroughs with populations of 5,000 or over returned sixty-one supporters of opposition against fifty ministerialists, those with populations between 4,999 and 1,000 elected sixty-seven oppositionists and 150 ministerialists, while those with less than 1,000 inhabitants were represented by only sixteen members of opposition against fifty-five supporters of government. The lists proved, said a prefatory note, 'beyond possibility of doubt that the influence of Ministers is in an inverse ratio to the population of the boroughs, so that in proportion as the numbers of the people diminish, the influence of the government increases'.[30] Further lists analysed divisions to show that support for the Whig party came in greater proportion than that for the Ministers from the larger, more open electorates.

Calculations such as these were to be highly important in converting the Whig leadership to the kind of reform which was ultimately achieved in the Act of 1832, with its stress on the full or partial disfranchisement of small boroughs, measured according to the population census, and the transfer of members partly to larger business communities, which were thus taken out of the county electorates, which in turn were increased in number to strengthen the landed and largely Whig aristocracy. Yet, if there was much calculation of party advantage behind the Whigs' conversion to reform in the 'twenties, it took more than that to make Fitzwilliam change the opinions of a lifetime and desert the principles of Burke. Milton, Fitzwilliam wrote to Grey in March, had clearly made out that government majorities were largely made up from the smaller boroughs. It was a different matter, however, to say, as Milton did, 'that without a partial demolition of these boroughs the liberties of the country must sink under the influence and consequent power of the Crown, at no very remote period of time'. On these grounds Milton had asked his father's approval of his 'unreserved and full support of Lord John Russell's plan of parliamentary reform'. No doubt, Fitzwilliam wrote, Russell's scheme would improve the system, 'but ninety other plans would do as much, and with me the question is, is it for the advantage of the country, and for the good of the public to moot the subject at all—where are you to limit alterations, at what point are they to stop?' Nor was this his sole objection. He feared that, as had often been argued and occasionally demonstrated, the reformers would be unable to agree on any single specific plan, and that any such plan would be defeated by a combination of government and some of the other reformers against it. As far as Milton was concerned, the issue was doubly painful:

I cannot bring myself to indifference, when I contemplate how much his influence and efficiency may be thrown away, when he becomes a prominent supporter of parliamentary reform, for from that instant he becomes the tool and slave of every worthless adventurer. He is born aristocratic, that is his station in the country; one that enables him if he acts in that sphere, to defend the rights and liberties of the people, whom he ought to consider as under his special care and guardianship.

Milton, however, had presented an ultimatum: if his father would not agree to his supporting the full extent of Russell's scheme, he would quit Parliament:

painful as the case must be to me: painful as the notoriety of so important a difference of opinion existing between him and me must be, I cannot concur in his support of a measure, not arising out of any particular event or case, but on the professed broad principle of improvement, one that can never cease, but if effected, would place the country in a state of turbulent restlessness, from which it would presently [e]merge in anarchy, and ultimately end in unlimited monarchy.

In the 'painful situation in which I feel myself placed', Fitzwilliam appealed not only to Grey's sympathy but to Burke's memory.[31] Like Abraham, he heard a voice bid him offer up his own son at the altar of principle.

The sacrifice was averted. Like Abraham, Fitzwilliam had misunderstood the situation. He had believed Milton to imply that he wished to second Russell's motion, and so identify himself completely with it. Milton, however, now made it clear that all he wished for was his father's permission to give the motion general support. 'To this,' Fitzwilliam informed Grey, 'I waive all objection; notwithstanding it does not agree with my own cautious maxims, with my strong opinions upon the case, I have indeed heretofore, as in Lambton's case, done as much, and without disapprobation seen Milton support the question generally.' There was no question, therefore, of Milton's retiring from Parliament. There was equally, however, no question of Fitzwilliam's conversion, forced or voluntary, to any but the most cautious, limited and well-founded reform, despite Grey's warning that 'with the feeling that now exists respecting it in the country, and after so many of the most considerable of our friends have pledged themselves to it, it cannot be avoided'. Fitzwilliam remained convinced that, not only would any attempt at reform divide rather than unite the party, and so be self-defeating in Parliament, but also that the raising of the issue would divert public attention from the more specific grievances which might be more profitably taken up against the government, especially on the report of the committee on the agricultural depression. Milton's conduct, therefore, had to be circumspect on the question.[32]

In the summer of 1822 Fawkes and some other Yorkshire reformers revived the plan for a county meeting to agitate for radical reform. Milton was asked to a preliminary meeting at York during the August races, but he had to confess that he felt 'in no ordinary difficulty upon this subject'. Though he stood by his vote for Russell's motion in April,

the events which have made me a convert to parliamentary reform have not had that effect upon my father, and though I have never had the slightest scruple about acting against his opinion upon common occasions, I do feel very great difficulty upon one which agitates him to a degree which cannot be conceived by those who have not been in the habit of conversing with him upon it. It is indeed the only subject I know which deprives him of his usual calmness, and of course it is always painful to me to discuss it with him.[33]

'My own principle with respect to parliamentary reform remains unmoved', Fitzwilliam wrote to Sir Francis Wood in August. Furthermore, Fawkes was on record as having declared the desirability of reducing 'the influence of aristocracy, or in other words of property', in the House of Commons; such a proposal was, to Fitzwilliam, the antithesis of all good Whig principles and an 'efficacious means of overturning the liberties of the country . . . [and] introducing either despotism or anarchy, indeed of both in their usual rotation.' In the circumstances, preparations for the county meeting went on slowly. Milton chaired the preparatory meeting at York on 4 November, despite his father's disapproval, but he suggested to Grey that a county meeting should be held only if it seemed that other counties might follow suit and that a general movement of the middle classes and gentry would follow. Althorp too wrote of his alarm lest Fawkes should attempt to draw the Whigs into support of the radical programme of annual parliaments and universal suffrage, and advocated 'a union of the moderate party with the violent one' to keep control of the meeting. Milton declared that his presence in the chair 'contributed to make the proceedings rather more rational than those which I found were in contemplation' and hoped that the 'grandees' would support the requisition for a county meeting strongly enough to avert its circulation among large numbers of less respectable people.[34]

The Yorkshire county meeting on 22 January 1823 was described by The Times as 'one of the most important domestic occurrences that have taken place in our time'.[35] Like the equally famous occasion in the Castle yard in March 1784, it was held in bitter weather and deep snow which, however, did not prevent the attendance of many reformers from the West Riding towns as well as gentry and freeholders from all over the county. Over 5,000 people were reported to be present. Fawkes opened with a speech 'no less argumentative than eloquent', and Milton 'explained the slow steps by which he himself had been induced to think a reform of the House of Commons right and indispensable', admitting that 'he had been mainly influenced by the evident want of sympathy between the House and the people on numerous great questions, from the year 1817 to that time'. He instanced the suspension of Habeas Corpus in 1817, the resumption of cash payments in 1819, the Peterloo affair, and the queen's trial. All these had convinced him that 'the opinions of the people had not that weight in the House of Commons which they ought to have'. He ended with a quotation from Burke and a recommendation of 'moderation and prudence'. Only Wortley opposed the petition for reform, framed in general terms in order to avoid those disagreements which always broke out when specific plans were advocated, and no less than 17,083 signatures were eventually collected.[36] Milton presented the petition to the Commons on 22 April.

So, for the first time since 1785, Yorkshire petitioned for reform, and the county 'resumed the role which Wyvill had always thought that it should play' in leading national opinion.[37] This time Whig aristocrats, gentry and the thriving business classes of the West Riding were in alliance; but there remained many strains and tensions amongst them. A few other counties followed Yorkshire's lead, but in some the radicals took charge and the general outcome was disappointing. Seven years were to pass before the Whigs were in a position to take the leadership, as a government in office, of the reform movement they had tried to capture in 1822–3. By then, Fitzwilliam had virtually retired from public life, so that his lifelong opposition to extensive reform was not to be put to the test. In the crisis of 1831 Grey, searching for every vote in the House of Lords, asked Milton if Fitzwilliam could be persuaded to come up to vote for the Reform Bill, but there is, perhaps intriguingly, no record whether Milton ever put the request to his father. His coming up would be 'really out of the question', Milton wrote:

His old opinions about parliamentary reform seem still to cling to him— the only decided observation he ever made was when the Bill was first explained to him and he said, 'Well this is a *new* constitution' and

N

though he is of course very anxious for the success of your administration I am not at all clear that he is equally anxious for the measure
upon which that success depends. The truth is that he never yielded at
all upon the question till my own opinions had become very strong and
perfectly unchangeable, and, even then, it was with the greatest difficulty
that he could be reconciled to my supporting the question.[38]

To the last, Fitzwilliam remained a true follower of Burke.

Fitzwilliam's and Milton's attitudes to reform were also affected
by, and in turn influenced, local politics in the West Riding. Here the
middle-class challenge to aristocratic leadership was exemplified in
the activities of the merchant community of Leeds, who were
beginning to demand more direct representation of their interests at
Westminster. If this could not be obtained by the enfranchisement
of the new commercial and manufacturing towns, they aimed at
taking control of one of the county seats. These were the men, or
their descendants, who had opposed Milton in 1807. They were
generally sympathetic towards the government of the day, and were
regarded as 'Tory' in political alignment. In 1818, they allied with
other government-orientated interests in Yorkshire to try to replace
Milton by a candidate from their own ranks. Milton was accused
of neglecting the commercial interests of his constituents, and preferring the diversions of country life to attention to constituency
business. Stress was also placed on disagreements between Milton
and the woollen interest over the export of woollen cloth. Unfortunately, too, Milton was seriously ill in the spring of 1818, and
when the dissolution was announced early in June he was conva-
lescing in the Isle of Wight. His friends and supporters were taken
by surprise when it began to seem that there might be a contest.
Lascelles, too, was suffering from ill-health, and had announced his
retirement. James Stuart Wortley, who had attempted to come
forward in 1812 in Lascelles's place, again declared his candidature,
and at first it was expected that he and Milton would have a quiet
walk-over. By mid-June, however, there were growing rumours of
activity by the Leeds merchants. In particular it was thought that
John Beckett, son of a prominent townsman and former Mayor,
was to be proposed. Beckett quickly realised that the commercial
towns were not yet strong enough to elect a member of their own.
The situation nevertheless caused much anxiety in Milton's camp.
His success in 1807 was based on the West Riding, but now, though
some reported that the landed interest in the other Ridings was more

favourable, it was feared that the West was no longer his safe stronghold. Wortley's home district was also in south Yorkshire and it was rumoured that he was in league with the Leeds faction to carry both seats against the Wentworth interest. Wortley discouraged these attempts as imprudent, however, and after last-minute attempts by the more hot-headed to find a third candidate the election passed off quietly. At the nomination Sir Francis Wood, proposing Milton, referred more confidently to 'the attempt of the five towns (an ominous dictatorship) to nominate fit persons to represent this county'.

The episode had, for a time, shaken Fitzwilliam's confidence in the security of his Yorkshire interest. 'I was in a figgit,' he confessed to Milton during the preliminaries to the election. '. . . We are still kept in hot water by the Leeds junto.' 'Had a person of any respectability, of the blue politics, come forward,' one of Stuart Wortley's principal helpers wrote, 'such is Lord Milton's present unpopularity the whole county would have been in a flame.' Fitzwilliam too confessed that, had a second Tory candidate appeared, he had considered starting a second Whig and repeating the contest of 1807, relying on the appearance of the struggle as one not between Whig and Tory but 'between the Yard and the Acre— between the banker's back parlour and the gentlemen at large— between the borough of Leeds and the county—between the monied and the landed interest'. After the collapse of the supposed Tory opposition, Fitzwilliam congratulated himself that

it has turned out not only satisfactory but useful, in a variety of points of view—It has embodied the country against the junto of Leeds—Whigs and Tory have united to keep down the assuming spirit and presumptuous pretensions of that little clique who in their arrogance thought all the gentlemen of the county were to be subordinate to the dictates of Beckett's back parlour. [The election] . . . brought together a vast concourse of the principal gentlemen, who came to vindicate their own honour by the support of you and Wortley.

the unprecedented crowd at the Castle yard, he believed, was evidence that 'the sense of the county was truly taken on that day'.

Such confidence was blind to the future. As Liverpool informed Canning, Milton could well have been turned out 'if it had not been the interest of the gentlemen of the county to keep things quiet'. Aristocratic disdain of the Leeds merchants and their 'back parlour' intrigues paid too little attention to the rising tide of middle-class political ambition.[39]. The 1820 election passed off quietly, Milton reporting that he was well received at Leeds, where Edward Baines, editor of the influential *Leeds Mercury*, was on his side. Wortley, Milton noted, was attended in his canvass of the town by no stronger force of merchants than was to be found in Milton's train.[40] The 1826 election, however, took place in the new situation created by the addition of Grampound's two former seats to the county. It soon became clear that at least one, if not two, of the four members would be claimed as primarily the representatives of the commercial and manufacturing interests, while the alliance of the merchants with the anti-Catholic faction also menaced the Whig hold on the county. They were 'critical, feverish times', Fitzwilliam agitatedly wrote to Milton. He feared that the Tory interest intended to try for three members, and warned Milton that their hostility was 'against *you*, and originates in Leeds'. The Whigs countered by putting up Carlisle's son, Lord Morpeth, with Milton. 'I have written,' Fitzwilliam informed Milton, '. . . to state, that we, the Whigs, claim one of the two [new members]: that we fix on Lord Morpeth— that with respect to the Tory candidate, we have nothing to do with that concern—it is the Tory business.' Milton, however, was alarmed at his father's impetuosity and at the prospect of the vast expense of a second Yorkshire contest. He urged him to refrain from precipitate action. He was willing to contribute up to £30,000 towards the cost of the election, but could not agree to spend any- thing more. 'I am induced to speak to you thus early and decidedly,' Milton wrote, 'because I know how over ready you are to embark on undertakings of this kind without consideration.' His own view was that the challenge would peter out because of the rift between the pro- and anti-emancipation Tories, and that it would therefore be rash to do anything that might stir up a contest. 'Matters are settled in the West Riding,' he wrote, 'and there are other principles and feelings that work far more actively in the populous districts than religious antipathy. We found that in 1807, we shall find it so in 1826.'[41]

By early November, six potential candidates were in the field; two Whig, two 'liberal Tory', and two anti-Catholic Tory. The next few months witnessed a battle of nerves, of bluff and counter-bluff, with the aim on all sides of frightening off the other and avoiding the threatened contest. 'All will depend on who has the *best pluck*', Sir

John Ramsden wrote, and, of course, on who was able to command enough money. Morpeth was relying on his uncle, the Duke of Devonshire, to finance him, but the Duke was wary and refused to stand the expense of a contest. 'He had no objection to his nephew taking the sweet of a quiet election, but now that there may be a smattering of the sour, he declares off,' Fitzwilliam wrote bitterly. '. . . It is really provoking, for Lord Morpeth is a delightful young man, and made to be a Whig.' Morpeth's retreat distressed Milton, who was hoping for a Whig colleague to share the expense. He declared to his friend Althorp that

I shall feel no great disposition to enter the next Parliament the only Whig member for Yorkshire. My great object in continuing to stand is not to obtain for myself a seat in Parliament (which I can have at Higham Ferrers), but to maintain Whig preponderance or at least Whig equality in Yorkshire and if that object is not attained I had rather not stand.

However, as Althorp pointed out, there was a limit to the value even of a seat for Yorkshire:

You always view the importance of politics in a stronger light than I do, and estimate much higher than I do the duty of making personal sacrifices to promote one's political principles, but I can hardly think that on reflection even you will say that it is a duty incumbent upon any man to spend seventy, sixty, fifty, forty, thirty or even twenty thousand pounds to secure an equal division between the Whigs and Tories in Yorkshire.

Sir Francis Wood, too, declared that Milton's friends would prefer to secure his safe election than to engage in a dubious contest to win two seats.[42]

The search for a second Whig candidate went on nevertheless, and in February the name of John Marshall, a wealthy Leeds flax-spinner and Whig supporter, was mentioned with approval. He was, Thomas Tottie informed Fitzwilliam, 'a man of intellect, knowledge and integrity . . . and his politics are decidedly hostile to those of the Tories'. Besides being 'an enlightened and independent legislator' and an advocate of Catholic emancipation, he would be a very suitable man to cope with the heavy local commercial business which increasingly burdened the members for Yorkshire and he would bring support from the trading towns. The main difficulty was, as before, the financial one. Milton still wished to limit the prospective expense, and would have liked, if possible, to raise a subscription in the county. Despite, however, the acknowledgement of 'how much the county owes to the noble and successful struggle made by yourself in 1807 to liberate it from the entire predominance of Tory interests', Sir Francis Wood wrote to Milton, the prospects were 'very discouraging . . . In the highest quarters little or nothing was to be expected, amongst the more opulent of the gentry the temporary distress and want of money was urged as conclusive against their present exertion, the more liberal talked of hundreds where perhaps thousands were expected from them and . . . the total would be found extremely inadequate to the expenses of a contest'. 1826 was indeed a bad year to try to raise money for elections, for the country was in the grip of a financial crisis which had led to the failure of many country banks, and money was difficult to raise at short notice. Fitzwilliam, therefore, had to find the money unaided, though Marshall agreed, Milton wrote, 'to add 30,000 to our 30,000'. Milton hoped that the joint expenses of his and Marshall's election would be limited to £80,000. This would not have covered the cost of a poll, but fortunately a contest was avoided. Wortley and Bethell, the two 'liberal Tory' candidates, withdrew, leaving Milton and Marshall to share the representation with the 'no-Popery' candidates Wilson and Duncombe. 'I could have wished that the no-Popery cry had not found two representatives,' Carlisle wrote, 'but it is a great point that you and Milton have been spared much trouble and expense, and that the commercial and manufacturing interest is adequately represented.' The expense, however, was over £50,000. The contest had been carried to the very last moment before the election meeting, and preparations for a poll had been taken to an advanced stage. Large numbers of Milton's supporters had been summoned and brought up to York for the election day. 'I never had election accounts to settle before,' Thomas Tottie wrote, 'and what I have experienced on the present occasion, will I think deter me from ever undertaking them again, [but] . . . I think your Lordship will allow that no means could . . . have been safely relied on to secure the return of a Leeds merchant, along with your Lordship, . . . but those which were adopted.'[43]

It was the last time Milton was to be elected as member for Yorkshire. Not only could such repeated costs be disastrous even to the Fitzwilliam fortune, but by 1830 Milton's tenure of the seat could clearly not be expected to be a long one. His father was 82, and the succession to the House of Lords could not be far off. 'To have incurred the risk of expending any more money on the county would under all the circumstances have been very absurd,' Francis Maude wrote in July 1830. The preservation of the Whig interest among the West Riding manufacturers had been his principal achievement. The trustees of the Leeds Coloured Cloth Hall regretted the end of a connexion which had 'produced if we may so term it a kind of intimacy which will perhaps never again be realised between them and any other member'. The Whig party cause in the county, too, owed much to his and his father's efforts over the years since 1807. 'I consider the County at large is under deep obligations to Lord Fitzwilliam and yourself for the great exertions you have made and for the intrepid defence of liberal and right principles—during periods of great danger,' wrote George Strickland, chairman of Milton's committee in 1826.[44] No Fitzwilliam sat again for Yorkshire in the unreformed Parliament. Milton's parting advice to the trustees of the Leeds Cloth Halls was that his successor ought to be 'a friend of civil and religious liberty' and 'he should be taken from among the landed proprietors . . . because . . . they are less liable to be influenced by partial views than any other class of man'. The candidate nominated for his seat was, however, Henry Brougham, a 'stranger' with no property in the county. His support lay amongst the West Riding liberals and was largely the product of 'anti-colonial slavery' opinion. Despite the preference of Yorkshire gentlemen for what Lord Dundas described as 'a regular game-preserving Yorkshire squire', Brougham obtained the support of the Wentworth interest. Milton wrote frankly to Brougham that his election would be 'an anomaly' and that though 'pure country gentlemen are not always very wise or well informed legislators . . . taking them *as a mass* . . . power and authority cannot be deposited in safer hands'. The election of 'ambitious Ministers' for counties with which they had no natural connexion might, he feared, tend to increase the power of the Crown. Nevertheless, he assured Brougham of his support on political grounds. Brougham's candidature was due to political feeling rather than traditional deference; but that Whigs continued to fill two of the seats for England's largest and most influential county was largely Fitzwilliam's achievement.[45]

By 1830 Milton had largely taken over the management of Fitzwilliam's electoral interests, so that their history in the 1820s belongs more properly to his biography than to his father's. Fitz-

william, however, remained as keenly interested as always in electioneering. Since the days when he had offered to come back in the
middle of his grand tour to encourage his supporters at Peterborough,
he had infused energy and method into the administration of the
family's election interests in Yorkshire and Northamptonshire. He
had also extended his operations into constituencies such as Retford
and Lincoln, and had begun to energise the flagging and weakly
based Whig interest in Huntingdonshire, where Milton house itself
lay. That county was politically under the total domination of the
Montagu family, allied with most of the gentry houses. The Whig
interest was mainly among the yeomanry and independent freeholders, and consequently it lacked the backbone of organisation
usually supplied in the unreformed counties by the professional
estate stewards of the larger landowners. It was also difficult to
find a suitable candidate, for there were few resident gentlemen both
Whiggish and respectable enough to qualify. 'Nothing can be done
without you,' Lord Carysfort, the leading Whig landowner in the
county assured the Fitzwilliams. In 1820 the Whigs won one seat for
Lord John Russell without a poll, the Duke of Manchester having
decided not to put up a rival candidate, but in 1826 the Montagus
opposed him and he was defeated. The Whig interest in Huntingdonshire was weak and far from united, and despite Milton's financial
support no permanent success was achieved.[46]

Peterborough, the quietest and safest of seats since 1790, became
unexpectedly troublesome in the 1820s. The 1818 election was quiet,
Elliot and Lamb being returned again. Elliot died shortly after the
election and was replaced by James Scarlett, a Whig lawyer, while
Lamb vacated his seat in 1819 to stand for Hertfordshire. To replace
Lamb, Fitzwilliam put forward Sir Robert Heron, a country gentleman from Lincolnshire with reformist views and an irritable temper,
assuring him that their variance on the subject of reform was
unimportant:

Upon this subject no one can be more decided than I am: I think it
impossible that anything should ever persuade me not to oppose every
theoretic reform [Fitzwilliam wrote]: but . . . I should never request a
friend who has once had the misfortune to let unlucky words drop from
his lips to recant, but I should say to him, be not prominent, stir not up
a subject that disturbs the ignorant and unwary and renders men's minds
dissatisfied and suspicious.

Heron assured Fitzwilliam that his support of reform had been very moderate indeed, and that he had 'never been a friend to annual Parliaments, universal suffrage or election by ballot', and that if in future he did find himself at variance with his patron on the subject he would at once take the Chiltern Hundreds. On the following day he added to Milton that 'my respect for Lord Fitzwilliam and knowledge of his opinion' would make him even less prominently a reformer in future.[47]

The difficulty arose not over any variance between Heron's principles and Fitzwilliam's but over Heron's reception at Peterborough. Heron was believed to be an opponent of the Church establishment, and even hostile to religion itself, and the Cathedral clergy were not slow to point out that a man with such a reputation was no fit representative of their city. The Archdeacon of Northampton, Dr William Strong, and twenty-five electors signed a letter to Fitzwilliam urging that Heron would not be acceptable 'either to us, or, as we are taught to believe, to a large portion of the other electors', and declaring that they would feel themselves 'most lamentably degraded' by his nomination. Milton addressed a scorching rebuke to Strong, remonstrating that his family had for many years 'uniformly manifested a desire to consult the honour and dignity of [the] inhabitants' in the selection of candidates, and that, if Heron were not so distinguished as the normal run of Peterborough's representatives, he was an honourable and respectable gentleman of unimpeachably Whig views. The only imputation against him must be an account of his moral and religious opinions, and here his own enquiries had satisfied him as to Heron's character. He was dismayed that such imputations could be made against Heron, and, by implication, against himself and his father, by one 'who has known me from my cradle, and my family from the earliest periods of his own recollection'. Strong stoutly replied that not twenty voters would support Heron, and in support of his contentions on Heron's religious views cited the recent appearance on Peterborough walls of such graffiti as 'No bishops, No parsons'. 'No such placards ever before disgraced this city,' he declared.

Fitzwilliam thought it a storm in a teacup, and believed the real opposition to Heron was 'because he votes through thick and thin in opposition—is therefore an improper representative of the ever loyal city of P.—no longer then the holy city—politics override religion'. Though Heron was elected quietly and without open dissent, however, this election marked the beginning of trouble for the family interest. Henceforward the Fitzwilliams had to contend with secret or overt opposition from the Cathedral. In March 1825 the Dean and Chapter petitioned Parliament against Catholic emancipation. In 1826 the lease of some property belonging to the cathedral expired, and Milton refused the large fine demanded for its renewal. It was therefore granted to supporters of a rival interest, and from this time a Tory opposition arose which led to contested elections in the city in the 1830s. In 1823, when James Scarlett vacated one of the seats to stand for Cambridge University, there was a flurry of excitement when a radical candidate contested the by-election, but he gained only 31 votes against 517. The first real challenge from the Tory interest came in 1835, though it was unsuccessful until an alliance with the radicals captured one seat in 1852.[48]

Malton remained quiet after 1818, though the agricultural distress of the time had to be alleviated by rent reductions on the estate to keep the tenantry in good political order. Here Fitzwilliam's power as a landlord had been too convincingly demonstrated in 1807 to encourage further rebellion, though there were still occasional reports of political disaffection among the tenantry. The electorate had nevertheless to be treated with generosity, and the customary 'attentions' to their needs and appetites continued to be paid well into the later nineteenth century.[49] York continued to be corrupt and turbulent, with contests in 1818, at which one of Fitzwilliam's candidates was defeated by Sir Mark Sykes, the old enemy, and in 1820, when two Whigs were at last returned after a sharp contest. The two elections and a by-election in 1820 altogether cost Fitzwilliam £25,000.[50] In 1826 one of the seats had to be conceded to the Tories again without a poll. Hull was always more difficult to manage even than York, and equally expensive, but in 1818 Fitzwilliam was able to secure the return of J. R. G. Graham of Netherby by thirty-eight votes, after an expensive scrutiny of the poll which cost Fitzwilliam an extra £2,000 and (fortunately) bankrupted the rival candidate. 'Throughout this transaction I have considered myself . . . entirely your lordship's instrument, and have rested so . . . much on your assistance and support,' Graham wrote. In 1820 Graham resigned for family reasons and because of his fear of expense. Daniel Sykes took over the Whig seat in an unusually quiet election costing only some £2,600, and retained it after a much more costly contest in 1826. In 1830 William Battie Wrightson succeeded Sykes in another contest, and from 1832 onwards Hull became a regular battle ground for the parties. It was, Graham wrote in 1820, 'a pit of fathomless corruption' where hardly a handful of the 3,000 electors would ever vote without payment of two guineas.[51] Here, as in the county and at York, Fitzwilliam had striven for many years to uphold a Whig interest at great personal cost. At Retford in 1826 he similarly financed the party attempting to break the Duke of Newcastle's hold on the borough, in a contest as violent as it was expensive and which ended with the Whig candidates taking to their heels to escape the fury of a mob which came near to lynching them.[52] All these efforts represented a substantial service to the party cause. Over the years many hundreds of thousands of pounds had been poured into elections from the Wentworth and Fitzwilliam fortunes, yet, despite the corrupt practices—from a more modern viewpoint—which that vast expenditure had often fostered, Fitzwilliam's own political ethics had never been convincingly disputed. He accepted the political conventions of his day, but showed that they were not incompatible with the highest standards of personal integrity.

Family changes occupied much of 1822–3. In August 1821 Charlotte was seriously ill, and despite an apparent recovery by Christmas she became weaker again in the Spring of 1822. She died on 13 May. 'She . . . died by inches having death upon her for weeks before the fatal stroke,' Fitzwilliam later wrote. His depression was increased by serious trouble with his eyesight, which was to be dealt with by a series of operations—no small undertaking at the age of 74. Fortunately the first operation, though destroying the sight of the left eye, unexpectedly led to so marked an improvement in the sight of the other that it was decided to go no further with them. 'His sight is now perfectly good for all common purposes and his anxieties are relieved,' Milton wrote on 29 August. Fitzwilliam's domestic life, too, was briefly restored again in July 1823 when to the astonishment of many friends and of the public, he remarried. His second wife was Louisa, Lady Ponsonby, a close friend of many years, widow of his old friend William Ponsonby and Charlotte's cousin by marriage. Grey's wife was her daughter, so that the marriage made Fitzwilliam Grey's father-in-law. He had been fond of Mary, now Lady Grey, from her infancy, and he now wrote to her of his delight that the hour had come 'when I am called upon to love you with that affection which such a connexion requires'. To

Grey too he wrote of his confidence that Louisa's 'life will be devoted to render mine happy, [and] I venture to assure those who love her most that her happiness will be the first object of mine—I like it the better,' he assured Grey, as making their own relationship 'more manifest and not to be misunderstood by the world'. Louisa, Grey replied, was 'a person, whom I have always loved as my own mother', and it was gratifying indeed that she should link him more intimately with Fitzwilliam and strengthen 'all those ties of confidence and attachment which had previously subsisted between us'. The marriage took place quietly at the Ponsonby home at Bishop's Court in Ireland, and was performed by Louisa's son Richard. The only other persons present were Fitzwilliam's Wicklow agent, Haigh, and Louisa's maid, 'Old Barnes'. Milton's friend Lord Althorp feared that it would be prejudicial to the former close relationship between Milton and his father.

I am afraid [Althorp wrote] it will place you in a very difficult situation, a more difficult one indeed than almost any other son would be placed in in similar circumstances; for in proportion to the extraordinary degree of confidence existing between you and your father heretofore, will the change be greater which I fear must now take place. . . . I must say I think you hardly used and it is no great encouragement to men in our situation to make sacrifices for those who are older than ourselves.

Louisa was introduced to Yorkshire society as the new Lady Fitzwilliam at the great musical festival held in York Minster in August 1823, an assembly described by Fitzwilliam as 'a general meeting of the whole county'. Shortly after reaching Yorkshire, however, she became ill. A cold, or possibly an attack of gout or rheumatism led to a long, slow decline and her death on 1 September 1824.[53] Fitzwilliam was a widower for the remaining years of his life.

During these last nine years, though he became increasingly infirm physically, Fitzwilliam's interest in political affairs remained lively and he watched with committed interest the progress of liberal causes always close to his heart. The Catholic question and the associated Irish problem continued to be the chief of these. In December 1824 he wrote to Grey of his dismay at the continued repression in Ireland. The consequence, he declared, must be to rouse up Irish separatism.

I am old enough to have lived through the American business [he wrote] from its first commencement to the ultimate result, and remembering how this unfortunate country was led on from one little step to another, I know our only chance of salvation must be stopping the very first. Having lost thirteen provinces to compliment the overbearing prejudices of a king, shall we throw away half our empire to compliment the rash folly of an heir presumptive—are we never to grow wise, does experience work nothing in our favour?

In February 1825 he went up to attend the Lords' debate on the Catholic question and later in the year he attended a meeting of Protestant peers with estates in Ireland to address the king on the subject of emancipation. He was now a more frequent visitor to Ireland than earlier in his life, often staying at the Bessborough's home, and in the summer of 1826 a deputation of Catholic representatives came to honour him there, saying that 'they hailed my short administration as the forerunner of a new system'. To Grey, however, Fitzwilliam expressed his anxiety at the continued delay in carrying Catholic relief. 'If this lack of emancipation is to go on,' he remarked, 'till you have war with a foreign power, from that instant you lose Ireland,' and a hostile Ireland would cut British communication with her new allies in South America. He had thought of asking an audience with the king, to warn him that persistence in the anti-Catholic policy would lead to an explosion. 'I do not advise him to change his Ministry, far from it,' he told Grey; 'but I do advise him to let his Ministers know what is fit for *their interests* that they should advise.' In January 1829 the recall of Lord Anglesey, the Lord Lieutenant of Ireland, for expressing disagreement with Wellington's anti-Catholic policy brought Fitzwilliam's experience in 1795 back to mind. Fitzwilliam was among those English peers and politicians invited to the mass meeting at Dublin on 20 January to call for emancipation, but he declined on 'a full consideration of the circumstances and my ignorance whether other persons similarly situated will be disposed to go over in such numbers as to give them weight'.[34] The battle was now won, however, and at the opening of the new session the Ministers announced that the Emancipation Bill was to be introduced as a government measure. Fitzwilliam's policy of 1795 was at last vindicated.

In other respects he still showed his attachment to an older world and its ways. The advance of the railway age filled him with apprehension, despite the benefits it was to bring to his family's mining and industrial interests during the next century.

o

Good roads are very good things, and greatly tend to the improvement of a country, [he wrote] but . . . these railroads can't be made without cutting up and disfiguring, without deteriorating the cultivation of the country by cutting down the hills and filling up the valleys to make levels just as much, perhaps . . . more even than the canals, which however are already made, and those mischiefs already done. But who can think that any important national benefit is to be derived from transporting half a hundred of cotton goods quicker from Manchester to London—but for this important purpose, all of us who have property between these two points, are to have it at the mercy of jobbing trustees and mendicant engineers.

He himself had been approached to become an honorary director of the 'Royal Hibernian General Railroad Company'—'my answer has been that whatever I could do to prevent the establishment of such a company, I would do—think of placing at the mercy of a set of London capitalists all the landed property of Ireland'. The movers of these schemes were 'traffickers in money—a very useful class, I grant—but are we quite sure, that the setting afloat such projects, putting them in newspapers, may not be converted into swindling means?'[55] By the late 1820s the pace of change was moving too fast for those who had grown up in more leisurely times.

Politics too were changing. The unexpected collapse of Liverpool's ministry in 1827 created something of a political revolution that seemed likely to lead to a reconstitution of party alignments, creating a moderate Tory–Whig alliance of the centre. This was a prospect Grey did not relish. He had always considered Canning as not only personally ambitious and untrustworthy, but socially unacceptable as a Prime Minister—his well-known sneer that the son of an actress was *ipso facto* debarred from becoming Prime Minister of England reflected a lifetime's adherence to the aristocratic principle. Grey declared that he himself would take no office under him, though he would not actively discourage his followers from doing so if the new government were to pledge itself to Catholic emancipation. Fitzwilliam, however, took a more generous view, and urged Grey to forget Canning's old offences of twenty years ago, and rather to rejoice at

the dismissal of that proud oligarchical faction who have so long overridden us and have with their chancellor at their head attempted to override the king also—they have failed, and we owe to Canning (at the risk of every thing important to him) that they have so failed —this therefore is a merit which we owe to him and which we ought to repay, by giving him . . . the silent support of not opposing.

Grey replied with a long justification of his attitude, stressing that his disapproval arose not mainly from personal dislike but from a suspicion that Canning's government would be formed on the same principles as its predecessor, and that in particular offers had been made to prominent anti-Catholics.[56] The offer, therefore, of the Attorney-Generalship to one of Fitzwilliam's members, James Scarlett, tested the Whig attitude to Canning's appointment. Fitzwilliam advised Scarlett against acceptance, but 'at the same time giving my own determination to give every support in my power to Canning's administration'. Grey, not unnaturally, remarked that he could not see, in that case, why Scarlett should not accept. Scarlett himself, who was eager for the office, argued that unless Canning were supported by the Whigs he would have to capitulate to the Tories. Lansdowne was in favour of acceptance, provided 'that the great Tories were not to be restored to the Cabinet', as 'a pledge to Canning that the Whigs would support him so long as his government was conducted upon principles of which they approved'. Milton and Fitzwilliam both nevertheless wrote that they could not advise it unless there was a positive pledge on the Catholic question. Scarlett pointed out that to make such stipulations was

like a man fainting for a particular fruit but who magnanimously resolves to die under the tree with his mouth open if the fruit will not fall into it, rather than climb the tree to gather it. . . . Can the Whigs ever expect to possess the government if they convince the nation as well as the king that they are determined never to have it unless all their wishes are *at once* accomplished?

Milton replied that 'If you think that by accepting office the Catholic question will be advanced, you are not only justified, but called upon to accept', and, with Fitzwilliam's approval, Scarlett did so, despite the breakdown of negotiations between Canning and Lansdowne over the Catholic issue. Hopes were dashed, however, when Canning died a few weeks later and, after a short interlude with the ineffective Goderich at the Treasury, Wellington reconstituted a Tory government early in 1828. Milton declared strongly against Scarlett's remaining a member of 'the very worst government I ever remember, or even heard of, there is no vice belonging to a government which is not to be found in it'. Fitzwilliam took a similar view, and consoled himself with the thought that 'We are open again to good old Whig principles and practices—they never can be wrong—at least

I am sure they never will be wrong, as long as I live—I was born in them, and in them I shall die'.[57] Despite the passing of emancipation by Wellington's government, the years 1828–9 saw the reconstitution of the old Whig-Tory lines of division in politics, and Wellington's defeat in 1830 on reform therefore resulted in Grey's becoming head of a predominantly Whig administration for the first time since 1807.

Fitzwilliam was, of course, too old to take part in political affairs after 1830, and Milton too declared his retirement from public life after the sudden death of his wife in childbirth on 1 November. In fact Milton was soon persuaded to return to politics, and he fought the battle for his favourite measure of parliamentary reform alongside his friends throughout 1831. His father, however, was too feeble to take any part in Parliament after 1830, and after a slow, gradual decline in health Fitzwilliam died on 8 February 1833, at Milton, in the house where he was born almost eighty-five years before.[58]

Fitzwilliam's was a life devoted to causes and to public duty. Brought up with the traditions of Rockingham Whiggery always in mind, he remained a man of the late eighteenth century. Adherence to principle, which, like his uncle and his friends Burke and Fox, he identified with the cause of the Whig party, was the guiding rule of his life. He lacked the political drive and flair which made great statesmen, but he stood always in the front of the second rank, dependable, reliable and steadfast. That consistency which was his chief claim to political virtue could also, on occasion, be his greatest liability. He lacked the flexibility to accommodate means to ends, and the patience, or deviousness, to take the longer way round. In Ireland in 1795 or in the House of Lords during the next decade, he stuck to the principles he believed to be right at the cost of political ineffectiveness and even of immediate failure. But his life was not an unsuccessful one. He rescued the Whig political interest in Yorkshire from the disasters which Fox, and his own inexperience, brought upon it between 1782 and 1784, and built up a formidable electoral machine which maintained Whig influence there for nearly thirty years. He devoted many thousands, indeed hundreds of thousands, of his income to political and public causes. In return, he received affection, respect and reputation, but he never sought tangible or financial rewards, nor honours for himself or any of his family. But above all, his political career bore witness to the strength which uprightness and friendship could exert in the supposedly corrupt world of eighteenth-century politics. A man who could win the lasting affection of Charles James Fox, the unshaken devotion of Edmund Burke, and the respect of a host of lesser but not unperceptive men, was not a political failure. 'Lord Fitzwilliam is one of the very few men that there is but one opinion of in the world,' Lady Shannon wrote in 1823. Fox's nephew, Lord Holland, wrote of Fitzwilliam in his *Memoirs:*

With little talent and less acquirements, he was, throughout life, one of the most considerable men in the country and a striking instance of that most agreeable truth—that courage and honesty in great situations more than supply the place of policy or talent. It was not his relationship to Lord Rockingham, though no doubt an advantage, nor his princely fortune, though a yet greater, which conferred the sort of importance he enjoyed for half a century in this country. He derived it more directly and more certainly from his goodness and generosity, and from the combination of gentleness and courage which distinguished his amiable and unpretending character. Such unblemished purity and such unobtrusive intrepidity, such generosity of feeling, firmness of purpose, and tenderness of heart, meeting in one of high station and princely fortune, commanded the affection and confidence of the public; and Lord Fitzwilliam enjoyed them, beyond even those of his own class who united much greater reach of understanding and more assiduity of business to superior personal accomplishments and advantages.[59]

Notes

[1] H. Parker to Fitzwilliam, 15 April 1812 (F 45f); Fitzwilliam to Milton, 24 August [1819] (N x1636). For 'Peterloo' see D. Read, *Peterloo: the 'Massacre' and its Background* (Manchester, 1958) and R. Walmsley, *Peterloo: the Case Reopened* (Manchester, 1969).

[2] *The Life and Times of Henry Brougham* (1871), II, pp. 341–44 (25 August 1819); Fawkes to Milton [September 1819] (N); Milton to Wood, 17 September (Hickleton MSS, A. 4. 10); Lord George Cavendish to Fitzwilliam, 2 October 1819; Devonshire to Fitzwilliam, October 1819 (N).

[3] Fitzwilliam to S. A. Beardsley, 17 October 1819, quoted in Walmsley, *op. cit.*, p. 325; Fitzwilliam to T. Garforth, 4 June 1802 (Y 16).

[4] Fitzwilliam to Sidmouth, 25 July 1812 (F 52); to Lord Pelham, 27 September 1802 (F 45d); to Sidmouth, 21 and 31 July 1819 (Y 10). On 25 September Fitzwilliam reported a lack of enthusiasm even among the unemployed for the speeches of orators on Hunslet Moor (*ibid.*), and on 6 August he assured Lady Ponsonby that people went to these meetings only as a form of free entertainment: 'the people go to hear them as they would go to see Punch, if Punch would make them laugh for nothing'. A few prosecutions of radical orators would soon end the business (Hickleton MSS, A. 1. 2. 9/5).

⁵ Fitzwilliam to Lady Ponsonby, 5 October 1819 (*ibid.*, A. 1. 2. 9/6); to Lord Holland, 18 September (B.M. Add MS 51593, f. 4); Draft requisition, F 52–57. B. Cooke to Fitzwilliam, 18 September 1819 (F 48d) refers to Fitzwilliam's instructions that a moderate tone should be adopted.

6 Fitzwilliam to Grey, 10 and 15 October [1819] : Grey MSS. There is correspondence regarding Mitchell and his activities in 1819–20 in F 52c.

⁷ E. Phipps, *Memoirs of the . . . Life of Robert Plumer Ward, Esq.* (1850), II, p. 18; R. Price to Milton, 25 October 1819; Holland to Fitzwilliam, 25 October 1819 (N); Fitzwilliam to Holland, 4 November 1819 (B.M. Add. MS 51593, ff. 42–3).

⁸ Brougham to Milton [3 October 1819]; W. Lamb to Fitzwilliam, 24 October; J. R. G. Graham to Fitzwilliam, 24 October 1819 (N).

⁹ Fitzwilliam to Lady Fitzwilliam, 'Monday' (N x515). The Duke of Kent was another of the Regent's brothers to express his respect for Fitzwilliam. In 1819 he appealed to him for financial assistance to pay off his large debts. Fitzwilliam contributed £2,500. The sum raised allowed the Duke and Duchess to return to England for the Duchess's confinement. Fitzwilliam was thus partly responsible for enabling the future Queen Victoria to be born on English soil (letters in F 134).

¹⁰ Read, *Peterloo*, pp. 195–7; Fitzwilliam to Sir F. Wood, 18 December 1819 (Hickleton MSS, A. 4. 10); Grey to Holland, 24 October 1819, and to Lady Ponsonby, 4 December 1819 (Grey MSS). On the Whig party's divisions over reform see Austin Mitchell, 'The Whigs and parliamentary reform before 1830', in *Historical Studies (Australia and N.Z.)*, XII (1965), pp. 22–42.

¹¹ 3 and 10 January 1820 : Grey MSS.

¹² Quoted in S. Reid, *Life and Letters of Lord Durham* (1906), I, pp. 129–30. Read (pp. 199–200) and H. W. C. Davis, *The Age of Grey and Peel*, pp. 212–3, suggest that Grey's hesitation was due to his anxiety to conciliate the Grenvilles, but it was much more because of his anxiety not to offend Fitzwilliam.

¹³ Grey to Holland, 26 December 1819 (copy) : Grey MSS.

¹⁴ Tottie to Milton, 20 December 1819 (N); Lamb to Fitzwilliam, 17 January 1820 : F49b.

¹⁵ Fitzwilliam to Holland, 14 February [1820] (B.M. Add. MSS 51593, f. 12) and to Sir F. Wood, 13 February 1820 (Hickleton MSS, A. 4. 10). George III's funeral took place on the night of 16 February in St George's Chapel.

¹⁶ Fitzwilliam to Lady Fitzwilliam, n.d. (N x515); A. Aspinall, *Lord Brougham and the Whig Party* (Manchester, 1927), pp. 101, 106–10.

¹⁷ Quoted in *ibid.*, p. 111.

¹⁸ Princess of Wales to Fitzwilliam, 21 July 1814, and reply (F 115h); Fitzwilliam to Queen Caroline, 29 June 1820; Caroline to Fitzwilliam, 28 June, and Sefton and Fitzwilliam to Brougham, 15 June (F 84); Fitzwilliam to Wood, 17 February 1821 (Hickleton MSS, A. 4. 19. 9).

¹⁹ Fitzwilliam to Milton [23 October 1820] (G 14), and [19 November 1820] (N); to Grey, [9 July 1820] (Grey MSS), and to Wood, 9 November (Hickleton MSS, A. 4. 19. 9).

[20] D. Sykes to Fitzwilliam, 8 December, and R. Chaloner, 6 December 1820; H. Gally Knight to Milton, 5 December 1820 (N); Fitzwilliam to Lady Ponsonby, 4 December 1820 (Hickleton MSS, A. 1. 2. 9/7), and to Grey, 6 and 10 December [1820] (Grey MSS).

[21] Grey to Sir Robert Wilson, 5 December (quoted in Aspinall, *Brougham*, p. 115); to Holland, 6 December 1820 (copy) (Grey MSS); to Fitzwilliam, 6 December (N), and reply, 10th (Grey MSS).

[22] Lady Grey to Lady Ponsonby, Wednesday [1821]; Fitzwilliam to Grey, [c. 11 January 1821]; Lambton to Grey, January 1820 (Grey MSS); Fitzwilliam to Wood, 12 and 17 February 1821 (Hickleton MSS, A. 4. 19. 9).

[23] Fitzwilliam to Milton [3 March 1821]; Milton to Sir G. Cayley, 11 March 1821 (copy) (N). Caley had writen to Walter Fawkes on 14 November 1812 defending his support of Milton's re-election, despite his then hostility to reform, remarking that 'so long as 500 such men could be sent to Parliament at each general election, there would indeed be no need of reform' (copy in Hickleton MSS, A. 4. 19).

[24] *The Times*, 3 March and 31 May 1821.

[25] See *infra*, pp. 372–6.

[26] *The Times*, 18 April: *Parl. Deb.*, n.s., v, 359–453.

[27] *Life of Edward Baines*, p. 118.

[28] *The Times*, 2 April 1821. Fitzwilliam proposed the thanks of the meeting to the High Sheriff (the chairman) and the proceedings closed with three cheers for the queen and three for Lord John Russell.

[29] Grey to Fitzwilliam, 13 January 1822 (N). Fitzwilliam had told Grey that he had ordered a general reduction in his rents (6 January: Grey MSS).

[30] N x515, dated February/March 1822 from internal evidence. A further list, dateable to February/March 1823, produces a similar picture: boroughs with populations of over 5,000 returned seventy-three supporters of opposition and sixty-six ministerialists, while those with less than 1000 inhabitants returned twelve and forty respectively.

[31] Fitzwilliam to Grey, 24 March 1822: Grey MSS.

[32] Fitzwilliam to Grey, 4 April (*ibid.*), and Grey to Fitzwilliam, 6 April (N).

[33] *Parl. Deb.*, n.s., VII, 51–141. The motion included a proposal for the partial disfranchisement of 100 small boroughs and the addition of seats to the manufacturing towns.

[34] Milton to Fawkes, 10 August 1822 (N); Fitzwilliam to Wood, 12 August, and Milton to Wood, 6 November (Hickleton MSS, A. 4. 19); Milton to Grey, 22 October 1822 (Grey MSS); Althorp to Milton, 9 August (N).

[35] 25 January 1823.

[36] *Life of Edward Baines*, pp. 118–9; *The Times*, 24 January 1823; Mitchell, *The Whigs in Opposition*, p. 180.

[37] J. R. Dinwiddy, *Christopher Wyvill and Reform*, 1790–1820 (York, Borthwick Papers, No. 39, 1971), p. 31.

[38] Grey to Milton, 14 September 1831 (G 83) and reply, 16th (Grey MSS).

[39] On the 1818 election see correspondence in F 48c and G 1; Liverpool to Canning, 6 July 1818 (Harewood MSS); S. Corbett to Lady Caroline Stuart-Wortley, 15, 21 and [22] June (Wharncliffe MSS); Fitzwilliam to Wood, 22 June (Hickleton MSS, A. 4. 19. 3).

[40] Milton to Fitzwilliam, 5 March 1820 (F 48).

[41] Tottie to Milton, 6 June 1825: (N); T. Wilson to Fitzwilliam, 2 December, and enclosure: Downe to Fitzwilliam, 3 December (F 33d); H. Allen to Milton, 29 November (N); Fitzwilliam to Milton, 20 November (N x 515), 29 November (x 516/35), [n.d.] (x 515); Milton to Fitzwilliam, 1 December (N).

[42] Sir J. Ramsden to Milton, 6 December 1825; Devonshire to Fitzwilliam, 17 December (N); Fitzwilliam to Grey, 19 December (Grey MSS); Milton to Althorp, 27 December (Althorp MSS, third earl, box 3); Althorp to Milton, 1 January 1826; Wood to Milton, 14 January (N).

[43] Tottie to Fitzwilliam, 13 March and 1 April 1826 (F 132), and to Wood, 1 June (Hickleton MSS, A. 4. 14); Wood to Milton, 20 May 1826 (N): Milton to Wood, 17 May (Hickleton MSS, A. 4. 19. 6); Althorp to Milton, 4 June (E 237); Carlisle to Fitzwilliam, 15 June [1826]; Tottie to Fitzwilliam, 28 June, and enclosures, and to Milton, 11 November (N). Wortley was created Baron Wharncliffe on 12 July. For Marshall see A Gooder, *Parliamentary Representation of the County of York* (Yorks. Arch. Soc. Record Series, vol. XCVI, 1938), II, p. 117.

[44] Maude to Milton, 5 July 1830 (G 2); address to Lord Milton, 6 July (G 3); Strickland to Milton, 14 October 1829 (G 83).

[45] Milton to Trustees of Leeds Cloth Halls, 15 July 1830 (G 3); Dundas to Milton, 27 July; Strickland to Milton, 31 July (G 2); Milton to Brougham, 29 July (N) and Brougham's reply [30 July] (G 2). Brougham prided himself on his 'universal popularity' with all Yorkshire interests.

[46] For Huntingdonshire see, *inter alia*, Carysfort to Fitzwilliam, 11 July 1818 (F 64f); E. Maltby to Milton, 21 July 1818, and 17 March 1820; Carysfort to Fitzwilliam, 12 January 1826 (N).

[47] Fitzwilliam to Milton, 28 [December 1817] (N x 516/43); Fitzwilliam to Heron, 3 November 1819, and reply, 6th; Heron to Milton, 7 November (N).

[48] W. Strong *et al* to Fitzwilliam, 17 November 1819; Milton to Strong [20 November], and reply 21st; Fitzwilliam to Lady Fitzwilliam [1819] (N); Sir J. Scarlett to Fitzwilliam, 5 February 1820; Heron to Fitzwilliam, 14 March 1820 (F 46b); Duncannon to Grey, 29 May 1820 (Grey MSS); W. Simpson to Milton, 26 October 1826, and enclosure; W. Lawrence to Hon. G. W. Fitzwilliam, 21 July 1859 (N). The petition of 1825 is in *Journals of the House of Lords*, LVII, pp. 123–4.

[49] W. Allen to Fitzwilliam, 4, 17 February, 6 April 1818 (F 107k); F. M. L. Thompson, *English Landed Society in the Nineteenth Century* (1963), p. 274.

[50] Alderman Hotham to Fitzwilliam, 2 November 1820: F 48d.

51 Graham to Fitzwilliam, 21 August, 3 September, 12 November 1818, 8, 26 January, 1, 3 April, 11 May 1819 (F 36c); D. Sykes to Fitzwilliam [24 March 1820] (F 49a); Graham to Fitzwilliam, 4 February 1820 (F 49b).

52 J. Parker to Fitzwilliam, 23 May 1826 (F 64) and 10 June [1826] (N).

53 Lady Milton to Lady Grey, August 1821 (Hickleton MSS, A. 1. 4. 9); Fitzwilliam to Milton, 22 November [1822] (N x 515); Milton to Grey, 29 August 1822 (Grey MSS); Fitzwilliam to Lady Grey, 24 July 1823 (Hickleton MSS, A. 1. 4. 2/8); to Grey, 1 August 1823; Grey to Fitzwilliam, 27 July (Grey MSS); Althorp to Milton, 20 July 1823 (N); Fitzwilliam to Lady Grey, 29 August [1823] (Hickleton MSS, A. 1. 4. 7/4); Grey to J. Ponsonby, 5 September 1824 (Grey MSS).

54 Fitzwilliam to Grey, 23 December [1824] (Grey MSS); Duke of Buckingham and Chandos to Fitzwilliam, 8 July 1825, and 'Resolutions of the Meeting of Protestant Peers' (F 87); Fitzwilliam to Lady Grey, September 1826 (Hickleton MSS, A. 1. 4. 7/7), and to Grey, 28 January 1827 (Grey MSS); Fitzwilliam to Rev. E. Groves, 6 January 1829 (The Times, 24 January).

55 Fitzwilliam to Grey, 20 January 1825; Grey MSS.

56 Grey to Holland, 14 April 1827 (copy); Fitzwilliam to Grey, 17 April, and reply, 18th; Fitzwilliam to Grey, 22 April, and reply, 23rd (Grey MSS).

57 Scarlett to Milton, [20/21 April 1827] (G 15), and enclosure (n.d.) (N); Milton to Scarlett, 22 April (N), and reply [23rd] (G 15); Milton to Scarlett, 25 April (N); Scarlett to Fitzwilliam [25 April], and to Milton [27 April] (G 15); Milton to Scarlett, 24 January 1828 (N); Fitzwilliam to Grey, 21 January 1828 (Grey MSS). Scarlett remained in office under Wellington but kept the seat at Peterborough till 1830 and then moved to Malton. In 1831 he voted against the Reform Bill and was ordered by Milton to take the Chiltern Hundreds (25 March 1831: N).

58 Fitzwilliam was buried on the 24th in the family vault at Marholm, with Charlotte and Louisa.

59 Lady Shannon to Lady Ponsonby, 27 July [1823] (Hickleton MSS, A. 2. 1. 29); Holland, Further Memoirs of the Whig Party 1807–21 (1905), p. 255.

CONCLUSION

The Whig party of the 1820s was a very different body from the group which had followed Rockingham in opposition to the American war and the 'influence of the Crown' half a century before. Though still in some respects an aristocratic party, it could no longer represent simply the aristocratic principle. Fifty years of economic and social change were too far reaching for that. Public opinion was no longer the tentative and deferential body which the Whigs had sought to recruit for their political campaigns in pamphlets and newspapers in the 1780s. Now there were powerful social and economic interests, experienced in independent political activity and determined to exert their own direct influence on governmental policy. The masses, too, were beginning to respond to public agitation and to make their own demands for social and economic justice. No longer were they prepared to wait for an aristocratic lead before expressing a view on public affairs. On the contrary, politicians had now to be acutely conscious that their activities were subject to constant public scrutiny and that their policies had to be formulated in terms acceptable to a wide spectrum of political opinion. Not all the Whigs welcomed such a development, but there was a growing number amongst them who realised that it was irreversible and that the party had to come to terms with it. The legacy of the Foxite opposition of the later 1790s reinforced that view. The experience of the post-1794 period led the Whigs to be a party devoted to public principles, and taught them that they could have no other justification for independent existence. As Fox had observed to Fitzwilliam in March 1792, there was nothing to distinguish Whigs from Tories unless they put forward an alternative to the prevailing Tory principles of government. Despite, therefore, the party's continued dependence on aristocratic patrons for much of its parliamentary strength, despite Grey's decreasing enthusiasm for reform after 1807 and despite the dislike which the conservative wing of the party felt for the radical tendencies of men like Whitbread, Lambton and Brougham, the Whigs found themselves by the 1820s becoming a new kind of party—a party that could survive only by reflecting, rather than leading, public opinion, and which could get into power not by 'storming the closet' from a platform in the House of Commons but by presenting the public with a new political programme. By the 1820s, opposition had to be the alternative government, or it was nothing.

Nevertheless, the Whigs of the 1820s still looked back to the time of Rockingham, and were conscious of a historic continuity of principles. None was more representative of this view than Fitzwilliam, who as Rockingham's heir, Burke's most complete disciple and Fox's closest friend, summed up in his own person the most deeply felt Whig traditions. Fitzwilliam's attitudes were still those of the enlightened Whig aristocracy of the later eighteenth century, and in the 1820s he was still influential and respected enough to make the party respond to its historical legacy. If that tradition was aristocratic, in Fitzwilliam's hands it was the expression of a socially responsible and benevolent governing class. Both parties, after all, were still largely aristocratic in leadership and composition, and the Tory resistance to reform in the 1820s and 1830s was nowhere more strongly rooted than in the House of Lords. Fitzwilliam's creed, however, differed from that of the Wellingtons and Eldons. His aristocratic principle was not simply an attempt to protect and prolong the dominance of landed wealth and hereditary privilege, though he believed that both still mattered. His attitude was that privilege and high position were justified only by public service, and by the extension of protection to those lower in the social scale and of inferior political or economic power. As he wrote of Ireland in 1796, a 'completely aristocratical' system 'leaves the lower orders without protection; and in that example we may learn what tyrants we aristocrats can be when there is no check whatever on the selfish bent of the human mind. Happy the country where there is such an alloy of democracy as brings the overbearing inclinations of the great to a fellow-feeling for the low'. (See chapter eight)

Whether as a private landlord, directly involved in the running of his estates, or as a public man, transferring to national affairs the creed of a partnership between property and dependence, Fitzwilliam represented the best in the eighteenth-century aristocratic system. His

activities and attitude as Lord Lieutenant of the West Riding during
the troubles of the second decade of the nineteenth century vividly
illustrate the principle: firm in the administration of the law, he
remained always humane and practical in his assessment of the
conditions which gave rise to popular agitation. His willingness to
give up the policy of repression in 1817, which differentiated him
from his Grenville allies and brought about the final reunion of old
Whig connexions, was founded on a conviction that the old bonds
between property and the people could be preserved as the core of
national unity against both reactionary militarists and irresponsible
demagogues. His stand over Peterloo in 1819 was, as has been shown,
a largely politically-inspired affair, but at its root lay principles that
looked back to the Rockingham–Burke ideal of a responsible governing class and a government which founded its authority on consent
and not on armed coercion. If his initial support for the suspension
of Habeas Corpus in 1817, like his acceptance of Pitt's repressive
measures in the 1790s, represented a fear of Jacobin subversion, his
opposition to the 'Six Acts' more truly indicated the fundamentally
liberal views which epitomised a lifetime's dedication to Whig
principles. Yet those views were not favourable to the concession
of constitutional reform: it was in some respects ironic that Fitzwilliam's stand over Peterloo, more than any other circumstance,
prevented the Whig party's commitment to parliamentary reform in
the early 1820s. In this respect alone Fitzwilliam could be claimed
to be a major influence on Whig thinking and strategy in the last
decade of his active life. Here it was Fitzwilliam's son who saw
more clearly the path to which his father's principles were inexorably leading. Milton's conversion to reform not only marked his
political maturity, and the end of his complete dependence on his
father's views: it also represented a logical development out of the
Rockinghamite principles of the 1780s. Rockingham himself had
declared against parliamentary reform less on principle than because
of its contingent difficulties: he had always been in favour of the
reform of proven abuses. It was on similar grounds that the Whigs
advocated the Reform Bill in 1831, and it was significant that a
Fitzwilliam was to be found amongst them.

Other Whig causes and principles were transmitted to the party of
the 1820s by Fitzwilliam's agency. Foremost among these was the
old Whig creed of 'civil and religious liberty all over the world'—
and, not least, in Ireland. As Fitzwilliam's martyrdom over Peterloo

profoundly affected Whig attitudes to reform, so his earlier martyrdom in Ireland helped to make the Whigs steadfast advocates of
Catholic relief, even against the hostile mood of English public
opinion and the determined resistance of George III and his eldest
son. Both Burke and Fox influenced Fitzwilliam's mind on this issue.
Fox contributed a passionate involvement in the principle of toleration; Burke supplied both pragmatic and philosophical justification
in an age of political polarisation. To Fitzwilliam the penal laws
against Catholic and Protestant dissenters were akin to repressive
measures against Jacobins. They could be justified for a short time,
in the context of an immediate political crisis; once the threat of
subversion of the constitution was over, no justification remained
for continuing them merely on the principle that nothing should
ever be changed. In 1795 his hope that the king and the Cabinet
would accept this argument in relation to Irish Catholicism was
dashed: he nevertheless continued to advance it in later years, .
speaking almost invariably in the Lords whenever the Catholic question was debated, and always in the same spirit: that the anti-
Catholic laws were originally justified solely on the grounds that the
Catholics of Ireland in the later seventeenth century represented a
threat to the Protestant constitution of England, but that over a
century later more was to be gained from cementing their loyalty,
and that of their English co-religionists, to the cause of order against
atheistic radicalism. In relation to religious toleration in general,
Fitzwilliam was a pragmatist: even though he shared in the widespread impression that Protestant Nonconformity had sinister connexions with Jacobinism in the 1790s, he consistently advocated the
granting of civil equality to religious dissenters on the grounds that
the denial of civil rights created rather than contained the political
disaffection which was the real threat.

Here as always, Fitzwilliam's consistent creed was the cause of
free civil government—government which assumed equality of civil
rights, yet reflected the inevitable social inequalities of an ordered
and hierarchical society: government that operated not directly
upon the people, but through the intermediate agency of a propertied
but responsible aristocracy whose interests were fundamentally those
of the whole nation. Burke's political writings, and his own career,
had promoted and illustrated this principle and had confirmed it as
the dominant one in Fitzwilliam's political thinking. In the later
eighteenth century it had led to a concentration on opposition to

the 'influence of the Crown' as the major threat to the natural
balance of social interests in the political system. By the 1820s,
although the sovereign still retained a considerable personal weight
in politics, no one could seriously pretend that the old type of
'influence' was any longer a real threat to liberty—rather, the
balance of the constitution might be menaced in the post-Waterloo
years by a creeping and insidious militarism—a tendency to identify
the civil government with military strength, in face of the supposed
threat of democratic rebellion from starving peasants or unemployed
weavers infected by Paineite ideas of equality. Fitzwilliam stood for
a calmer assessment of the situation. Civil government, as he wrote
in 1802 (see chapter eleven), should be kept out of the hands of the
military—the 'men in red coats'—and be entrusted only to civilians
—'men in brown coats'—whose interests lay in the preservation of
free institutions. The people, in any case, were fundamentally loyal:
that they were susceptible to the promises of a few agitators was no
surprise, if their true friends and protectors—the aristocracy and men
of wealth—seemed insensitive to their conditions. The remedy was
not wholesale and indiscriminate repression, but a return to true
Whig principles—the cementing of the social order by the union of
protection from above with deference from below. As he had suggested to the Rev. Henry Zouch when writing about the 'Proclamation Society' in 1787, the governors should accept the dignity and
the rights of the governed, and should set them a better example. If
this creed lacked political sophistication, and was out of touch with
the developing demands of an industrialising and increasingly urban-
ised society, it nevertheless was a responsible and benevolent
principle.

Fitzwilliam's career was therefore all of one piece. The causes and
principles to which he dedicated his political and public life came
from one mould. Never an original thinker, he showed unusual
tenacity in holding to and applying the ideals which he believed the
Rockingham inheritance had placed in his care. Few public men of
the period maintained this level of consistency over so many issues
and for so long a period. Fitzwilliam's fate as an office-holder, of
course, reflected this attitude. He was an obstinate man, with a high
sense of his duty and, therefore, of public rectitude. Compromise
was not in his political vocabulary, and since politics is largely the
art of successful compromise Fitzwilliam was the most unsuccessful
of politicians. His natural home—as he himself frequently pro-

claimed—was out of office, acting as the local representative of the Whig party in the limited area of his own 'natural' influence. Here in south Yorkshire he succeeded, in time, in that most difficult of tasks—capturing the loyalty and the affection of men to whom he came as a comparative stranger, and at first as a rather heavy-handed one, in place of a widely loved and respected 'native prince' of the north. In his person and in his view of the needs of society Fitzwilliam formed a link between old and new, helping to carry forward into the new post-industrial revolution England of the nineteenth century the liberal constitutional creed of the old aristocratic England which gave it birth. The Whig party of the later 1820s was still the product of this thinking, despite the attempt of its more radical members to hurry it into a closer alliance with new social forces. Fitzwilliam's career illustrates how much the party could still respond to its historic role.

INDEX